CW01084332

Mark Huish and the London & North Western Railway

Mark Huish and the London & North Western Railway

a study of management

T. R. Gourvish

Lecturer in Economic History   University of East Anglia

Leicester University Press   1972

First published in 1972 by Leicester University Press
Distributed in North America by Humanities Press Inc., New York

Copyright © T. R. Gourvish 1972

All rights reserved. No part of this publication may be reproduced,
stored in a retrieval system, or transmitted, in any form or by any
means, electronic, mechanical, photocopying, recording or otherwise, without the
prior permission of the Leicester University Press.

Designed by Arthur Lockwood

Set in 'Monotype' Scotch Roman and Grotesque 215/216
Printed in Great Britain
by W & J Mackay Limited, Chatham
Bound by James Burn (Bookbinders) Ltd, Esher
ISBN 0 7185 1101 8

Preface

Captain Mark Huish, "power-politician of the iron road", has excited the attention of a great many writers on railways. But while the colour of a highly competitive period for the industry is amply represented by this leading executive manager of the Victorian age, the precise nature of his management, and the mechanics of the railways' decision-making and business organization, remain largely neglected. This book examines the major problems of British railway management in the nineteenth century, using Huish's career as a model. The growth of the internal organization of railway companies is a subject of considerable importance in British business history. It involves the first concerted attempt to solve many of the problems of large-scale business, and the first opportunity to train a large body of administrators in such problems. In this context the choice of Huish as a case-study is particularly apt. His managerial experiences provide perhaps the best illustration of railway management's transition from a haphazard phenomenon on the small lines of the 1830s to the complex administrations of those giants of Victorian business enterprise, the large companies which appeared after the 'Railway Mania' of 1845–6. It is intended that the material presented here will serve as a guide not only to the several managerial problems facing the railways, but also to the reactions of management to these problems.

This work is based upon a Ph.D. thesis accepted by the University of London in 1967. An extensive revision of the text was undertaken in the Summer of 1970 and completed in April 1971. I should like to acknowledge the assistance given by the staffs of the several archives, museums, and libraries, in providing me with the information necessary to this study. Special mention must be made of Mr E. H. Fowkes, Archivist of the British Transport Historical Records Collection in London, and Mr G. Ottley, of Leicester University, former Superintendent of the British Museum's State Paper Room. Without their help and encouragement much of the vital material relating to railway management would have eluded me. Research and publication were greatly facilitated by most generous grants from the Twenty-Seven Foundation, the Carnegie Trust for the Universities of Scotland, and the University of Glasgow. I should also like to thank the editors of *Business History* for permission to reproduce material from my article on Huish, published in 1970; the British Transport Historical Records Office for permission to reproduce map 5 and the excursion bills on pp. 189 and 191; the University of London Library for permission to reproduce the Grand Junction Railway fare schedule on p. 75; London Midland Region (B.R.) for permission to reproduce plates 1, 2, 3, 4, 5 and 6; Western Region (B.R.) for permission to reproduce plate 7; and George Allen & Unwin Ltd for permission to reproduce plate 8 (from Charles Grinling's *The History of the Great Northern Railway*). The patience and encouragement of Mr P. L. Boulton and his staff at the Leicester University Press made the task of presenting the work for publication a pleasure.

In the course of my work on railway management I have been fortunate to receive the active encouragement of several historians, and, especially, my former teachers at the London School of Economics, and my former colleagues at the University of Glasgow. I owe a particular debt to Professor D. C. Coleman, who not only supervised my original thesis, but read and commented upon the revised manuscript. For his constructive criticisms and long-term support I am deeply grateful. I should also like to thank Dr D. H. Aldcroft, Dr M. C. Reed, Mr G. L. Turnbull, Mr M. B. English, and Mr D. C. H. Robson for particular kindnesses.

T.R.G.

Contents

Maps and line illustrations

Tables

Further statistical tables (44–63) are contained in the first part of the Appendix.

Plates

Abbreviations

BTHR	British Transport Historical Records, London
G.P.O.R.O.	Post Office Records Office, London
H.L.R.O.	House of Lords Records Office, London
I.O.R.	India Office Records, London
P.R.O.	Public Record Office, London
S.R.O.	Scottish Record Office, Edinburgh
P.P.	Parliamentary Papers
S.C.	Select Committee
Ctee	Committee
Mins	Minutes

Railway companies, canal companies, etc.

B. & D.J.	Birmingham & Derby Junction Railway
Cale.	Caledonian Railway
C. & B.	Chester & Birkenhead Railway
C. & H.	Chester & Holyhead Railway
E. Cos	Eastern Counties Railway
E.D.P.	Edinburgh Dundee & Perth Railway
E.C.C.	Ellesmere & Chester Canal
E. & G.	Edinburgh & Glasgow Railway
E. & W.I.	East & West India Dock Railway
E.L.	East Lancashire Railway
G.J.	Grand Junction Railway
G.J.C.	Grand Junction Canal
G.N.	Great Northern Railway
G.P.G.	Glasgow Paisley & Greenock Railway
G.P.J.	Glasgow & Paisley Joint Railway
G.P.K.A.	Glasgow Paisley Kilmarnock & Ayr Railway
G.S.W.	Glasgow & South Western Railway
G.W.R.	Great Western Railway
I.O.W.	Isle of Wight Railway
L. & B.	London & Birmingham Railway
L. & Br.	London & Brighton Railway
L. & C.	Lancaster & Carlisle Railway
L. & M.	Liverpool & Manchester Railway
L. & Y.	Lancashire & Yorkshire Railway
L.N.W.	London & North Western Railway
L.S.W.	London & South Western Railway

M. & B.	Manchester & Birmingham Railway
M. & L.	Manchester & Leeds Railway
Mid.	Midland Railway
M.S.J.A.	Manchester South Junction & Altrincham Railway
M.S. & L.	Manchester Sheffield & Lincolnshire Railway
N.B.	North British Railway
N.E.	North Eastern Railway
N.M.	North Midland Railway
N.U.	North Union Railway
N.W.	North Western Railway
O.W.W.	Oxford Worcester & Wolverhampton Railway
R.C.H.	Railway Clearing House
S.A. & M.	Sheffield Ashton & Manchester Railway
S. & B.	Shrewsbury & Birmingham Railway
S. & C.	Shrewsbury & Chester Railway
S. & D.	Stockton & Darlington Railway
S.C.	Scottish Central Railway
S. & H.	Shrewsbury & Hereford Railway
S.E.	South Eastern Railway
S.U.	Shropshire Union Railway & Canal
S.V.	Birmingham Wolverhampton & Stour Valley Railway
Y.N.B.	York Newcastle & Berwick Railway
Y.N.M.	York & North Midland Railway

For Susan

It is the unhappy lot of those connected with the management of Railway property to be continually obnoxious to various and contradictory charges. On the one hand, they are taxed with being monopolists, having but one view, viz., to extract the 'uttermost farthing' from a suffering public. On the other, they are suspected by the Proprietors of not so regulating the fares, freight, and accommodation, as to obtain the largest possible dividend which the line is capable of producing.

Mark Huish, 1848

The major requisites for successful management are a first-rate planning system, charisma, and a sense of competitive urgency.

G. A. Steiner, *Top Management Planning*, 1969

PART ONE

PART
ONE

1

Problems of early railway management

What were the major problems facing railway management, when Mark Huish entered the railway service in 1837? Certainly by the late 1830s the railway had established itself. Large numbers of passengers and goods were being conveyed by locomotive power, and almost 1,000 miles of line were constructed before 1840, including a great portion of the trunk routes which came to dominate the 1840s.[1] The advantages of this new form of transportation with its faster and often cheaper facilities were

1 H. G. Lewin, *Early British Railways, 1810–1844* (1925), 186.

clearly recognized.[1] But the industry was still in a transitional phase, having achieved only a partial ascendancy over its competitors. Moreover, the railway companies were slow to master the management problems which confronted them. The importance of several issues was little appreciated until the later 1840s, when, for example, it was seen that earlier theories and anticipations of capital costs, organization, traffic management, and pricing had been far from accurate.[2] By 1840, too, Parliament had begun seriously to investigate the rôle of railways in the economy. The Select Committee on Railways of 1839 had conceded that the railway possessed a quasi-monopolistic position in the transport sphere. It had established that a railway was essentially different from a turnpike or canal, and could not therefore be operated in the same way. The implications of these concessions, in terms of further government action, were a serious unknown factor for the railway administrators.

I

The excessive and unexpected cost of railway promotion and construction not only caused concern before companies opened their lines, but proved a pressing and enduring problem thereafter. Capital accounts usually came to exceed the original estimates presented to Parliament, and many lines were compelled to seek fresh capital by subscription or loan. A measure of undue optimism, together with a general lack of experience of construction costs, was no doubt partly responsible. But early managements were also frustrated by the waste of capital resources caused by the system of promotion, with its burden of parliamentary and legal expenses, and the high price of land and compensation. In the long run, the initial failure to estimate with any accuracy the operating costs of a railway (early opinions on the life of rails are a good example) proved equally important, but it is certain that the high capital costs of construction and the accumulation of unproductive elements in the capital account greatly affected managerial attitudes to the subsequent organization of traffic.

Parliament was frequently criticized for contributing to the railways'

1 R. Z. Mudge, *Observations on Railways, with reference to utility, profit, and the obvious necessity for a national system* (1837), 2–12; N. W. Cundy, *Inland Transit. The practicality, utility, and benefit of railroads* . . . (1834), 1, 16–23; H. Fairbairn, *A Treatise on the Political Economy of Railroads* . . . (1836), 1–3, 49–57.
2 E. D. Chattaway, *Railways, their Capital and Dividends* . . . (1855–6), 3–5.

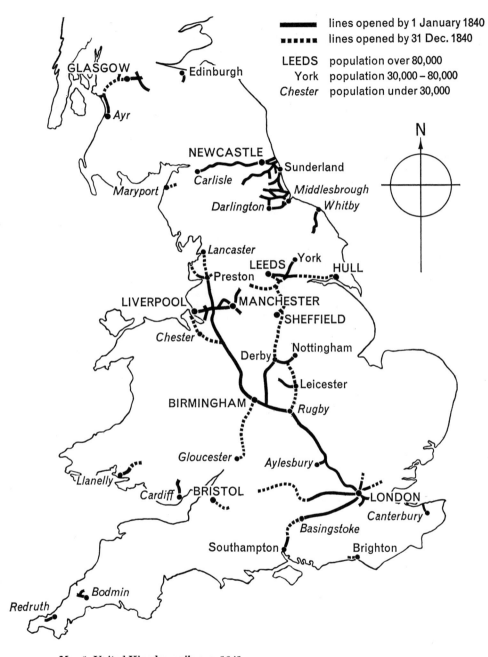

Map 1. United Kingdom railways, 1841

Legend:

———	lines opened by 1 January 1840
▪▪▪▪▪▪	lines opened by 31 Dec. 1840

LEEDS — population over 80,000
York — population 30,000 – 80,000
Chester — population under 30,000

Map labels: GLASGOW, Edinburgh, Ayr, NEWCASTLE, Carlisle, Sunderland, Maryport, Middlesbrough, Darlington, Whitby, Lancaster, York, LEEDS, HULL, Preston, LIVERPOOL, MANCHESTER, SHEFFIELD, Chester, Nottingham, Derby, Leicester, BIRMINGHAM, Rugby, Gloucester, Aylesbury, Llanelly, Cardiff, BRISTOL, LONDON, Canterbury, Basingstoke, Southampton, Brighton, Bodmin, Redruth

N

difficult financial position. The House of Lords Select Committee on the Management of Railways, 1846, reported that much unnecessary expense could be traced to the restrictions of Parliament's standing orders, and many important schemes were hindered by opposition founded on trivial mistakes in the plans. The London & Birmingham Railway, for example, experienced great difficulty, and its committee of management continually sought the advice of those who had promoted railways before themselves.[1]

Contemporaries were also alive to the mistakes of internal management, and in particular to the 'extravagance' of construction—the result, it was alleged, of the exalted position in the 1820s and 1830s of engineers and contractors. While the railway was in its first stage of development, with only small industrial lines open and the trunk lines under construction, the civil engineer was a popular choice for manager, being well-respected by inexperienced management boards. But pamphlets such as *An Exposure of the costly fallacies of Railroad Engineering* (1837) and *Railways: their Uses and Management* (1842) voiced a growing concern that extravagance in the use of labour and materials

> has not only been a blot on the profession itself . . . but has proved their [*the engineers*] utter incapacity, not only for economical construction, but economical and thus profitable working. The entire ignorance of Directors of even the principles or details of the works . . . throws them completely into the power of the engineer.[2]

Engineering problems were, of course, initially almost overwhelming, and Britain as the pioneer was forced to buy her experience dearly. But there is also no doubt that works were often the subject of lavish ornamentation, and that men of little practical knowledge were sometimes employed by directors unaware of the full implications of provision for mechanical transport. A notable engineer of the 1830s doubted whether railways had always been constructed "upon the best model", and the Select Committee on Railways of 1839 suggested that engineers had taken insufficient care in the preparation of estimates.[3] The problem lingered on into the 1840s, with the *Railway Times*'s statement that managements had been at first too easily influenced by lawyers and engineers, who retained a direct interest in swelling the expenditure.[4] The extravagance

1 Carr Glyn, and Creed, letters to Edward Cropper (Liverpool & Manchester Railway), 1833, Historical Letters, HL2/R2–14, BTHR.
2 Anon., *Railways: their Uses and Management* (1842), 15.
3 P.P.1839, X, Second Report, vi.
4 *Railway Times*, 9 and 23 Jan. 1841.

of the Great Western was strongly criticized, and Charles Saunders, secretary of the company, admitted in 1846 that the control of funds by engineers was potentially detrimental to its interests.[1]

Some railways avoided the high construction costs which had helped to provide the Liverpool & Manchester and London & Birmingham railways with a capital expenditure of over £50,000 per mile. The Grand Junction, for example, was praised for its "modesty of style", and the Newcastle & Carlisle was also constructed cheaply, in view of the engineering problems which it faced.[2] Nevertheless, the estimated capital cost of English railways in 1846 was about £31,000 per mile, a figure almost double that for the Belgian state railways, and there was much speculation as to the cost of railways had the government supervised both promotion and construction. As early as 1822, Thomas Gray had petitioned for a system of railways controlled by the state, and later observers such as Laing and Morrison thought that this would have produced a capital saving of at least 30 per cent.[3]

The railway manager of the 1840s had to deal with circumstances as they were, however, and as more companies opened their lines to traffic, the engineer was found lacking in the specialist knowledge and aptitude required by commercial operation. Although influential figures such as Robert Stephenson, Joseph Locke, and Isambard Brunel continued to enjoy considerable prestige, companies began to look elsewhere for their executive officers and sought men who would not only discourage further expenditure but also provide business acumen and organizing ability. Captain Mark Huish was one of the men called in during the later 1830s to deal with a situation which had created railway lines at high cost.

II

Further difficulties resulted from the early organization of railway companies. Fluidity of procedure was still general in 1840, and as the pioneers struggled to deal with the unprecedented size and complexity of the new joint-stock concerns they had created, strong criticism was levelled at the

1 Saunders's evidence to *House of Lords S.C. on the Management of Railway Promotion*, P.P.1846, XIII, Q.896.
2 F. Whishaw, *The Railways of Great Britain and Ireland* (1840), 337–8.
3 T. Gray, Petitions to Parliament, 29 Mar. 1822 and 27 May 1823, cited in T. Wilson, *The Railway System and its author, Thomas Gray* (1845), 25–7, and J. Morrison, *Observations illustrative of the defects of the English system of Railway Legislation* . . . (1846), 13.

Board system, and in particular at the "irresponsible power" enjoyed by directors.[1] It appeared that the first railway directors were very much amateurs, rarely devoting sufficient time to their duties. Share qualifications were quite small,[2] and this attracted men who for political, commercial, or even social reasons wished to be connected with important railway companies. Indeed, some managements welcomed the inclusion of prominent businessmen who, although unable to contribute much towards the actual running of the concern, could by their presence provide an atmosphere of honesty and prosperity. Although a great deal of criticism was ill-informed, the early Boards were far from perfect. They were frequently unaware of the need to concentrate on matters of general policy, to avoid the trivial, and to leave executive details to full-time staff. At first, many attempted to handle the 'out-door' management of the line in addition to their customary duties. Certainly, by modern standards, the power wielded by directors was excessive. This may have been necessary in the early stages of a company's history, but malpractices were facilitated, and the task of a railway manager was hampered by the publicity given to examples of mismanagement at Board level.[3] Parliament, in its attempts to deal with the railways, was aware of the effects of the authority which the directorate assumed within infant companies,[4] and of the manner in which shareholders were often prevented from discerning the true state of the companies' business. Free use of the proxy system at general meetings, and on occasion a blatant refusal to give information, enabled certain managements to keep their shareholders silent, or evade their enquiries.

Directors with large holdings naturally had an interest in raising the market value of the company's stock. Sometimes, unremunerative traffic

1 Anon, *Railways* . . . (1842), 17–18; W. Galt, *Railway Reform, its expediency and practicability considered* . . . (1844), 17; S. Laing, referred to in J. Whitehead, *Railway Management. A Letter to George Carr Glyn. Esq., Chairman of the London & North Western Railway* (1848), 20–1.

2 Analytical Table in Appendix 31, *S. C. on Railways*, P.P.1839, X: Qualification for Grand Junction, Liverpool & Manchester: 5 shares; for London & Birmingham, Great Western : 10 shares (share: £100).

3 The *Railway Times* was particularly critical of the Manchester & Birmingham, Eastern Counties, Midland Counties, and North Midland railways: *Railway Times*, 9–16 Jan., 6 Mar., and 16 Oct. 1841, 20 Aug. 1842. See also J. Whitehead, *Railway Prostration. Causes and Remedies. A Letter to the Rt. Hon. Sir Robert Peel* (1849), 9, 19–20; A. Smith, *The Bubble of the Age: or the Fallacies of Railway Investments, Railway Accounts, and Railway Dividends* (1848), 3–15; and D. Lardner, *Railway Economy: A Treatise on the New Art of Transport, its Management, Prospects, and Relations, Commercial, Financial, and Social* (1850), 513–14.

4 Stanley: "all railroads must be more or less partial monopolies in the hands of directors", *Hansard*, 4 Feb. 1841.

was retained in order to increase the published weekly traffic returns (which affected Stock Exchange prices). A second expedient was to create artificially high dividends, either by using capital funds to meet operating costs, or by paying the dividends themselves out of capital. Expenditure could be concealed by the improper charging of items to the capital account, and variations in the presentation of accounts were often deliberately made in order to hide deficiencies, or to prevent unfavourable comparisons with the performance of other railways. Speculation was frequently encouraged by the issue of new stock, and there was ample opportunity for patronage and even corruption: the Report of the Select Committee on the South Eastern Railway Petition of 1845 clearly illustrated the possible dangers.[1] This is not to say that all managements were corrupt, but even scrupulous Boards knew that the share position could influence their decisions and that completely honest acts would be scrutinized closely by those suspicious of their motives. The salaried officer might very often be caught up in such controversies, which threatened his integrity, or at least reduced his opportunity for freedom of action. Frauds of the kind committed by George Hudson on the Eastern Counties and York & North Midland railways were exceptional, but this did not prevent a deluge of suggestions aimed at all companies and intended to improve organization and efficiency. Boards were considered to be large and unwieldy, and although the creation of committees was a sound step to alleviate difficulties, commentators continued to prefer compact, well-paid groups to large and often self-perpetuating bodies.[2]

Concepts of adequate organization were slow to gain acceptance, although these had been advocated from the early 1830s. Peter Lecount, in his *Treatise on Railways* of 1839, reported that little progress had been made to perfect the directorial system of control, while George Carr Glyn, chairman of the London & Birmingham Railway, exposed the inadequacies of his company's organization in his Memorandum on Management Division of 1836, proving to be fully alive to the need to define authority and assess responsibility within the company structure. He wrote that:

> each department should be directed by a *responsible* officer . . . to him should be left the management of the details of the business in each department . . . that each department should from time to time

1 P.P.1845, X, Report, xiv–ix. The Committee found that an M.P. had been rewarded for aiding the company in Parliament, and that shares had been given to the solicitor of the Board of Ordnance for his favour in connection with competing railway projects in north Kent.
2 P. Lecount, *A Practical Treatise on Railways* . . . (1839), 253–7.

report to the Committee of Management upon the matters connected with the same and should suggest such changes in the arrangements as may appear expedient, bringing the consideration of them before the Ctee. of Management, from which each head of department would receive his orders and instructions.[1]

Carr Glyn's recommendations were not generally followed, however, and the matter was as pertinent in the 1850s when raised by McDonnell as it had been in the 1830s.[2] Many companies retained a slovenly attitude towards the definition of executive duties, and failed to enforce adequate rules of responsibility.

Carr Glyn's conception of responsibility rested not only upon the appointment of one superior officer, but also upon the idea that each head of department should be answerable only to the Committee or Board:

> The Committee only cannot effectively check the operation and arrangements of such an undertaking and with such an establishment as that upon the L. & B., and it therefore becomes necessary that it should have the assistance of a confidential superior officer, whose principal duty it must be generally to superintend the working of the system and to observe the working and operations of each outdoor department . . . all orders should be issued direct to the head of the dept., while at the same time the effectual inspection and efficiency of the superior officer is secured by his immediate reference to and connection with the Ctee. of Management . . . [which] will avoid much cumbersome detail, through the responsible heads of each department being charged with the details of their respective office.[3]

The companies, however, came to appoint both a 'secretary' and a 'manager' between whom responsibilities were often ill-defined. The London & Birmingham intended to confine their secretary to the finance and audit department, but because Richard Creed took an active part in the general supervision, as did Henry Booth on the Liverpool & Manchester, and, later, Captain Huish on the Grand Junction, the example was followed elsewhere. When a company employed both a secretary and a manager, there was often doubt as to which matters the subordinate officers should refer to them. The position was complicated by the varied terminology used by the railways. When McDonnell wrote this had

1 Glyn, confidential 'Memorandum on Management Division', 1836, Historical Letters, HL2/R306, BTHR.
2 G. McDonnell, *Railway Management, with and without Railway Statistics* (1854).
3 Carr Glyn's 'Memorandum'.

crystallized, but in the 1840s 'secretaries', 'engineers', and even 'directors' assumed general executive responsibility.[1] On the smaller railways, one official was often able to undertake both secretarial and managerial duties. But when such a man took charge of a larger company, or his own company extended its operations, this was rarely possible. In this situation, delegation of authority was very reluctantly conceded by an executive whose forceful personality had launched a new line, or whose experience had accustomed him to responsibility for the entire sphere of operations.

Carr Glyn's suggestions, had they been adopted, would have solved many departmental crises, and eased the anxiety of chief executives when urgent matters arose. Some companies found a temporary solution in allowing tenacious characters such as Huish, Saunders, and Laws to assume responsibility for as many matters as possible. These more decisive managers took upon themselves the task of issuing orders and preparing reports for the consideration of the Board, especially when cases of accident or neglect by railway servants occurred. But on lines where practice differed, some matters might pass unsupervised. Cases of negligence or incivility were not settled promptly because of doubt as to which officer or company department was concerned. The absence of adequate reports on the day-to-day running of the various branches of the railway company's organization was a further serious defect.[2]

No real definition between the operating and commercial aspects of management was made while railways could still be worked as a whole, under the aegis of one or two officials. The departmental system, with a chain of responsibility linking clerk and director, was not a reality.[3] Since the organization of railways was in this uncertain state, it was necessary for a successful concern to employ men of integrity able to deal with varied and often unforeseen circumstances. Following the reduced influence of the engineer in executive management, men with military backgrounds became popular. The captain and lieutenant from both army and navy had experience of accounts and book-keeping, and were also familiar with the control of large staffs. Captain Huish entered the railway industry after service with the East India Company's army, but it was the navy which provided the majority of these important railway recruits.[4]

1 E.g. Capt. John Laws, Managing Director of the Manchester & Leeds; Charles Saunders, Secretary and Superintendent of Traffic, Great Western.
2 McDonnell, *op. cit.*, 20ff.
3 M. R. Bonavia, *The Economics of Transport* (1954), 81–2.
4 This was due, it appears, to an excess supply of young naval captains with very poor

Executives recruited from the armed forces were not universally welcomed, however, since they tended to lay stress on staff discipline and to
neglect the organization of goods traffic, with which they were initially
unfamiliar.[1] Some of the new executives of the 1840s were obtained,
therefore, from rival transport undertakings, or from commercial sources.
Men such as Braithwaite Poole (Grand Junction) and Moseley (Eastern
Counties), recruited from large carrying firms, were invaluable in organizing early goods traffic.[2] Men with business experience often became
secretaries: Henry Booth, Richard Creed, and Charles Saunders are
examples.[3] But few companies were fortunate enough to acquire such able
men, and the simultaneous creation of several companies after the first
'Mania' of promotion, 1836–7, put great pressure upon available resources. The Midland Counties, North Midland, and Birmingham &
Gloucester were among the railways which suffered particularly from a
lack of competent management in the late 1830s and early 1840s.[4] The
shortage of trained administrative staff and the consequent strain placed
upon directors were among the industry's greatest problems.

III

The *Railway Times* echoed a widespread criticism when, in an editorial of
23 January 1841, it called for the "most rigid economy in the future
management of railways". The pressure upon companies associated with
the high capital cost of railways invited a dangerous policy of parsimony
once they began to operate services, and the writings of the *Railway*

---

chances of promotion: M. A. Lewis, *The Navy in Transition, 1814–1864: A Social
History* (1965), 78–80. In the 1840s there were several ex-military men in important
posts in railway management, including, besides Huish (Grand Junction), Capt.
J. M. Laws and Capt. C. H. Binstead (Manchester & Leeds), Capt. J. E. Cleather
(Grand Junction, Manchester & Birmingham), Capt. J. W. Coddington (Caledonian),
Capt. W. O'Brien (Great North of England), and Capt. C. R. Moorsom and Lieut.
H. P. Bruyeres (London & Birmingham).

1 'Thesis', in *Railway Times*, 23 Jan. 1841; G. P. Neele, *Railway Reminiscences* (1904),
  author's anotated copy, BTHR, 8.
2 Poole was recruited from Crowley & Co., Moseley from Pickford & Co.
3 Booth (Liverpool and Manchester) was the son of a corn merchant, Creed worked for
  the firm of Fauntleroy & Creed before joining the London & Birmingham, and
  Saunders (Great Western), educated at Winchester and Oxford, possessed mer-
  cantile experience in Mauritius.
4 See, for example, *Railway Times*, 17 Apr. and 16 Oct. 1841, 29 Jan., 4 June, and
  6 Aug. 1842.

Times and others did little to discourage this. An attitude of cheeseparing harmed many lines, especially in their first few years of working, when repair and maintenance costs were particularly high.[1] The companies were often torn between reducing operating costs, and thus meeting the demands of those investors who desired temporary high dividends, and using profits to offset future expense, thereby securing a steadier but lower return upon capital. Nevertheless, discerning companies did realize that "arbitrary reductions encourage evil results" and that the reduction of costs in order to maintain dividends was "false economy", even if the process was slow.[2]

It was only to be expected that operating matters would be perplexing, while the technical problems of railway management were but partially understood. Practice grew up rather haphazardly, drawing upon experience derived from canals, road-coaches, carriers, and the mineral plateways, and as late as 1835, actual knowledge of working trains by locomotive was confined to a few companies only: indeed, the Stockton & Darlington Railway, one of the pioneers, was consulted by several companies seeking advice on working and management.[3] It was also significant that the London & Birmingham Railway, in its first years of operation, called upon Joseph Baxendale of Pickford & Co., and A. Bagster, who possessed coaching experience, to organize its traffic departments.[4] Men of the canal and turnpike order were necessarily bound up with the formative years of railway practice, and although their presence was often invaluable, efficient railway operation was sometimes impaired by executives and directors who retained interests in canals or carrying firms which were brought into direct competition. It was the partnership of private carriers and railway companies, for example, which complicated the early management of goods traffic and led to divided control on some lines.[5]

Further problems arose from the failure of the early companies to provide for adequate maintenance of the rolling stock and permanent way. Economy in the construction of branch lines, difficulties with the supply of labour, and, above all, faulty track, not only endangered the

1 Lardner, *op. cit.*, 39.
2 Chattaway, *op. cit.*, 28.
3 E.g. letters from Sandars (Liverpool & Manchester) to Pease, 1826, SAD8/108, BTHR. Later, the practice of the Liverpool & Manchester acted as a model for many companies.
4 Baxendale was Superintendent of Traffic, April–November 1839, L. & B. Mins, 1839, LBM1/34, BTHR. See also G. L. Turnbull, 'The Railway Revolution and Carriers' Response: Messrs Pickford & Company 1830–50', *Transport History*, II (1969) 54.
5 See below, Chapters III and V.

working of services but encouraged governmental interference in internal
management. Here, Isambard Brunel, in his evidence to the Select Committee on Accidents of 1841, represented the industry as a whole in its
opposition to the discretionary powers acquired by the newly-constituted
Railway Department of the Board of Trade.[1] But supervision, if unwelcome, was perhaps desirable. Many erroneous technological assumptions continued to affect managerial conduct. The optimistic opinion, for
example, that iron rails would last for a century or more influenced the
provision for repairs for some time. It was not until the slump of 1847
that a more critical analysis of permanent way costs was made.[2]

Efficiency was also hindered by the lack of a complete and universally
recognized system of accounts and an uncertain attitude towards cost
accountancy. There was little in a company's Act of authorization to
guide it, either in the keeping of accounts, or in the determination of
profits.[3] Great difficulty surrounded such problems as the allocation of
expenditure between capital and revenue accounts, and the nature of
depreciation. It was not sufficient for a railway with heavy capital investment to calculate profits merely by matching cash receipts and expenses,
delaying provision for deterioration and obsolescence until replacement
became unavoidable. The crude cash accounting methods employed by
eighteenth-century business were clearly unsuitable,[4] but the early railways produced only the most rudimentary of accounts and displayed
little or no interest in the implications for future costs of extensive capital
formation. There was an immense variety in accounting practices, and,
indeed, misleading statements were often issued to prevent inter-
company comparison and to encourage continuing investment. The mistakes of the 1830s and early 1840s, encouraging the misallocation of
resources, eventually resulted in a demand for the independent audit of
railway accounts.[5] There was, however, no really satisfactory exposition
of financial and administrative practice to guide railways until Lardner's
Railway Economy of 1850, which drew heavily upon Huish's experience
as contained in confidential reports of 1848–9 to the London & North
Western.[6]

1 P.P.1841, VIII, QQ.772–83. See also H. Parris, *Government and the Railways in
  Nineteenth Century Britain* (1965), 28–60.
2 See Chapter V.
3 H. Pollins, 'Aspects of Railway Accounting before 1868', in A. C. Littleton and
  B. S. Yamey (eds.), *Studies in the History of Accounting* (1956), 337.
4 R. P. Brief, 'The Origin and Evolution of Nineteenth-Century Asset Accounting',
  Business History Review, XL (1966), 3–4.
5 Carr Glyn's Digest, 16 Jan. 1843, Glyn, Mills & Co. Archives, and the *House of
  Lords S.C. on the Audit of Railway Accounts*, P.P.1849, X, Third Report, xiii–xv.
6 See Chapter V.

IV

Traffic management was to become the principal task of the executive officer, but in the early stages of railway development, his duties fluctuated with the changing conception of the nature of the railway as a means of conveyance. At first it was assumed that railways would be used in the same way as canals and turnpikes, with independent concerns—freight carriers, coaching companies, and industrialists—supplying their own power and waggons and paying a toll to enable them to pass onto the line.[1] Early railway legislation, both private and public, obviously regarded railways as merely a more efficient development of existing transport modes. The Stockton & Darlington Railway Act of 1823, which authorized the use of steam power on the line, clearly intended that both passenger and goods traffic would be conducted by independent parties.[2] However, the evolution of the locomotive in the 1820s as a practical means of providing power caused a change, and it became usual, from about 1825, for new railway Acts to include a clause allowing the company to supply steam haulage and to charge a 'locomotive toll'.

It was soon found that safe and efficient working was impaired by the appearance of competing users, employing a mixture of horse and locomotive power and a variety of rolling stock. The experience of the Stockton & Darlington Railway quickened the transition from independent to company control of conveyance. On opening in 1825, the company entrusted the organization of both the coal and the less important passenger traffic to independent firms. The resulting scramble for railway facilities brought with it a poor level of service, and after eight years of unsatisfactory working the company decided to assume total responsibility for the conveyance of traffic by adopting locomotive power. This was achieved between October 1833 and April 1834.[3] The position of the Liverpool & Manchester Railway was also significant. Its Act of 1826 created an important precedent in requiring the company to

1 The best general account of the railway's transition from toll-taker to operator of complete transport services is in W. T. Jackman, *The Development of Transportation in Modern England*, vol. II (1916), 461–602.
2 A. K. Butterworth, *A Treatise on the Law Relating to Rates and Traffic on Railways and Canals* . . . (1889), 4–5; W. W. Tomlinson, *The North Eastern Railway, its rise and development* (1914), 84–5.
3 Tomlinson, *op. cit.*, 117–23, 364–5, 384–5. Some goods traffic remained in private hands and was horse-operated, *S.C. on Railways*, P.P.1839, X, Second Report, ix; Butterworth, *op. cit.*, 5.

take full responsibility for (i.e. 'carry') both passenger and goods traffic, and the extensive use of locomotives from the opening in 1830 was a serious blow to those who wished to run private trains. From about 1833, therefore, it became established practice to allow for conveyance by the railways. In the ensuing private Acts companies were authorized, "if they shall think proper", not only to provide locomotives for the use of others, but also to employ these themselves.[1]

Parliament had not at first sought to restrict locomotive and conveyance charges, since it was envisaged that competition would safeguard the public interest. By 1839, however, it was forced to admit that its original conception of railway carrying had broken down. The Select Committee of that year reported that

> [although] it does not appear to have been the intention of Parliament to give to a Railway Company the complete monopoly of the means of communication on their line of road . . . the safety of the Public . . . requires that upon every Railway there should be one system of management, under one superintending authority . . . On this account it is necessary that the Company should possess a complete control over their line of road, although they should thereby acquire an entire monopoly of the means of communication.[2]

The Committee had been influenced by Carr Glyn, who had stated that "several accidents have occurred in consequence of that divided authority",[3] but it was also clear that quality of service and the level of rates had been affected. Independent operators had been unwilling, for example, to invest in engines and stock comparable with the standards demanded by company regulations. The railway companies had to some extent encouraged the situation by withholding vital facilities, such as water and siding accommodation, from private firms, while the maximum tolls fixed by Parliament in each Act for use of the railway were high enough to ensure that these firms could be prevented from running trains profitably.[4] Passenger traffic thus soon came under complete railway control, and rates for this service were limited. But the same was not true of goods traffic, and at first Parliament set no limit on charges for the conveyance of goods, except that they should be 'reasonable'. After 1840, however, the problem of the railway as a means of conveyance had been

1 Butterworth, *op. cit.*, 9.
2 P.P.1839, X, Second Report, vi–vii. This was repeated in the *S.C. on Railways*, P.P.1840, XIII, Third Report, 3–4.
3 P.P.1839, X, Q.132.
4 Jackman, *op. cit.*, 573–4.

largely settled, and thereafter railway Acts contained a new clause which fixed the amount of an increased toll, applicable when the company conveyed goods traffic.[1] Charges regulated by Parliament were thus threefold—for the use of the line, for the supply of locomotive power, and for conveyance. Competition alone had proved insufficient to ensure control of railway rates.

Goods traffic was complicated by the continued presence of independent carrying firms. These merely employed the railways to convey traffic which they otherwise organized. It was this extended sense of the concept of railway carrying (involving all the essential ancillary services connected with the carriage of goods) which caused railway managers the most problems, and led Huish to remark that "perhaps no question connected with the practical detail of railway management has given rise to a greater diversity of opinion."[2] The theory of a railway as a public highway lingered on, notably in the Railway Clauses Consolidation Act of 1845, which sought to regularize future private Acts.[3] But as certain companies directed their attention to complete control of goods traffic, including collection and delivery, loading, and insurance,[4] it became widely believed that "there are defects inherent in the practice of conveyance of goods by intermediate carriers which must of necessity act as a discouragement to the increase of traffic."[5] Huish, as secretary of the Grand Junction, was one of the executives who stressed an economic justification for the railways' integrating all aspects of goods traffic. By 1845, in fact, many railways had subordinated the carrying firms, but the controversy as to the advisability of this step raged for some years.

V

On railways opened in the 1820s and early 1830s the chief profits were expected from goods and mineral traffic, and many companies began

1 E.g. the Acts of the Warwick & Leamington and Yarmouth & Norwich railways, 1842, cited in Butterworth, *op. cit.*, 10.
2 M. Huish, 'Confidential Report to the Chairman and Directors of the London & North Western Railway, upon the Working of the Merchandise Traffic for the Half-Year Ending 31 Dec. 1847', 1848, Historical Letters, HL2/R99B, BTHR.
3 8 & 9 Vic. c.XX, s.92.
4 By 1839 the Liverpool & Manchester, Newcastle & Carlisle, and Leeds & Selby railways had become sole carriers on their lines, *S.C. on Railways*, P.P.1839, X, Second Report, viii–ix.
5 J. B. Williams, *On the Principles of Railway Management* . . . (1846), 127.

operation without providing for passengers. This notion was speedily
contradicted by the unexpected success of passenger locomotion, particularly on the Liverpool & Manchester Railway, where after only four
years of operation receipts for this traffic were five times higher than the
original estimates. From about 1835, therefore, many managers devoted
most of their attention to passenger and parcels traffic, and several companies neglected goods traffic. The trunk railways in particular carried
only the lighter and more profitable items of freight, leaving much to be
transported by road and canal.

In the 1830s the railways faced an extensive and well-organized coaching trade. Competition, however, was generally short-lived. The long-
distance coaches were soon defeated, because of their comparatively slow
speed and high fares. The heavy taxes to which they were subject,
especially before 1842, also hampered their efforts to compete, although
railway companies were also affected by a similar imposition upon their
passengers.[1] It is generally accepted that coach travel was costlier than
rail transport and that under pressure of competition coach fares were
drastically cut. However, it is also true that many railways were forced to
reduce their charges, and that, for a time, third-class rail fares exceeded
the 'outside' coach fare on a number of major routes, including that from
London to Birmingham.[2]

The coaching interest adapted to the superiority of the railways far
quicker than did the canals and carrying firms. The leading concerns spent
little money in financing opposition to railway projects in Parliament,
and having realized the futility of trying to match their rivals in speed
and comfort, they attempted to turn the situation to their own advantage
by providing feeder services to connect towns lacking direct rail communication. The 'branch coach' was important to the railways from about
1835 to 1850, after which the extension of the rail network rendered it
largely superfluous. The railway executive sought to augment traffic by
organizing through rail-coach services for towns not served by his line.
In this task, he found that the negotiation of contracts with coaching
firms was a harassing problem. The London & Birmingham Railway,
whose policy in the later 1830s was followed by the Great Western and
London & South Western companies, decided that the most advantageous system would be to confine the interchange of traffic to certain

---

1 See below.
2 In 1841 the rail fare was 14s., the coach fare 12s.: *Bradshaw's Railway Companion*,
1841, TT1/16, BTHR. Some companies raised their fares after coaches had been
defeated, e.g. the Manchester Bolton & Bury: Ritson's evidence, *S.C. on Railways*,
P.P.1839, X, QQ.4143–9.

privileged firms.[1] Agreements were made on this basis, but the attempts of the privileged coach firm to undercut its rivals, and discrimination in the granting of access to railway premises, evoked sharp criticism. It appears that although the railways escaped the disadvantage of delays occasioned by touting for custom at stations, discrimination against small coaching firms discouraged passenger travel from many of the intermediate stations.[2] In the early 1840s the Great Western was criticized for its operations at Slough, Steventon, and Cirencester, where a great deal of inconvenience was caused to passengers travelling from London to Oxford and Cheltenham.[3] Nevertheless, the policy of exclusive advantage remained, and the railways secured an orderly if not an optimum interchange of traffic.

One of the major tasks of passenger traffic management was the choice and provision of accommodation. The early railways accepted the example of the coaches in providing more than one class of travel, but many companies began by catering almost exclusively for the wealthy. In doing so, train capacities were not maximized, and the lack of uniform services made safe and reliable operation difficult to achieve.[4] The early contempt for lower-class passengers distressed writers in the later 1830s and early 1840s, particularly since the defeat of the road coach had enabled the railways to ignore the interests of the poorer long-distance traveller.[5] However, the deliberate emphasis on first-class travel, especially on the trunk lines, and the reluctance to provide adequate third-class trains at reasonable times and with reasonable comfort, gave the companies only a short-term benefit. Many managers saw by 1845 that second- and third-class passengers formed the major potential source of

1 W. Chaplin's letters to R. Creed, 16 Oct. 1837, and to E. Mills, 20 Oct. 1837, Historical Letters, HL2/R33, BTHR.
2 G. Briggs, letter to L. & B., July 1838, and Stephen's letter to Moorsom, 28 Aug. 1838, complaining of a railway monopoly, and citing the example of the disappearance of the Thame–Tring coach, due to lack of facilities provided by the railway, HL2/R68, BTHR.
3 Bruton, of the Three Cups Inn, Oxford, letters to Saunders, 30 July and 11 Aug. 1840; T. Cole to S. Clarke, 22 Oct. 1840; and G. R. Phillips to G.W.R., 5 and 24 Feb. 1842, HL1/29, BTHR.
4 Single-class trains were popular, and discrimination against lower-class passengers was exercised by varying the speed of services. It appears that the road coaches were also operating below capacity before the railways' emergence: H. J. Dyos and D. H. Aldcroft, *British Transport* (1969), 76.
5 Poor Law Commissioners' letter to S. Laing, Railway Department, 3 Jan. 1842, MT11/2, P.R.O.; Third Report of *S.C. on Railways*, P.P.1844, XI, 3, 6. Railways often inserted clauses in agreements with coaching firms in which the latter promised not to run competing services: see Laing's letter to Saunders, 15 Apr. 1842, MT11/2, P.R.O.

revenue and that a continued resistance to public demands and government action (the Act of 1844 required newly-sanctioned companies to provide at least one third-class train daily[1]) would prove disadvantageous.

A distinction should be drawn between the large trunk railways and the smaller railways serving the thickly-populated industrial regions. On the former, almost all timetables lacked lower-class trains at peak periods until the mid-1840s. Joseph Baxendale's evidence to the Select Committee of 1841 showed the impossibility of travelling second-class from Lancaster to London in one day, due to the structure of the Grand Junction timetable: of six trains each way, only two provided this type of accommodation.[2] Travel from London to the North was similarly affected by poor connections for all but first-class passengers, as table 1 shows.

Table 1
Connecting passenger services from London to the North at Birmingham, 1841

London & Birmingham trains	First and Second cl.	First cl.	Mail (First)	First, Second and Third cl.
Birmingham, arrive	1.45 p.m.	2 p.m.	2.30 p.m.	3.30 p.m.

Grand Junction trains		First Cl.	Mail (First)	First and Second Cl.
Birmingham, depart		2.15 p.m.	2.45 p.m.	3.30 p.m.

Source: *Bradshaw*, TT1/16, BTHR.

Even when the major trunk railways introduced third-class travel, the trains were made inconvenient. Speeds were unnecessarily slow,[3] and travel was further discouraged by spartan carriage designs and by running at night.[4] Railway staff denied third-class passengers the full railway service—porterage duties were not carried out—and often deliberate intimidation was employed in an effort to force travel by a higher class.

1 7 & 8 Vic. c. LXXXV.
2 *S.C. on Accidents on Railways*, P.P.1841, VIII, QQ.1813–15; Grand Junction Railway timetables, 1839–40, *Bradshaw*, 25 Oct. 1839 and 1 Jan. 1840; TT1/6, 9, BTHR; and *Liverpool Courier*, 25 Dec. 1839.
3 The L. & B.'s third-class train departed at 7 a.m. and was detained at Roade from 10.40 a.m. to 12.30 p.m. to allow higher-class trains to pass it: it arrived at Birmingham at 3.30 p.m. (The 9.45 a.m. Mail train arrived at 2.30 p.m.)
4 The G.W.R. ran third-class trains to Faringdon in 1840 at 4 a.m. and 9 p.m. *Bradshaw*, TT1/10, BTHR. The same company provided open unsprung waggons on their 'goods trains', placed next to the locomotive, and consequently prone to accident.

Evidence supplied to the Railway Department in 1842 revealed that passengers had been carried on luggage trains, in horse or cattle waggons which were insufficiently sprung and had dangerously low panellings.[1] The Great Western and Grand Junction companies also provided a poor second-class service, with slow speeds and insufficient accommodation.[2]

It is not surprising that most of the trunk lines' passenger receipts came from first-class traffic before the later 1840s. Table 2, which shows the passenger receipts of two important companies, indicates that first-class receipts formed by far the largest sector, especially on the Grand Junction.

Table 2
London & Birmingham and Grand Junction railways: passenger receipts, by class, July 1841–July 1842

Railway	Year	First cl.	%	Second cl.	%	Third cl.	%	Total receipts
L. & B.	1841–2	£225,000	50.0	£204,000	45.4	£20,500	4.6	£449,500
G.J.	1841–2	£211,500	69.3	£66,800	21.9	£26,900	8.8	£305,200

Source: Accounts & Papers, P.P.1843, XLVII.

Indeed, for the United Kingdom as a whole, passenger receipts for the year ending in June 1843 showed a first-class share of over 44 per cent.[3]

The smaller railways did, however, cater for the lower fare-paying passenger. As early as 1842 it was realized that there was a valuable third-class traffic in the industrial areas of northern England and central Scotland. Many companies provided third-class carriages on all their trains. Here, the greater part of passenger revenue came from passengers paying 'third-class fares' of about 1*d*. to 1½*d*. per mile. This policy was of course encouraged by the Act of 1844: the Railway Department's specific intention was to protect the poorer travellers against the possibility of high fares, such as had been charged on the Grand Junction and London & Brighton railways, and to improve the standard of accommodation.[4]

1 BT6/280, P.R.O.
2 Wainewright, letter to G.W.R., 25 June 1839, HL 1/29, BTHR; M. Huish, letter to Railway Dept, 7 Jan. 1842, BT6/280, P.R.O.
3 First class, 44.58%: second class, 41.83%: third class, 13.59%; taken from Lardner, *op. cit.*, 273.
4 7 & 8 Vic. c. LXXXV: companies deriving at least a third of their revenue from passengers were required to provide at least one third-class train daily, stopping at all stations on the line, at a speed of not less than 12 m.p.h., with fares not to exceed a penny per mile. At the Board of Trade's discretion, the provisions could be dispensed with in special circumstances, except re fares. The revenue from this traffic was exempt from passenger duty; see Parris, *op. cit.*, 57.

The Act of 1844 at first damaged the organization of many companies' services, however, and in order to prevent loss of traffic on normal trains, efforts had to be made to improve standards, or at worst, to discourage travel by creating inconvenient departure times for third-class trains. Laing, in evidence to the Select Committee on Railways of 1844, stated that "securing the means of decent accommodation by one train daily at a low fare does, to a certain extent, involve the necessity of the company improving the accommodation by other trains, in order to prevent the traffic being drawn into this train".[1] Indeed, as soon as the Act became operational, in November 1844, many companies experienced great difficulties, owing to a sudden increase in demand for travel which severely taxed their resources.[2] By 1846, however, the accommodation of most companies in the United Kingdom had become more diversified, and the encouragement of improved carriage designs by the Railway Department had not only proved beneficial to the customer, but had also shown managers the long-term importance of the lower-class passenger.[3]

The comparative crudity of pricing techniques in the 1830s and 1840s was a further managerial problem. Erroneous assumptions pervaded railway pamphlets and must have affected the decisions of the early railway companies, who at this time possessed only a rudimentary knowledge of the means to adjust fares in order to maximize profits. As long as parliamentary restrictions on maximum rates were too generous to be really effective, and there was an absence of railway competition, the trunk lines in particular were content to maximize revenue without reference to the costs of transporting the traffic. Indeed, it may be argued that the inability of companies to calculate their costs with accuracy prevented sophistication in the method of pricing.[4] It is likely that certain traffics were carried at a working loss, a fact which would be undetected if a large revenue were obtained.

A few companies appeared to master more advanced ideas of fare manipulation at an early stage, often using expedients close to the concept of charging according to what the traffic would bear. The timetable of the Northern & Eastern Railway in 1841 showed, for example, that fares were not charged on a strict mileage basis, but were adjusted to

1 P.P.1844, XI, Q.1532.
2 T. L. Hunt, *The Rationale of Railway Administration, with a view to the greatest possible amount of accommodation, cheapness, and safety* (1846), 18–19.
3 Parris, *op. cit.*, 93–7.
4 This would seem to explain the apparent reluctance to maximize profits, detailed by G. R. Hawke, 'Pricing Policy of Railways in England and Wales Before 1881', in M. C. Reed (ed.), *Railways in the Victorian Economy* (1969), 79–80.

meet road competition.[1] There was also great debate upon the comparative advantages of a small traffic at high fares and a large traffic at low
fares. Following the experience of the Leeds & Selby Railway in 1835,
it was commonly believed that the former course was preferable, but
many companies operated in areas where high fares attracted only a very
small traffic. It was only on the major trunk routes that a small traffic
with high average fares could be maintained, but even the Grand Junction, Great Western, and London & Birmingham railways were forced
to alter their policy, in accordance with Robert Stephenson's dictum that
"the reduction of fares produces a maximum income".[2] By the time of
the second 'Mania' of 1845–6, the possibility of railway competition had
so alarmed the established lines that fare cuts were introduced as part of
the armament used in battles fought in parliamentary committees.

The pricing of passenger traffic was affected also by the government's
passenger duty, of one-eighth of a penny per passenger-mile, which was
introduced in 1832 to place railways on an equal footing with coaches.[3]
Although the English trunk lines paid the greater part of the tax (in
1840, for example, five companies paid £53,000 out of a total yield of
£72,000), the position of the smaller companies in the north of England
and in Scotland was particularly affected. The pricing policies of these
companies were complicated by a duty which in some cases formed as
much as 14 per cent of the fare, and the Treasury's decision to suspend
the allowance of a composite rate from 1839 caused many companies to
petition the government for redress. Huish, as secretary of the Glasgow
Paisley & Greenock Railway—a company affected by the decision—
stated that "Scotch railway companies . . . feel this tax more than any
other, inasmuch as they are compelled from the comparative thinness of
the population and the poverty of the districts to carry at a much lower
fare than the great English railways."[4] Sudden increases in the amounts
demanded of smaller companies seriously damaged their business positions, and after much publicity, Sir Robert Peel intervened, and an Act
of 1842 changed the duty to a five per cent tax on the gross revenue from
passenger traffic.[5]

1 Fares: Shoreditch–Ponders End, 2s., Shoreditch–Tottenham 1s., but Tottenham–
  Ponders End only 8d.: timetable, Dec. 1841, MT6/1, P.R.O. Passengers were not of
  course allowed to book twice in a journey from Shoreditch to Ponders End: A.
  Langford, letter to Railway Department, 8 Jan. 1842, BT6/280, P.R.O.
2 Stephenson's evidence, *S.C. on Railway Promotion*, P.P.1846, XIII, Q.481.
3 2 & 3 Will. IV c. CXX.
4 Huish's evidence, S.C. on Railways, P.P.1840, XIII, Q.4212. The Treasury's decision
  had been occasioned by a reduction in the mileage duty on coaches.
5 Peel's budget speech, *Hansard*, 11 Mar. 1842, and 5 & 6 Vic. c.LXXV.

The trunk lines were not at first concerned about the duty, for as long as they were able to maintain fares of over twopence a mile, the amounts paid were equivalent to a revenue tax of only five per cent. However, the proliferation of lines after the second 'Mania' necessitated a downward revision of fares, and this, together with much lower maximum charges enforced in private Acts, reduced the companies' potential profit margins on passenger traffic. Thus, all companies found that the passenger tax was, with local rates, an important and unavoidable element in working costs.[1]

VI

Goods traffic presented managements with parallel problems, involving road and water competition, accommodation, and pricing, but it was generally recognized from an early date that the goods department was far more difficult to organize than its passenger counterpart. The railway companies' inexperience of the carrying trade, and the complications of collection, loading, sorting, invoicing, and delivery, were no doubt responsible for this. During the 1830s and early 1840s most of the important companies concentrated their attention upon the profitable passenger and parcel traffics, and although the smaller railways in industrial areas derived most of their revenue from heavy mineral traffic, the trunk lines were at first sceptical of the advantage of extending the work of the goods department to bulky low-tariff goods. There are in fact several examples in the late 'thirties and early 'forties of complaints by manufacturers of prohibitive railway charges.[2] The goods business also developed more slowly because the railway did not possess the same advantage over the canal or coastal steamer as it enjoyed over the stage-coach. The carrying firms, with considerable expertise and experience, were for a time successful opponents. During the 1840s, however, the new transport by rail began to attract goods, and the traffic increased steadily at the expense of both road and water conveyances. In particular, the higher-priced items, such as groceries, teas, and luxury goods, were drawn to the railway.

The early management of the goods business was influenced to a con-

1 Despite the remission of duty allowed on 'parliamentary' third-class passengers under the Act of 1844.
2 E.g. Bass & Co., letter to the L. & B., 28 Nov. 1839; G. Jones (Ricketts & Co.), letter to G.W.R., 26 Apr. 1842: HL2/R272, HL1/29, BTHR.

siderable extent by the position of the independent carrying firms, such as Pickford & Co. and Crowley & Co., which had become accustomed to forwarding goods by canal or road under their own management. The carriers wished to continue to control the direction of goods traffic, by conducting the duties of collection, delivery, loading, and risk themselves, employing the railways to convey goods from point to point. The most vehement and protracted struggle of the early railway age resulted from the railways' efforts to secure responsibility for the carrying of goods in all its aspects. Many problems were caused by the admission of independent carriers on the lines of inexperienced companies. The important firms were able to send by railway only those items where speed of transit was important, leaving other goods to the canals and roads, on which they also carried. The flow of goods traffic thus tended to reflect the interests of these firms (especially in terms of capital invested in established routes) rather than those of the railway companies. As a result, the railways found it difficult to reduce the carriers to the status of 'feeders' for a traffic under full railway control.

Opposition to the carriers not only alienated certain sections of the public, but also hindered the development of traffic on some lines. The larger firms possessed considerable influence and had built up an important clientele, while their knowledge of the trade was at first clearly superior to that of the railways. These factors induced companies such as the London & Birmingham to persist in encouraging carriers to use the railway.[1] Of course, the relative advantages to the public of carriage by railway company or by carrier were a matter of controversy. It was alleged that competition among private firms encouraged low rates, but this was questionable, and a number of letters addressed to the London & Birmingham urged the company to take control of the goods business. Chance Brothers of Birmingham were particularly concerned, informing the company on 5 June 1839: "We take the liberty of submitting for your consideration the effect which your not acting as carriers on your own railway has on the cost of conveyance of the articles we manufacture".[2] The motives of railways such as the Grand Junction, which from its opening was eager to control all goods traffic passing over its line, were much criticized by contemporaries. Admittedly, the Grand Junction, champion

1 The L. & B. formed a close relationship with Pickford & Co.: Turnbull, 'The Railway Revolution . . .', 54–5. The company, having flirted with the possibility of giving Pickford total monopoly of goods traffic, eventually opened the line to all carriers. See the proposed agreement with Baxendale, 24 Nov. 1837, Report to the Ctee of Management, 12 Sept. 1838, and L. &. B. Mins, 5 Oct. 1838, HL2/R316 and R48, LBM1/3, BTHR.
2 HL2/R277, BTHR.

of the railways' cause, was not always honest either in its professions or actions, but it was certainly of value to the railway to eliminate the 'middlemen', and the policy was not entirely without advantage to the public.[1] The company's position as a trunk line, and its importance as one of the first railways to carry over another line (the Liverpool & Manchester), made the struggle for supremacy an event of some significance for future railway management. The Great Western and London & South Western railways were among those who followed its example in seeking to exclude carriers, and, for a time, an unsatisfactory 'mixed' system of control operated.[2] One of the major points in dispute between the railway and the carrier was the right of an arbitrary charge for 'smalls', that is, small parcels or packages. The railway companies were able to price freely for such articles, and resisted strongly the carriers' attempts to avoid the parcel tariff by packing together several parcels for different consignees in one package. On the other hand, the carriers were distressed by the railways' efforts to take from them this lucrative part of their business. They were also concerned by the use by some companies of one or two privileged firms as their agents, who received preferential allowances, a device which was clearly aimed at the independent carriers. These and other disputes embittered the rivalry, and the manager of the 1840s faced an extremely difficult situation, accompanied by expensive litigation.[3]

The regulation and classification of goods rates again provided the managements with more problems than those surrounding passenger fares. Initial rates varied widely between the different companies, as did the stipulations of the special Acts regarding maximum tolls and rates. It is not easy therefore to make positive judgments on detailed problems which would be applicable to the railway industry in general, particularly since it is often hard to determine 'tolls' for the use of the railway only, and 'tolls' which included a charge for locomotion and waggons. It can be said that the earliest schedules of rates were fairly uniform, railways following the example of the canals in relating charges to the value of the articles carried. This was particularly true while the carriage of goods was restricted to a few commodities: the Select Committee of 1839, for example, provided information which showed a close correlation between

1 Huish's evidence, *S.C. on Railways*, P.P.1844, XI, QQ.6640–50.
2 Where carrying was undertaken by both the railway and, under certain controls, by carriers on the same line, e.g. the London–Lancashire traffic: see the Grand Junction's agreement with Robins & Co., 10 Apr. 1839, Robins's evidence, *S.C. on Railways*, P.P.1840, XIII, Q.1973.
3 For further details see Chapter III.

charges allowed on a number of railways for limestone, dung, coal, sugar, timber, and cotton.[1] However, only a few years later, William Hodges, writing after the second 'Mania', remarked that the private Acts contained very great differences in the maximum charges allowable.[2] The increasing complexity of setting maximum rates had made for a greater variety in the charges, a situation encouraged by the absence of a uniform classification of goods and minerals.

Despite the differences in the maximum rates enforced by Parliament, the Select Committee of 1844 suggested that by 1842 the principal railways had achieved a broad uniformity in the merchandise rates charged to the public.[3] However, the nature of the services covered by these rates varied on each railway, and Braithwaite Poole, in his pamphlets supporting railway carrying, claimed that there were marked differences in the charges on railways which did not carry.[4] In the absence of adequate information, it is difficult to test these statements, but the evidence seems to point to disparity rather than uniformity. In practice, the position of water and road competition affected the great majority of goods hauls, making a uniform tariff based upon mileage unworkable. Companies under pressure from canals or coastal shipping soon found it necessary to reduce rates for certain classes of goods. The Grand Junction, for example, made a number of reductions from April 1840 aimed at the canal carriers.[5] On the other hand, maximum rates were sometimes illegally exceeded: the Liverpool to Manchester timber rate of 1840 was, for example, higher than the limits set by Parliament.[6] It rapidly became clear that the haphazard arrangements for the control of freight charges, based upon canal practice, bore little relation to the complex traffic situations facing the railways.

The canals had exercised a rudimentary principle of charging according to value. The Sheffield Canal in 1815 had, for example, a 2d. toll per ton-mile for potatoes and a 4d. toll for apples, although the costs incurred

1 Limestone and dung, 1d. per ton-mile; coal, $\frac{1}{2}d$.–$1\frac{1}{2}d$.; sugar and timber, 2d.–$2\frac{1}{2}d$.; cotton, 3d.: P.P.1839, X, App. 31.
2 Maximum rates for coal varied between 1d. and 4d., corn between $1\frac{1}{2}d$. and 6d., 'general merchandise' between $2\frac{1}{4}d$. and 6d.: W. Hodges, *The Law Relating to Railways and Railway Companies* . . . (1847), 432.
3 P.P.1844, XI, App. 2: a charge of about 3d. per ton-mile was reported.
4 B. Poole, *Twenty Short Reasons for Railway Companies being themselves the Carriers of Goods* . . . (1844), 3–12, and *A Dozen More Short Reasons why Railway Directors should now dismiss those middle-men, who have intruded themselves upon some lines of railway* . . . (1844), 5.
5 G. J. Mins, 1840–1, GJR1/3, BTHR.
6 Henry Booth, letter to Charles Saunders, 10 Aug. 1840, HL1/29, BTHR.

by both traffic were similar.[1] But the canals were not authorized to carry goods themselves until 1845, and other considerations did not enter into their pricing of tolls. The railways, on the other hand, discovered other considerations in fixing charges. An article's bulk, liability to damage, the risk of fire, and ease of loading and handling became important, and there is evidence to show that some companies adjusted rates to meet such contingencies at an early stage. Inevitably, the railway companies' inexperience led to complaints of arbitrary pricing methods unrelated to the circumstances of individual traffics. The railways were also hindered by the obligation to charge equally to all customers, while private carriers were able to vary charges and offer preferential rates for bulk consignments. J. R. Chorley, in his evidence to the Select Committee on Railways of 1840, claimed for example that Pickford's charged 80*s.* for the carriage of wines and spirits from London to Birmingham, but privileged customers (e.g. 'tradesmen') were quoted only 45*s.*[2] The Equal Rates Clause of 1845 modified the situation affecting railways, such that an equal charge was defined as relating to the same section of railway *under the same circumstances.*[3] This enabled an interpretation which in fact encouraged the railways to negotiate preferential agreements for large and regular consignments, although the legal position remained uncertain.

The demand for through traffic encouraged a degree of uniformity of rates, and this was cemented by the creation of the Railway Clearing House in 1842, an organization which expanded rapidly during the 1840s to provide leadership in the classification and pricing of goods traffic.[4] Gradually, rates became as uniform as traffic conditions would allow. Companies in general followed the practice of the Clearing House, but altered their policy where special local circumstances were considered important.

The railway manager of the early railway was thus confronted with a wide variety of problems. The most important of these were variations in company organization, pressing financial constraints, and a traffic management complicated by inexperience, changing competitive conditions, and the unsatisfactory nature of government intervention. This infant industry, adjusting both to itself and its environment, provided great opportunities for executive responsibility, and a competent manager

1 W. M. Acworth, *The Elements of Railway Economics* (1932), 110–11.
2 P.P.1840, XIII, Q.4994.
3 Railway Clauses Consolidation Act, 8 & 9 Vic. c.XX, s.90.
4 See P. S. Bagwell, *The Railway Clearing House in the British Economy, 1842–1922* (1968), 33–89.

could often enjoy an extraordinary control over a railway company's business affairs. The career of Captain Mark Huish affords an example of such an official, who entered railway service during the later 1830s and came to dominate the affairs of railway management for nearly two decades.

Captain Mark Huish
1808-67

Mark Huish was born in Nottingham on 9 March 1808. He was the elder son of Eliza, daughter of John Gainsford of Worksop, and Mark Huish, a hosier, and for many years Deputy-Lieutenant of Nottinghamshire.[1] Very little is known about his childhood, though it was apparently uneventful. But it is clear that he was influenced by the Nonconformist beliefs of his parents, who attended the Church of Protestant Dissenters in High Pavement. Mark was sent to the school of Mr Taylor in Castle

1 *Illustrated London News*, 4 Dec. 1858. Previous confusion as to the date of Huish's birth arose from the record of his baptism, 6 Apr. 1809.

Gate, where he was reported to have received a "classical education". It seems likely, however, that his schooling involved a thorough acquaintance with the principles of Dissent.[1]

Huish's boyhood ended with his entrance into the service of the East India Company. In 1823 he became a cadet in the company's army, on the recommendation of Mrs Bird, a family friend. 'Passing the committee' on 10 March 1824, at the age of 16, he sailed for India the next day aboard the *Larkins* of Portsmouth. On 23 March he was registered as an ensign with the 67th Regiment, Bengal Native Infantry.[2] The 'Indian Army' was a later development of the duties of the trading company. In the early nineteenth century, officers "were generally sent out to India very young, without training or supervision, to live in discomfort on meagre salaries, starting at £120 per annum. No share of the fabled riches of the East came their way, especially in time of peace."[3] This is a forthright view, certainly, but it does not appear to exaggerate either the general conditions, particularly at the time of the Burma War, 1824–6, and the Mysore Rebellion, 1830, or the experience of Huish himself.

In July 1824 the young ensign reached Fort William, Calcutta, the centre of operations for both the company and its army, under the supervision of Lord Amherst.[4] Active service did not come Huish's way, and his education and abilities soon led him into administrative work. In July 1825 he benefited from a transfer to the newly-raised 6th Extra Regiment —later known as the 74th—with which he remained until his resignation. Promotion was customarily automatic, and on 24 August, at the age of 17, he became a lieutenant. From August 1826 he acted as personal escort to Lord Amherst, and from January 1830 he performed the duties of quartermaster and acting interpreter for the regiment. It was in this post that he learned the rudimentary lessons of administration.

Huish spent five years at Chittagong as quartermaster. But life there was rigorous, and the opportunities limited. In 1834, at the age of 26, he took his furlough, a three-year period of leave granted to officers with ten

1 East India Cadet Papers, 1823, L/MIL/9/153, fos. 144–7, I. O. R. Huish remained a staunch Dissenter. It was reported that he was an enthusiastic supporter of the London City Mission, and that "his house was often thrown open for religious meetings", see Memoir of Captain Huish, *Mins of Proceedings, Institution of Civil Engineers*, xxvii (1867–8), 602.
2 V. C. P. Hodson, *List of the Officers of the Bengal Army 1758–1834*, vol. II (1928), 495–6; E. Dodwell and J. S. Miles, *Alphabetical List of the Officers of the Indian Army from the year 1760* . . . (1838), 142.
3 C. E. Carrington, *The British Overseas* . . . (1950), 193.
4 Royal Governor-General of Bengal Province, 1823–8.

years' service,[1] and although promoted to captain while absent in England, he remained unsympathetic to the cause of India and its army. In fact, there was little to induce him to return. He was faced with the prospect of a 26-year period of service without leave, and while the 1820s and 1830s marked the beginning of a serious deterioration in the East India Company and its relations with the Indians, in Britain commercial and industrial advances offered exciting opportunities for men of his experience. He came to live at 12 Clarence Street, Liverpool, and was immediately attracted by the first 'Mania' of railway promotion and building, which followed the success of the Liverpool & Manchester Railway.

The progress of railway promotion in Lancashire, the construction of major trunk routes, and an introduction into commercial society, all induced Huish to enter railway management. His education, knowledge of book-keeping, and the recently-acquired status of captain were accomplishments in his favour. The Indian Army ended payments to him in July 1837, and from this time he began seriously to consider railway employment.[2] By 1837 the locomotive had become the accepted means of conveyance, and although the initial efforts to link the main population centres in England had, on the whole, been satisfied (in terms of promotion if not construction), there was fresh activity to promote railways in Scotland. The majority of posts on English lines had been filled, and thus it was to Scotland that Huish turned.

In October 1837 Huish answered an advertisement for a secretary to the Glasgow Paisley & Greenock Railway:

WANTED a PERSON to Act as SECRETARY to this COMPANY. He must be qualified to conduct the general business and correspondence of the Company, and to take a general superintendence and management of all the Books and Accounts, and be able to give his undivided time and attention to the duties of the office.

James Turner, Interim Secretary
October 17th, 1837.[3]

The Greenock company, authorized in July 1837, was in English eyes a comparatively minor venture. Only 22½ miles in length, it was intended to serve a dense, but predominantly poor population, already enjoying an

---

1 *The New Arrangement, with respect to the Rank and Promotions of the Army* . . . (1796), 30–1; *The Furlough Regulations of the Indian Army* . . . *By An Officer of the Bengal Artillery* (1852), 5.
2 Huish did not formally resign his commission until July 1838.
3 *Greenock Advertiser*, 19 Oct. 1837.

extensive steamboat service on the Clyde, and dominated by a landed
interest hostile to railways. Such was the interest in the post, however,
that Turner, the temporary secretary, was able to write that "applications
for the Secretaryship are pouring in from all quarters".[1] Over 60 were in
fact received, and from a short-list composed mainly of Scotsmen the
Board of Directors chose Huish, on 3 November 1837. His salary was to
be £200, and securities of £1,000 were required.[2] He was informed of the
decision on the 4th, in a letter from Turner, who had for some time been
anxious to transfer the burden of work in order to concentrate on the
company's legal affairs. Huish immediately proved to be a keen, almost
too keen, successor, who was anxious to give a good impression and eager
to start work.[3] On 17 November Huish named as his securities John Ray
of Heanor Hall, Derbyshire, Mrs I. B. Smith of Bridgford House, Nottingham, and James Gilfillan of Liverpool. Moving to Glen House in
Greenock, he began work as secretary on 24 November, continuing with
the company until 7 July 1841: from January 1838, he also acted as one
of the joint secretaries to the Glasgow & Paisley Joint Line Committee,
created to undertake the construction and management of the first seven
miles of the line, and in July his salary was increased to £400 per annum.

Huish's duties had been described as follows: "to conduct the correspondence of the company, take a general superintendence and management of the Books, and Accounts, prepare the business for the meetings,
and to take the minutes".[4] It will be seen that he carried out these duties
efficiently, and that his talent for negotiation was particularly useful. At
a time when the duties of railway officials were fluid, Huish, supported
by an enthusiastic Board, was allowed great freedom both to express and
to implement his views, and even to dictate policy.[5] He was also entrusted
with various missions to England to meet Joseph Locke, the consulting
engineer, and to discuss modes of working, and the plans of the English
companies in relation to Scotland.

As secretary to the Glasgow & Paisley Joint Committee, Huish possessed a less direct influence. He mainly reported the intentions of his
Board to the representatives of the Glasgow Kilmarnock & Ayr Railway,
which was to share the line, and carried out routine tasks as directed.

1 Turner to Stewart, 24 Oct. 1837, G. P. G. Letter Book, BR/GPG/4/2, S.R.O.
2 G.P.G. Mins, 3 Nov. 1837, BR/GPG/1/1, S.R.O. It appears that the Board were
   unaware of Huish's captaincy at this time.
3 Turner to Huish 4 Nov. 1837; Huish to Turner, 6 and 9 Nov. 1837; BR/GPG/4/2,
   S.R.O.
4 Turner to Geibie, 26 Oct. 1837, BR/GPG/4/2, S.R.O.
5 See Chapter III, and Huish's relations with the Chairman, Ker.

Nevertheless, by working hard, and dealing with diverse railway problems at first hand, he was able to study all the facets of promotion, construction and working—an invaluable experience and an important grounding in railway management.

Huish visited Liverpool "on private affairs" in May 1841, and was approached by representatives of the Grand Junction Railway. The company had been experiencing difficulties with its existing executive structure, and in particular, was dissatisfied with Captain J. E. Cleather, the Outdoor Superintendent and Secretary; recognizing Huish's competence, and his talents as a negotiator, they offered him the post. On 29 May the Grand Junction Board proposed that he be "called in",[1] before the Greenock directors had been informed of the approach.[2] Huish professed a reluctance to leave Scotland, where he had been treated well, and he defended the Greenock company with his customary tenacity until his departure in July 1841. It is important to note, however, that on the opening of the railway throughout in March, Errington, the resident engineer, acted as manager, and the secretaryship became a more mundane post. In these circumstances the Grand Junction offer was far too attractive to be rejected, as Huish admitted, and he tendered his resignation on 4 June. His eventual successor was Wyndham Harding, another notable railway figure.[3]

Returning to Liverpool with an enhanced reputation, Huish was plunged into the turmoil of English railway politics. The Grand Junction Railway, opened throughout on 4 July 1837, was part of the main trunk route between Lancashire and the South, and was in consequence at the centre of fierce controversies concerning through traffic. But Huish was far from overawed by this prospect, and, indeed, he asserted himself confidently from the beginning. After a formal introduction to the Board on 14 July, he began work as secretary, with an outdoor manager, Norris, under his instructions, and 28 July found him busy with statements of loans and liabilities, and with arrangements for a goods agency at Chester.[4] The directors were quick to realize his value, and at the General Meeting of 6 August 1841 they referred to the "appointment of Cpt. Huish to the office of secretary and general manager . . . In Cpt. Huish the Directors have . . . secured for the company a valuable officer, and

---

1 G. J. Mins, 29 May 1841, GJR1/3, BTHR.
2 The Greenock Company's Chairman, Robert Ker, had been notified in private.
3 Harding was appointed on 23 September 1841 at £300 p.a. On his contribution to early railway management, see his *Facts bearing on the progress of the Railway System* (1848), and *The Gauge Question. Evils of a diversity of gauge and a remedy* (1845).
4 G. J. Mins, 14–28 July 1841, GJR1/3, BTHR.

one who from his previous connexion with railway concerns will be found prepared at once for the able discharging of the varied and important duties now committed to his care.''[1] It seems, therefore, that the directors considered Huish well worth his large salary, which must have been initially in the region of £700–£1,000. When the company was enlarged in 1845, Huish's salary was raised to £1,250, a very large salary at the time, and proof of his predominance as a railway executive.

Huish's career with the Grand Junction affords ample evidence of his efficiency, both as an administrator, and as a tactician in struggles between rival companies. He took on many new duties, in comparison with his work for the Greenock company, and was thus able to demonstrate a far wider range of abilities. The Grand Junction proved an ideal employer for the ambitious secretary, for it was in many ways a pioneer in railway management. It led the campaign in favour of the control of goods traffic by railway companies, and took part in the early negotiation of traffic and running agreements. Huish proved a competent negotiator, for example, in connection with the 'West Coast' (Caledonian) project, where his experience of Scottish railway affairs was invaluable. He was also quick to suggest policies to the Board. As early as August 1841 he sponsored the experiment of low fares in the Wolverhampton area.[2]

Huish became involved in a nation-wide controversy as the champion of the Grand Junction in its dispute with Pickford & Co. over the place of carriers in railway goods traffic.[3] His attitude had important repercussions later, when he was manager of the London & North Western, but was of significance in the early 1840s in placing him among the foremost managers in the country. His position was also due to a mastery of inter-railway affairs, which became increasingly important as new schemes threatened the supremacy of the established companies. The Grand Junction secretary was an able strategist, and although some of his triumphs had damaging effects later (his encouragement of the Great Western's broad gauge in the west Midlands, though beneficial to the Grand Junction, created problems for the London & North Western in the 1850s) he was a most important influence behind the company's amalgamation with the Liverpool & Manchester and other railways in 1845,[4] and the diplomatic manœuvres which led to the formation,

1 G. J. General Meeting, 6 Aug. 1841, GJR1/7, BTHR. Shortly after his appointment, Huish was married, to his first cousin, Margaret Huish, on 12 August 1841. There were no children.
2 G. J. Mins, 3 Aug. 1841, GJR1/3, BTHR.
3 See Chapters I and III.
4 From 11 August 1845 Huish became manager, with Henry Booth secretary, of the enlarged company.

sanctioned on 16 July 1846, of the London & North Western Railway.

On 10 October 1846 the directors of the newly-formed company, an amalgamation of the Grand Junction, London & Birmingham, and Manchester & Birmingham railways, appointed Huish "General Manager for both divisions of the railway". He moved from Liverpool to Euston in April 1847, and his salary was increased to £2,000 per annum. Whilst manager, he lived at Harlesdon House, Harlesdon Green, in Middlesex, close to the present Willesden Junction station.[1] The change in his status signified an important extension not only of his powers and responsibilities but also of the company for which he acted. From 1846 to 1858 he was the executive head of the largest and most important railway in the country, and one of the leading figures of his day. His managerial abilities were notable, and the successes he achieved compare with those of Allport, Saunders, Watkin, and Findlay, and cause him to be ranked with the foremost railway managers of the Victorian age.[2]

Huish's strong personality and close acquaintance with the intricacies of traffic management enabled him once more to exert a powerful influence over the councils of his employers, and there were many instances of his dictating to the Board and its several committees. The 'Euston Confederacy', a series of traffic agreements aimed at securing traffic from competitors, was very much his creation, and a startling answer to the difficulties facing the established lines as a result of Parliament's sanction of duplicate projects. His independence was subject to limits, however, for the Board was the best-informed in the country, and directors such as George Carr Glyn, Lord Chandos, Richard Moon, and Admiral C. R. Moorsom could not easily be brushed aside. Nevertheless, there was no doubt that the manager was frequently too close to the heart of railway matters to be seriously challenged: his work at the Railway Clearing House and his attendance at all the important select committees on railway affairs were testimonies to his great standing. His reports, which covered a wide range of subjects, from accident control and telegraphic communication to permanent way costing and traffic management, commanded great respect. He perfected a goods system which excluded independent control of terminal duties, and his efforts to secure a wider and more uniform acceptance of principles of through traffic were outstanding. He also led the way in the participation of executives in financial management and in rudimentary cost accountancy.

1 *Middlesex Directory*, 1855, Guildhall Library, London.
2 James Allport (Midland), Charles Saunders (Great Western), Edward Watkin (Manchester Sheffield & Lincolnshire), George Findlay (London & North Western).

Although in charge of an extensive business Huish was also eager to interfere in minor problems, which tended to incur the resentment of his fellow officers, and to weaken his position as administrative head.[1] Certainly he contributed to the solution of many problems which might have been delegated, including the provision of postal facilities and the organization of royal trains. But his attitude was also symptomatic of a zealous regard for all questions involving the company.

The London & North Western found itself increasingly under attack from powerful competitors, and even Huish's monumental efforts could not avert the inevitable decline of its predominance. The collapse of his 'pooling' agreements, and of the company's alliances with the Midland and Manchester Sheffield & Lincolnshire companies in 1857, led to his fall from grace, and eventual resignation, on 11 September 1858. This move, although forced upon him as a result of the course taken by competing lines, had been occasioned by the scheming within his own company, and his successor, William Cawkwell, general manager until 1874, was appointed chiefly because it was felt that he would be more amenable to pressure from the directors.

The opposition of Richard Moon, C. R. Moorsom, and Edward Tootal, with the acquiescence of Carr Glyn, proved to be decisive factors in Huish's downfall. Indeed, as early as 1856, Carr Glyn, in a letter to Lord Chandos, stated:

> The extent of the business through the manager's office is so large and multifarious that not only does Capt. Huish require assistance, but it really becomes of great importance that some one under him should be capable of carrying on the business and its details in the event of his retirement or anything happening to him . . .[2]

On 5 September 1858 he wrote to Chandos:

> I felt for some time past the isolated position in which the L. & N.W. has been placed . . . I have been particularly struck by the position in which the Manager . . . is left at the Railway Clearing House meetings. No-one supports or co-operates with him and even those companies connected with the L. & N.W. leave the individual unsupported. I have wondered that he did not feel this and tender his resignation . . . I am quite disposed to admit great talent and pains-

---

1 Note George Neele's account of Huish's intervention in the case of a lost dog:
  G. P. Neele, *Railway Reminiscences* (1904), 57–8.
2 Carr Glyn to Chandos, 14 Jan. 1856, Glyn Mills & Co. Archives.

taking on the part of Cpt. Huish . . . but he has drawbacks which have interfered with his good qualities . . . Cawkwell always appeared to me a plain small man and generally respected . . .[1]

Further letters show opposition to Huish, but the coup was not welcomed by all, and Samuel Ashton, who had objected to Huish's rivalry with Watkin of the Manchester & Sheffield company, told a fellow director on 14 September:

I cannot contemplate on our own proceedings at the N.W. Board with all the satisfaction I could desire. We have made Huish the scapegoat for the difficulties we are under, & why?—because he has too pertinaciously stood up for our interests against our adversaries . . . We are now at sea for another manager, and be he ever so clever, it will require a long period before he can know a tithe of what Huish has at his fingers end . . .[2]

Huish's letter of resignation combined contrition with a certain self-justification. He wrote:

The present difficulties, as you are aware, have been brought about by circumstances wholly beyond my control, but I feel that I am acting in accordance with a duty which I owe to the Board and to the interests entrusted to your care, by resigning my charge, in the hope that, by a change of management, some progress may be made towards a settlement of the present embarrassments.[3]

This self-sacrifice was poorly rewarded, however. Huish received 18 months' salary, a free pass for life, and an address and testimonial from over five thousand employees of the company. But he was given no pension, and the reward was niggardly for a man who had worked so hard to defend the company's interests. He moved in retirement to the seclusion of Combe Wood, Bonchurch, Isle of Wight, and soon ceased to have any dealings with his former employers. During these years he took an interest in several companies with which he was connected. He was persuaded to become a director of the Isle of Wight Railway, thus returning to a concern not unlike the Glasgow Paisley & Greenock in its size and scope. He also acted as chairman of two important non-railway companies—the Clifton Suspension Bridge and the Electric and International Telegraph—and his influence as a railway authority, although damaged,

1 Carr Glyn to Chandos, 5 Sept. 1858, HL2/R307/4, BTHR.
2 Ashton to Smith, 14 Sept. 1858, HL2/R383, BTHR.
3 Huish, 11 Sept. 1858, HL2/R373/7, BTHR.

did not disappear altogether. He was an important contributor to the Royal Commission on Railways of 1867, gave evidence to the Select Committee on the Cornwall Railway, was active in the problems of Irish railways, and acted as arbitrator in a number of inter-company disputes.[1]

Huish died on 18 January 1867, aged 58. The *Railway Times* commented simply "De mortuis nil nisi bonum", and there was no mention of his railway career on his tombstone, which ironically, or perhaps at his own wish, bore the following inscription:

> In Memory of Mark Huish, Esq., of Combe Wood, Bonchurch Formerly Cpt. 74th B.N.I. who died 18th January 1867 aged 58 Years. "Them also which sleep in Jesus will God bring with him". 1 Thess. 4. 14.[2]

1 See Chapter VIII.
2 St Boniface's Graveyard, Combe Wood, I.O.W. I am indebted to Mr M. B. English for this information.

3

Huish's early railway career 1837-46

Huish's first experience of the railways coincided with the formative period of the industry's history described in Chapter 1. In this chapter an examination is made of the major management problems which he faced in his early career—as secretary of the Glasgow Paisley & Greenock Railway, 1837–41, and secretary and general manager of the Grand Junction, 1841–6. Special attention is paid to his place in the organization of these companies, his involvement with passenger and goods traffic, and his contribution to overall business efficiency. A similar pattern of analysis will be followed in succeeding chapters.

1　Company organization

The complex technical requirements of railway companies ensured a considerable variability in the organization of executive authority, and the duties of paid officials differed with the circumstances and ideas of each company. At first, basic precepts of organization had been broadly similar, since they were borrowed from the same sources, and in particular from canal companies. The 'Agent' or 'Superintendent' of the early-nineteenth-century canal performed supervisory duties over tolls, accounts, and working which acted as a precedent, especially for smaller railways. Further, the techniques of early railway management bore some comparison with the demands made of the coal 'viewer' in the north-east.[1] But the railway company soon demonstrated its essential difference from earlier industrial businesses. In particular, its size and the extent of its capital investment helped to alter the prevalent concept that company control should rest upon direct ownership. The early railways, therefore, helped to stimulate interest in the delegation of management to paid officers, and Captain Huish was one of the early executives who benefited from this change. As secretary of both the Glasgow Paisley & Greenock and Grand Junction companies, he performed duties which extended over a far wider area than had been generally expected of such an official.

Organizational differences between the Glasgow & Greenock and Grand Junction railways, which affected Huish's attitude to managerial problems, stemmed from the respective positions of the two companies. Huish joined the Scottish railway "before a spade was put in the ground",[2] and although chiefly concerned with general administrative tasks, he was expected to deal with problems of construction and land purchase. On the Grand Junction, these duties were delegated to engineers and solicitors, and the work was not pressing, since the company was well established when Huish became its secretary.

The Greenock Railway derived its strength from the local nature of its Board of Directors—a fact well thought of by contemporaries and held to secure economy and honesty.[3] It also had the benefit of a small but closely-knit executive which was constantly in touch with Board policy.

1 S. Pollard, *The Genesis of Modern Management* (1965), 127–8.
2 Huish's evidence, *Royal Commission on the Gauge of Railways*, P.P.1846, XVI, Q.4614.
3 "There is entirely a local board, the best guarantee against extravagance", *Railway Magazine and Annals of Science*, IV (1838), 18.

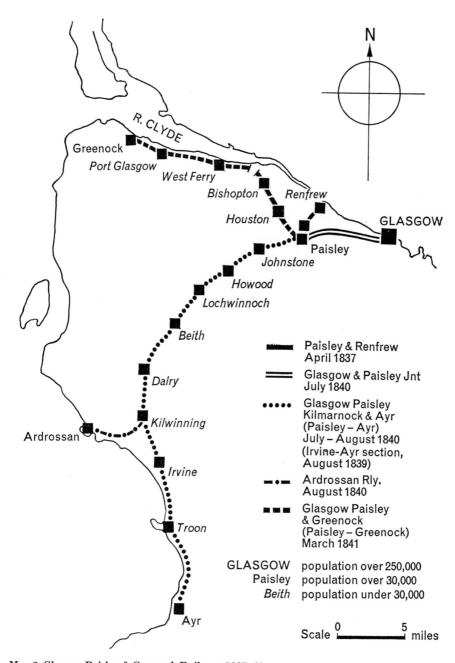

N

R. CLYDE

Greenock
Port Glasgow
West Ferry
Bishopton
Houston
Renfrew
GLASGOW
Paisley
Johnstone
Howood
Lochwinnoch
Beith
Dalry
Kilwinning
Ardrossan
Irvine
Troon
Ayr

Paisley & Renfrew
April 1837

Glasgow & Paisley Jnt
July 1840

Glasgow Paisley
Kilmarnock & Ayr
(Paisley – Ayr)
July – August 1840
(Irvine-Ayr section,
August 1839)

Ardrossan Rly.
August 1840

Glasgow Paisley
& Greenock
(Paisley – Greenock)
March 1841

GLASGOW population over 250,000
Paisley population over 30,000
Beith population under 30,000

Scale 0 — 5 miles

Map 2. Glasgow Paisley & Greenock Railway, 1837–41

Management problems were thereby eased, and any initial difficulties which existed centred mainly upon the organization of the Glasgow–Paisley section of the railway, which was managed by an inter-company joint committee.[1] On the whole, enthusiasm, and the comparatively small size of the company, compensated for the lack of a well-defined system of authority.

It was certainly Huish's experience that, while the early companies were small, or in the construction stage, an official could often exercise a patriarchal, almost a dictatorial, control of business. According to the Greenock Board, the secretary was to deal with the minutes and supervise the books and accounts.[2] In fact, Huish's rôle became very close to that envisaged by the Canterbury and Whitstable Railway in its advertisement for a manager in 1831:

> He will have the superintendence of every department and it will be his duty to bring into focus from time to time the entire situation of the undertaking and business. It will be his particular office to consider of and adopt every means in his power to increase the company's business and to afford facilities to passengers and persons in the transit and delivery of goods and merchandise . . .[3]

The Greenock company, however, tended to equate operation with the engineering department, and in February 1841, shortly before the opening of the line, it was decided to appoint Errington, the resident engineer, as traffic manager, "with the assistance of Captain Huish".[4] This decision, which can also be seen in the Glasgow & Paisley Joint Line Committee's definition of a manager's duties, certainly affected Huish's position, and may well have influenced his decision to resign.

The Grand Junction had by 1841 a developed organization, based upon the committee system. This had evolved from the practice of the Stockton & Darlington and Liverpool & Manchester railways, where the Board of Directors divided into smaller groups to handle specialized matters such

1 This section was shared by the Glasgow Paisley & Greenock and Glasgow Paisley Kilmarnock & Ayr companies.
2 Turner to Geibie, 26 Oct. 1837, BR/GPG/4/2, S.R.O.
3 *Kent Herald*, 28 July 1831, quoted in R. B. Fellows, *History of the Canterbury and Whitstable Railway* . . . (1930), 39; the company's experiment with a manager was abandoned in 1832.
4 G. P. G. Mins, 9 Feb. 1841, BR/GPG/1/2, S.R.O. This had also been the policy of the Stockton & Darlington Railway, whose engineer, Thomas Storey, acted as traffic manager.

as traffic, finance, and construction.[1] The Grand Junction benefited from the fact that many of its directors fulfilled the same function for the Liverpool & Manchester Railway itself, a company which had experienced many problems of control, even before 1830.[2]

Huish was recruited largely because Captain Cleather, the Outdoor Superintendent and Secretary, had been unable, in the face of increased business, successfully to combine operational and secretarial duties.[3] To ease this situation the Board also created a separate post of 'Manager of the Outdoor Department', and R. S. Norris was appointed. He was, however, to receive his orders from Huish, who was clearly intended to be the executive head of the company: at the general meeting of 6 August 1841, for example, he was specifically referred to as "Secretary and General Manager".[4] Huish, in fact, conferred constantly with the directors, advised them on general policy, and became responsible for traffic management. He dealt with labour problems, and represented the company in legal disputes and before select committees dealing with railway matters. His responsibility thus extended to the general welfare, efficiency, and overall business performance of the company, and in planning for the market and making routine supervision of the several departments he performed functions which were close to the managerial precepts of later Victorian, and even modern, times.[5]

One executive does not create a successful organization, however, and the delegation of authority, not only from director to manager, but also from manager to subordinate officer, was necessary for the smooth running of a railway as large as the Grand Junction. Huish, indeed, was entrusted with the problems arising from the performance of all company staff, including matters of discipline, and a system of executive res-

1 The committee system was not of course novel to railways: banks, turnpike roads, and canals also developed this type of management.
2 L. & M. Mins, 1826–30, LVM1/1, BTHR.
3 G. J. Mins, 29 May 1841, GJR1/3, BTHR.
4 G. J. Mins, 28 July 1841; G.J. General Meeting, 6 Aug. 1841, GJR1/3, GJR1/7, BTHR.
5 See J. Parsloe, *Our Railways* (1878), 115–16; anon., 'The Lot of the Railway Manager', *Financial News* (14 Nov. 1889); anon., *Railways and Railway Men* (1892), 9–28; Sir G. Findlay, *The Working And Management of an English Railway* (1899), 58–70. On modern theory, see W. S. Barry, *Managing a Transport Business* (1963), 119–26; D. S. Beach, *Personnel: The Management of People at Work* (New York, 1965), 191–221, 459–87, 538–606; P. F. Drucker, *The Practice of Management* (1955), 4–13, 301–9; F. E. Folts, *Introduction to Industrial Management* (New York, 1963), 16–31; F. Harbison and C. A. Myers, *Management in the Industrial World. An International Analysis* (New York, 1959), 8–20; A. E. B. Perrigo, *Modern Management Techniques* (1968), 18–37; G. A. Steiner, *Top Management Planning* (1969), 87–104; etc.

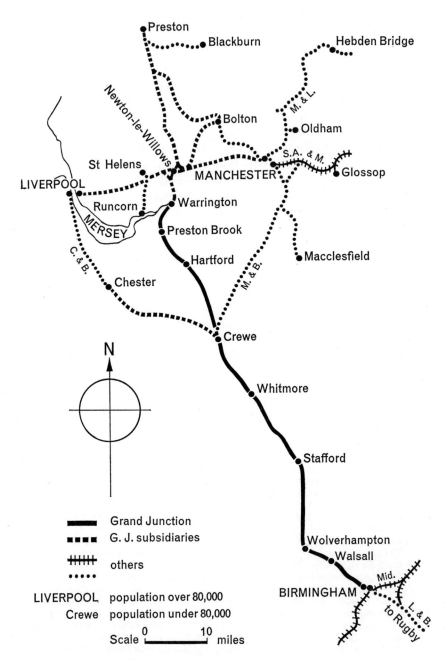

Map 3. Grand Junction Railway, 1833–46

ponsibility was clearly defined. This suggests that the company was being managed in a relatively sophisticated way and that the demands on the railway as a business enterprise caused it to lead in the delegation of powers to paid officials.

Huish's position may be compared with that of two other early officials, Captain John Laws, of the Manchester & Leeds, and Henry Booth, of the Liverpool & Manchester. Laws, the superintendent of the line from 1839, worked mainly on outdoor matters, although these paralleled much dealt with by Huish. In April 1839, for example, he reported on the cost of works at Rochdale, just as Huish investigated the expense of a loading wharf at Walsall in August 1843.[1] Laws, indeed, was occupied with a variety of problems affecting passenger and goods traffic. However, although his opinion carried weight with the directors, many ideas were referred to the committees of management and finance. He did not enjoy Huish's freedom of action, especially with regard to negotiations with outside parties, and from the beginning, in fact, he had been intended to work in close conjunction with Gill, a director.[2] Huish possessed a far wider range of responsibilities than did Laws, whose work at times overlapped with that of the traffic superintendent. Henry Booth, as secretary and treasurer of the Liverpool & Manchester, also differed from Huish, in this case in his interest in financial affairs. But he also enjoyed considerable freedom in his activities, and was, like Huish, interested in traffic matters and staff problems.[3]

The managerial structure of the Grand Junction developed further during Huish's period of office, and this contributed to the company's success in the 1840s. Its system of executive responsibility can be seen in both letters and Board minutes: in particular, Huish became involved in the practice of compiling and examining reports, a process related to Carr Glyn's ideas of a "departmental system".[4] But although the Board recognized its inability to deal with all management matters as business increased, its meetings continued to be cluttered with trivialities even after Huish's appointment,[5] and it was many years before the distinction between 'direction' and 'management' was properly understood, even by the leading companies. A change took place in August 1844, however,

1 M. & L. Mins, 22 Apr. 1839, LY1/2, G. J. Mins, 9 Aug. 1843, GJR1/5, BTHR.
2 M. & L. Mins, 7 Jan. 1839, LY1/2, BTHR.
3 L. & M. Mins, 9 Aug.–16 Dec. 1841, etc. LVM1/5, BTHR.
4 G. J. Mins, 8 Dec. 1841, 18 May and 29 June 1842, GJR1/4, BTHR, and cf. Glyn's memorandum in Chapter I.
5 A £50 claim for a dead horse was refused (G. J. Mins, 3 Nov. 1841) and a 13s. 6d. claim for butter was considered (G. J. Mins, 5 July 1843, GJR1/4, BTHR).

inspired by John Moss, the Chairman, and Huish, and thereafter minor matters were delegated to a newly-formed working committee. In 1845, further developments resulted in the creation of fixed rather than rotating committees responsible for the main items of management, under Huish's co-ordinating control.[1] The company thus moved towards a departmental system, with responsible executive officers controlled by directors generally conscious of their duties.[2]

Other companies appear to have created organizations similar to that of the Grand Junction, often with a proliferation of committees, but this is in no way proof that management was conducted on the lines of effective responsibility. Minute books are often misleading,[3] and certain companies which enjoyed a working success in the early 1840s—before the spread of railway competition—were able to conceal administrative defects and haphazard control. Ideas of responsibility varied markedly. The Manchester & Leeds Railway, for example, required weekly reports from all its officers during the early 'forties, while on other, smaller lines, such as the North Union, the Board supervised the entire system without this aid. The Grand Junction, although by no means a faultless company, benefited from its intelligent application of the theory of practical management by railway officials who were closest to problems of day-to-day working. There was little comparison here with the complicated structure of the Eastern Counties Railway, for example, which encouraged internal dissension and inadequate traffic management.[4]

2 Passenger traffic

From the mid 1830s provision for passenger travel became the major preoccupation of most railway executives. In Scotland, the Greenock Railway, with the Glasgow Paisley Kilmarnock & Ayr and Edinburgh & Glasgow companies, brought the first inter-urban routes to that country, and Huish played a leading rôle in this development. Not only did he help to formulate the policy of his own company, but he also participated in

1 G. J. Mins, 14 Aug. 1844, 5 Feb. and 4–14 June 1845, GJR1/5, BTHR.
2 Meetings were, however, sometimes inquorate, e.g. 27 and 29 July, 3, 5, and
    9 August, and 14 September 1842, GJR1/4, BTHR.
3 Those of the Eastern Counties and North Midland railways suggest a sophisticated
    management system, but as events proved, these lines were notoriously mis-
    managed.
4 E. Doble, 'History of the Eastern Counties Railway . . .', unpublished London
    Ph.D. thesis (1939), 119–25; and E. Cos Mins, e.g. EC1/5, EC1/37, EC1/56, BTHR.

the discussion of general issues affecting passenger traffic in the west of Scotland at a time when precedents were few.

Financial and engineering difficulties, which delayed the opening of the railway to Greenock, ensured that Huish's experience of Scottish passenger traffic was confined mainly to the planning stages. He was actively involved in the purchase of rolling stock and the planning of services, for both the Joint Line and the Greenock Railway proper. As early as August 1838, for example, he reported to the Joint Line Committee, with Humphrey, the Glasgow & Ayr secretary, on the mode of operation to be followed, and the rolling stock required.[1] In late 1840 plans were made to begin operation on the Greenock line. Here Huish was mainly concerned with the formulation of timetables and train frequencies, matters complicated by the fact that the company shared its Glasgow terminus and the line to Paisley with the Glasgow & Ayr Railway. By means of patient negotiation he secured an advantageous position for the Glasgow & Greenock: he insisted on reserving the even hours of departure for his company, and his timetable proposals were close to those eventually adopted.[2]

The precise nature of the company's facilities should be made clear. Although the initial services provided first- and second-class accommodation only, the fares charged for first-class approximated to those for *third-class* on the English trunk lines, while comfort was scarcely equal to second-class on the Grand Junction. Later, the Greenock company became the most significant 'third-class line' of the 1840s, and as early as 1842 64 per cent of its passenger traffic was third-class. In the year ending June 1847 the figure was 83 per cent. Such a policy was not, of course, freely chosen, for the nature of demand dominated the company's decisions. The Greenock management did exercise choice, however, in refusing to provide season tickets, and in rejecting Sunday travel. Although there was strong criticism of the latter, the practice was widespread in Scotland in the 1840s, and it is clear that local religious interests in Greenock exerted a direct influence. The majority of English railways, on the other hand, provided Sunday trains.[3] There is no evidence to show that Huish approved of Scottish policy, despite his religious sentiments.

Huish's experience of pricing policy in Scotland was again limited.

1 G.P.J. Mins, 2 Aug. 1838, BR/GPJ/1/1, S.R.O.
2 G.P.G. Works Ctee Mins, 3 Aug. 1840; G.P.J. Ctee Mins, 17 Dec. 1840; G.P.G. Mins, 22 Jan. 1841; BR/GPG/1/6, BR/GPJ/1/1, BR/GPG/1/2, S.R.O.
3 By 1847 only four small railways in England and Wales closed on Sundays, but in Scotland the G.P.G. was one of 13 which did so: Accounts & Papers, P.P.1847, LXIII.

He did, however, work with the Glasgow & Ayr company on the Joint Line's fare table of 1840, and was later instructed to draft the Greenock Railway's first fare schedule of March 1841.[1] But the Board of Directors severely reduced his freedom of action, setting a fare of 2s. 6d. first- and 1s. 6d. second-class for the Glasgow to Greenock journey. These fares were still in use in 1847, any experiments in pricing being limited to the lower-class sectors.

The low fares quoted by the Clyde steamboats had a pronounced effect upon company policy, and Huish's schedule of fares included some constructed on a strict mileage basis, others adjusted to meet the needs of special 'competitive' areas. Most of the short-distance fares (up to four miles) were similar, being 1.71d. first- and 1.14d. second-class per mile: fares from Glasgow to Paisley, Houston to Bishopton, and Port Glasgow to Greenock are examples.[2] But the Board's stipulation for the Glasgow–Greenock journey involved a fare of only 1.33d. and 0.88d., reflecting the competition by river. The relative freedom from alternative transport explains the higher charges quoted for the Paisley–Houston and Bishopton–Port Glasgow journeys—2.4d. and 1.6d., 2.0d. and 1.6d. per mile, fares which the company would no doubt have liked to extend over the entire schedule. Joint rail-steamer fares further illustrate the effect of competition on pricing policy: here, the company was forced to make substantial concessions to steamboat companies co-operating with the railway.[3] The company's relations with the Glasgow Paisley & Ardrossan Canal were also important in this context. In 1841 the canal's 'swift' boats were said to be carrying about a thousand passengers daily between Glasgow and Paisley for sixpence.[4] The railway company introduced a third-class fare of sixpence to meet this challenge, but with mixed success, and when the canal proposed a reduction to fourpence, a controversy arose as to the best plan of action. Humphrey and Bass, the Joint Line's manager, wished to reduce the railway fare to fourpence, but Huish, who had played a prominent part in abortive negotiations with the canal, instead favoured a cut in goods rates of between 20 and 30 per cent.[5] The Greenock Board supported Huish's view, the Glasgow & Ayr Board sup-

1 G.P.G. Mins, 4 Dec. 1840, 23 Feb., 5–12 Mar. 1841, BR/GPG/1/2, S.R.O.
2 Calculated from Huish's memorandum on fares, 23 Feb. 1841, and his revisions of 5–12 Mar., BR/GPG/1/2, S.R.O.
3 T. R. Gourvish, 'The Railways and Steamboat Competition in Early Victorian Britain', *Transport History*, IV (1971), 10–11, 16–17.
4 R. S. Skey, *Report to the Committee of the Birmingham and Liverpool Junction Canal on the present state of the competition between the canal carriers . . . and the Grand Junction . . .* (1841), 15.
5 G.P.J. Mins, 1–15 July 1841, BR/GPJ/1/1, S.R.O.

ported that of Humphrey and Bass, but Huish left Scotland at this stage (July 1841) and eventually the railway did cut its fare (in November). In retrospect, Huish's policy appears to have been the sounder, for not only did the fare reduction make the Glasgow–Paisley services scarcely remunerative, even using the company's rudimentary costing calculations,[1] but freight reductions might well have embarrassed the canal without prejudicing the railway's passenger system. Wyndham Harding, Huish's successor, remarked in 1844 that the railway's superior speed eventually proved decisive, even when the canal fares were lower.[2]

There were early advocates of the economic advisability of full train loads to be achieved by low fares,[3] but the Greenock company's fares were too low to yield anything but a very small profit on the large capital sum invested. The working costs proved higher than expected, and the experiments with third-class fares and accommodation merely attracted passengers from the first and second classes.[4] Nevertheless, Huish's knowledge of the pricing difficulties in Scotland was useful to him in later circumstances. He clearly understood, for example, that a low fares policy undertaken merely for the sake of increasing the traffic might result in reduced profits, since working costs were often increased disproportionately. He also undertook traffic-forecasting: his estimates of likely passenger traffic made in 1838 proved very close to the actual figures in 1841, a fact which was very valuable for the company in planning its services.[5] A manager's success was dependent upon the skill with which he responded to actual transport demands and tested traffic elasticity. The evidence suggests that Huish followed a consistent and practical policy in Scotland, despite the comparatively short time he had to prove his worth.

When Huish joined the Grand Junction, its passenger services were already established. At first, the practice followed was that of the Liverpool & Manchester, with whom a through service to Birmingham was

1 A 4*d.* fare from Glasgow to Paisley amounts to 0.57*d.* per mile: the Greenock company estimated that costs for the first three months of operation amounted to 0.61*d.* per passenger-mile: G.P.G. General Meeting, 2 July 1841, BR/GPG/1/2, S.R.O.
2 Harding's evidence, *S.C. on Railways*, P.P.1844, XI, Q.5365.
3 E.g. P. P. F. Degrand, *On the Advantages of Low Fares and Low Rates of Freight* . . . (Boston, U.S.A., 1840), 1–39.
4 Harding's evidence, *S.C. on Railways*, P.P.1844, XI, QQ.5342–57, and see Gourvish, 'The Railways and Steamboat Competition . . .', *loc. cit.*, 11.
5 In the company's report of December 1838 the number of daily passengers was put at 2,000: BR/GPG/1/2, S.R.O.; the returns for the first 40 days' operation gave 88,750 passengers: *Herapath's Railway Magazine*, 5 June 1841.

organized. Two types of train were introduced—the 'First Class' and the 'Mixed' (first and second class)—and there were three types of carriage design, all with covered and seated accommodation. Third-class travel was discouraged, but by 1841 there were precedents for three classes on the railway. Travelling comfort was superior to that provided by nearly all other railways, but coaching effects lingered on in the second-class carriages, which were fitted with roof-seats "for those who prefer riding outside".[1] The company's stations, referred to by Whishaw as "economical", were, however, rather drab: the Board received frequent complaints, and Huish himself criticized the state of the company's buildings, especially in 1841.[2] But while railways remained in what Robertson termed the "parochial stage",[3] they were not obliged to provide facilities of any particular kind, and the possibility of vandalism certainly affected managerial decisions.

The encouragement of first-class travel was popular on the trunk lines of the early 1840s, and many of Huish's policies followed this course. Until 1844 the privilege of through booking was limited to first-class passengers, and it took prolonged negotiations with the London & Birmingham and membership of the Railway Clearing House before the Grand Junction extended this facility.[4] Separation of the classes, although not taken to the lengths of segregation practised by the Great Western, can be seen in several decisions.[5] As late as 1846 Huish made a stolid defence of the practice of providing third-class carriages on 'third-class trains' only, to prevent traffic draining away from higher classes.[6] At the same time he admitted that his company still encouraged first-class travel and that policy towards the second-class had until September 1844 been very restrictive.[7] The Grand Junction's continued reluctance to cater for poorer passengers was also apparent in its attitude to the Act of 1844, which marked the first serious interference with the free determination of services.[8] After the Board of Trade had informed the com-

---

1 *Wyld's Guide to the Grand Junction and Liverpool and Manchester Railways* (1838), 4. Smoking was strictly forbidden, both in the carriages and stations, the predominant reason being fire risk: C. E. Lee, *Passenger Class Distinctions* (1946), 35–6.
2 Whishaw, *op. cit.*, 128; G. J. Mins, 9 Aug. and 29 Sept. 1841, GJR1/3, BTHR.
3 W. A. Robertson, *Combination among Railway Companies* (1912), 2.
4 G.J. Mins, 31 July 1844, GJR1/5, BTHR.
5 E.g. in the refusal to allow a North Union second-class carriage to travel through with a G.J. mail train, G.J. Mins, 24 Aug. 1842, GJR1/4, BTHR.
6 Huish's evidence, *S.C. on Railway Acts Enactments*, P.P.1846, XIV, Q.2081. The practice had been introduced in 1844 at Moss's suggestion, following L. & B. policy.
7 *Ibid.*, Q.2082.
8 See Chapter I. Some early Acts contained restrictions, e.g. the L. & B.'s Peterborough

pany that it lay within the Act's scope, the management extended third-class travel to Sundays, but at extremely inconvenient hours.[1]

Further evidence, however, shows that Huish was concerned with the *extension* of facilities. During his period of office the timetables began to show a broader class stratification, and several attempts were made to extend the opportunities for poorer passengers to make long-distance journeys. In 1842, for example, Huish both suggested and implemented important retimings which gave the second-class passenger an extra through train from Liverpool to London, and enabled the third-class passenger, for the first time, to travel from Liverpool to London in one day.[2] Negotiations with the London & Birmingham in 1844, in which he was prominent, resulted in a trebling of second-class accommodation and a $33\frac{1}{3}$ per cent increase in the number of Liverpool–Birmingham trains.[3] Special and excursion services were a further area of interest. When Huish joined the company, special cheap-fare trains were already in existence, following developments on the Whitby & Pickering and Newcastle & Carlisle railways.[4] The Grand Junction had organized similar trains for race meetings at Wolverhampton and Chester, and for the local assizes at Stafford. Huish was soon made responsible for these facilities, and for holiday excursions where the company arranged with private agents on a contractual basis.[5] The revision of the passenger duty in 1842 led to an extension of excursions: the Grand Junction took a full part in this development, but, in doing so, escaped the criticism levelled at other railways, whose anxiety to accommodate the public brought a spate of accidents.[6]

---

branch Act of 1843, 6 & 7 Vic. c.lxiv, stipulated that third-class carriages were to accompany all trains with second-class accommodation.

1 G.J. Mins, 6–25 Mar., 12 June, 21 Aug., 25 Sept. 1844, GJR1/5, BTHR. Until 1846 Sunday third-class trains ran at 4 a.m. (London–Birmingham) and 7.30 a.m. (Birmingham–London).

2 G.J. Mins, 18 May, 22 Apr. and 19 Oct. 1842, GJR1/4, BTHR; *Midland Counties Herald*, 26 May and 10 Nov. 1842.

3 *Midland Counties Herald*, 5 Sept., 15 Aug., and 3 Oct. 1844; *Liverpool Courier*, 14 Aug. 1844.

4 The first organizers of excursion trains appear to have been the Glasgow & Garnkirk (1834), Dublin & Kingstown (1835), and Bolton & Kenyon (1836). Facilities of a more regular kind were provided on the Whitby and Newcastle & Carlisle lines from 1839: Lee, *op. cit.*, 9.

5 E.g. Huish arranged times and fares for the Birmingham Mechanics Institute, 1841, the Birmingham Musical Festival, 1843, and Crisp's Excursions to Paris, 1844 and 1845.

6 The *Railway Gazette*'s congratulations on the company's working of its Eccles race trains contrast with reports of dangerous operations in *The Times*, 17 Sept. 1844, and the *Liverpool Courier*, 18 Sept. 1844, 17 Sept. 1845.

In evaluating Huish's policies it should be remembered that decisions affecting passenger services were rarely taken in isolation. Parliament's policy towards railway promotion alerted all established companies to the importance of convincing public opinion that new, competitive railways were unnecessary. Relations with other railway companies were often crucial, and the Grand Junction's position as the centre portion of north–south traffic made complicated manœuvres inevitable. Direct competition affected the Grand Junction as early as August 1842, when the Manchester & Birmingham Railway opened its line to Crewe, providing a shorter route to Manchester. Traffic arrangements were thus complicated by the need for inter-company agreement. In 1843, the Manchester & Birmingham, which had reluctantly agreed to share the traffic to Birmingham, complained that the train timings were restricting the development of its traffic to Crewe and Chester. As a result Huish introduced two 'experimental' first-class trains on the Grand Junction, but these proved unremunerative and were soon abandoned.[1] In 1843, too, there were frequent alterations of the Liverpool–Birmingham services, in response to the demands of other companies. Indeed, constant vigilance was required of Huish and his fellow officers to maintain connections for passengers from both north and south.[2]

Pressure from outside bodies was also effective. The Post Office was of particular importance, persuading the Grand Junction to spread the times of trains more evenly through the day, and to accelerate its services, in some cases by as much as 40 minutes.[3] Membership of the Railway Clearing House also caused changes in policy. Prior to joining in July 1844, the company had only encouraged the interchange of traffic with other railways when its own interests were paramount. The management had always attempted to carry traffic which would travel a maximum distance over its line, regardless of the interests of the passenger,[4] and long-distance travel by any but first-class was impeded. But the growing demand for through booking and travel by through carriage eventually

1 G.J. Mins, 7 Dec. 1842, 18 Jan., 12 Apr., 6–20 Sept. 1843, GJR1/4, GJR1/5, BTHR; *Midland Counties Herald*, 27 Apr. and 2 Nov. 1843.
2 A minor alteration in the timing of a London–Birmingham train, for example, caused Huish and a committee of directors considerable work: G.J. Mins, 12–17 Apr. and 24 May 1843, GJR1/4, BTHR; *Liverpool Times*, 25 Apr. 1843, *Midland Counties Herald*, 27 Apr. 1843.
3 G.J. Mins, 13 Mar., 24 Apr., 5–20 June, 14 Aug. 1844, 21–7 May 1845, GJR1/5, BTHR.
4 Thus Huish made every effort to secure Derby–Liverpool and Preston–Liverpool traffic, but until 1843 refused to provide adequate arrangements with the Chester & Birkenhead Railway, which gave a second route to Liverpool: *Railway Times*, 12 Feb. 1842; G.J. Mins, 1 Feb. and 19 Apr. 1843, GJR1/4, BTHR.

induced the company to overcome the extra costs of Clearing House membership, and thereafter, a more liberal policy towards long-distance travel by all classes was adopted.[1]

Huish played a dominant rôle in the company's pricing policy. With its high dividends, the Grand Junction was one of the exceptional railways of the 1840s, and its traffic position was such that a considerable freedom to experiment was enjoyed. Huish took advantage of this situation to test demand in three major areas: the main-line and through fares, short-distance fares, and excursion fares.

In 1841 the Grand Junction's long-distance fares, increased to offset reductions in the goods rates, were between 5 and 12 per cent below the maxima allowed in the company's Act,[2] and fairly close to the average per-mile charges of 13 principal railways (table 3).

Table 3
Comparison of Grand Junction and other long-distance passenger fares, 1841–5

| Railway Co. | Date | Journey | Fares per mile in pence | | | |
			Mail	First	Second	Third
Grand Junction	1841–2	Liverpool–Birmingham	3.07	2.83	2.21	1.35
Thirteen co.s*	1841–2	Weighted average of several journeys	—	2.94	2.00	1.35
Grand Junction	August 1842	Liverpool–Birmingham	3.38	3.20†	2.21	1.60
Thirteen co.s	1842–3	Weighted average . . .	—	2.92	2.09	1.49
Grand Junction	July 1845	Liverpool–Birmingham	2.83	2.46	1.97	1.00
Thirteen co.s	July 1845	Weighted average . . .	(2.62)		1.87	1.07

Source: *Bradshaw*, 1841–5, TT1/16–45, BTHR.
*London & Birmingham, Great Western, London & South Western, London & Brighton, Manchester & Leeds, North Midland, Liverpool & Manchester, Birmingham & Gloucester, Newcastle & Carlisle, Northern & Eastern, Hull & Selby, Great North of England, and Birmingham & Derby Jnc.
†The G.J. also quoted a further first-class fare which amounted to 3.01*d.* per mile.

1 R.C.H. Ctee Mins, 1 July 1844, RCH1/2, BTHR. The G.J. Board had previously declined to join owing to the necessity of adopting the costlier Edmondson system of consecutively numbered card tickets; see Bagwell, *op. cit.*, 42–3.
2 The G.J.'s Act contained the following maximum charges: mail trains, 3½*d.* per mile; covered carriages, 3*d.*; uncovered carriages, 2½*d.*; 3 & 4 Will. IV, c. xxxiv.

At this time Huish seems to have been content merely to implement the policy of the directors, who were unwilling to reduce fares.[1] Indeed, in August 1842 fares were raised by a further 10–18 per cent, in an attempt to offset the loss of Manchester–Crewe traffic to the Manchester & Birmingham: company charges then stood well above the average.[2] In pursuing this policy Huish was a party to what the *Railway Times* called a "discreditable specimen of railway management".[3] The company, in its anxiety to compensate for lost revenue, was discovered planning to charge fares in excess of the legal limits of its Act.[4] Although hasty adjustments were made, the management emerged with its high fares policy exposed and its public image tarnished.[5]

Huish was now actively concerned about the effects of high fares on the company's revenue. In the autumn of 1842 he made a number of attempts to persuade the directors to revise their policy, but without success,[6] and his disquiet was vindicated by the traffic accounts, where 'coaching' receipts fell by about 17 per cent after June 1842 (table 4).

Table 4
Grand Junction Railway 'coaching' receipts, 1841–5

Year July–June	Coaching receipts*	Index 1841–2 = 100
1841–2	£353,795	100
1842–3	294,421	83.2
1843–4	294,892	83.4
1844–5	312,679	88.4

Source: Company Accounts, GJR1/7, BTHR.
*'Coaching' includes receipts from carriages, horses, mails, and parcels. Extracted from table of statistics, see Appendix, table 44.

1 At the General Meeting of August 1841 Moss claimed that although the prospective revision of the passenger duty would give scope for lower fares, cuts required corresponding action by other companies. However, the G.J. does not appear to have actively pursued the matter at this time.
2 See table 3.
3 *Railway Times*, 20 Aug. 1842.
4 On 5 August Huish issued a new farebill containing a Liverpool–Birmingham fare of 26s. first class (3.2d. per mile): *Midland Counties Herald*, 11 Aug. 1842. The maximum legal rate for covered carriages was 3.0d.
5 On 9 August – the day before the new fares were to come into effect – an inquorate Board discovered the error, and a revised scale was speedily drawn up: G.J. Mins, 3–13 Aug. 1842, GJR1/4, BTHR.
6 Huish referred specifically to a loss of London–Carlisle traffic to the rival East Coast route.

Eventually the Board agreed to Huish's demands. Fares were first reduced on routes specifically affected by competition—such as Birmingham–Holyhead and Liverpool–Derby—then, following the reorganization
of services in 1844, lower fares were applied to the entire system. Alterations to the Liverpool–Birmingham fares in October 1844 and May 1845
involved cuts of between 11 and 37 per cent according to class,[1] and in
July these fares were once again close to the average of the major railways. In September a further 12–19 per cent reduction was made in the
first and second classes,[2] and Huish was thus able to inform the Select
Committee on Railway Acts Enactments that the company's fares were
only slightly above the maxima contained in the Bill for the amalgamation with the Manchester & Birmingham and London & Birmingham
railways.[3] The threat of competition had clearly been a strong inducement to reduce fares, but Huish was also eager to test demand and at the
same time secure a more uniform, simplified pricing system. He opposed,
for example, the variety resulting from pricing according to both carriage
and train description,[4] and had several arguments with the London &
Birmingham over lack of uniformity.[5] Moves towards a less complicated
system certainly aided traffic management, while the lower fares were of
obvious benefit to the public. However, the new policy seems to have
caused little change in the company's revenue position. The report of
February 1845 revealed an increase in passenger volume of 37 per cent,
but gross revenue rose by only $5\frac{1}{2}$ per cent. In 1846 Huish claimed that
the gross revenue of 1845 was about 22 per cent higher than in 1844, and
that the increase had been "more than sufficient" to offset increased
operating costs. But the Grand Junction was no longer operating solely
in the highest profit sectors, and there was even a suggestion that profits
from goods traffic were being used to meet additional passenger costs.[6]

The company's short-distance fares were broadly fixed according to
distance travelled, rising by increments of 6d. or 1s., but minimum fares of
1s. 6d. first and 1s. second class ensured high charges per mile for journeys
under six miles. In the schedule of 1838, for example, the Warrington–

1 The reductions were 16 per cent (Mail), 23 per cent (first), 11 per cent (second) and
  37 per cent (third), *Bradshaw*, 1844–5.
2 *Liverpool Courier*, 3 Sept. 1845. The revised fares were equivalent to 2.46d., 2.09d.,
  1.60d., and 1.00d. per mile.
3 P.P.1846, XIV, Q.2029: maximum fares were to be 2d. first, $1\frac{1}{2}$d. second, and 1d.
  third per mile.
4 G.J. Mins, 17 Jan. 1844, GJR1/5, BTHR.
5 E.g. re night mail, second-class express, and third-class through fares: G.J. Mins,
  14–28 Feb., 25 Mar., 3 Apr., 14–21 Aug. and 2 Oct. 1844.
6 G.J. Special General Meeting, 1 Feb. 1845, GJR1/7, BTHR.

Moore fare amounted to 6*d*. first and 4*d*. second class. There were several complaints, but the practice occurred on other lines, and was perfectly legal.[1] Indeed, as late as 1842 fares from Perry Barr to Birmingham exceeded 5½*d*. and 3½*d*. per mile, and most of the Birmingham 'short' fares were higher than those of other leading railways.

Table 5
Comparison of Grand Junction and other short-distance passenger fares in 1842 and 1845

Railway co.	Date	Journey	Fares per mile in pence		
			First	Second	Third
Grand Junction	1842	Birmingham–Perry Barr	5.53	3.69	—
Grand Junction	1842	Birmingham–Newton Road	3.55	2.66	—
Grand Junction	1842	Birmingham–Walsall	3.78	1.89	—
Grand Junction	1842	Birmingham–Wolverhampton	2.06	1.65	—
Eight co.s*	1842	Weighted average of several journeys	2.96	1.92	1.21
Grand Junction	1845	Birmingham–Perry Barr	2.77	1.84	1.23
Grand Junction	1845	Birmingham–Newton Road	2.66	1.77	1.03
Grand Junction	1845	Birmingham–Walsall	2.53	1.57	1.05
Eight co.s	1845	Weighted average . . .	2.47	1.68	1.01

Source: *Bradshaw*. early 1842, July 1845, TT1/25 and 45, BTHR.
*London & Birmingham, Great Western, London & South Western, London & Brighton, Northern & Eastern, Birmingham & Derby Jnc., Birmingham & Gloucester, and Manchester & Bolton.

Huish again favoured fare experimentation in a downward direction. As early as August 1841 he suggested that Wolverhampton race trains be used to test reductions, and he later made Wolverhampton a special low-fare station.[2] His enthusiasm caused the audit committee to sanction a series of cuts in the Birmingham–Stafford, Chester–Crewe, and Warrington areas in the autumn of 1841, though the results appear to have been mixed.[3] Competition was a further complication. The opening of the

1 G.J. Act, 1833, 3 & 4 Will.IV, c.xxxiv, section clx: "for a less distance than six miles, the said company are hereby empowered to demand and receive the aforementioned rates and tolls for six miles."
2 See table 5.
3 The available evidence is imprecise. In January 1842 Huish claimed an increase in traffic in most of the experimental areas, but the directors subsequently reported only a "doubtful success", and the Warrington and Stafford results were disappointing. See G.J. Mins, 15 Sept., 6–20 Oct., and 10 Nov. 1841, 12 Jan. 1842, G.J. Special General Meeting, 1 Feb. 1842, GJR1/3–4, GJR1/7, BTHR; *Staffordshire Gazette*, 7 Oct. and 2 Dec. 1841.

92 **Fares and Distances from**

WARRINGTON STATION.

Places lying West of this Station. Runcorn, 4 miles.

Places lying East of this Station. Altrincham, 12 miles.

Distances.	Stations.	2d.cls.		1st.cl.		mail.		car.	horse.
miles		s.	d.	s.	d.	s.	d.	s.	s.
78	BIRMINGHAM ..	11	6	16	6	19	6	50	26
74½	Perry Barr	11	0	15	6				
71¼	Newton Road	10	6	15	0				
68½	Bescot Bridge ..	10	0	14	6				
67¾	James's Bridge.. ..	10	0	14	0				
66	Willenhall	9	6	14	0				
63¾	WOLVERHAMPTON	9	6	13	6	16	0	43	22
58	Four Ashes	8	6	12	0				
56½	Spread Eagle ..	8	0	12	0				
54	Penkridge..	8	0	11	6				
48¾	STAFFORD	7	0	10	0	12	0	33	17
45¼	Bridgeford	6	6	9	6				
43	Norton Bridge ..	6	6	9	0				
34¾	WHITMORE	5	0	7	6	9	0	25	12
32	Madeley	4	6	6	6				
24	CREWE	3	6	5	0	6	0	16	8
21	Coppenhall	3	0	4	6				
19¼	Minshull Vernon ..	3	0	4	0				
16¾	Winsford	2	6	3	6				
12¼	HARTFORD	2	0	2	6	4	0	9	5
9¾	Acton	1	6	2	0				
5½	Preston Brook	1	0	1	6				
3	Moore	1	0	1	6				
	WARRINGTON ..								
4¾	Newton Junction ..	1	0	1	6				
7¾	Collin's Green	1	0	1	6				
9¼	St. Helen's Junction	1	6	2	0				
11¼	Top of Sutton Incline	1	6	2	6				
12	Rainhill..	2	0	2	6				
14	Bottom of Whiston In.	2	0	3	0				
15	Huyton Lane	2	0	3	0				
15½	Roby Lane	2	6	3	0				
17	Broad Green	2	6	3	6				
19½	LIVERPOOL.. ..	3	0	4	0	5	0	15	7
	Stations to Manchester.								
5¼	Newton Bridge.. ..	1	0	1	6				
6	Parkside	1	0	1	6				
8	Bolton Junction ..	1	0	1	6				
10¼	Bury Lane	1	6	2	0				
12½	Lamb's Cottage.. ..	2	0	2	6				
13¼	Barton Moss.. ..	2	0	3	0				
15½	Patricroft	2	6	3	0				
17	Eccles	2	6	3	6				
17¾	Weaste Lane	2	6	3	6				
18	Cross Lane	2	6	4	0				
19½	MANCHESTER ..	3	0	4	0	5	0	15	7

Grand Junction Railway fare schedule 1838 at Warrington, from *Osborne's Guide to the Grand Junction, or Birmingham, Liverpool & Manchester Railway* (1838)

Manchester & Birmingham led the Board to increase fares north of Whitmore, but Huish opposed the move, and was successful in persuading the directors to return to the former schedule. The extensive changes of 1844 brought the short fares closer to a strict mileage system, and fares such as that between Birmingham and Perry Barr were reduced. By July 1845 a much more uniform and generally lower pricing scheme was in operation.[1]

Huish was also entrusted with the general pricing of special and excursion trains. However, he usually negotiated within limits set by the Board, informing it of the tenders offered, and acting on instructions received.[2] Particular arrangements were made in the Chester–Crewe area, where competitive conditions from 1842 caused a succession of fare cuts, and in 1844 day return tickets were introduced. But with the exception of the Wolverhampton and Chester race trains, these concessional tickets were not extended to other areas until November 1845, despite their recognized success on other railways—notably on the London & Brighton. Indeed, it was the action of the London & Birmingham, which adopted day returns in January 1845, that probably led the Grand Junction to follow suit.[3] Here again, the company was reluctant to risk its ordinary, high-tariff business.

Passenger pricing was thus a complex and often crude process, but it was particularly crucial to companies like the Grand Junction, whose passenger traffic contributed the major portion of gross revenue (table 6).

Table 6
Grand Junction Railway gross receipts for 'coaching' and goods traffic, 1841–5 (in percentage terms)

Year July–June	Coaching receipts* %	Goods receipts %
1841–2	73.2	26.8
1842–3	75.9	24.1
1843–4	73.1	26.9
1844–5	69.3	30.7

Source: Company Accounts, GJR1/7, BTHR.
*'Coaching' receipts included receipts derived from mails, parcels, horses, and private carriages.

1 See table 5.
2 E.g. re Crisp's cheap trips from Liverpool to Paris, 1844 and 1845, which involved negotiations with the L. & B.: Huish, letter to Creed, 20 July 1844; Crisp, letter to Creed, 16 Dec. 1844, HL2/R175, BTHR.
3 Creed's evidence, *S.C. on Railway Acts Enactments*, P.P.1846, XIV, Q.1746.

Huish's main achievement lay in his persistent support for lower fares. He helped to lead the English trunk lines towards the carriage of larger traffic volumes at revised tariffs, a necessary development if competition were to be forestalled, and later justified by Parliament's action in imposing much lower maximum fares after the second 'Mania'. Inevitably, this change of policy brought considerable management tensions. The Board naturally wished to protect its 10 per cent dividend, and at first Huish was instructed to follow a high fares policy. The change of heart in 1844, seen by the directors as a device to persuade Parliament to reject applications for new, competing railways, was welcomed by Huish as a chance to test traffic elasticities. As a result, the company moved significantly away from its bias towards first-class traffic. Although information is scant and lacks complete comparability,[1] the following example clearly illustrates the trend. In 1841–2 first-class traffic made up about 69 per cent of total passenger revenue:[2] by 1845–6 this had become only 45 per cent, a change that had national importance, since the company enjoyed 10 per cent of the United Kingdom's traffic earnings.

Table 7
Analysis of Grand Junction passenger revenue by class, 1845–6 (July–June)

	First %	Second %	Third %	Parlt. %	Total %
G.J. passenger traffic revenue	44.8	32.3	22.1	0.8	100.0
G.J.'s share of total U.K. passenger traffic revenue	12.7	7.9	14.1	1.2	10.0

Source: Accounts and Papers, P.P.1847, LXIII.

Huish also showed himself to be a master railway 'diplomatist' with undoubted negotiating talents. It was in these years that he began to participate in inter-company affairs, being involved in the efforts of the Grand Junction to defeat rival projects, such as the Trent Valley, Chester & Holyhead, and Shrewsbury lines. This entailed attendance at parliamentary committee meetings, and meetings of proprietors, with a view to encouraging lines which would feed the Grand Junction, and

1 The surviving data were compiled after the G.J.'s amalgamation with the L. & M. and Leigh railways in 1845, and include the unseparated receipts of these companies prior to their absorption.
2 See Chapter I, table 2.

scotching those which threatened competition. Huish's contribution to early railway diplomacy included his sponsorship of the Caledonian project, in an effort to retain the valuable northern traffic;[1] and the organization of a traffic agreement between the Grand Junction, Midland, and Manchester & Leeds railways in 1845, which helped to stabilize the competition for traffic from Lancashire to the south, by dividing receipts in fixed percentages. This was the first railway 'pool' of this kind, and useful experience for Huish's later work with the London & North Western.[2] Finally, Huish engineered a cunning rapprochement with Saunders of the Great Western, which finally induced the London & Birmingham to consider amalgamation.[3] Co-operation in traffic management was also an important feature of Huish's work. The Grand Junction and London & Birmingham railways acted together on a number of occasions, applying an agreed policy to mutual traffic problems. Thus, Huish negotiated for a common approach towards the carriage of mails for the Post Office, and discussed a variety of special passenger fares, including those for soldiers and convicts.

Huish's authority was wide-ranging. He was involved in all facets of traffic management, and his desire to manage was supreme. Sometimes, perhaps, he assumed too much responsibility. His interference with subordinates at Birmingham and with enginemen in the observation of regulations may well have encouraged dissension.[4] Nevertheless, profits were retained, punctuality and safety—the main criteria in judging quality of service—were maintained,[5] and much of this may be attributed to Huish's skill as a traffic manager. He was able to secure an increase in gross revenue which, although modest, was quite an achievement in the circumstances of increasing competition. His ability to respond to changes in public demands, and to alter services to meet changed circumstances, provided the flexibility necessary to maintain profitable operation.

1 See Huish, letter to Creed, 3 Sept. 1842, and Creed's reply, 6 Sept. 1842, PROS/1/18, BTHR.
2 The 'pool' prevented wasteful competition between the Birmingham and Normanton routes. See C. H. Grinling, *The History of the Great Northern Railway 1845–1902* (1903), 92–3.
3 See Huish's letters to Saunders, Mar. 1845, etc., HL1/30, BTHR; Huish, in a published Circular of 11 June 1845, simulated encouragement of the Broad Gauge in the Midlands, a policy which had unfortunate repercussions later.
4 Veritas Vincit, *Railway Locomotive Management* . . . (1847), 134–40.
5 Huish was able to report, for example, that in over six months' operation to January 1843, only $1\frac{1}{2}$ per cent of trains had been late: G.J. Mins, 18 Jan. 1843, GJR1/4, BTHR.

3 Goods traffic

Huish's experience of goods traffic management was at first very limited. The Glasgow Paisley & Greenock had barely commenced the carriage of goods when he resigned, and at that time only cotton, parcels, and light articles were carried, and these by passenger train, for the company had no separate goods department.[1] He was, however, involved in the several discussions to decide the mode of working future traffic, especially on the Joint Line.[2] The Greenock Railway eventually decided to admit carriers on the line, since its capacity to carry was severely restricted. A special Board meeting in 1840 resolved that "it would be greatly for the advantage of the Co., if carriers could be induced to use the road, paying a toll therefor [sic] . . . the co. finding locomotive power, and if necessary wagons, but taking no charge of collecting, packaging, or delivering the goods."[3] Accordingly, in May 1841, McDougall, a local carrier, was appointed Goods Agent for the company at Glasgow.

But when Huish joined the Grand Junction, managerial attention was firmly focused upon the attempt to *exclude* independent carriers from the goods business. In December 1838 the company began to undertake the collection and delivery of goods, and on 6 November 1839 the Board resolved to take further action against the "objectionable proceedings arising from the admission of carriers on the railway". The Grand Junction soon became the sole carriers of Birmingham–Lancashire traffic, and there followed a series of measures designed to discourage the independent collection and delivery of goods sent to and from London. The conflict, which culminated in the notorious legal battle with Messrs. Pickford & Co., had thus progressed far before the arrival of the new secretary. Nevertheless, Huish was to become deeply concerned in defending the company's position.

The case of Pickford v. Grand Junction of 1841[4] involved two major issues. First, Pickford, which organized its own collection and delivery services, claimed a rebate similar to that allowed to Chaplin & Horne, the Grand Junction's London 'agents', for performing these services for the railway company.[5] Second, the carriers demanded that aggregate packets

---

1 G.P.G. Mins, 9 June 1841, General Meeting, 2 July 1841, BR/GPG/1/2, S.R.O.
2 G.P.J. Mins, 23 July and Oct. 1840, BR/GPJ/1/1, S.R.O.
3 G.P.G. Mins, 1 July 1840, BR/GPG/1/2, S.R.O.
4 This has been summarized by Jackman, *op. cit.*, 744–9, and more recently by Turnbull, 'The Railway Revolution . . .', *loc. cit.*, 61–5.
5 From June 1840 Chaplin & Horne handled G.J. goods passing over the L. & B. to

of 'smalls' ('packed parcels'), a lucrative part of the goods traffic, should not be charged at the small parcel rate of 1*d*. per pound, but at a much lower tonnage rate.[1] Although both sides professed a willingness to negotiate, the dispute was exacerbated by concerted efforts to obstruct each other's business. Pickford had its contract with the Grand Junction terminated, was denied the use of certain railway facilities, and faced high charges for waggon-hire.[2] On the other hand, the carriers made a number of false declarations of goods presented for conveyance, especially of 'smalls' carried in locked hampers, which certainly encouraged the railway company to seek control of the entire goods business.[3] Both parties claimed that goods were being misdirected.[4]

The court's decision of July 1842 went against the Grand Junction. It was held that although a railway company could vary tolls according to circumstances, it should not do so in order to "prejudice or favour particular parties, nor for the purpose of unfairly creating a monopoly". Judgment was that "responsibilities are diminished for a railway company if smalls are bound up in one package with one consignee", and "if a carrier wishes to receive his goods on their arrival at the railway terminus, the company are *not* entitled to charge him the same sum for carriage as they charge to other persons whose goods are delivered to the consignee". The outcome appears to have been a policy decision, designed to protect the public interest against 'railway monopoly'.

But the exact circumstances of equality of charge and the means to enforce it remained vague. The Grand Junction did modify its policy, such that a compliance with the court's decision could be claimed. A rebate was allowed to Pickford, though it was less than the sum granted to Chaplin & Horne, and the charging of packed parcels at 1*d*. a pound was abandoned in favour of a tonnage rate, though this was high.[5] Huish, in his notable letter to the *Railway Times* of February 1843, remarked

---

London, enjoying a 10*s*. rebate on the railway's charge, which was refused to other firms. See G.J. Mins, 28 Nov. 1839, 15 Jan., 22 Apr., and 30 May 1840, GJR1/3, BTHR.

1 The G.J. was free to charge for smalls weighing under 500 lb., and had set a rate of 1*d*. per lb. for parcels under 112 lb. On 24 November 1840 Pickford presented their notorious hamper, containing several small parcels. The G.J. quoted a charge of 81*s*. 8*d*., the carriers offered 26*s*. 6*d*.

2 Baxendale's evidence, *S.C. on Accidents on Railways*, P.P.1841, VIII, Q.1749, and G.J. Mins, 23–30 Sept., 3 Oct. 1840, GJR1/3, BTHR.

3 Jackman, *op. cit.*, 630, n. 1; Saunders's evidence, *S.C. on Railways*, P.P.1844, XI, QQ.3941–50, 4025; Moss's letter, 17 Feb. 1841, in *Railway Times*, 20 Feb. 1841.

4 *Railway Times*, 6 Mar. 1841; G.J. Mins, 16 Feb. 1842, GJR1/4, BTHR.

5 The rebate granted to Pickford was 6*s*., later 7*s*., and the revised tonnage rate was 4*s*. per cwt.

that these were the "real questions at stake", and suggested that the Grand Junction was acting in accordance with the court's directive. But if the company did not quite continue its "existing policy of discrimination",[1] its actions scarcely provided equality of treatment. The latitude offered by the court's decision and the known limits of the carriers' financial resources enabled the company to harass its rivals.[2] The agency question was not finally resolved until 1858,[3] and although succeeding railway Acts usually contained an additional clause preventing the company from charging separately for each parcel contained in a package of parcels,[4] nothing was done to establish a fair rate for packed parcels.

The controversy continued, and the Grand Junction was frequently accused of not submitting to law. Pamphlets, letters, and articles were legion, and both sides had persuasive points to make, although much was hidden in bombastic harangue.[5] The Grand Junction defended both its actions and the need for railway control, and there was bickering on both sides, the company complaining of evasion of just rates, the carriers of damage and delay. Later railway policy can be traced from Huish's evidence to Select Committees in 1845, where it is clear that private firms were still discouraged in a number of ways.[6] Eventually a settlement was declared at the Board meeting of 11 February 1846, and from 1847 the London & North Western made use of both Pickford and Chaplin & Horne as its agents. Thereafter the competition of private carriers on railways virtually disappeared.

In the dispute with Pickford the Grand Junction relied heavily on its successive chairmen, Moss and John Lawrence, and on Swift, the company's solicitor, whose advice on methods to evade the intentions of the court's vague rulings was extremely important.[7] What, then, was Huish's

1 As Jackman alleged, *op. cit.*, 748.
2 The conflict took place at a time when "the idea of enforcement by administrative means outside the courts was only just beginning to take root", and when it was freely admitted that the carriers would wilt if forced to undertake constant litigation to recover damages: Parris, *op. cit.*, 6.
3 By the 'Reading Case', Baxendale v. Great Western Railway, 5 C.B. (N.S.), 336: see Butterworth, *op.cit.*, 155.
4 E.g. in the Oxford Railway Act of 1843: Butterworth, *op.cit.*, 142.
5 This was partly the result of the actions of ex-carriers, such as Braithwaite Poole, Comber, and Eborall (all of the G.J.), in turning against their former employers. See, for example, Poole, *Twenty Short Reasons* . . . (1844), and J. Shipton, *A Letter addressed to Railway and Canal Directors on the subject of Carrying Goods* . . . (1844).
6 *R.C. on the Gauge of Railways*, P.P.1846, XVI, QQ.4645, 4664–5, 4691–6; *S.C. on the Oxford Worcester and Wolverhampton Railway, and Oxford and Rugby Railway Bills*, P.P.1845, XI, QQ.11035–42, 11085, 11163.
7 Swift's evidence, *S.C. on Railways*, P.P.1844, XI, QQ.2432–40, and G.J. Mins, *passim*, and especially 15 Apr. 1840, GJR1/3, BTHR.

contribution? First of all, he was particularly concerned with public opinion, and his spirited defence of the company's standpoint was a valuable asset. He informed the Select Committee of 1844, for example, that carriers were not needed on a railway, and told the Morrison Committee of 1846: "I think the system of introducing carriers upon a line is fraught with very great evil, is unsound in itself, and is making the public pay double profits to a middleman".[1] Further, his grasp of the details of traffic management enabled him to keep the Board informed of developments. He reported, for example, on the circumstances of delivery from the Vauxhall Depot, Birmingham, which led to a reduction in the carriers' allowance.[2] In February 1842, it was he who mentioned the complaints that Pickford was forwarding by canal goods intended for the railway. Huish was also involved in the many negotiations with Joseph Baxendale and other representatives of the carrying firm. But his major contribution was to encourage the extension of the Grand Junction system to other lines. He organized the deputations which sought to end private carrying on the Birmingham & Gloucester Railway,[3] and made several suggestions to increase the railway's traffic and improve operating efficiency. His efforts were such that the London & North Western Board later declared him "a gentleman of great ability, and experience in those carrying arrangements, and in that system of operations peculiarly applicable to a long line of railway."[4] Certainly, the Grand Junction's example was followed by other railways. Samuel Salt in his *Facts and Figures* of 1848 stated that private carriers had declined in number since the "memorable fight between the Grand Junction Railway and Messrs. Pickford & Co.",[5] and in Salt's book of 1850 there were favourable reports of railway carrying from several railway companies.[6]

The railways claimed an economic justification for the control of goods traffic. Huish himself indicated the possibilities of economies of scale and suggested that the railways would benefit if the use of waggon capacity were maximized.[7] The companies also made much of the argument that independent carriers would divert merchandise to the canals, where they were well established, and would take advantage of the increasing diversity of the rail system to influence charges and direct

1 P.P.1844, XI, Q.6673, P.P.1846, XIV, Q.2066.
2 G.J. Mins, 27 Oct. 1841, GJR1/4, BTHR.
3 G.J. Mins, 6–20 Sept. 1843, 25 Sept. 1844, GJR1/5, BTHR; *Liverpool Courier*, 2 Oct. 1844.
4 L.N.W. General Meeting, 12 Feb. 1847, LNW1/1, BTHR.
5 S. Salt, *Facts and Figures, principally relating to Railways and Commerce* (1848), 64.
6 S. Salt, *Railway and Commercial Information* (1850), 105–6.
7 Huish's evidence, *S.C. on Railways*, P.P.1844, XI, QQ.6659–60, 6711.

traffic flows. Certainly, the Grand Junction had suffered from Pickford's diversion of Liverpool–London goods traffic to other railways from 1842, and Huish gave forceful expression to his ideas on this subject. But fears that the carriers would use canals to embarrass railways appear to have been largely unfounded: such a policy would have been feasible only when speed of transit was of little importance.[1] Indeed, it is difficult to take the railway's position at face value, when so much can be seen as propaganda designed to win parliamentary support. Huish's remarks to the Select Committee of 1844 on the effects of canal competition on railway rates included a firm denial that any formal agreements had been made with rival canals, but the minutes show that he had himself played a prominent rôle in negotiations leading to agreements with the Ellesmere and Liverpool Junction canals which sought to maintain higher rates.[2] The Grand Junction's emphasis upon the need for a single carrying authority was also undermined by the admission that three independent coal firms worked trains over the line.[3]

Litigation continued, stimulated partly by public sympathy for the carriers, and partly by the failure of the courts to provide a definitive judgment on the several issues affecting the railways and their customers. But there is little to suggest that the railway companies were subjected to serious restrictions.[4] The carriers certainly continued to perform useful service on a local level, and their experience was often valuable over long journeys, before the Railway Clearing House developed sufficiently to control transit over a number of separate railway lines. However, both these advantages were diminishing in importance by the time of the 'Mania' of 1845, and Huish later spoke of the inevitability of the railways' tendency to "extend the principle of doing as much as possible for themselves": it is clear that once they had learned about the carrier business they would seek to assume control of it.[5]

The Grand Junction was thus firmly committed to the carriage of

1 See Turnbull, 'The Railway Revolution . . .', *loc. cit.*, 66.
2 Huish, QQ.6701–3, and G.J. Mins, 9 Nov., 14–21 Dec. 1842, 4 Oct. 1843, GJR1/4–5, BTHR.
3 Huish, QQ.6718–19, 6728–9, and Huish's evidence, 8 June 1846, on the Amalgamation Bill, H.C.1846, Vol. 84, H.L.R.O.
4 Some judgments did nevertheless reflect a strong fear of abuses arising from 'railway monopoly', e.g. in Huntingdon v. G. J. Rly, where the latter was held responsible for the fraud committed by a dealer's servant while on railway property. See Anon., *Carrying Question: remarks on the memorial presented to the Railway Commissioners by some of the merchants of Birmingham* (1847), 7–8.
5 Carriers' Memorial, 3 Apr. 1845, BT6/280, P.R.O., and Huish, quoted in W. H. Chaloner, *Social and Economic Development of Crewe, 1780–1923* (1950), 42.

goods, and under Huish's management the traffic grew steadily. Merchandise, livestock, and coal traffic increased by over 50 per cent between 1841–2 and 1844–5, a much faster rate than that of passenger traffic, and accordingly, the sector's share of total traffic revenue increased from 24 per cent in 1842–3 to 30 per cent in 1844–5.[1] Indeed, although the company maintained its position as a passenger-oriented railway, its share of United Kingdom goods traffic was not small. Lack of data before 1845 prevents a complete analysis, but in 1845–6 the company collected over 13 per cent of the country's total receipts (including parcels and mails), a higher proportion than that enjoyed by its passenger traffic.[2]

An examination of the company's accounts reveals that general merchandise was the most important constituent element, averaging over 82 per cent of total receipts, 1841–6.[3] Although an unknown quantity of mineral traffic is included in the merchandise returns, this high percentage supports other evidence that the company concentrated upon the carriage of high-tariff consumer goods. Huish himself stated that general goods, "groceries and teas", were the main items carried, and his view was echoed by others, and for example by Richard Foss, who in evidence to the House of Commons Committee on the Trent Valley Railway Bill in 1845 indicated that this company expected its goods revenue to be derived from similar sources.[4] Cotton, milk, and fish were also important traffics for the Grand Junction, especially in the Liverpool and Birmingham areas, and Braithwaite Poole's analysis of the tonnage carried by the company in 1844 showed grain, cotton, fish, eggs, and butter as important elements, although the receipts were not given.[5]

Livestock traffic was also of some importance, its average share of goods receipts in the period to 1846 being 13.4 per cent. Huish made special provision for its encouragement, particularly in the Midlands. As early as November 1841 he pressed for a reduction of cattle rates, presumably to attract business which still used the roads. In March and September 1842 he revised pig rates and, in an attempt to defeat canal competition, offered drovers the inducement of free passes.[6] Although the traffic's share of total receipts fell after 1843, actual receipts rose, and the manager often had to remind the Board that existing stock was insuffi-

1 See Appendix, table 46.
2 Accounts & Papers, P.P.1847, LXIII, and cf. table 7 on p. 77.
3 See Appendix, table 46.
4 Huish's evidence, *R.C. on the Gauge of Railways*, P.P.1846, XVI, QQ.4692–5; Foss's evidence, 29 Apr. 1845, Trent Valley Bill, H.C.1845, vol. 82, p. 347, H.L.R.O.
5 Salt, *Facts and Figures* . . ., *op. cit.*, 89–90.
6 G.J. Mins, 10 Nov. 1841, 9 Mar. and 7 Sept. 1842, GJR1/4, BTHR.

cient to cope with the increased business, and that the men were 'overworked'. By 1845–6 the enlarged company handled about 25 per cent of the country's livestock rail traffic, including 40 per cent of the traffic in pigs.[1] Statistics for Liverpool alone, 1841–5, show a similar pattern of growth, corresponding with an increased general demand for meat, both home produced and foreign.[2]

The Grand Junction, in common with other trunk railways, was slow to show interest in the heavier traffic in minerals and agricultural produce. Sea and canal competition was powerful and almost universal, but managements at first tended to concentrate upon goods which would yield the highest rates, and especially the luxury and perishable items which required speedy transit. In the mid-1840s attitudes changed, and Huish certainly encouraged the carriage of minerals. He arranged a number of special contracts at concessionary rates, for example with the iron works at Chillington, near Wolverhampton, in 1843 and 1845, and with parties offering bulk consignments of stone and salt.[3] Unfortunately, details of tonnages and revenue have not survived, and only coal receipts are distinguished in the accounts. But here the coal owners provided their own trains, and as the Grand Junction did not itself carry coal, Huish had no experience of the mode of working.[4] Indeed, the volume of traffic remained fairly stationary until late 1844, and was increased principally by the amalgamation of 1845, which gave the enlarged company control of Lancashire coal traffic.

Huish's interest in goods management, in common with chief executives of other railways, extended to the maintenance of plant, provision for new traffic, and anticipation of future demands. Just as Henry Booth, Charles Saunders, and John Laws supervised their goods managers with these aims in mind, so Huish directed the activities of Braithwaite Poole, at Liverpool, and Eborall, at Birmingham. In general, managers acted on the advice of the men on the spot, and Huish was again no exception. The letters from Eborall to Huish of 1841 show a clear link between policy initiation at the lower managerial levels and Huish's rôle in transmitting ideas to the Board. For example, it was Eborall who suggested the idea of a canal connection at James Bridge,

1 Hyde Clarke, *Contributions to Railway Statistics* . . . (1849), 9–11, and the return in *S.C. on Railway Acts Enactments*, P.P.1846, XIV, Appendix 1.
2 Salt, *Facts and Figures* . . ., *op. cit.*, 57; Clarke, *op. cit.*, 17.
3 G.J. Mins, 1 Feb., 15 Mar., 7 June 1843, 1 Oct. 1845; 30 Nov., 28 Dec. 1842, 17–27 Jan., 10 July 1844, GJR1/4–5, BTHR.
4 Huish's evidence, *R.C. on the Gauge of Railways*, P.P.1846, XVI, QQ.4645–53, and re Amalgamation Bill, H.C.1846, vol. 84, H.L.R.O.

which was later brought to the notice of the directors.[1] But the Grand Junction's drive to control the goods business and extend its operations led Huish to act on his own authority, which was rare on other lines. There are several examples. He can be found accelerating goods trains, modifying rates, and altering the basis of the agency agreement with Chaplin & Horne—all without the direct intervention of the directors.[2] In September 1842 the Board decided to leave to his discretion the fixing of special rates for bulk pig traffic, and in January 1844 he ordered coke supplies on his own authority, in response to reports of colliery turn-outs.[3]

Huish, in fact, assumed prime responsibility for certain important areas of good management. These were inter-company traffic, canal competition, and general pricing. The first was particularly crucial. It was in the 1840s that trunk railways began to encourage inter-regional traffic with the intention of increasing average hauls, and this involved a constant battle against the shortcomings of an undeveloped railway system and its conflicting methods of management. The Grand Junction faced considerable difficulties in that the prevention of traffic losses to other routes frequently depended upon the co-operation of all companies forming a connection between the points of acceptance and delivery. The management was necessarily involved in negotiations with connecting railways, and especially with the London & Birmingham. In 1844, for example, Huish requested the company to help in accelerating Liverpool–London goods trains, for without its assistance successful competition from other railways could not be prevented.[4] Indeed, the London & Birmingham was the subject of frequent criticism, on the grounds that its high tolls tended to divert traffic to the canals.[5] As early as December 1841 Huish asked Creed, the London & Birmingham secretary, to cut rates between Rugby and Birmingham for the convenience of the Leicester cattle trade, and throughout the period there were complaints of hindrances suffered by the Grand Junction. Indeed, Huish was once led to suggest that south-bound goods, on reaching Birmingham, be transferred to the canal.[6]

Huish was well aware of the adverse effects of disagreement among the railway companies. He had seen Scottish-bound goods diverted from

1 G.J. Mins, 4 Aug. and 7 Sept. 1841, 16 Oct. 1844, GJR1/4–5, and letters from Eborall to Huish, 3 and 5 Aug., 11 Sept. 1844, found in GJR1/4, BTHR.
2 G.J. Mins, 7 Sept. and 1 Dec. 1841, 10 Aug. 1842, 9 Aug. 1843, GJR1/3–4, BTHR.
3 G.J. Mins, 28 Sept. 1842, 3 Jan. 1844, GJR1/4–5, BTHR.
4 G.J. Mins, 8 May 1844, *et seq.*, GJR1/5, BTHR.
5 Huish's evidence, *S.C. on the O.W.W. Railway Bill*, P.P.1845, XI, QQ.10997–11000, and re Amalgamation Bill, H.C.1846, vol. 84, H.L.R.O.
6 G.J. Mins, 15 Dec. 1841, 5 Oct. 1842, 24 May 1843, GJR1/4, BTHR.

Liverpool to Leith, and Liverpool–London goods sent via Normanton and the Midlands. The desirability of reaching agreement with competitors to avoid damaging 'rate wars' was also paramount. In June 1844 negotiations with the Manchester & Leeds Railway resulted in an agreement by Huish and Laws to create a 'frontier' for goods traffic.[1] This was, however, an exceptional method of solving inter-company disputes before 1845. Too often, railways employed discriminatory tactics to defeat rivals, and the Grand Junction itself was guilty of this in its relations with the Manchester & Birmingham in 1843, when it offered special rates below those quoted to its rival.[2] Nevertheless, despite its difficulties, the Grand Junction built up an impressive supremacy in goods handling at Birmingham, which was an early focal point for traffic interchange. Progress was such that in February 1844 the Birmingham & Derby and Birmingham & Gloucester railways asked to join the Grand Junction's central goods office, which had proved most successful in redirecting goods and facilitating inter-regional collection and delivery.[3] There were also other examples of efforts to extend long-distance traffic. In October 1843 Huish attempted to build up the Irish trade, and new rates between Liverpool and the west of England and Derby were suggested as a means of attracting business. He contracted with the Midland Counties and Birmingham & Derby companies for cattle traffic at reduced rates in 1842, and often met the company agents, Chaplin & Horne, to discuss measures to increase traffic.

Huish's dealings with the canals merit some attention. The Grand Junction was in a less fortunate position than many of the early trunk lines in facing a strong challenge, notably from the Duke of Bridgewater's, Ellesmere & Chester, Birmingham, and Birmingham & Liverpool Junction canals. Although the railway often possessed the upper hand, especially in winter, canal competition demanded considerable respect, and for a time rates were cut and traffic dislocated. But agreements negotiated by Huish, and signed in the winter of 1842, alleviated the position. In November Huish presented a list of rates for Chester–Manchester traffic, compiled 'in unison' with the Ellesmere Canal, in which certain articles were raised by as much as 2*s.* 6*d.* a ton. Further cuts were made in December.[4] Nevertheless the continuing anxiety about canal competition

1 G.J. Mins, 26 June 1844, GJR1/5, BTHR. The M. & L. agreed not to allow M. & L. and L. & M. waggons south of Derby; the G.J. agreed not to receive goods for places north of Derby.
2 G.J. Mins, 24 June 1843, GJR1/4, BTHR.
3 G.J. Mins, 28 Feb. 1844, GJR1/5, BTHR.
4 G.J. Mins, 9 Nov. 14–21 Dec. 1842, GJR1/4, BTHR.

is evident from the Board's demand to be consulted before special rates
for bulk consignments were agreed. Certainly, the Grand Junction's rivals
continued to operate with a degree of profit. The Ellesmere Canal, for
example, recovered from a setback in 1842 to gain an Act enabling it to
undertake the carriage of goods, thus anticipating the general Act of
8 & 9 Vic. c.42.[1]

The complex problem of rate-fixing also engaged Huish's attention.
In the 1840s goods pricing proved to be much more difficult than passenger
pricing, owing to the greater variety of rates and the interference of outside interests. Not only was competition for goods traffic stronger, neces-
sitating a separate schedule of rates for each area, but manufacturers and
mining interests sought to use their influence in Parliament to secure
lower maximum charges. The success of the coal interests in reducing
railway rates was an important example.[2] Despite these difficulties the
Grand Junction moved towards a more sophisticated policy, under
Huish's leadership. Rates were broadly based upon the differential
ability of each traffic to pay the price demanded, variations from a strict
mileage schedule being determined by several considerations, including
value, loading problems, and liability to damage.[3] There was also evidence
that the company took into account the quantity offered, realizing the
importance of encouraging full train loads.[4]

These developments took place, ironically, at a time when the managers of trunk lines were little tempted to attract low-class traffic in bulk.
Huish was firmly committed to the encouragement of goods traffic, however, as his evidence in 1845 illustrates,[5] and his efforts were important in
preparing the ground for the rapid increase in traffic carried after 1846
by the London & North Western. In support of his policy, he claimed that
the company had made nine successive rate reductions by 1844, and that
the "rates for goods are far below those which are authorised by the
Act".[6] Complete evidence does not survive, but it is certain that the
Grand Junction altered its general rates at least five times during his
period of office—in 1842, 1843 (twice), 1844, and 1846. These changes did

1 E.E.C. General Ctee Orders, 25 Aug. 1842, EEC1/5, BTHR. Carrying powers were
  also obtained by the Birmingham & Liverpool Jnc. Canal, see F. C. Mather, *After
  the Canal Duke* (1970), 150.
2 See the effects of this lobby on L.N.W. coal rates, in Chapter V.
3 The schedule of 1843, for example, fixed separate rates for old and new potatoes,
  glass in boxes and glass in crates, and iron and "damageable iron": G.J. Mins,
  28 Dec. 1842, GJR1/4, BTHR.
4 Huish's evidence, Amalgamation Bill, H.C.1846, vol. 84, H.L.R.O.
5 *S.C. on the O.W.W. Bill*, P.P.1845, XI, QQ.11020, 11152-4.
6 Huish's evidence, *S.C. on Railways*, P.P.1844, XI, QQ.6652-4; letter to *Railway
  Times*, 27 Aug. 1842.

not always involve reductions over the whole range of goods,[1] but the rates of January 1846 were certainly lower than ever before, and involved a more simplified classification.[2]

Huish aided Poole, Eborall, and occasionally Swift, in dealing with specific problems surrounding goods rates. He helped Poole, for example, to draw up a revised scale of charges in February 1842, and played the major rôle in the changes of August, which were framed to offset competition from the Manchester & Birmingham.[3] Other minutes reveal his collaboration with the goods managers in connection with rates to Worcester and Bristol, cuts in the rate for pottery in 1843, and revised rates for horses in the same year. These duties were additional to his abovementioned work with livestock and canal rates.

Huish's general attitude towards pricing was to work towards charging what the traffic would bear. This can be seen in his frequent suggestions to alter the general schedules, according to the level of receipts produced. Thus in May 1844 he offered to reduce the seventh-class rate, because "the receipts were poor".[4] Huish also claimed experience in costing as an aid to pricing, although no-one possessed a clear understanding of railways costs at this time. Generally, goods receipts as a whole paid the expenses as a whole. Huish, when asked whether any traffic was carried at a loss, admitted: "It is difficult to pick out any one article in a large merchandise traffic, and say that identical article produces a loss to the company."[5] It was also difficult to show that a specific article made a profit. Huish conceded that some items were carried at "very little profit", and that the Grand Junction's rates had been reduced almost to the point where fresh traffic would be unremunerative, since additional outlay in operating expenses would be necessary. His management of goods pricing was, however, generally capable. He pronounced against a rigid rate system for the country as a whole, pointing to the crux of the problem—the peculiarities of local traffic conditions.[6] The different tariffs in force between 1841 and 1846 showed that the company priced according to both value and susceptibility to damage, as well as following rough equity principles in basing the general schedules on a mileage basis. Huish appeared determined to use the rating system to maximize

1 The schedule of January 1843, for example, was slightly higher than that of
  November 1840 in the highest and lowest classes (Liverpool–Birmingham traffic).
2 Four classes were instituted, Huish's evidence, Amalgamation Bill, H.C. 1846,
  vol. 84, H.L.R.O.
3 G.J. Mins, 2 Feb., 10 Aug. 1842, GJR1/4, BTHR.
4 G.J. Mins, 1 May 1844, GJR1/5, BTHR.
5 Huish's evidence, *S.C. on Railway Acts Enactments*, P.P.1846, XIV, Q.2011.
6 *Ibid.*, Q.2071.

revenue, and although relative traffic costs do not seem to have been isolated for pricing purposes, the Grand Junction policy appears as advanced as any in the early 1840s.

4   Management and business efficiency

So far this Chapter has concentrated upon Huish's rôle in the organization and traffic management of the companies he first served. But how effective, in overall business terms, was his personal management? Such a question is more readily posed than answered. The manager's contribution to the business performance of a railway company before the twentieth century is very difficult to evaluate with any certainty, and a detailed comparison of the activities of the early companies, with a view to gaining an overall picture in which to place the individual manager, is almost impossible. The nature of the surviving data precludes a comprehensive analysis of such problems as the assessment of productivity (however crudely it is to be measured) or the determination of a relationship between costing and pricing decisions. There is a further serious difficulty: that of deciding the creative source of company decisions where evidence is largely circumstantial. Finally, there is a problem of analysis, in that Huish performed widely differing functions in Scotland and England for companies of contrasting size and in different stages of development. No attempt will be made to evaluate the comparative importance of Huish's two rôles. Here we shall be limited to a brief examination of his contribution to the efficient operation of the two companies.

In Scotland Huish was prominent in financial affairs, being concerned especially with investment and land purchase during the Greenock company's construction. Here, peculiar problems were added to the familiar difficulties of an infant rail concern.[1] The company had been promoted at the end of the first investment 'Mania' and was thus faced with construction during the depression of 1837–42.[2] Further, the company encountered high construction costs related to disturbance of the urban environment,[3] and rightly anticipated intense competition from

1 See Chapter I.
2 See R. C. O. Matthews, *A Study in Trade Cycle History: Economic Fluctuations in Great Britain 1833–1842* (1954), 212, and B. R. Mitchell, 'The Coming of the Railways and United Kingdom Economic Growth', *Journal of Economic History*, XXIV (1964), 329.
3 For an account of these problems see J. R. Kellett, *The Impact of Railways on Victorian Cities* (1969), 4–14, *et seq.*

the steamboats of the Clyde.[1] In these circumstances effective operation in the future depended greatly upon the skill with which an inexperienced management handled its financial problems. It was essential for the company both to retain the investment promised in the share deposits and to control its budget during a period of dear money.

Huish, who had acquainted himself with the financial management of the Liverpool & Manchester, assumed responsibility for almost all the Scottish company's financial problems, suggesting lines of policy to the Board and its Finance Committee. Much was routine, of course, and he can be found compiling the share lists, issuing circulars announcing further calls on shares, writing to agents in Liverpool, Dublin, Manchester, and Birmingham in connection with arrears, and checking accounts.[2] Nevertheless, these were very necessary functions since prior to 1837 Turner, Huish's predecessor, had allowed the accounts to become a tangle of discrepancies and errors.[3]

For a time the company's affairs created little anxiety. The management enjoyed significant local support, especially in Greenock and Glasgow,[4] and a Lancashire investment common to most early projects. Share calls were paid promptly, which suggests not only that financial organization was effective but that many subscribers became firm rather than speculative shareholders.[5] But the prolongation of the depression produced a financial crisis in 1839. Forfeitures of shares, caused by non-payment of calls, began to trouble the Board as soaring construction and land costs swallowed up the assets. In April Huish revealed that the company was overdrawn on its account.

Loans could legitimately be raised only when half the share capital had been called up, and so the management turned first to the Scottish banks. In the autumn of 1839 the company was supported by five banks to the extent of £35,000 in overdrafts.[6] Subsequently, loan capital proved its worth, as with many other railways, in providing most of the

1 See Gourvish, 'The Railways and Steamboat Competition . . .', *loc. cit.*, 1–4, 8–12.
2 G.P.G. Mins, 2 Feb. and 24 Sept. 1838, 19 Apr. and 8 Nov. 1839, and Huish, letters, 24 Nov. 1837, *et seq.*; BR/GPG/1/1–2, BR/GPG/4/2, S.R.O.
3 G.P.G. Mins, 12 Apr. 1838, BR/GPG/1/2, S.R.O.
4 The original subscriptions amounted to £134,475 from Greenock and £16,900 from Glasgow, Mins of Evidence, Glasgow Paisley & Greenock Railway Bill, H.C.1837, vol. 13, H.L.R.O. However, local interest in the company should not be exaggerated: see T. R. Gourvish and M. C. Reed, 'The Financing of Scottish Railways Before 1860 – A Comment', *Scottish Journal of Political Economy*, XVIII (1971), 210–11.
5 Between 1837 and 1841 at least 70 per cent of each call was paid before the following balance sheet, and the remaining arrears paid within six months: Accounts, BR/GPG/1/1–2, S.R.O.
6 G.P.G. Mins, 2 Aug. and 25 Oct. 1839, BR/GPG/1/2, S.R.O.

emergency capital needed. The company made extensive use of this facility after September 1839, and Huish's support for large loans certainly influenced the Board's decisions.[1] Loans contributed 53 per cent of the capital raised between June and December 1839, and 45 per cent in the same period of 1840. However, the unpreparedness with which expenses for the joint line were met indicates the partial failure of the company to anticipate expenditure, even in the short run.[2] In spite of every effort, including loans by directors' guarantee, deficits continued to rise in subsequent accounts,[3] until in September 1840 Huish warned the Board that the company's liabilities were very heavy, and recommended that the cost of the works contracts be investigated. In the following month he stated that the company, in spending £535,958, had exceeded the terms of its Act.[4] This was hidden from the shareholders, and the balance sheet for 30 November showed an expenditure of only £514,000. In the company's favour, costs had certainly been unexpected, and there is evidence that the tenders for loans had not always been acceptable at the rates of interest offered.[5]

The problems faced by the Glasgow & Greenock were similar to those encountered elsewhere, of course. Land prices were frequently high, money market conditions were generally unfavourable, and several companies underestimated their expenditure. But the company escaped charges of malpractice levelled at railways such as the Eastern Counties, and only met harsh criticism with the allegation that the Board had distorted traffic prospects in order to raise the value of new shares.[6] Much of the company's success in handling its financial difficulties was due to Huish's coolness, which contrasted strongly, for example, with the threatened resignation in 1840 of Errington, the engineer. Indeed, the crisis gave him ample opportunity to demonstrate his talents. Although irregularities did occur, he was generally in command of the situation and made several positive suggestions to improve financial policy. In particular, he was anxious that the company should proceed on a legal basis. He was determined not to borrow money until half the share capital had

1 Note G.P.G. Mins, 15 Nov. 1839, referring to a loan of £30,000 from the Royal Bank of Scotland, BR/GPG/1/2, S.R.O.
2 E.g. Huish was pressed to meet arrears of £8,500: G.P.G. Mins, 17 Sept. 1839, BR/GPG/1/2, S.R.O.
3 £12,500, account of 30 June 1840; £42,900, account of 31 Dec. 1840, BR/GPG/1/2, S.R.O.
4 G.P.G. Mins, 16 Oct. 1840, BR/GPG/1/2, S.R.O. The Act provided for share capital of £400,000 and loan capital of £133,333: 1 Vic. c. cxvi.
5 G.P.G. Mins, 10 Jan. 1840, BR/GPG/1/2, S.R.O. Loans totalling £5,000 were offered, but only £500 proved acceptable.
6 'Anti-Humbug from Liverpool', letter, *Herapath's Railway Magazine*, 29 May 1841.

been raised, and pressed for the charging of costs to the appropriate account. He recommended, for example, that maintenance costs be charged to revenue and management costs to capital.[1] He also influenced the Board's decision to transfer its share of the Joint Line's working profits for July–November 1840 to the interest debt on loans. This sound decision followed two years of deficit on current expenditure, when many companies, similarly placed, would have been strongly tempted to use the money to enhance an artificial dividend.[2] Finally, he led the company in seeking a more permanent solution to its difficulties in a further application to Parliament.[3] In April 1841 the company gained authorization to raise a further £100,000 to cover deficits and provide for extensions.

Huish's involvement in the purchase of land was also highly important. Although, in general, land and compensation costs did not form a large proportion of the railways' total expenditure,[4] for the Glasgow & Greenock the problem was unusually acute. Inexperience of railway land purchase in Scotland, a multiplicity of landowners within a small area (as many as 130 in five miles), and the disputes which normally accompanied a railway projected through residential areas and large estates, caused the management considerable difficulty. The Greenock company was, like the Eastern Counties, hindered by the intransigence of landowners, and although the majority of land was acquired prior to July 1839, deliberate obstructionism and inflated rates of compensation caused substantial expenditure after this date. Land costs, therefore, proved a considerable burden, especially before the railway was opened, and the eventual expense was nearly double that of the estimate.[5]

The Secretary's value as a mediator and negotiator was soon apparent. He was frequently involved in meetings with land agents, solicitors, and arbitrators, and his close relationship with the Chairman, Robert Ker, enabled him to express his personal views on policy.[6] His methods were

1 G.P.G. Mins, 7 Nov. and 4 Dec. 1840, BR/GPG/1/2, S.R.O.
2 G.P.G. General Meeting, 2 Jan. 1841, BR/GPG/1/2, S.R.O.
3 Huish's report, 5 Nov. 1840, G.P.G. Mins, 6 Nov. 1840; BR/GPG/1/2, S.R.O.
4 See H. Pollins, 'A Note on Railway Constructional Costs 1825–1850', *Economica*, New Ser. XIX (1952), 395–407, and S. A. Broadbridge, 'The Finances of the Lancashire and Yorkshire Railway 1835 to 1873', unpublished London Ph.D. thesis (1957), 16–18. Pollins, *op. cit.*, 407, provided a table which gave an average percentage of land to total costs of 14.2 per cent for 18 railways opened in or before 1841, at the time of opening. J. R. Kellett has recently challenged the methods adopted by Pollins. His own calculations yield a somewhat higher figure of 16.5 per cent in 1849: *The Impact of Railways on Victorian Cities* (1969), 11, 427–31.
5 By November 1839 land costs, including conveyancing and valuation, were 33.9 per cent of total costs. In May 1841 the figure was still 21.9 per cent: Accounts, BR/GPG/1/2, S.R.O.
6 E.g. Huish's letter to Ker, 29 Mar. 1838, BR/GPG/4/2, S.R.O.

on the whole successful, for although there was much opposition and dispute, his stress upon the convenience of arbitration agreements helped to ensure that there was only one jury trial over land, and that was forced upon the company by Paisley Corporation.[1] Certainly his realistic attitude contrasted with that of the other officers. Thus, in 1838 he told Turner, the company solicitor:

> You must set your face against taking the whole of a person's property if part is touched. They no doubt make up very plausible stories about the uselessness of the remainder to them. It is far more useless to us . . . I do beg you to stir your stumps, for we are sadly behind, and the new delay in Lord Blantyre's case will hamper us much.[2]

The company's relations with Charles Stewart, guardian of Lord Blantyre's estates in Erskine, presented Huish with his most difficult assignment. The Act of 1837 contained special instructions for the railway's three-mile route across the estates, involving considerable restrictions upon the company's freedom of action.[3] Engineering problems accentuated the difficulties, and Huish's tactful advances to Stewart were frequently spoiled by the mistakes of the engineer and contractors.[4] The importance of the dispute for Huish's career lay in the opportunity to demonstrate a wide variety of managerial skills. His ability to surmount opposition was evident. The attitude which he adopted also suggested a kind of 'entrepreneurial' involvement, possible only on a small line.[5] His letters to Stewart and Errington reveal a skilful implementation of the company's plans, a control of the executive, and a grasp of the dangers of incurring litigation. In spite of his efforts, however, the works at Bishopton were delayed, although engineering disputes were also to blame.[6] Nevertheless, Huish's activities in the financial sphere showed that he possessed a wider horizon than was customary among officials. Executives normally tended to concur in the policy of the directors, even to the extent of co-operating in frauds. Few secretaries would have dared

1 G.P.G. General Meeting, 5 July 1839, BR/GPG/1/2, S.R.O.
2 Huish to Turner, 18 May 1838; in a letter to Errington, 15 May 1838, he was strongly critical of Turner; BR/GPG/4/2, S.R.O.
3 1 Vic. c.cxvi, sections xxi–xxiv.
4 Huish, letter to Stewart, 5 Dec. 1837 and to Errington, 26 Apr. 1838; BR/GPG/4/2, S.R.O.
5 Huish lent the company £500 during the financial crisis: G.P.G. Mins, 6 Sept. 1839, BR/GPG/1/2, S.R.O.
6 Errington's Report, 28 June 1839, Locke's Report, 30 Dec. 1840, read at G.P.G. General Meetings, 5 July 1839 and 2 Jan. 1841, BR/GPG/1/2, S.R.O. Huish admitted later that his experience of the actual work of construction had been limited: evidence, *R.C. on the Gauge of Railways*, P.P.1846, XVI, Q.4615.

to urge the investigation of engineering accounts as Huish did in 1840.[1]

Huish's participation in the financial affairs of the Grand Junction was much more limited, for by 1841 the company had created a treasurer's department, supervised by an audit committee, and controlled by the directors. Matters affecting share and loan capital were normally left to these bodies, and Huish was chiefly concerned with the presentation of balance sheets and traffic statistics. However, the minutes reveal that he sometimes did rather more than act as intermediary between the treasurer, Thomas Goalen, and the directors, and he can be found assuming the temporary post of treasurer for subsidiary companies. In December 1841 he was appointed honorary treasurer of the Caledonian project, and in January 1844 was asked to act as temporary treasurer to the Lancaster & Carlisle Railway.[2] But in normal circumstances Huish's activities touched finance only in so far as traffic experiments affected revenue, or repairs and the payment of compensation for loss or injury were reflected in working costs. Traffic management proved to be Huish's forte, and it was only later that he acquired the experience to enable him to pronounce upon technical problems relating to cost accountancy and the determination of profits.[3]

Huish was also involved in the Grand Junction's labour management. He had organized the recruitment programme for the Glasgow Paisley & Greenock,[4] and was able to use his experience to effect in England. His duties included the establishment of discipline, and the supervision of subordinates. The enforcement of rules, the settlement of grievances, the imposition of fines, and the award of gratuities were all dealt with in an effort to solve recruitment problems accentuated by a high wastage rate.[5] His rôle was not of course a novel one, but the degree to which he influenced policy was unusual for an executive.[6]

Since the Grand Junction was well established, the main labour problems were those concerning working rules, dismissals for negligence, and replacements. It is clear that Huish assumed responsibility for a great

1 G.P.G. Mins, 7 Nov. 1840, BR/GPG/1/2, S.R.O.
2 G.J. Mins, 15 Dec. 1841, 17 Jan. 1844, GJR1/4, GJR1/5, BTHR.
3 See Chapters V and VII.
4 G.P.G. Mins, 31 Aug. 1838, 28 June, 7 July, and 1 Sept. 1840, BR/GPG/1/2, S.R.O.
5 For further information on the railways' early labour problems see P. W. Kingsford, 'Railway Labour 1830–1870', unpublished London Ph.D. thesis (1951), 1–2, 31–72, and his 'Labour Relations on the Railways, 1835–1875', *Journal of Transport History*, I (1953), 65–82.
6 The work of Green (L. & M.), Laws (M. & L.) and Hudson (Y.N.M.) is useful for comparative purposes.

many of these problems. Instances of dismissal, promotion, and recruitment frequently came before the Board, and were then referred to
the general manager. Although the 'paternal' system of recruitment was
still very much in evidence,[1] Huish often acted on his own, and he frequently arranged staff changes. Indeed, it was he who, in his first year of
office, caused regulations to be made for the appointment of staff, subject
to his approval, and after a month's trial.[2]

Examples of Huish's intervention in staff affairs suggest that increased
efficiency was his aim. After resignation or dismissals had upset the
organization of a department, he often attempted to improve the system
of working, altering the duties of the remaining officials, and saving
recruitment. In 1842 and 1843, this was done at Preston Brook, Whitmore, Liverpool, and Crewe.[3] Indeed, a crude attempt to relate labour
costs to revenue by means of staff cuts was made as a result of the opening
of the Manchester & Birmingham Railway.[4] But such activities were
never consistent before the 'Mania' of 1845, and most Boards attempted
to reduce costs elsewhere and to retain experienced staff while these were
at a premium.

Further evidence reveals the Grand Junction's labour management as
a mixture of 'paternalism' and restriction. The company made extensive
use of the system of bonuses and gratuities to encourage loyalty, and
Huish often acted as the representative of men deserving special attention.[5] He also requested money for distribution to the relatives and
dependents of men killed or injured while on duty, and participated in
the scheme for a railway community at Crewe, which matched those at
Wolverton and Swindon.[6] The company was particularly anxious to
follow the practice of the London & Birmingham Railway at Wolverton,
and Huish was entrusted with the study of cottages, cheap fares, and
general services, for use at Crewe. Thus, the resultant church, school,
bank, cottages, and other services were not innovations, but they did help
to create a contented staff. The management also provided cottages elsewhere, and it appears that good labour relations were seen as a vital
factor in the maintenance of operational efficiency.

1 I.e. recruitment by the choice of individual directors in rotation; see G.J. Mins,
  11 Oct. 1843, GJR1/5, BTHR, and Kingsford, *op. cit.*, thesis, 16–20.
2 G.J. Mins, 1 Dec. 1841, GJR1/4, BTHR.
3 G.J. Mins, 16 Feb., 6 July, 23 Nov. 1842, 19 Apr., 5 July, 6 Sept. 1843, GJR1/4–5,
  BTHR.
4 G.J. Mins, 10 Aug. and 14 Dec. 1842, GJR1/4, BTHR.
5 E.g. the overworked cattlemen who received £5 in 1842: G.J. Mins, 23 Nov. 1842,
  GJR1/4, BTHR.
6 See Chaloner, *op. cit.*, 40–66.

On the other hand, hours were long, discipline was harsh, and the wages policy was a dangerous one. The cuts of 1842 and 1843 caused great dissatisfaction, for example, although the company's rates of pay remained higher than the average paid by other major companies.[1] Huish's contribution to wage policy is uncertain, but it is clear that he helped to implement it, even if the stimulus to economize in this way came from the directors.[2] The manager was, however, actively engaged in the investigation of 'misdemeanours', taking upon himself the responsibility for sacking men in minor positions. The company, in common with others, took a firm stand on drunkenness, and there were several cases of dismissal on this account, some involving prison sentences.[3] Cases of fraud, theft, and negligence also came before Huish, and an effort was made to reduce accidents and costs arising from "carelessness", "irregularity of conduct", and offences connected with book-keeping.[4] However, efficient management had its dangers in the early 1840s. With the existing scarcity of trained staff, strict controls and wage cuts could cause headaches. In March 1845, for example, the company's locomotive superintendent reported with alarm that the company had lost 16 men in a fortnight (mainly to other railways) as a result of wage cuts. Unskilled men were easily replaced, but it was at times almost impossible to find skilled, and even semi-skilled men. The Grand Junction, in common with other railways, was forced on occasion to replace staff with men who had been dismissed from service with other companies.

Huish was compelled to rely upon the advice of subordinate officers responsible for the various departments, and as business increased, he gave them more scope for individual action. There was a gradual change from the clumsy and unsatisfactory referral of minor staff matters to the Board of directors, to a more sophisticated system, in which the executive officers under Huish dealt with staff arrangements, and were instructed by a working committee.[5] The effects of this change are difficult to assess but, given the relative inexperience of the management, the supervision of what must have been a very inexperienced clerical and operating staff must be counted one of Huish's achievements in the encouragement of efficient operation.

In seeking a final assessment of Huish's early management experience, the attempt to quantify may well be a fruitless exercise. Certainly, many

1 G.J. Mins, 22 Sept. 1842, 26 Apr. 1843, GJR1/4, BTHR.
2 G.J. Mins, 19 Apr. 1843, GJR1/4, BTHR.
3 G.J. Mins, 11 Jan., 6 Sept. 1843, 24 July 1844, 18 June 1846, GJR1/4–6, BTHR.
4 G.J. Mins, 15 Dec. 1841, 9 Nov. 1842, 18 Jan. 1843, 27 Mar. 1844, GJR1/4–5, BTHR.
5 Especially from August 1844.

of the activities described above do not easily lend themselves to such an approach. There is little to be gained from an investigation of the working record of the Glasgow Paisley & Greenock, since Huish's participation was limited. It is, however, possible to measure the trends of the Grand Junction's income, although the accounts are far from satisfactory, and may distort the attempt to evaluate managerial achievement. Statistics of traffic revenue show a recovery from the year 1842–3 until amalgamation, and may be attributed to Huish's expansionist policy after the failure of the Board's rate increases in 1842. A table of net income estimates, compiled from the company accounts, indicates that the Grand Junction's favourable trading position was maintained despite increasing competition from other railways (table 8).

Table 8
Grand Junction net income estimates, 1841–6 (1841–2 = 100)

Year July–June	Net income: Railway traffic only	Net income: all business operations
1841–2	100	100
1842–3	95.3	89.5
1843–4	97.3	95.1
1844–5	106.0	104.8
1845–6*	336.9	315.2

Source: Company Accounts, GJR1/7, BTHR, compiled from figures in Appendix, table 45.
*Includes returns from the constituent companies of the enlarged Grand Junction (principally the Liverpool & Manchester), and for the six months of 1846, returns from the constituent companies of the London & North Western (London & Birmingham, Manchester & Birmingham).

Dividends remained high, and since prices fell during the period (the table is expressed in current prices), the achievement of the company in maintaining its net income level was a substantial one.

An analysis of the company's annual rate of return on receipts in table 9 indicates a healthy position, and although the traffic returns were no higher than those obtained by the London & North Western between 1846 and 1851,[1] the return on total business revenue was far better, and quite steady, until the amalgamation.

Further analysis is not practicable. Nevertheless, the rough measures of managerial performance presented above do suggest that Huish's

1 See Chapter V.

work, particularly as traffic manager, was important in maintaining the company's sound business position.

Table 9
Grand Junction annual percentage rate of return on receipts, 1841–6

Year July–June	Gross traffic receipts	Net traffic receipts	Percentage rate of return on traffic receipts	Operating costs %
1841–2	£443,566	£275,817	62.2	37.8
1842–3	388,108	262,880	67.7	32.3
1843–4	403,395	268,269	66.5	33.5
1844–5	451,206	292,400	64.8	35.2
1845–6*	1,412,579	929,305	65.8	34.2

Year	Total revenue	Net income	Percentage rate of return on total revenue	Total costs %
1841–2	£449,451	£250,488	55.7	44.3
1842–3	392,930	224,242	57.1	42.9
1843–4	408,373	238,296	58.4	41.6
1844–5	455,495	262,445	57.6	42.4
1845–6*	1,437,538	789,697	54.9	45.1

Source: Company Accounts, GJR1/7, BTHR.
*Additional returns as in table 8.

PART
TWO

4

The London & North Western Railway 1846-51
Managerial adaptation and reorganization part I

Chapters Four and Five cover the period from the formation of the London & North Western in 1846 to the reorganization of its managerial structure in 1851. To divide in this way both the company's history and Huish's career is justified not only by the need to assess the initial organization, but also because the period coincides with a change, both in management and in railway affairs generally.

Railway management was greatly affected by the 'Mania' of 1845–6—the second and major outburst of speculation in railways, which involved the indiscriminate sanction by Parliament of new railway projects, many of them destined to failure.[1] This, and the ensuing financial crisis of 1847, influenced managerial conduct in two ways: firstly, the established companies were induced, reluctantly, to adopt potentially unproductive schemes, as a protective measure. The ingenuity of managers was thereby severely taxed, in the attempt to gain profits from such ventures. Secondly, railways had to adjust to a situation of doubt and suspicion— the legacy of the 'Mania'—where the public, and in particular, the shareholders, called for a close inspection of accounts and made efforts to interfere in the management of both capital and traffic. Accusations of dishonesty were aimed chiefly at railway directors, but charges were also made against solicitors, engineers, and managers. Hostility showed itself in uncompromising, often vicious pamphlets, claiming to prove mismanagement, and in rumours that lines were unsafe.[2]

Railways were passing from the constructional stage of development,[3] and investors were impatient for the fruits of investment. It was in this period that the shareholders sensed that there would be a difference between their expectations and actual earnings.[4] With pessimism rife by 1848, it was necessary for the companies to release more detailed financial statements of their position and prospects. The lead came from the London & North Western, with its public statement of 28 October 1848, and this was followed by similar revelations by all the leading railways. But the exposure of Hudson's arbitrary financial management of various companies (and especially the Eastern Counties, and York & North Midland) brought further discredit on the industry. Some companies had indeed acted in flagrant disregard of their investors, profiting from the sale of shares at inflated premiums. Even the London & North Western did not escape criticism, and there is no doubt that the writings of influential pamphleteers gained wide acceptance, however accurate or inaccurate their allegations may have been.

The companies also faced a Parliament which wavered between allow-

---

1 Of the railway mileage sanctioned from 1845 to 1847, some 1,500 miles were abandoned under the Act of 1850: E. Cleveland-Stevens, *English Railways: Their Development and Their Relation to the State* (1915), 164.

2 See, for example, Smith, *The Bubble of the Age* . . . (1848), *Herapath's Railway Magazine*, 15 Jan. 1848.

3 In terms of men employed, the peak year of construction was 1847: P. Deane and W. A. Cole, *British Economic Growth, 1688–1959* (1962), 231. 1850 was the first year in which the numbers employed in operation exceeded those in construction.

4 The declared dividends of 17 major companies averaged, in the years 1847–50: 6.3 per cent, 5.3 per cent, 3.4 per cent, and 3.3 per cent, M. Slaughter, *Railway Intelligence*, VI (1852), 55. Allowing for artificial dividends declared by railways controlled by Hudson, a more realistic average earning would seem to be about 4 per cent in 1847 and 2 per cent in 1850.

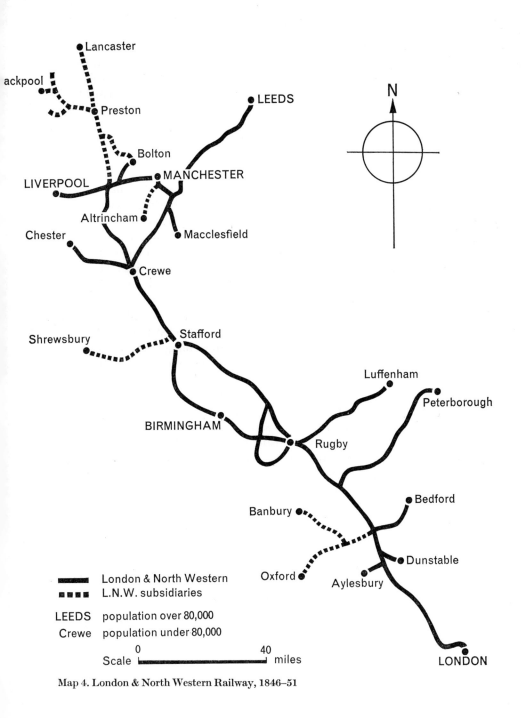

Map 4. London & North Western Railway, 1846–51

ing freedom and advocating control. The abandonment of the Railway Board experiment and its reports on schemes helped to encourage the increase in new projects, which had an adverse effect on companies such as the London & North Western. Government responsibility passed to the Railway Commissioners between 1846 and 1851, but it was mainly inside Parliament that attempts to restrict managerial freedom originated. Lord Monteagle's Audit Bill of 1848, and Ricardo's Bill of February 1850, envisaged serious interference with business freedom, for example, but proved abortive.

Under the new conditions of close investigation of managerial performance, the companies directed their attention to such enduring problems as that of determining with accuracy the long-run costs of operation, a necessary task if they were to control future earnings. The distinction between capital and revenue accounts, provision for depreciation, and working expenses were all given closer attention. Huish, with the London & North Western, made a decisive contribution towards a codification of theory and practice. A second problem—the rapid increase in capital expenditure—was not handled so successfully, for not only was money required for new lines, but heavy expenses attended the adaptation of existing routes to meet a larger traffic. Station enlargements, new sidings, warehouses, wharves, and additional tracks were all found to be necessary. These problems, together with more familiar burdens (such as pricing restrictions, local rates, and passenger taxes) ensured that few companies prospered: only the London & North Western and Great Western could claim in 1851 a position remotely similar to that enjoyed in 1846, and even here, dividends had been halved.

Another striking feature of the period was the rapid expansion of the railway system, and the inter-company competition which it created. In the five years to the end of 1851, the mileage in operation in the United Kingdom more than doubled, and with nearly 80 per cent of this in England and Wales,[1] managers such as Huish suffered considerable problems of traffic control. The London & North Western, for example, which in 1846 was relatively free of competition and enjoyed a monopoly of traffic from London to the North, was soon threatened by the Great Northern and Great Western, in addition to the challenge of many smaller railways in local areas. The establishment of the Shrewsbury & Birmingham, Shrewsbury & Chester, North Staffordshire, South Staffordshire, and Manchester Sheffield & Lincolnshire lines caused many difficulties,

1 United Kingdom mileage was 3,036 at the end of 1846, and 6,890 at the end of 1851, when the figure for England and Wales was 5,306: Accounts & Papers, P.P.1847–8, XXVI, 1852, XLVIII.

and Huish found it his main task to dispel the antagonism which accompanied competition for the same traffic. Under his management rate-wars gave way to the devices of agreement, lease, and pooling of receipts. Although squabbles were intermittent throughout the period, intercompany relations were characterized by Huish's creation of the 'Euston Confederacy', a series of traffic agreements aimed against the Great Northern, and with the object of maintaining the London & North Western's hold on the London traffic for as long as possible. Between 1846 and 1851 Huish drew the Midland, Lancashire & Yorkshire, East Lancashire, and Manchester Sheffield & Lincolnshire into alliance with him, a partial and shortlived achievement, but the most striking feature of railway diplomacy at this time.

A further result of the proliferation of railways was the development of the Railway Clearing House, which became both wider in its scope and more effective in its operation. Membership grew steadily once the Grand Junction and associated companies joined in 1845, and in 1850 the voluntary body gained an Act which granted it legal powers to sue for default.[1] Huish participated fully in its business. He sponsored, for example, the first meetings of goods managers in 1847, the success of which not only helped to accelerate uniformity of operation and pricing on connected railways, but also demonstrated what might be achieved by communal action, thus encouraging thoughts of amalgamation.[2]

The period also saw the development of ancillary activities, increased stress upon the recruitment and promotion of officials from within railway ranks, and greater attention towards goods traffic. Many companies, for example, assumed control of canals, and worked the traffic: the London & North Western decided to become a canal carrier in 1850.[3] In these years, the electric telegraph was generally applied to assist in traffic management, and the larger companies sought to control certain vital resources, such as coke and water. Efforts were also made to improve the service offered to the consumer, and the provision of refreshment rooms, bookstalls, and later, hotels, served this end, in addition to the feeder services by road and water already established on several lines. In stressing the advantages of recruiting trained railwaymen where possible, the companies demanded that candidates for higher posts in the executive should possess a working knowledge of railway business, a qualification

1 The Act had the unfortunate effect of restricting the powers of the Clearing House, although proving successful in its principal aim, viz. to enable the House to recover debts: Bagwell, *op.cit.*, 120–2.
2 See W. E. Simnett, *Railway Amalgamation in Great Britain* (1923), 9–10.
3 L.N.W. Special Meeting, 22 Feb. 1850, LNW1/1, BTHR.

which had hardly been possible a decade earlier. There were also developments in staff control, wage schedules, and apprentice training. A closer attention to the possibilities of goods traffic helped to widen the market, but the process was very gradual, and some market-creating opportunities were deliberately missed because of the dictates of railway diplomacy. However, the London & North Western led the way in the movement towards a larger goods traffic, which provided a valuable if controversial addition to revenue.

For Huish, who had become general manager of the enlarged Grand Junction in August 1845,[1] 1846 was as much a turning-point as it was a watershed in the history of railway development. On 10 October he was appointed manager of the entire London & North Western system, and from this time his influence in railway affairs increased considerably. But the London & North Western deserves study for reasons other than that Huish was its executive head. Its very size gave its management a character of more than ordinary interest. It was, indeed, one of the pioneers in the change from small to large business units, and the period 1846–51 may be viewed, therefore, as a time when the initial attempts to solve problems of size were made in the railway industry. The company, an amalgamation of the Grand Junction, London & Birmingham, and Manchester & Birmingham, was not the first important merger: that distinction was enjoyed by Hudson's Midland Railway of 1844. It was, however, the most significant, and also the first of a series which saw the creation of the Lancashire & Yorkshire, Caledonian, and York Newcastle & Berwick companies. Working 500 miles of railway in 1846 and over 800 by 1851, the London & North Western played a decisive part in all railway activities. In 1846–7 its share of United Kingdom passenger receipts amounted to 23 per cent (including over 30 per cent of first-class receipts) and this was achieved with fares below the country's average.[2] Similarly, nearly 25 per cent of the country's goods and total traffic receipts was enjoyed by the company. Its share of United Kingdom capital, manpower, and stations was again not only significant in itself but much larger than that of other railways. Indeed, this position of predominance was maintained, at least until the early 1850s.[3]

In fact, the company was the largest joint-stock concern of the day, and its capitalization, which exceeded £29 million in 1851, was far beyond that of any other company, whether railway or non-railway. The largest

1 Huish's salary was £1,250. Henry Booth (ex-Liverpool & Manchester) became secretary.
2 See tables 12 and 15 on pp. 118 and 123.
3 Cf. table 21 on p. 165.

canals, for example, had rarely spent over a million pounds (the Grand Junction was exceptional in its expenditure of £1.6 million by 1811)[1] and important industrial concerns show smaller sums: the "exceptional" Dowlais ironworks had an estimated capital of only £1 million at mid-century, and the "giant" coal companies, such as the Powell Duffryn Steam Coal Company, possessed capital assets of only £0.5 million in the 1860s.[2] Indeed, as late as 1905 there were only three British industrial companies with a capital in excess of £10 million.[3]

The London & North Western, therefore, was an exceptional business, with a wide coverage of the country, and with its subsidiaries and associates it carried in most of the major markets north of London. Its goods system was both successful and controversial, being a development of the Grand Junction's model, in which private carriers were excluded, and the company also led in the operation of mail, parcel, and other traffics. Strength was drawn from the fact that until 1850 Euston remained the only terminal for northern traffic in London, and the prestige of the constituent companies was also a valuable asset. It was not until 1851 that other railways, such as the Great Northern and Great Western, began to develop improved services and techniques to threaten the company's supremacy.

1 Company organization

The managerial structure was built upon the existing systems employed by the constituent railways. That of the London & Birmingham was probably the most influential, but the Grand Junction had in 1845 altered its organization, and this had become similar to that of the London company. As business increased further delegation from Board to committees had taken place, in order to save the leading directors from overwork, and to avoid wasted effort on trivialities. The Grand Junction's chairman, Moss, had, following the changes of August 1844, made fresh efforts to unload some of the burden of work, and in February 1845 he had suggested the formation of standing committees and monthly Board meetings.[4]

---

1 E. C. R. Hadfield, *The Canals of the East Midlands* (1966), 116.

2 P. Mathias, *The First Industrial Nation. An Economic History of Britain 1700–1914* (1969), 267, 269; A. S. Birch, *The Economic History of the British Iron and Steel Industry 1784–1879* (1967), 203–4; J. H. Morris and L. J. Williams, *The South Wales Coal Industry 1841–1875* (1958), 151–2.

3 P. L. Payne, 'The Emergence of the Large-scale Company in Great Britain, 1870–1914', *Economic History Review*, 2nd ser., xx (1967), 539.

4 G.J. Mins, 5 Feb. 1845, GJR1/5, BTHR.

Huish had also pressed for a new management system along the same lines, with fixed rather than rotating committees of directors for road and traffic, goods, audit, and finance,[1] and when the company absorbed the Liverpool & Manchester in August 1845 this system was put into effect, with Huish responsible for traffic and general working—a rôle of co-ordination. Huish also participated with Swift and Lawrence (successor to Moss) in talks with the London & Birmingham prior to the fusion of interests.[2] He had thus moved with his company, before 1846, towards a more divided management; in so doing he anticipated the requirements of the London & North Western, where the chief officer's task was to co-ordinate a number of committees and departments, rather than to execute policy details himself. For Huish, as for most other leading officers, the days of patriarchal control were over. Although he continued nevertheless to exert a tremendous influence over a wide variety of railway activities, the manner of execution was different, and the limits of his jurisdiction necessarily more closely regulated.

The company's organization was arranged in considerable detail before the Act received the Royal Assent and, as Huish stated, the parties acted "in anticipation of the Bill".[3] The first meeting of a joint London & Birmingham and Grand Junction 'Board' was held as early as 13 December 1845, although until 16 July 1846—the date of the Act—both companies continued as separate bodies with their own meetings. This was important, since the Act provided for a tripartite organization until February 1851, each of the three railways retaining a permanent local committee composed of ex-Board members.[4] The Board of Trade appears to have wished to divide the management in order to guard against the possible misuse of privileges. The report on the Bill, 11 June 1846, stated that the Lords of the Privy Council for Trade "consider that the companies have sufficient identification of interests . . . [but that] . . . it by no means follows that an entire and permanent fusion of the three companies is absolutely necessary to allow them to effect all they desire . . .".[5] The companies agreed to the formation of local committees but, as Carr Glyn afterwards stressed, it was of practical convenience to do so: to fuse suddenly and completely would have caused chaos, as well as basing the company too closely on London.[6] He remarked in 1849: "Parlia-

1 G.J. Mins, 4–14 June 1845, GJR1/5, BTHR.
2 G.J. Mins, 22 Oct. 1845, GJR1/6, BTHR.
3 Huish's evidence, Amalgamation Bill, H.C.1846, vol. 84, H.L.R.O.
4 9 & 10 Vic. c. cciv, section 50.
5 Minutes of Evidence, 15 June 1846, Amalgamation Bill, H.C.1846, vol. 84, H.L.R.O.
6 Glyn, L.N.W. Chairman, at L.N.W. General Meeting, 7 Aug. 1846, LNW1/1, BTHR.

ment thought, and we agreed, that it was a prudent and wise step that the great interests at Liverpool, Manchester, and elsewhere . . . should still retain for the consolidation of interests their local committees".[1]

The committees, however, were to be controlled by a central Board of 18 members, which was to meet monthly at Euston. The management envisaged a great advantage to be gained from the "uniformity of system and concentration of authority".[2] The period to 1851 was a formative one, in which the London & North Western was managed on a federal basis, and although there were difficulties in this policy, and integration proved slow to achieve, the decision was on the whole sound. Certain long-standing disputes were eliminated, as, for example, that between the Birmingham and Liverpool directors of the Grand Junction, and certain decisions, especially those relating to traffic, could be applied to all sections of the railway. Separatism remained, however, not only at Board level, but within the executive, and this was encouraged to some extent by the division of secretarial duties, and by the creation of superintendents and traffic committees for each branch of the railway (table 10).

The management, therefore, having been constructed out of a federation of three companies before the amalgamation was authorized, continued to divide responsibilities on a geographical basis, the railway having a Northern and Southern division, and, from the opening of the Leeds and Dewsbury lines, a North-Eastern division. It was thus hardly surprising if on occasion certain officers or committees administered part of the railway without reference to the interests of the whole.[3] The benefits of delegating affairs over a prescribed area outweighed such disadvantages.

Huish as general manager acted as a link between the many and diverse instruments of administration. After October 1846 he supervised the entire line, and was able to direct to some extent the work of local committees of directors. His reports to the General Board on the proceedings of regional management were always received with great attention, and it was intended that he bring about the "harmonious working of the whole of the traffic".[4] This rôle was strengthened by his move from Liverpool to Euston in April 1847, at a salary of £2,000, an immense sum for an executive.[5]

1 L.N.W. General Meeting, 16 Feb. 1849, LNW1/1, BTHR.
2 L.N.W. General Meeting, 7 Aug. 1846, LNW1/1, BTHR.
3 Robert Dockray, the company's resident engineer (Sthn. Div.), 1846–52, was critical of McConnell in this context: R. M. Robbins, 'From R. B. Dockray's Diary – II', *Journal of Transport History*, VII (1965), 114, entry of 21 Mar. 1850.
4 L.N.W. Mins, 16 Oct. 1846, LNW1/20, BTHR.
5 L.N.W. Mins, 9 Jan. 1847, LNW1/20, BTHR; *Midland Counties Herald*, 8 Mar. 1847.

Table 10
Major executive structure of the London & North Western, 1848

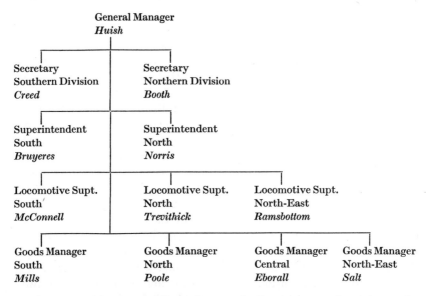

Conduct of business followed a continuing pattern throughout the
period, although the slump of 1847 caused a tightening of certain procedures, especially those relating to expenditure, and the growth of the
company added to the number and scope of committees. Generally,
supervision was effected locally by regional committees of directors and
by paid officers who were responsible for the various departments of
business. Both reported periodically to fixed general committees (such as
the audit committee, and finance committee) and to the General Board,
which met at Euston. The latter acted in much the same way as the committee of the Railway Clearing House, that is, as a central sorting office,
considering and delegating matters, and originating ideas and plans for
future conduct. The committees operated as periodic (usually fort-
nightly) meetings, where outstanding business was discussed and settled.
Instructions could then proceed either via Huish or direct to the subordinate officers concerned.[1] Some bodies were not only fixed but had
responsibility for an activity involving the whole of the company's operations: these included the audit, general finance, stores, general locomotive
and merchandise, and works construction and estate committees, all of
which were established by 1848. These were followed in importance by

1 E.g. L.N.W. Southern Road & Traffic Ctee Mins, 26 Aug. 1846, LNW1/141, BTHR.

the regional committees, with responsibility for road and traffic, and locomotive power, on each division of the railway.

As the company's activities increased, numerous *ad hoc* bodies were created by the General Board. These were composed of two or three directors, who were entrusted with the settlement of a particular question or dispute: other railway companies were usually involved.[1] In fact, after 1848 the Board delegated more and more of the company's business, both to standing and *ad hoc* committees. The minutes read almost as a catalogue of the various transactions of subordinate bodies, which were then either approved or amended.

There was, in this period, some internal comment on the London & North Western's organization, which was referred to as a "curious system" of "intermittent management".[2] Specific reference was made to the absence of directors at regional committee meetings, and although it was true that the success of the organization depended partly upon the diligence of the directors (both central and local), the officers were intended to provide day-to-day continuity of management. Organization was sound, if not faultless, and whatever its shortcomings, it acted as a model for the other major railways. The management of the London & North Western in the later nineteenth century differed from its predecessor only in a reorganization of committees, an increase of divisions, and a creation of officers' meetings. The way in which business was conducted remained basically the same. Indeed, the views of George Findlay, general manager at that time, upon what constituted an efficient management, coincided with those of Huish and Carr Glyn: a "definition of duties, and an active, vigilant supervision" were characteristic of both periods.[3] Reports were scrupulously made from the beginning, the control of expenditure and requisition procedure was carefully defined, especially after 1848, and everything possible was done to prevent waste or fraud.

Huish's duties were many and varied. In short, his task was to link the work of committees, to preside over the passenger and goods departments, and to make arrangements with other companies: but since this involved advising the directors on general policy, supervising subordinates entrusted with the execution of decisions, and negotiating with railwaymen over most of Britain, his responsibility was clearly considerable. The General Board was particularly dependent on Huish for much of its information and working papers. An outstanding feature of his work was

1 E.g. re G.W.R., L.N.W. Mins, 9 Sept. 1848, LNW1/20, BTHR.
2 Robert Dockray's Diary, 8 Jan. 1850, in R. M. Robbins, 'From R. B. Dockray's Diary – I', *Journal of Transport History*, vii (1965), 2.
3 Findlay, *op. cit.*, 68.

the monthly report to this body, dealing with the "general working of the line". The first was presented on 14 November 1846, and, with succeeding reports, dealt with questions of traffic, public relations, efficiency, and improvements. Since business arising from committees was also included, the reports were the main instrument by which Huish informed the Board of the company's activities. The operation is made clear in a minute of 1851, where it was stated that "In regard to the General Traffic, and Locomotive and Carriage Departments, the Board has been kept cognizant of their proceedings through the reports of the General Manager, and the minutes of the general or combined locomotive committees in London."[1] Huish's reports were, for busy directors, the most useful, and, indeed, they indicate not only that Huish had a far wider grasp of the details of management, but that, in this situation, it was difficult for the Board to resist his recommendations.

Huish attended the meetings of many committees, and was therefore closely acquainted with the practical details of management over a wide area. He was prominent in the minutes of the Road and Traffic, and General Locomotive and Merchandise committees, and his importance as a link between these and other committees can be seen, for example, in 1849, when he was instructed by the Liverpool Traffic Committee to inform the Chester Station Committee about the poor state of the permanent way.[2] There were many such examples, which gave Huish an opportunity to press his own ideas on both traffic and administrative improvements. Often, a matter which he brought up at a general Board meeting caused the formation of an *ad hoc* committee,[3] and, as non-routine business increased, a system of dual authority was born, in which a director and the manager would deal with a particular problem. Thus, Huish acted with Carr Glyn over the North Staffordshire dispute, and with Barrow during the Great Northern negotiations of 1849.[4] Generally, the Board created a temporary committee of two or three directors with Huish as executive adviser: the North Staffordshire talks of June 1849, were, for example, arranged in this way.[5] Further methods of decision-making illustrate the diversity of the dual authority system. A committee was formed in July 1848 to consider traffic with the Eastern Counties Railway, "Capt. Huish, in the meantime being authorised to act in cases of urgency, under the advice of the Chairman"; and while Huish was

1 L.N.W. Mins, 14 Feb. 1851, LNW1/21, BTHR.
2 L.N.W. Northern Road & Traffic Ctee Mins, 5 Oct. 1849, LNW1/158, BTHR.
3 E.g. re the Night Mail, L.N.W. Mins, 13 Oct. 1849, LNW1/21, BTHR.
4 L.N.W. Mins, 17 Feb. 1848, 13 Jan. 1849, LNW1/20, BTHR.
5 L.N.W. Mins, 9 June 1849, LNW1/21, BTHR.

negotiating with Saunders of the Great Western in 1849, a committee was created "to advise the manager".[1] Clearly, in these cases, the management was organized as an effective partnership of director and officer.

It can be suggested, therefore, that although Huish's influence and individuality were apparent, efforts were made to exercise control over him, especially on important matters. This does not alter the fact that in many ways Huish was an exceptional figure. Naturally, one would expect subordinates to carry out the minor duties he had once performed for the smaller Grand Junction: Eborall, for example, dealt with staff problems in Birmingham, the superintendents with timetable adjustments, and a committee with station buildings. But Huish was extremely reluctant to delegate matters, and although sometimes a weakness, this did appear to accelerate executive decision.[2] Further, his ability to deal with technicalities of the kind usually reserved for specialists such as engineers, suggests a competent manager attempting to understand the whole process of railway operation. His general reports were an important contribution to railway management science, as well as proving useful to the North Western Board. The most outstanding were his reports on moving stock and permanent way, 1848–9,[3] and on goods and passenger traffic, 1848–50.[4] Huish also dealt with technical matters in the day-to-day management, and despite a suggestion that he interfered too much in the work of his subordinates, the knowledge gained was a valuable asset. Other duties that on the surface appear trivial were also part of the manager's task—to ensure that the railway's actions did not create adverse public opinion. It is in this light that Huish's involvement with memorials, complaints, compensation, and accidents should be judged.

Huish continued, then, to act on his own authority and deal directly with certain spheres of railway business. He helped to create the company

1 L.N.W. Mins, 15 July 1848, 10 Feb. and 24 Nov. 1849, LNW1/20–1, BTHR.
2 E.g. re staff cuts, L.N.W. Sthn. Road & Traffic Ctee Mins, 25 Aug. 1847, LNW1/141; re Norton Bridge staff needs, Nthn. Road & Traffic Ctee Mins, 19 May 1848, LNW1/158; and re Rugby Refreshment Room, L.N.W. Mins, 7 July 1848, LNW1/20, BTHR.
3 'Report to the Directors of the London & North Western Railway Company on the Present Condition of Their Moving Stock . . .', June 1848, and 'Report to the General Works Committee on the Present Condition of the Permanent Way . . .', April 1849, confidential printed reports subsequently published as *On Deterioration of Railway Plant and Road; In Two Reports to the Directors of the London & North Western Railway Company* (May 1849).
4 'Confidential Report . . . upon . . . the Merchandise Traffic . . .', February 1848, HL2/R99B, and 'Report on the Passenger Traffic,' April 1850, confidential printed report to the L.N.W. Road & Traffic Ctees, Company Reports, LNW1/716 BTHR.

rule book of September 1847,[1] took sole responsibility for the various Post Office contracts, became the company expert on the electric telegraph, undertook the opening arrangements of new lines, and participated fully in the work of the Railway Clearing House, which for the first time made a deep impression on general traffic policy. Huish's standing in the railway world can further be seen in his discussions with the Railway Commissioners on train communication, and on working-class accommodation for the Great Exhibition.[2] His influence in railway diplomacy cannot be overstressed, and it was largely due to his ideas that the 'Confederacy' was created. He was fully committed to the policy of economy in working, and aided the Moorsom Committee in suggesting improvements in 1848, following the decline of railway fortunes. The policy of rationalizing departmental work, cutting salaries, and reducing expenses, which he helped to create, proved a necessary if sometimes dangerous response to more difficult conditions.

Huish's tactics and personality did not always enable the company to be run as smoothly as was possible. His supreme confidence gradually turned into arrogance, and although it may be true that an unpleasant and demanding manager "often teaches, and develops more men than anyone else",[3] Huish's arbitrary actions did not always endear him to his chief subordinates. Company success in management also depended on the executive as a team of officers, each important in his own right, but Huish tended to ignore this when it suited him. Admittedly, his first duty was to the Board, but his high-handed approach was resented, in particular by Poole and Dockray. It is significant that as early as 1850 Dockray predicted Huish's decline,[4] and that when the company's direction was reorganized in 1851, the men who were to effect this came to the fore, by joining an enlarged General Board of 30 members.[5] Huish was, then, a manager of the intuitive type, and although great strides were made towards a more scientific approach to decision-making, there was still room for action both individual and arbitrary.

1 L.N.W. Mins, 11 Sept. 1847, LNW1/20, and RB1/100, BTHR.
2 L.N.W. Mins, 9 Oct. 1847, 11 Sept. 1850, LNW1/20–1, BTHR.
3 Drucker, *op.cit.*, 307.
4 Dockray, writing of Bury's resignation on 7 March 1850, stated: "I doubt whether he acts sufficiently upon general principles so as to enlist the sympathy of a large section of those by whose assistance alone any management can be successful. Captn. Huish will fail in the same way – when the pinch comes, he will find everybody ready to give him a kick, to rejoice in his failure and displacement"; quoted in Robbins, *Journal of Transport History*, VII, 1965, 111.
5 Note the rise of Richard Moon and Edward Tootal, L.N.W. Mins, 11 Sept. 1850, 1 Mar. 1851, LNW1/21; L.N.W. General Meeting, 21 Feb. 1851, LNW1/1, BTHR.

2   Passenger traffic

The general problems facing railways in their passenger business were fully described in Chapter Three, and further elaboration of similar processes for 1846–51 is unnecessary. The spread of the railway network, however, made it difficult to detach passenger policy from inter-company diplomacy, and decisions therefore became more complex and prone to unwelcome repercussions.

Between 1846 and 1851 passenger traffic in the United Kingdom expanded, and both numbers carried and gross receipts increased (see table 11).

Table 11
United Kingdom passenger traffic, 1846–7 and 1850–1

Year July–June	Numbers carried	Gross receipts	Mileage open*
1846–7	51,352,163	£5,148,002	3,036
1850–1	78,969,623	£7,177,340	6,621

Source: Accounts & Papers, P.P.1847–8, XXVI, 1851, XXX.
*Mileage taken at 31 Dec. 1846 and 1850.

The dominance of passenger traffic in total railway receipts began to decline, however, and by 1851 goods receipts (including mails, parcels, and horses) formed almost half of the total.[1] Within this framework, the London & North Western suffered in that its passenger traffic became less profitable, because of increased competition and the reduced scale of maximum fares imposed by the Act of 1846.[2] However, the company's share of United Kingdom passenger traffic declined very little in the period, and one may therefore suppose that not only was the trend towards reduced passenger profits more general, but that the London & North Western was operating in the highest profit sector, as had been true of the Grand Junction, and London & Birmingham. As table 12 shows, in 1846–7 its 17 per cent share of United Kingdom first-class passengers yielded over 30 per cent of total receipts.[3]

1 Statistics for U.K.:
   1846–7: Passenger Receipts 60.5 per cent, Goods 39.5 per cent.
   1850–1: Passenger Receipts 51.6 per cent, Goods 49.4 per cent.
   Accounts & Papers, P.P.1847–8, XXVI, 1851, XXX.
2 9 & 10 Vic. c. cciv, section lxiii: maximum fares: $2\frac{1}{2}d$. Express, $2d$. First, $1\frac{1}{2}d$.
   Second, and $1d$. Third, per mile.
3 The comparatively long distances travelled by L.N.W. passengers were an important
   factor.

Table 12
London & North Western's share of United Kingdom passenger and goods traffic and receipts, 1846–51

Year July–June	Share of U.K. passenger traffic (numbers) BY CLASS					Share of U.K. passenger receipts BY CLASS					Share of U.K. goods receipts	Share of U.K. total traffic receipts
	First %	Second %	Third %	Parlt. %	Total %	First %	Second %	Third %	Parlt. %	Total %	%	%
1846-7	17.2	12.4	7.2	14.7	10.9	30.7	22.0	9.9	25.3	22.8	24.8	23.6
1847-8	14.2	12.3	5.7	14.6	11.2	29.0	20.6	5.2	22.8	21.8	25.5	23.3
1849-50	12.9	9.5	5.3	13.0	9.9	26.9	16.9	4.4	18.8	19.0	20.7	19.8
1850-1	11.4	9.5	5.5	12.1	9.6	24.9	16.5	4.8	19.3	18.0	19.9	18.9

Source: Accounts & Papers, P.P.1847–8, XXVI, 1850, XXX, 1852, XLVIII.
Note: the figures supplied to the Government differed from those in the Company's Revenue Account, and if the latter were used, the percentages would be slightly, though not significantly, different. The goods statistics used include in this case mails, parcels, horses, and dogs.

Service problems remained acute, and Huish's experiments with the London & North Western trains can be seen in the context of adaptation to the new competitive atmosphere surrounding railway operation. In his quest to maintain passenger receipts, he was in favour of increasing the number of express trains, and he made several efforts to impress their necessity upon the Board.[1] Such a policy did not find favour with those who considered the long-run costs of high-speed operation to be far too high, but Huish saw expresses not only as prestige trains in a tactical battle with the Great Northern and Great Western, but as attractive services which could be charged at higher fares than the normal first-class trains.[2] His ideas were implemented in 1848, when the company organized fast, direct trains to Scotland. An improved service to Glasgow and Edinburgh began in May, taking $12\frac{1}{2}$ hours, and was reported by Huish to be "very popular and punctual"; and from August these expresses ran on to Perth (in 14 hours) and Dundee (in 15).[3]

Despite such advances, the company faced the criticism that its accommodation was too narrowly based on first-class travel. In fact, the available traffic statistics, supported by Huish's own analysis in his report on Passenger Traffic of 1850, indicate that although services were certainly aimed at the first-class passenger and few non-compulsory third-class trains were run, the 'parliamentary' trains, provided under the Act of 1844, contributed an increasing amount of the company's passenger receipts. This sector was, moreover, similar in its extent to the average parliamentary sector in total United Kingdom passenger receipts (table 13).

Furthermore, the company dealt with 12–14 per cent of the country's total parliamentary passengers and about 19–25 per cent of the receipts, despite running only the minimum number of such trains on the main line.[4] Huish was no working-class patron, however, and his confidential remarks to the Railway Clearing House Committee in September 1849 showed that he intended to maintain first-class returns, even to the extent of reducing second- and third-class carriage standards, to prevent their

1 L.N.W. Mins, 19 June, 10 July, and 12 Aug. 1847, LNW1/20; General Locomotive & Merchandise Ctee Mins, 14 Aug. 1846, LNW1/221, BTHR.
2 Norris and Dockray were among those who believed that speed, as well as train weight, affected permanent way wear. See below, pp. 152–3.
3 L.N.W. Mins, 15 Jan., 15 Feb., and 13 May 1848, LNW1/20, BTHR; *Midland Counties Herald*, 27 Apr., 4 May, and 10 Aug. 1848.
4 See table 12 above, and Report of the Railway Commissioners, 31 Mar. 1848, P.P.1847–8, XXVI, Appendix 39: in 1847 many companies operated only the minimum services, including the Caledonian, Lancaster & Carlisle, South Eastern, Eastern Counties, and London & Brighton railways.

Table 13
**London & North Western and United Kingdom passenger
receipts—percentage distribution by class, 1846–50**

Year July–June	Sample	Percentage distribution of receipts by class				
		First %	Second %	Third %	Parlt. %	Total
1846–7	London & N.W.	43.8	38.4	6.2	11.6	100
1846–7	United Kingdom	32.6	39.8	14.3	10.5	100
1847–8	London & N.W.	41.8	39.0	2.7	16.5	100
1847–8	United Kingdom	31.3	41.1	11.6	15.8	100
1849–50	London & N.W.*	45.1	35.3	2.7	16.9	100
1849–50	United Kingdom	30.5	40.1	10.7	18.7	100

Source: Accounts & Papers, P.P.1847–8, XXVI, 1850, XXXI.
* Statistics for the six-month period January–June only. The United Kingdom total includes a small percentage of mixed traffic receipts.

use by richer passengers.[1] In his Report of 1850 he revealed the attention being given to first-class, and especially express, accommodation, the latter yielding between 15 and 19 per cent of total passenger receipts, 1847–9 (table 14).

He also maintained that the policy was sound. First-class passengers generally travelled further than others—an indication of potential profitability—and express travel accentuated this tendency. It appears that well over half the receipts came from under 20 per cent of passengers, those who travelled 50 miles or over.[2] It should be noted, however, that Huish failed to give any indication of the relative loads of each type of carriage. If first-class stock was not being fully utilized, revenue might have been increased by introducing other types of carriage. Unfortunately, no information survives to enable this to be tested.

The company's policy was not on the whole restrictive, although during the slump some of Huish's suggestions for improving the service were vetoed by the Board.[3] Timetable alterations were made as a result of the decline in business, especially during the winters of 1847–9, but the overall impression is one of expansion of what was the world's largest passenger service. Huish, as in his previous posts, made efforts to secure more profitable stops for trains, and drew the Board's attention to a

1 R.C.H. Ctee Mins, 14 Sept. 1849, RCH1/2, BTHR.
2 Huish, 'Report on the Passenger Traffic', 30–1.
3 L.N.W. Mins, 11 Nov. 1848, LNW1/20, BTHR, re proposal to put lighting in express trains.

miscellany of public requests for facilities. He also assumed responsibility for the timetables of newly-opened lines, and continued to arrange the timings of prestige trains, although, of course, most timetabling problems were left to the Road and Traffic committees and the traffic superintendents.

Table 14
London & North Western passenger receipts by class, 1847–9

Year July–June	Express %	First %	First day* %	Second %	Second day* %	Third %	Total
		Percentage distribution of receipts by class					
1847–8	14.60	23.05	4.28	33.11	5.83	19.14	100
1848–9	18.78	21.20	3.78	31.05	5.35	19.85	100

Source: Huish, 'Report on the Passenger Traffic', 32.
* Receipts from day tickets.

With Huish's firm support, through booking and excursions were greatly extended to cover the north of Scotland, and parts of Ireland. The importance of a regular holiday traffic was also realized, and the Board announced its intention to encourage travel to the English spas and lakes, the Welsh resorts, and Killarney.[1] In a letter of 1850 Huish revealed his personal enthusiasm for excursion traffic, and the numerous advertisements in both local and national newspapers are a testimony to his success in providing trains, despite the tortuous inter-railway negotiations involved.[2]

Huish was once again concerned with the effects upon passenger services of demands from the Post Office, and from rival railway companies. He was closely acquainted with both problems, and his attendance at the Railway Clearing House enabled him to meet other executives regularly and discuss traffic matters with them. The meetings of officers of the West Coast companies also fulfilled this function, although on a smaller scale.[3] Often, when one company altered its services, reciprocal action was necessary elsewhere, and Huish was usually asked to deal with emergency measures of this kind. In 1850, for example, he was called upon to rearrange services at Peterborough in response to changes made

1 L.N.W. Mins, 14 Apr., 9 June, and 30 Oct. 1849, LNW1/21, BTHR.
2 Huish to Gilmer, 5 Mar. 1850, HL2/R373, BTHR; *Midland Counties Herald*, 20 Apr. 1848, 21 June 1849.
3 L.N.W. Mins, 13 Oct. 1849, etc., LNW1/21, BTHR.

by the Eastern Counties Railway.¹ Some actions were not in the public interest, but it was Huish's duty to maintain the company's position rather than provide loss-making facilities. Given the circumstances of depression, the company in fact maintained a high level of service, and escaped criticisms levelled at some of the major companies for their 'economies'.²

As regards pricing, Huish at first continued to follow the policies he had employed before 1846. But the London & North Western's favourable traffic position was soon threatened, first by lower maximum fares, then by the slump, and not least by the increased competition of other railways. Huish's report of 1850 is the most comprehensive account of policy and experience at this time. In discussing the details surrounding the fall in passenger revenue to 1849, he not only outlined previous pricing activity, but indicated the lessons to be drawn, making several suggestions to improve future practice.

His initial task was to create uniformity over the amalgamated line. Until June 1847 fares varied on each of the company's sections, and were also slightly higher than the maxima permitted in the Act. Thereafter, fares were unified and, for the main-line, fixed at the legal maximum. Nevertheless, the fares were lower than had been customary on both the London & Birmingham and Grand Junction Railways in the early 'forties, and, with the exception of the third-class, remained lower than the average of the other major companies (table 15).

As business conditions worsened the company experimented with fares, particularly for intermediate and short distances, in an attempt to retain previous levels of income. Huish was given the task of arranging detailed analyses of traffic response, especially in the Lancashire area, where losses appeared heavy.³ The Board was particularly concerned about the fall in Liverpool–Manchester receipts in 1849, and Huish's Report indicated that the Manchester–Stockport, Peterborough, and Coventry areas also received particular attention, and were compared with statistics for other railways, when these scarce documents could be acquired.⁴

1 L.N.W. Sthn. Road & Traffic Ctee Mins, 3 Oct. 1850, LNW1/144, BTHR.
2 The G.W.R., for example, was strongly criticized in January 1849 for abandoning its concessionary return ticket facilities.
3 L.N.W. Mins, 10 Nov. 1849, LNW1/21, BTHR.
4 L.N.W. Mins, 14 Feb. 1850, LNW1/21, and Huish's Report, 36–7, 40–2, BTHR. Huish acquired valuable, though more rudimentary, statistics from Capt. J. M. Laws, on the Manchester & Leeds passenger traffic, 1845–7, and from C. P. Roney on the Eastern Counties passenger traffic, 1847–9.

Table 15
Average fares per mile of the London & North Western and seven major United Kingdom railways, 1847, 1848, 1851

Period	Sample	Fares by class in pence per mile			
		First	Second	Third	Parlt.
Jan.–June 1847	7 railways excluding the L.N.W.	2.38	1.61	0.97*	0.96
Jan.–June 1847	Stated L.N.W. average	2.18	1.45	0.91	0.95
1847	From Huish's Report†	2.13	1.59	0.98	—
Jan.–June 1848	7 railways excluding the L.N.W.	2.45	1.71	0.97‡	0.98§
Jan.–June 1848	Stated L.N.W. average	2.08	1.43	1.00	1.00
1848	From Huish's Report	2.00	1.50	1.00	—
Jan.–June 1851	7 railways excluding the L.N.W.	2.38	1.58	0.80‖	0.93
Jan.–June 1851	Stated L.N.W. average	2.16	1.41	0.93	0.98

Source: Accounts & Papers, P.P.1847–8, XXVI, 1849, XXVII, 1852, XLVIII;
Huish, 'Report on the Passenger Traffic', 33. The seven railways are: Great Western,
Lancashire & Yorkshire, Midland, South Eastern, London & South Western,
London & Brighton, and Eastern Counties.
*5 railways.
†Excluding day tickets.
‡5 railways.
§6 railways.
‖5 railways.

Huish, in considering the various pricing changes of the period, rejected the idea that either an increase or a reduction in fares would prove a general solution. His experience of the Glasgow–Greenock area led him to favour, for local traffic, a pricing system firmly based upon "what the traffic will bear", i.e. adjusted to the peculiar circumstances of each district.[1] He supported the overall policy of keeping long-distance fares higher than the short, and also of charging the former on a mileage basis, but he wished to exempt the low-class London to Scotland fares,

1 Huish noted in his Report that abstract fairness of charge had little effect on the public, and that short-distance fares could be affected by a great many factors, including road competition: Report, 35.

because of strong competition by sea. The company could not raise fares beyond the parliamentary limits, of course, and Huish also suggested that, were this possible, the results would not necessarily prove beneficial. The experiment with Manchester–Stockport fares had failed, and it appeared that companies known to have a high tariff policy were "suffering more".[1] The general manager also explained that the increase in day ticket rates from two-thirds to three-quarters of the full fare, begun in January 1848, had not met with success, and had probably excluded large sections of the public. On the other hand, the increase of Night Mail fares in November 1849 was not criticized, for, in comparative terms, it meant little to such a traveller over a long distance.[2]

The effects not only of the general traffic situation but also of pricing decisions had been to reduce the company's second- and third-class revenue. Huish favoured neither a reduction in accommodation nor abstract fare reductions in the lower classes of traffic. He explained that on certain sections of the railway, low fares and improved third-class accommodation had merely caused a decrease in returns, especially on the Liverpool–Manchester line. Referring to Laws's experience on the Manchester & Leeds, he also suggested that net returns could decline even if the gross receipts were maintained.[3] Clearly, no general rule could be found: whereas reductions on the Manchester–Stockport line had rectified the position, a deliberate restriction of facilities had been needed in the Liverpool area.[4]

Huish was critical of a system which he had helped to create. What, in fact, were his positive suggestions to improve receipts? In the latter pages of his Report he stressed the "primary importance" of improving express services in order to free mixed-class trains for duty in the local areas. He considered that the short-distance local traffic could be improved, and receipts would come not only from a less prescribed pricing system, but also from extensions in special concessional rates, especially those related to season tickets, and period excursion fares. This attitude did not, of course, mark a startling departure from the company's previous policy, for much of what Huish stressed had been started in 1848

1 The G.W.R.'s share of U.K. passenger receipts fell by 37 per cent (cf. the L.N.W.'s loss of 20 per cent), 1846–51; see Appendix, table 49.
2 L.N.W. Mins, 9 June 1849, LNW1/21, BTHR.
3 Laws' statistics showed an increase of 1½ per cent in gross receipts but a fall of 20 per cent in net revenue, 1845–7: Huish, 'Report on the Passenger Traffic', table XI, 41. Liverpool–Manchester statistics were given in table XII, 42.
4 In 1846 there were three third-class trains, Liverpool–Manchester, and in 1849, seven in each direction. On 1 February 1850, the number was reduced to two each way, and the results were favourable: *ibid.*, 41–2.

and 1849. Nevertheless, he did show the management where its policy should ideally be directed for maximum profit, and, in indicating where his own sentiments lay, tried to offset the handicap of having more than one policy-maker.[1] His work was also exceptional in that it was supported by a mass of detailed statistics: in his Report he provided tables showing passenger receipts *at each station* over four consecutive years— a rare level of sophistication at this time.[2]

After April 1850 the company modified its pricing plan on the lines suggested by Huish. A concerted attack upon local traffic was initiated, but without recourse to low fares in areas which could not make them work.[3] Lower tariffs were introduced in areas threatened by road competition, and certain "agricultural" districts were given the benefit, on an experimental basis, of "extremely low fares".[4] Tests of demand elasticity were thus continued, but only in areas which seemed to promise new traffic. As Huish pointed out, there was little to be gained from further experiment with the Liverpool–Manchester fares, for "let the fare . . . be what it may, few will travel but on business, and the distance . . . is too great to permit of continued intercourse" [i.e. commuting].[5] Of course, certain fare cuts were a response to reductions by rival companies. The Shrewsbury–Wellington fares were generously cut during the dispute with the Shrewsbury & Birmingham Railway, and the experiment with Preston–Liverpool fares was occasioned by a contest with the East Lancashire company, which was later rectified by an agreement involving a traffic division.[6] The incursion of inter-railway considerations into short and intermediate distance pricing was certainly a problem which had rarely existed before the 'Mania'.

Huish's plans for excursions, season tickets, and other concessions, were also implemented. The pilot Killarney scheme of mid-week 14-day return tickets was extended to Scotland, and, after a meeting of officers of interested companies in June 1850, it was decided to extend the availability of third-class tickets from London to Scotland, and to make

1 Smith, one of the directors, was keenly interested in pricing, and much work was done by the Road & Traffic Ctees, and by the Audit Ctee.

2 Huish, 'Report on the Passenger Traffic', 8–27. The only evidence of similar enquiry that I have found is a reference to a statement of weekly station receipts made by a Ctee of Investigation on the more modest London & Blackwall Railway, 1841–3, RAC1/227A, BTHR.

3 L.N.W. General Meeting, 16 Aug. 1850, LNW1/1, and Sthn. Road & Traffic Ctee Mins, 13 June 1850, LNW1/144, BTHR.

4 L.N.W. General Meeting, 16 Aug. 1850, LNW1/1, and Sthn. Road & Traffic Ctee Mins, 3 July 1850, LNW1/144, BTHR.

5 Huish, 'Report on the Passenger Traffic', 42.

6 *Ibid.*, 43; *Midland Counties Herald*, 23–30 Jan. 1851.

concessions to family parties.[1] The season ticket rate, which Huish had reduced in the London area in 1848, was further reduced from January 1851, and in September 1850 the company followed others in extending its half-price children's tickets to those under 12 years of age. Huish also stressed the importance of ancillary aids in attracting passengers. For example, he mentioned the lack of a first-class hotel between London and Scotland.[2] Pricing alterations also stemmed from his direct intervention. He altered the Stamford branch fares in 1850, and reintroduced day tickets on an express train. In fact, the fare tables for all new lines were sent to him for his approval.

In the short run, Huish's policies appear to have been financially successful, although the increase in travel both before and after the Great Exhibition of 1851 clearly affected gross revenue. The company could not expect to continue unaffected by the trends of the period, and it was therefore expedient to concentrate firstly upon high-speed long-distance services, and secondly upon building up short-distance services. Competition was diversifying traffic channels, and as Huish stressed, it was not merely price, but "hours, convenience, and service" which were important in determining passenger demand.[3] The manager, in fact, gave much of his time to settling difficulties caused by rival companies. The North Staffordshire caused many headaches, especially at Whitmore, and the Lancashire & Yorkshire and East Lancashire railways vied with the London & North Western in the Liverpool and Manchester areas, until an agreement to divide traffic was made. Huish's letters to Gilmer in 1850 are an excellent example of the lack of trust between rivals, and the incredible intricacies of competitive pricing. Despite the existence of traffic agreements, Huish stressed the importance of undercutting the Midland and Lancashire & Yorkshire in their London–Huddersfield fares, and of ensuring that the latter did not encourage traffic to go via the Great Northern by quoting a cheaper fare for westward journeys than for those eastward.[4] He was also guilty of duplicity in his traffic arrangements with other companies. When cross-examined in 1858, during his evidence to the Committee considering the Great Northern and Manchester Sheffield & Lincolnshire Bill, he admitted that despite the exist-

1 This was a meeting of L.N.W., Midland, Y.N.M., Y.N.B., Cale., and N.B. companies, "to concert united measures for improving the traffic between Scotland and London", L.N.W. Sthn. Road & Traffic Ctee Mins, 3 July 1850, LNW1/144, BTHR.
2 Huish, 'Report on the Passenger Traffic', 44.
3 *Ibid.*
4 Huish, letters to Gilmer, 21 Sept., 15 Oct., 9–28 Oct. 1850, HL2/R373(13), BTHR.

ence of complex arrangements for traffic in the Lancashire area, companies had frequently diverted traffic from each others' lines: his agreement with the North Staffordshire company in 1850 promised traffic from Liverpool to East Anglia which had already been agreed as falling to the Manchester Sheffield & Lincolnshire and Midland lines, by prior agreements.[1]

Similar work was involved in Huish's efforts to protect the West Coast route to Scotland. Regular meetings of the interested companies, led by Huish, considered fares and services. The incursion of a fresh competitor always created great difficulties, as was the case in 1850 when the Shrewsbury & Birmingham challenged the London & North Western's Birmingham–Liverpool and Chester routes by quoting very low fares. Similar skirmishes with the East Lancashire and Lancashire & Yorkshire companies were troublesome, but every effort was made to settle problems involving rate-wars as speedily as possible. Throughout the period, Huish met the representatives of various companies, with the intention of stabilizing prices. The tangled negotiations with the Lancashire & Yorkshire were his special province, for example.[2] His involvement with the determination of both services and fares was considerable, and his increasing interest in inter-company affairs gave him considerable scope to determine the direction of London & North Western policy.

1 *S.C. on the Manchester Sheffield & Lincolnshire, and Great Northern Railway Companies Bill*, P.P.1857–8, XV, QQ.5999, 6093–106.
2 L.N.W. Nthn. Road & Traffic Ctee Mins, 2 Nov. 1849, etc., LNW1/158, BTHR.

5

The London & North Western Railway 1846-51
Managerial adaptation and reorganization part II

1 Goods traffic

Between 1846 and 1851 the railway companies gave increased attention to goods traffic. Receipts, while not quite keeping pace with the expansion of the rail network, increased more than those for passenger traffic, such that by 1851 most of the larger companies earned roughly equal amounts from the two traffics.[1] And as business increased, the Railway

1 See Appendix, tables 49–50.

Clearing House encouraged moves towards operational uniformity and the closer co-operation of its members in traffic organization. The available statistics, however, make it difficult to construct a detailed analysis of even one company's activities. But within the general context of growth it is clear that the contribution of the London & North Western, both in its share of total goods traffic, and in its general managerial policy under Huish, was paramount.[1]

The company's goods management was highly important because the Grand Junction's policy of excluding the independent carriers had been fully accepted, an important decision which influenced other companies and stimulated a controversy among both railwaymen and the public. Huish played a leading rôle in the extension of the Grand Junction system to the London & Birmingham line. The proceedings of the Merchandise Committee reveal not only his personal enthusiasm for the policy, but his concerted efforts to overcome the many points of difference between the company and its prospective agents.[2]

The company began to carry over the whole line in February 1847, and an agency agreement was applied from 1 July, by which Pickford & Co. and Chaplin & Horne undertook the collection and delivery duties for the Southern Division of the Railway. In September Pickford sold its Camden depot to the company.[3] The terms of the agency were similar to those previously made by the Grand Junction. It was, however, intended that the agents would perform their duties at near cost, and during the lengthy negotiations on the subject, Huish inspected the books of Chaplin & Horne to ensure that the agreed allowance would be fair.[4] By the eventual terms, the agents were to receive a service charge of between 3*d.* and 6*d.* per ton handled plus a salary of at least £7,500 per annum, with extra bonuses for efficient operation.[5] The company, while retaining overall control, was thus freed from the minutiae of goods organization over much of its system, while the charges made by the agents for terminal services were closely regulated. The agreement brought the accumulated experience and business of Pickford & Co. to the Railway, and in doing so saved the company capital expenditure. The implementation of the new

1 See Appendix, tables 49–50, and table 12 above.
2 L.N.W. General Locomotive & Merchandise Ctee Mins, 7 Aug., 14 Oct., 9–14 Nov. 1846, 5 Mar. and 9 Apr. 1847, LNW1/221, BTHR.
3 PIC3/2, BTHR. I am indebted to Mr G. L. Turnbull for this reference.
4 Huish stated that the actual cost of collection and delivery in London averaged 7*s.* 6*d.* per ton. The agents were eventually granted 8*s.* per ton (the Grand Junction had allowed 10*s.*): L.N.W. Loco. & Merchandise Ctee Mins, 9 Nov. 1846, LNW1/221, and Agency Agreement, LNW3/3, BTHR, summarized in the Appendix.
5 LNW3/3, BTHR.

system was also the occasion for a division of the goods executive into four areas, under experienced and competent officers, and following this step, the extent of the new agreement was freely advertised, with a list of places where collection and delivery services were to be performed.[1]

The agency agreement, together with the expulsion of the private carriers, was not, however, a complete solution, speedily executed and universally welcomed. Problems of interpretation remained, and there were frequent disputes over Pickford's share of the railway traffic and its alleged freedom to forward goods by canal. The agents continued to send goods by water from Tipton to Manchester, and from the Potteries, and were also caught dispatching goods from Liverpool via the East Lancashire Railway.[2] The many disputes were not fully settled until 1850, when Pickford finally agreed to abandon its canal boats.[3]

The London & North Western also experienced a hostile and unexpected attack upon its mode of conducting the goods traffic. This was an extremely important episode in railway management affairs. In particular, it demonstrated the extent to which the publication of pamphlets could cast doubt upon the internal management and profitability of railways, and affect subsequent policy. It also revealed Huish as the outstanding executive officer of the day, spokesman not only for his company but for the industry as a whole.

Huish, reporting to the Merchandise Committee after the introduction of the new goods system, declared at first that there had been remarkably little dislocation.[4] His more mature judgment, in February 1848, after six months' operation, remained optimistic.[5] He reaffirmed the advantages of the railway acting as carrier, stressed the necessity for unity of principle in working the line, and suggested that the toll system (formerly operated by the London & Birmingham) had been losing ground in the eyes of railwaymen. Admitting that "perhaps no question connected with the practical detail of Railway Management has given rise to a greater diversity of opinion", Huish claimed to have established the most profitable means of organizing the goods traffic. He mentioned a number of direct advantages. These included the fact that the company could

1 L.N.W. Loco. & Merchandise Ctee Mins, 22 Dec. 1846, LNW1/221, BTHR; *Midland Counties Herald*, 18 Nov. 1847. The Goods Managers were Braithwaite Poole, Mills, Salt, and Eborall.
2 L.N.W. Loco. & Merchandise Ctee Mins, 20 Nov. 1848, 12 Jan., 11 May, and 8 June 1849, LNW1/221, BTHR.
3 *Ibid.*, 11 Jan. 1850.
4 *Ibid.*, 9 Apr. and 11 Aug. 1847.
5 Huish, 'Confidential Report . . . upon . . . the Merchandise Traffic', HL2/R99B, BTHR.

command its own business, and that the end had come for the carriers on toll "with no ties, who were continually looking out for fresh outlets and advantages elsewhere . . . [and whose] personal advantage was best served by embroiling neighbouring companies in a contest for traffic held on a precarious tenure, and liable at any moment to be abstracted by the offer of more flattering inducements from other parties".[1] He also contended that greater profits had resulted from the company's control of the traffic in 'smalls'.[2] Finally, he pointed out that other companies north of the Thames had adopted the same principles, their "community of interest" being cemented by the existence of the Clearing House Goods Managers' Conferences (which he had helped to initiate).[3]

The Report contained some stirring words, but not all those interested in goods management shared Huish's optimism. The General Manager had himself admitted that the slump in trade would affect a comparison of revenue and costs before and after the introduction of the new system. He also referred to certain teething troubles, not the least of which was the fact that the 36 dispossessed carriers had attempted to divert traffic to the canals. Furthermore, his tabular analysis of the company's goods account was not completely satisfactory: in showing an increase in net profit of £7,500 for the period July–December 1847 (compared with the same months of 1846), he had not separated the costs of operating the coal and cattle traffics, although this had been done with the revenue.[4] Indeed, although Huish claimed that the new system had produced increased profits per ton, he was unable to give "authentic data" on tonnages carried, working expenses, and receipts, to show the position of any particular branch of the business. Thus, in spite of the overall increase in profit, and Huish's claim that some of the additional operating costs had resulted from a separate decision to run goods trains at night,[5] some doubts remained, especially as to the profitability of certain classes of goods carried. To be fair to Huish, he did admit that it would take longer to judge the new system, and he also posed the difficulty of isolating a separate underlying trend, detected at Liverpool, for the company's

1 Huish, 'Confidential Report . . . upon . . . the Merchandise Traffic', HL2/R99B, BTHR.
2 *Ibid.* Huish considered the 'smalls' traffic at Camden in September 1847, which amounted to 278 tons. The revenue collected was £1,582, compared with the £417 which Huish estimated as the probable return under the former toll system of the L. & B.
3 *Ibid.*
4 *Ibid.*, table 1, reproduced in the Appendix, table 51.
5 L.N.W. Special Ctee Mins and Reports, 11 July 1846, LNW1/50; L.N.W. Mins, 15 Aug. 1846, LNW1/20, BTHR.

additional traffic to be of the bulk, low-tariff type, which had the effect of reducing average receipts per ton.

The year 1848 proved a difficult one for railway managers, but although a short-run fall in receipts caused anxiety,[1] total goods receipts, unlike those for passenger traffic, grew steadily to 1851. The profitability of this larger traffic was, however, questioned, and the company was surprised to be confronted by serious criticism so soon after its reassuring financial statement of October. The principal attack came from a published pamphlet addressed to George Carr Glyn, the company's chairman, by John Whitehead, of the Stock Exchange, on 15 November.[2] The writer stated, with considerable elaboration, that the railway companies were hiding the facts from the shareholders, and that in particular, the abandonment of the toll system by the London & North Western had resulted in great losses, which were being met by profits from the passenger traffic. Whitehead explained that the new system had encouraged "ruinous" canal competition at low rates, and that the companies were guilty of carrying traffic without considering its profitability. He recommended that goods rates be doubled, in order to transfer unproductive items to sea or canal.[3]

The letter received much publicity. Although it was commendable to seek a more detailed analysis of profit and loss from the railways, Whitehead expected too much in his demand that this information should be provided for "each description of traffic carried on the line".[4] No railway company was in a position to do this, even for its own use. Many costs, indeed, were extremely difficult to allocate even to the much broader categories of 'passenger' and 'goods'. Whitehead's argument, moreover, purporting to show the company's failings, was itself riddled with misconceptions and imaginary statistics. Many of these surrounded his attempt to prove losses on the goods account by means of a comparison of the respective earning capacities of a passenger carriage and a goods truck.[5] Editorial comments in the *Morning Herald* and *Morning Chronicle* made use of these errors to defend the railway company. The former was very hostile to Whitehead, stating that his "knowledge of the practical working of a railway . . . is as lamentably deficient as his statements are

1 L.N.W. Loco. & Merchandise Ctee Mins, 8 Sept. 1848, LNW1/221, BTHR.
2 *Railway Management. A Letter to George Carr Glyn, Esq.* . . . (1848). Whitehead had been secretary of the South Eastern Railway during the corruption scandal of 1845, see above, p. 25.
3 *Ibid.*, 7–8, 11–12, 15.
4 *Ibid.*, 12.
5 *Ibid.*, 8–10.

erroneous and his suggestions ridiculous".[1] It was pointed out that the logic of Whitehead's argument was that "the company CANNOT earn a LITTLE by the goods traffic, because they do earn much by the passenger traffic."[2] The *Morning Herald* supported the railway's goods system, questioned the policy of doubling the rates, and in giving its opinion that the terminal costs at London were some 20–30 per cent lower than the 10*s.* per ton claimed by Whitehead, suggested a close personal contact with Huish.[3] The *Herald* also knew that the company had shown a net profit on goods traffic greater than that suggested by Whitehead, and provided statistics which sought to prove that goods earnings per mile were little less than passenger earnings.[4]

The argument thus developed from a general attack upon the goods system to the specific charge that the company was making a loss on its goods traffic. This outburst of discussion about an intimate part of the company's affairs provoked Huish to answer Whitehead himself. In a pamphlet entitled *A Letter to George Carr Glyn . . . On Some Points of Railway Management . . .*, he used the accounts for 1847–8 to demonstrate that the goods traffic could not have been worked at a complete loss, since the total operating costs (passenger *and* goods) were only about £30,000 more than the goods receipts.[5] He also stressed the fallacy in seeking profit by doubling the rates, while his defence of the coal traffic rates as admittedly low but remunerative was an important statement of railway policy:

> The Rates for Coal, as also those for Goods, are fixed as high as circumstances will permit. Railway Companies do not voluntarily prefer low to high charges, if the latter can be obtained. The question is, are the Coal *Rates* remunerative or not? That they are too low is admitted, and nothing but the bulk conveyed can make them answer . . . The amount of profit has nothing to do with the argument. I have a right to assume that the highest obtainable rate is charged, and this being so, the trade should be carried on so long as any margin of profit remains, even if the expense of working it be 90 per cent. of the receipts.

1 *Morning Herald*, 23 Nov. 1848.
2 *Morning Herald*, 21 Nov. 1848.
3 Cf. *Morning Herald*, 23 Nov. 1848, and Huish's investigation of the books of Chaplin & Horne, mentioned above. It is quite possible that Huish was himself the author of these newspaper articles.
4 *Morning Herald*, 21–3 Nov. 1848. Passenger receipts (Jan.–June 1848) were £670,107, and train-miles run were 2,132,176, = 6*s.* 3*d.* per train-mile: merchandise receipts were £339,800, train-miles 1,300,644, = 5*s.* 2$\frac{1}{4}$*d.* per train-mile.
5 Huish, *Letter to George Carr Glyn . . .*, 8. See Appendix, table 51 (2).

The total balance of profit is the point to look at, and although a percentage of working expenses is to some extent a useful guide, for ordinary purposes it would lead to error if adopted as a general test. . . . quantity is the essential element of Railway success. Without this, rates, however high, will never return a large profit . . .[1]

Huish's views were convincing, and were generally praised in the press. The *Morning Herald* spoke of a "very able letter", the *Morning Chronicle* of a "perfect refutation" of Whitehead's conclusions.[2] Unfortunately, Huish had not resisted the temptation to try to crush his opponent. In seeking to do so he too committed some statistical errors, and his bombastic claim to be able to demonstrate profit in all sectors of traffic—"It would not be difficult . . . to attach the cost of every item of railway expense to each particular description of traffic"[3]—was rash in the extreme. The impetuous way in which he over-emphasized the profitability of the goods traffic led to an escalation of the debate, which was hardly in the company's interest. Whitehead replied with two more letters,[4] and there were notable contributions from others.

Whitehead's second letter took up some of the weaker points of Huish's pamphlet, making some perfectly valid criticisms of the manager's rasher statements. He disputed Huish's claim that he could assign costs to each type of traffic, and used the statement that the most profitable railways had been those which had concentrated on the carriage of coal and minerals to reassert his support for the open system of carrying.[5] But in his general argument he shifted his ground, and ignoring his previous opinion that goods losses were subsidized by passenger profits, claimed instead that the receipts from 'smalls' were being secretly applied to hide losses on general merchandise charged by ton.[6] This allegation, based on a misunderstanding of Huish's comment that *coaching* parcels were not credited to the goods account, could not be substantiated, and was exposed by the *Morning Herald*.[7] Statistics were

---

1 *Ibid.*, 16–18.
2 *Morning Herald*, 28 Nov. 1848; *Morning Chronicle*, 29 Nov. 1848.
3 Huish, *Letter to George Carr Glyn* . . ., 11.
4 *Railway Management. A Second Letter to George Carr Glyn, Esq., in reply to Capt. Huish's letter*, 30 Nov. 1848, and *Railway Management. The Proof! A Third Letter to George Carr Glyn, Esq.* . . ., 5 Feb. 1849.
5 Whitehead, *A Second Letter* . . ., 5, 9, and Huish, *Letter to George Carr Glyn* . . ., 11, 17.
6 Whitehead, *A Second Letter* . . ., 6–8.
7 *Morning Herald*, 2 Dec. 1848, and Huish, *Letter to George Carr Glyn* . . ., 8. Whitehead had confused coaching parcels (which were in fact regarded as passenger traffic) and small parcels (which were credited to the goods account). The gross receipts from

provided to demonstrate the fallacies in Whitehead's work, and it was even suggested that the information which he sought was part of a plot to gain useful statistics for the canals.[1]

The disagreement over the earning capacities of passenger and goods trains occasioned by Huish's pamphlet need not concern us, except to notice that it was in part responsible for further publication, and in particular, the letters of Eckersley and 'A Sufferer'.[2] Eckersley, the 'Comptroller' of the Lancashire & Yorkshire Railway, provided his company's own figures to defend Huish's position, although his work was, of course, no proof that the London & North Western's system was profitable. The most obvious of Whitehead's mistakes—the confusion of earning capacity and actual earnings—was exploded again at some length, and it was shown that the Manchester & Leeds Railway (as it then was) had made sizeable profits on its goods business in 1847.[3] However, since Eckersley did not state whether his 'goods traffic' included mails, or parcels, his statistics of locomotive mileage could not be compared with Huish's estimates of train mileage, and, as Whitehead commented, he had appeared to neglect permanent way and stock renewal costs in his calculations.[4] Nevertheless, Eckersley defended Huish's view that "railway companies generally contrive to get as high rates as the circumstances of the traffic will permit", and he supported the view that the goods traffic, as then conducted, was profitable.[5]

The *Morning Herald* again intervened, to express doubts whether passenger and goods costs could have been as similar as Eckersley had claimed, while 'A Sufferer', in support of Whitehead, queried the expediency of expelling the independent carriers, and implied that capital had been used to maintain dividends, as operating costs rose.[6] This pamph-

---

'smalls' were put at *c*. £40–50,000 p.a. by the *Herald*: the balance available for
L.N.W. dividend (Jan.–June 1848) was £467,163; passenger receipts were £670,107,
and a very low estimate of operating costs of 2*s*. 9*d*. per train-mile gave a net working
profit of only £378,392. This still left £88,271 as the yield from goods traffic, and it
was clear that such a sum could not have come from the 'smalls' traffic alone.

1 *Morning Herald*, 2 Dec. 1848. Whitehead was also accused of being a sympathiser of
Joseph Baxendale, embittered opponent of railways and head of Pickford & Co.

2 P. Eckersley, *Railway Management. Observations on Two Letters to George Carr Glyn,
Esq.* . . . (1848); 'A Sufferer', *Railway Policy. A Letter to G. C. Glyn* . . ., 6 Dec.
1848.

3 Eckersley, *op. cit.*, 10. Passenger receipts were £165,764, goods receipts £185,610,
operating costs £58,737 and £74,076, leaving a 'profit' of £107,027 (passenger traffic)
and £111,534 (goods traffic).

4 *Ibid.*, 11; Whitehead, *Railway Management. The Proof!* . . ., as a 'P.S.'

5 Eckersley, *op. cit.*, 14–15, 22.

6 'A Sufferer', *op. cit.*, 5–7; *Morning Herald*, 12 Dec. 1848.

leteer, who was supported by the same publisher as Whitehead,[1] emphasized the strength of the canal competition, and referred to the "heavy
loss" made on some bulk traffics, and especially on the coal trade.[2] But
there were many mistaken assumptions here, too. 'Sufferer' did not
understand one of the basic facts, i.e. that the London & North Western
was still using carrying firms, but as agents, and that in this way a
stricter and more satisfactory control over both the firms and the traffic
they encouraged was obtained. He also failed to point out that the increased capital expenditure of which he complained was the necessary
outcome of a genuine extension of the company's activities.

Whitehead's final assault followed in February 1849, in the form of a
third, and lengthy, letter to Carr Glyn. Once more he challenged Huish to
reply to his charges. Investigating the London–Birmingham goods rates,
he showed that they were on the whole lower than had been charged by
the London & Birmingham, and claimed that some traffics were undoubtedly unremunerative. The accuracy of Whitehead's data on the
London & North Western rates of 1849 is borne out by the terms of a
secret agreement with the Grand Junction Canal, which came into operation in February, and, indeed, it appears that prior to this the rates had
been even lower than he had suggested.[3] However, Whitehead's figures
for the London & Birmingham were for tolls only, the actual cost to the
public being omitted. Further, it is doubtful whether his deduction of a
uniform 10s. per ton for terminal costs was accurate, especially since the
London & North Western had agreed a total cost, including agency fees,
of 9s. at Camden and 3s. 10d. at Birmingham. Nevertheless, Whitehead's
claim that the company's new classification of goods involved reduced
rates for many important articles required an answer, as did his accusation that Huish was ignoring the published rates by arranging lower
preferential terms for items such as sugar and coffee.[4]

Many of Whitehead's comments were no doubt valid. The company
had itself admitted that rates had been reduced, and it appears that full
advantage was taken of Huish's foolish remark to the contrary.[5] But low
rates did not prove financial losses, and Whitehead's attempt to show a
loss of over £27,000 on the goods traffic for 1847–8 was again based upon
hypothetical statistics, including the use of a crude and by no means

1 Smith, Elder, and Cornhill.
2 'A Sufferer', *op. cit.*, 10–11.
3 Whitehead, *Railway Management. The Proof!* . . ., 3–7. Cf. his rates, in the Appendix, table 51 (3), and those agreed by the railway and canal, table 51 (4).
4 *Ibid.*, 7.
5 Huish, *Letter to George Carr Glyn* . . ., 6.

universally accepted estimate of train operating costs. The *Morning Herald* once again took up the challenge on behalf of the railway company, Huish having decided to maintain a prudent silence. The newspaper questioned Whitehead's calculations, and was particularly critical of his attempt to make a judgment based upon a comparison of two vastly different traffic situations.[1] This was certainly a valid point, but some of Whitehead's criticisms nevertheless remained pertinent. His discovery, for example, of Huish's omission of allowances for depreciation in his analysis of February 1848, and his sponsorship of Dockray's report on the effect of a large traffic on the permanent way, were important.[2]

Huish suffered some criticism, therefore, and despite the overall persuasiveness of his case, some statements were injudicious, and were ably exploited by his opponents. His claim that goods trains were cheaper to work than passenger trains was questioned by the indefatigable *Morning Herald*,[3] and, indeed, ran counter to the estimates of locomotive power and coke costs presented to the Merchandise Committee, and with which he must have been familiar (table 16).

Table 16
London & North Western coke and locomotive costs, passenger and goods trains

Period six months ending	Division of L.N.W.	Coke cost per PASSENGER train-mile	Power cost per PASSENGER train-mile	Coke cost per GOODS train-mile	Power cost per GOODS train-mile
30 Nov. 1847	Sthn	5.30*d.*	12.22*d.*	7.41*d.*	15.56*d.*
30 Nov. 1848	Sthn	4.36	12.68	6.12	15.05
31 May 1849	Sthn	4.09	10.96	5.60	11.97
31 May 1850	Sthn	3.56	9.16	4.87	11.83
30 Nov. 1847	Nthn	2.30	7.22	3.90	11.07
30 Nov. 1848	Nthn	2.49	7.63	4.06	11.01
31 May 1849	Nthn	2.34	7.33	4.08	10.07
31 May 1850	Nthn	2.15	6.71	3.67	9.66

Source: L.N.W. Loco. & Merchandise Ctee Mins, LNW1/221, BTHR.

1 *Morning Herald*, 7–8 Feb. 1848.
2 Whitehead, *Railway Management. The Proof!* . . ., 18–48, citing Dockray's Report to the Committee of Way and Works on the effects of speed and weight on the permanent way, August 1848.
3 5 Dec. 1848.

However, the allegations that the goods traffic was being conducted at a loss had positive effects in stimulating Huish and his executive to make the first concerted efforts to measure the costs attributable to this sector.

There seems, then, to be a case for supposing that the London & North Western experienced short-term difficulties with the new goods system, probably in the direction of low marginal returns on additional traffic. Some items may indeed have been carried at little or no profit, as Huish had admitted earlier with regard to Grand Junction traffic, but the available accounts and estimates do not allow a firm conclusion to be made. In the long run, the company undoubtedly benefited from the application of the Grand Junction system over the whole line, and the seizure of bulk traffic was essential if, with increasing capital expenditure, a moderate dividend were to be maintained. Dockray's warning about the effect of a larger, heavier traffic on track costs was important, but it was no answer to give traffic to the canals, as Huish's critics seemed to suggest.

A considerable part of the company's short-term difficulties arose from a severe but transient canal competition. There were also occasional squabbles with railway companies, such as the Eastern Counties, but these were speedily settled.[1] The conflict with the Grand Junction Canal was frequently mentioned by the pamphleteers, and the minutes of the Merchandise Committee provide an insight into the attitude of Huish and his fellow officers to this challenge. Huish, for example, spoke of a canal 'confederacy', stretching from Lancaster to London, in September 1847, and warned that a contest with the Grand Junction Canal and its associates would be likely to follow the decision to commence carrying in December. Indeed, before the controversy with Whitehead, Huish had met Graham, the Canal's chairman, "in order to prevent the continuance of competition".[2] Poole and Gregson, the respective goods managers, met at Lancaster in August 1848 and drew up the basis of an eventual agreement. Negotiations were prolonged because the Canal wanted the Railway to charge only the maximum rates for coal, but a six-month agreement was operated from February 1849 and later renewed for a further nine months.[3] The canal company was pleased to announce that competition had been "confined within its legitimate bounds", but although the agreement fixed canal rates below those of the railway, it was the latter

1 L.N.W. Loco. & Merchandise Ctee Mins, 13 July and 10 Aug. 1849, LNW1/221, BTHR.
2 *Ibid.*, 11 Mar. and 8 Sept. 1848.
3 *Ibid.*, 20 Nov. 1848, 12 Jan., 9 Feb., 9 Mar., and 10 Aug. 1849. Cf. C. Hadfield, who in *The Canals of the East Midlands* (1966), 219, mentions the first rate agreement as being that of 1857.

who appeared to derive the most benefit. The London & North Western's special agreements with coal companies were not affected, and it was able to secure the Canal's concurrence in its arrangement of special contracts for bulk consignments. The dispute with the Canal was reopened in 1850, principally because of the Railway's coal trade, but by this time the railway was in a stronger position than before, while the Canal, although maintaining its gross revenue, was almost certainly experiencing reduced profits as operating costs rose.[1] Like the railways, canals had been forced to abandon a high-tariff policy for one embracing a larger traffic at lower rates.

The London & North Western suffered from the competition of other canals in this period, and a contest with the Duke of Bridgewater's Canal for the Liverpool–Manchester traffic lasted 18 weeks in 1849, after sporadic rate cuts in the previous year. Correspondence between Poole and Booth showed that the Canal had attracted valuable customers, including Samuel Lees, the Manchester cotton manufacturer, and Poole estimated that a 25 per cent fall in revenue at Liverpool had taken place in April 1848.[2] A further outbreak of rate-cutting began in July 1849, and Poole again complained of the effects on receipts.[3] The Bridgewater Canal eventually raised its rates in January 1850, but there is no doubt that the Railway's position had been damaged. In addition to the canal challenge, the London & North Western faced the disruption caused by the intervention of other railways. The low rates stimulated an increase in traffic, but revenue fell.[4] Conflict also arose in the Potteries, where for a time Pickford employed canals in defiance of the agency agreement. The anxiety with which the management viewed each instance of canal competition and its willingness to negotiate testify to the effect this had on profits. Eventually, the company sought a solution in the direct control of canal management. It assumed ownership of the Birmingham Navigation in 1846, leased the Shropshire Union in 1847 (which brought some two hundred miles of waterway under its aegis), and in 1851 shared in a lease of the Leeds & Liverpool Canal.[5]

A closer examination of the company's goods traffic shows more

---

1 For receipts, see Appendix, table 52.
2 Poole to Booth, 24 Apr. and 24 June 1848, HL2/R365, BTHR.
3 L.N.W. Loco. & Merchandise Ctee Mins, 13 July 1849, LNW1/221; Nthn. Road & Traffic Ctee Mins, 19 Oct. 1849, LNW1/158, BTHR.
4 L.N.W. Loco. & Merchandise Ctee Mins, 11 Jan. 1850, LNW1/221, BTHR. A detailed account of the contest, drawn from canal sources, is provided by F. C. Mather, *After the Canal Duke* (1970), 195–209.
5 9 & 10 Vic. c. ccxliv; 10 & 11 Vic. c. xxi; L.N.W. Mins, 13 July 1850, 14 Feb. 1851, LNW1/21, BTHR. The Shropshire Union was an amalgamation of the Birmingham & Liverpool Jnc. and Ellesmere & Chester canals.

clearly the trend of increasing gross revenue and short-term fluctuations in profits. Not surprisingly, overall goods receipts rose steadily, despite the trade depression, as the company extended its activities to other lines. But much of this growth can be attributed to the company's exceptional position. While Lardner's calculations suggested that the average distance travelled by the country's railway goods traffic was little more than 20 miles, the London & North Western was carrying traffic over a much longer average distance,[1] and, helped by the co-operation stimulated by the Clearing House, was able to meet the challenge of sea and canal more easily than many of the other major railways. The parliamentary returns are a further indication of the company's strength: the London & North Western enjoyed about 20–25 per cent of the total United Kingdom receipts, disregarding the earnings of other railways for which the company provided locomotive power and other services.[2]

One of the main trends apparent from the accounts is the declining share of total receipts commanded by livestock traffic, and the accompanying rise of coal traffic receipts. The merchandise sector (general goods) changed very little during the period, remaining close to the position it had held in Grand Junction days.[3] The figures, however, probably hide a movement towards heavier freight—minerals, and agricultural produce—which was suggested by Huish in 1848.[4] There is more evidence about coal, which increased its share of total goods receipts from about $4\frac{1}{2}$ per cent in 1846 to nearly 10 per cent in 1851.[5] Greater attention was also paid to iron, grain, cotton, and manure. Sand traffic became a matter of some interest, and the company used the Birmingham Canal to convey limestone, being thus in a position to transfer heavy minerals to the railway.[6] The lower maximum rates imposed on the company after 1846 may have encouraged firms to send goods previously handled by canal. Low coal rates certainly had this effect. So too did the use of special contracts for bulk consignments, which Huish continued to arrange. In 1847, for example, he agreed terms with Allsop of Birmingham for the carriage of ale to Camden, and in 1849 secured the shipment of 10,000 tons of iron pipes from Birmingham to the Thames.[7]

1 In the year ending 30 June 1847 the L.N.W.'s average was estimated to be 69.75 miles, compared with a national average of 22.5 miles: Lardner, *op. cit.*, 206–7.
2 See Chapter IV, table 12.
3 See Appendix, tables 46 and 53.
4 See above, pp. 132–3, and cf. Poole's Report to Huish, 7 Jan. 1848, LNW8/96, BTHR.
5 See Appendix, table 53.
6 L.N.W. Mins, 16 Dec. 1848, 13 Jan. 1849, LNW1/20, BTHR.
7 L.N.W. Loco. & Merchandise Ctee Mins, 12 Nov. 1847, 14 Dec. 1849, LNW1/221, BTHR.

Livestock traffic became an area of special responsibility. From November 1850 Fisher Ormandy, Cattle Manager for the company's northern division, organized the whole of the company's operations. His reports on the cattle traffic, of 1849, 1850, and 1851, were useful summaries of the railway's position, as well as clear indications of the several changes affecting the traffic.[1] Ormandy was given the task of arranging rates with other companies, and it appears that Huish was quite willing to delegate management of this sector of the traffic.

Ormandy's reports provide the background to a situation of falling livestock receipts, most apparent during the depression of 1847, and an increasing traffic—which suggests falling rates.[2] Nevertheless, the company's share of the United Kingdom's railway traffic in livestock, about 25 per cent in 1847, remained considerably higher than that of any other railway.[3] This predominance had been enjoyed by the Grand Junction too, but whereas pigs had proved the largest element of its traffic, it was cattle that provided the main source of revenue for the London & North Western. The pig traffic had, of course, been seriously affected by the aftermath of the Irish famine, which reduced supplies reaching the railway at Liverpool.

It is clear that, for the London & North Western, the Smithfield Market trade was the most important. The livestock brought south produced much more than traffic going eastward to Lancashire and Yorkshire, and in 1849 a third of the cattle and half of the sheep carried by the company was for the London area.[4] In this situation, Ormandy was able to demonstrate that the fall in receipts in 1849 could be traced mainly to a fall in the traffic carried south, a fact partly explained by the growth of the Manchester market, the decline in Irish exports, and the availability of meat supplies in London and the Midlands.[5] The slide was halted in 1850, and Ormandy's reports indicated how the railway actively encouraged livestock movement and kept abreast of new developments. The increase in traffic to Manchester was attributed to the new and spacious cattle station at Edge Hill, Liverpool, and concerted efforts were made to

1 F. Ormandy, 'London and North Western Cattle Traffic Report. Half-Year Ending December 31, 1848' (1849), and 'Report upon the Cattle Traffic of the London & North Western Railway for the Year 1850' (1851), confidential printed reports, HL2/R102(1–2), BTHR, and *idem*, 'Report upon the Cattle Traffic of the London & North Western Railway for the Year 1849' (1850), printed report, London School of Economics Library.
2 See Appendix, tables 47 and 54.
3 Table 54 (1).
4 *Ibid.*, (2, 3).
5 Ormandy, 'Report . . . for 1849', 11–14.

stimulate business from the West, Shropshire, East Anglia, the North-east, Aberdeen, and southern Scotland.[1]

Huish was more active in the management of coal traffic, although his inexperience of the business when with the Grand Junction explained the special responsibility enjoyed by Braithwaite Poole in Liverpool. Although a considerable proportion of the London coal trade was conveyed by sea—Poole estimated that over three million tons or 99 per cent of the total was sent in this way in 1847[2]—the railways were beginning to take the canals' share of the traffic, especially in other districts, and by 1848 the London & North Western was carrying over 850,000 tons annually, a great increase on the tonnage handled in 1846–7. Much of this increase may be attributed to Huish's intervention. Although the working of the Northern Division traffic (about 20 per cent of the total) was left to Poole, Huish arranged the conduct of the London coal trade, and in common with his Goods Manager urged the extension of this traffic, which was considered to be profitable despite the low rates enforced by the Act of 1846.[3] He advised the Merchandise Committee, and negotiated with the coal companies with the aim of securing large and regular consignments. In 1849, for example, he met representatives of the Clay Cross and Ince Hall colleries, obtaining promises of guaranteed annual tonnages in return for preferential rates.[4] He also concerned himself with coal accounts, and with the provision of extra accommodation at Camden, Kilburn, and Kensington. Although the capital required to provide for this increased London traffic was large, the regular consignments, the comparatively long distances travelled, and the provision of waggons by the coal-owners, suggest that Huish's policy of encouraging low-tariff bulk traffic was not necessarily as unprofitable as his opponents claimed. Unfortunately, material for a more sophisticated test of profitability does not survive.

Huish's rôle again included a general supervision of the company's traffic. With regard to local or internal traffic (i.e. that confined to the London & North Western's own network), he made several valuable contributions. He suggested that goods trains he operated at night to relieve congestion, and made extensive use of the Trent Valley route, to

1 *Ibid.*, 9–10, 30, and 'Report . . . for 1850', 51–9, 68–76.

2 B. Poole, *A Report to the Road and Traffic Committee of the Northern Division of Directors of the London and North Western Railway Company on Coal Traffic* (1849), 6.

3 Coal rates: up to 50 miles $1\frac{1}{4}d$. per ton-mile; over 50 miles, $\frac{7}{8}d$.; allowance for owners' waggons, $\frac{1}{8}d$., and for owners' locomotives, $\frac{1}{4}d$.

4 The Clay Cross colliery agreed to provide 45,000 tons p.a. in loads of not less than 150 tons; the Ince Hall colliery agreed to provide 10,000 tons: L.N.W. Loco. & Merchandise Ctee Mins, 12 Jan., 9 Feb., and 14 Dec. 1849, LNW1/221, BTHR.

free the Birmingham line.[1] He framed new regulations for brakesmen in 1846, created the general rulebook of September 1847, and having recommended successfully that it would be economical to move the Birmingham goods department from Vauxhall to Curzon Street, pressed for the conversion of the former premises into a factory for making waggon sheets.[2] Huish also inspired the purchase of the Haydon Square property in the city of London, an important decision, for the site was the only one "eligible and accessible as a city goods terminus".[3] The move gave access to the East & West India Dock Railway, and Huish and Horne arranged a goods agreement with that company to complete the line of communication.[4] Certain matters of detailed management were also Huish's province. In 1850, for example, he pressed for the purchase of new waggons for Camden, and was often prominent in the search for sidings and buildings necessary to provide for new business.

In the arrangement of through (i.e. inter-railway) traffic, the Railway Clearing House became increasingly important. From September 1847 it presided over the through goods traffic of most railways north of London, handling and adjusting the accounts and monies involved. Each company sent goods towards their destination, collecting the total rate for the through journey. This was then adjusted by the House, and divided among the interested companies on a mileage basis, with a charge of $\frac{1}{4}d$. a mile for the use of 'foreign' waggons, and a demurrage charge for waggons if detained on 'foreign' lines. The London & North Western's part in the creation and extension of this system was decisive. Huish was himself one of the creators of the Goods Managers' Conferences, and he chaired the first meetings, in 1847, which helped to secure acceptance not only of the London & North Western's own rate classification, but also of several other administrative details satisfactory to the company.[5] Furthermore, the leading figure behind the Clearing House idea was its secretary, Kenneth Morison, who until 1848 was a company official, and the offices were in Seymour Street, close to Euston Station. Goods traffic soon became the major concern of the Clearing House, as the accounts supplied by Morison

1 L.N.W. Mins, 15 Aug. 1846, LNW1/20; Special Ctee Mins, 11 July 1846, LNW1/50; Loco. & Merchandise Ctee Mins, 10 Dec. 1847, 14 Jan. 1848, LNW1/221, BTHR.
2 L.N.W. Loco. & Merchandise Ctee Mins, 8 Oct. 1847, LNW1/221; L.N.W. Mins, 10 June 1848, LNW1/20, BTHR.
3 L.N.W. Loco. & Merchandise Ctee Mins, 20 Nov. 1849, LNW1/221, BTHR.
4 An agreement was also made with the London & Blackwall: L.N.W. Mins, 21 Feb., 15 June, and 15 Aug. 1850, LNW1/21, BTHR.
5 R.C.H. Goods Managers' Conferences, 19 Jan., 16 Feb., and 2 Mar. 1847, RCH1/179, BTHR.

1. Captain Mark Huish

2. George Carr Glyn

3. Lord Chandos

4. Sir Richard Moon

5. Admiral C. R. Moorsom

6. Sir Edward Watkin

7. Charles Saunders

8. Edmund Denison

indicate,[1] and much of the inter-company discussion of the period centred upon the through-traffic arrangements, their adequacy, suggested improvements, and plans for a more sophisticated classification of commodities.[2] Huish was prominent only between 1847 and 1849, for Braithwaite Poole became the permanent chairman of the Goods Managers' Conferences in May 1848, and London & North Western interests were thus adequately safeguarded.[3] But these two years were the formative period in the system's development, and Huish was able to secure advantageous terminal rates for his company, as well as introducing his own ideas on invoices, forwarding notes, sheets, ropes, and all the various accoutrements of goods traffic organization. The success of his efforts may be seen in the way the smaller companies complained that the arrangements often worked unfairly against them. In particular, those small lines which brought traffic to a long trunk route claimed that they were not adequately remunerated.[4]

After Poole's appointment, Huish attended the Goods Conferences only when important matters of principle were raised. Thus, in July 1848, he helped to arrange small parcels rates and used his influence to secure the maintenance of terminal rates. He also attended in December 1848, to counter an attempt by the smaller companies to raise the rate for the use of waggons, and in November 1849, when the minor companies again tried to reduce terminal charges.[5] But in other matters, and particularly in the rearrangement of the goods classification, Poole was the company's spokesman.

Huish, in fact, directed most of his attention to the activities of the parent Clearing House Committee. Here, he was particularly interested in the need for uniformity in waggon design, and was, indeed, the first to point out the inhibitive effects of a lack of standardization.[6] When the organization was altered in late 1850 he became one of the Committees' delegates—a rare honour for an executive—and, in addition, he attended the increasingly important General Managers' Meetings.[7] In this way, he

1 R.C.H. Ctee Mins, 1846–51, RCH1/2, BTHR. In the six months to 31 Dec. 1848, £595,162 of £876,403 related to goods traffic: in the same period of 1851, £1,181,845 of £1,638,845 was for goods.
2 For further details of activity, see Bagwell, *op. cit.*, *passim*, esp. 72–89.
3 R.C.H. Goods Managers' Conferences, 26 May 1848, RCH1/179, BTHR.
4 *Ibid.*, 11 Nov. 1848.
5 *Ibid.*, 21 Dec. 1848 and 22 Nov. 1849.
6 R.C.H. Ctee Mins, 25 Feb. and 26 Aug. 1846, 22 Sept. 1847, 9 Mar. 1848, RCH1/2, BTHR.
7 Meetings began informally in 1849 and 1850, but no minutes were recorded until January 1851.

was able not only to influence general railway policy but also to secure a dominant position for his company within the framework of Clearing House regulations.

Pricing also engaged Huish's attention, and he was active in the arrangement of both internal and external rates. For the former, he was mainly occupied with the more important negotiations with large firms, rival canals, and railways: the goods managers at London, Birmingham, Liverpool, and Manchester arranged the minor and purely local rates. But despite this delegation of authority, occasioned by the complexity of company operations, there was still scope for the individual initiative that had characterized Huish's management in the early 'forties. The minutes show that he was given the task of securing a general uniformity of rate policy. He was also responsible for tolls charged on the Birmingham Canal, and other company waterways. But as time went on, he became chiefly concerned with the adjustment of rates in response to competition. He can be found negotiating with several railway companies in an attempt to improve the company's traffic prospects by means of agreement, rather than by cut-throat competition, and here he faced all the anomalies and complications arising from the application of untried techniques to specific traffic situations.[1]

The problem of external rates involved Huish and Poole in attempts to secure a greater degree of uniformity in company rate classifications. At almost all the Clearing House meetings of the period, some article or group of articles was discussed, and the way was paved for the first general classifications of September 1847 and January 1852.[2] Most of the minor items were settled by Poole, but Huish again intervened whenever important decisions were made.[3] Clearing House meetings also provided an opportunity to devise pooling agreements. Arrangements made for co-operation in the supply of materials (such as sheets and ropes) for inter-company use led companies to consider creating more limited traffic agreements on the same basis. Huish's 'confederacy', a union of companies hostile to the East Coast route to the North, was encouraged by meetings held under Clearing House auspices, and was in part a

---

1 L.N.W. Mins, 15 Apr. and 15 Dec. 1848, LNW1/20; Loco. & Merchandise Ctee
  Mins, 13 Oct. 1848, 13 July and 14 Sept. 1849, 11 Jan. 1850, LNW1/221, BTHR.
2 The classification of 1847 listed nearly 400 items, grouped into 5 classes: that of 1852
  is discussed in Chapter VII.
3 R.C.H. Goods Managers' Conferences, 21 July and 21 Dec. 1848, 22 Nov. 1849,
  RCH1/179, BTHR.

response to the convenience of concerted action discovered before 1851.[1]

However, the Clearing House did not exactly create order out of chaos. There was still a great deal of dispute over pricing matters, and especially over traffic-attracting concessions. Thus in December 1847 Huish objected to the decision of the Goods Managers to suspend return passes to cattle drovers and dealers, and the London & North Western continued to grant them on its Liverpool–Manchester line.[2] Internal disputes could also affect rate-fixing, as, for example, when the anticipated competition with the Great Northern Railway caused the company to revise its cattle rates.[3] Traffic agreements, such as that made by the Midland and London & North Western companies in 1849, brought with them the problem of altering rates to meet the changed circumstances, wherever traffic was pooled or divided.[4] There remained, then, a considerable diversity within and outside the company, and even where competition-limiting agreements were declared to be in force, there was ample room for manœuvre: special rates for large or unusual consignments, for example, often worked against the attempt to stabilize pricing procedures.

2   Management and business efficiency

The manager's contribution to the business performance of his company is once again difficult to evaluate with any certainty. As before, the evidence is limited, and does not easily lend itself to sophisticated analysis. A further complicating factor is that in the period after 1846 we must allow for the adverse effects of the trade cycle. But to correlate human endeavour and economic variables is a nigh-impossible task, and we must here be content with a more circumstantial approach. What, then, can be said of Huish's management? First, it is clear that the manager, in his efforts to maintain the company's position, helped to promote a greater cost-consciousness, especially in the traffic departments. His duties were undoubtedly intended to include a responsibility for restraint in operating and fixed costs, as the railway expanded its activities. But it was also

---

1 On the pooling of waggon sheets see *ibid.*, 17 Aug. 1847. The meetings of the Octuple Committee from September 1851 were organized with the help of the R.C.H., see Chapter VII.
2 R.C.H. Goods Managers' Conferences, 3 Dec. 1847, 14 Jan. 1848, RCH1/179, BTHR.
3 L.N.W. Sthn. Road & Traffic Ctee Mins, 19 June 1850, LNW1/144, BTHR.
4 L.N.W. General Meeting, 17 Aug. 1849, LNW1/2, BTHR.

intended that the quality of service be maintained. This managerial strategy should be clearly understood. Too many historians in the past have assumed that growth and high profits were the company's sole aims.[1]

The application of accounting knowledge to promote company efficiency was an important turning-point in Britain's industrial development.[2] The sheer size of railways such as the London & North Western acted as a stimulus, but the process was also set in motion by the difficulties of the post-'Mania' period, with its revelations of fraudulent practices, the indiscriminate sanction of new lines (causing increased capitalization and severe competition) and the government's imposition of stricter pricing controls after the Railway Clauses Consolidation Act of 1845. The railways were thus driven to tackle many of the innate difficulties of large-scale operation with a dispersed labour force and a high proportion of fixed capital. Public pessimism also forced the major companies to reveal more detailed statements of their position and prospects. From this time there was a greater effort to provide for depreciation, to compile more meaningful statistical analyses, and to estimate the long-run costs of operation. The London & North Western was one of the first railways to meet this challenge.

Huish's personal contribution to management accounting practice was outstanding. The fact that he was concerned at all with matters other than those relating strictly to the operation of the trains places him above all contemporary executives in the railway industry, both in Britain and America.[3] As stated above, the London & North Western quickly created a regular reporting system, exemplified by Huish's own monthly reports to the Board of Directors, which augmented the detailed statistical information essential to effective decision-making.[4] Moreover, Huish's reports on specific problems of management were not only a guide for his own company, but were often of theoretical value for the industry as a whole. For example, in his reports on moving stock and permanent way, 1848–9, he directed policy towards the effective spreading of replacement and renewal costs, synthesizing previous opinions

---

1 E.g. C. H. Ellis, *British Railway History 1830–76* (1954), 182ff., and R. Lloyd, *Railwaymen's Gallery* (1953), 47–51.

2 The following discussion is taken from my article, 'Captain Mark Huish: A Pioneer in the Development of Railway Management', *Business History*, XII (January 1970), 47–51.

3 This concern distinguishes Huish from the outstanding American railroad executives of the period, and in particular, D. C. McCallum of the Erie Railroad: A. D. Chandler, 'The Railroads: Pioneers in Modern Corporate Management', *Business History Review*, XXXIX (1965), 32.

4 See above, pp. 111–14.

about the problem of the depreciation of railway plant. His motives were clear: in his prefatory remarks to a published edition of the reports, he declared that "the distrust recently engendered in relation to Railway accounts . . . render[s] it imperative upon Railway managers to encourage a publicity which has not hitherto been considered essential".[1] His intention was to explain the difficulties surrounding the estimation of deterioration of both rolling stock and the permanent way, and, in particular, to remedy "the absence of any acknowledged principles for ascertaining its amount . . . [in terms of annual cost] . . . and the consequent diversity of practice which has resulted . . .".[2] It is clear from his discussion of past practice that the early railways, in common with other enterprises, had lacked a uniform definition of depreciation: some meant a fall in the market value of assets, others the cost of renewal, and others the cost of replacement.[3]

The report on moving stock was instrumental in settling a long-standing controversy on the valuation and maintenance of rolling stock. Huish recommended that the company's depreciation fund of £30,400 be abandoned, and that the stock be maintained out of revenue as part of a more even allocation of costs. He had grasped the modern conception of valuing plant in relation to its earning capacity (which he called 'effective value') rather than its current market value. This was a definite advance in accounting method, and a considerable improvement on the previous practice of railway companies. The report was notable for its appreciation of the problems of calculating costs for a company whose component parts were rapidly changing. Huish laid bare the danger of tempting railway executives to create illusory prosperity by neglecting the less tangible costs of operation. He also showed that excessive prudence in providing for future costs denied shareholders dividends that were properly earned. Early railway companies had been guilty of both: a balance between extremes was obviously necessary.[4] The report was praised as a notable contribution to railway management theory, and although the market valuation which he had made was criticized by a committee of directors, the Board implemented his recommendation.[5]

The report on the permanent way of 1849, compiled by a number of officials under Huish's leadership, recommended the retention of a

1 Huish, *On Deterioration of Railway Plant and Road* (1849), vii.
2 *Ibid.*, v.
3 *Ibid.*, 3–14. See also Pollins, in Littleton and Yamey, *op. cit.*, 343–9.
4 Huish, *On Deterioration of Railway Plant and Road*, 4–5.
5 *Ibid.*, 24–5; L.N.W. Special Ctee Mins, 8 Aug. 1848, LNW1/50; L.N.W. Mins, 15 July and 9 Aug. 1848, LNW1/20, BTHR.

depreciation fund (begun in July 1847) to meet the anticipated cost of replacing the track. Rails could not, it was said, be equated with rolling stock. Whereas parts of the latter could be systematically renewed by current repairs or gradual replacement, the permanent way deteriorated more slowly and equally, producing a sudden cost burden.[1] The report invalidated previous theories of a rail's average life,[2] using a more realistic estimate of 20 years to calculate the annual sum necessary to form the depreciation fund.[3] A figure of £20,700 at $4\frac{1}{2}$ per cent interest was suggested to replace the former sum of £16,000 per annum. The Works Committee subsequently modified the proposal to an annual appropriation of £22,050 at 4 per cent.[4] In this way, an arbitrary method of estimating costs was replaced by the careful use of statistics to probe the company's needs over time.

The reports are useful documents, therefore, not only for the statistics which they provide—virtually unobtainable elsewhere—but also as a firm indication of the London & North Western's lead in the attempt to master complex problems of financial management. But how progressive were the reports? Huish was certainly anxious that his company should exercise care in determining profits, and that permanent way costs in particular should be evenly spread. But the later 1840s were a time of general caution, encouraged by the Companies Clauses Act of 1845 and the Select Committee on the Audit of Railway Accounts of 1849.[5] Further, the period of caution was transient, and many companies soon reverted to the system known as "replacement accounting", that is, of charging all repair and replacement costs to revenue as they occurred.[6] Nevertheless, Huish's policy was progressive in the sense that financial management was employed to keep dividends more stable over time and to create a greater understanding of overhead costs. Other companies followed the London & North Western in charging rolling stock repairs to revenue, and in setting up permanent way renewal funds in 1849.[7] Huish

1 Huish, *On Deterioration of Railway Plant and Road*, 11, 40–1.
2 *Ibid.*, 31. It had been thought that rails would last 'for above a hundred years'!
3 *Ibid.*, 40–9. The rails of the L.N.W., which were on average $7\frac{1}{2}$ years old in 1849, were estimated to have a further life of $12\frac{1}{2}$ years.
4 L.N.W. Works Construction & Estate Ctee Mins, 11 May 1849, LNW1/281, and see L.N.W. General Meeting, 17 Aug. 1849, LNW1/1, BTHR.
5 8 & 9 Vic. c. xvi, and P.P.1849, X.
6 See below, Chapter VII.
7 Such companies included the London Brighton & South Coast, South Eastern, Eastern Counties, Midland, York Newcastle & Berwick, and York & North Midland railways: M. Huish and others, 'Report to the Permanent Way Committee on the Renewal Fund', confidential printed report, April 1853, L.N.W. Company Reports, LNW1/716, BTHR, 4.

had therefore helped to introduce a policy of 'Maintenance Equalization' on railways, if only for a short time. His use of statistics to measure the way in which costs reacted to traffic changes was a longer-lasting example to other companies, while the stress upon maintaining the track and stock in good order contrasted with the practice of many railways, which made arbitrary reductions in their current liabilities to enhance dividends. Huish's reports were certainly used by Dionysius Lardner in compiling his notable treatise on *Railway Economy* of 1850, and comments upon the originality of this work need to be modified.[1] Lardner, in fact, was indebted to Huish for the release of a great deal of both published and unpublished material on the London & North Western.[2] He borrowed substantially from this source, and his investigation of railway costs— particularly the sections on rolling stock and rails—owed much to ideas in Huish's reports of 1848–9. He followed Huish, for example, in distinguishing between the depreciation of rolling stock and that of rails, in exposing the erroneous opinions of a rail's life, and in showing the effect of train speed in track deterioration.[3] Huish married an appreciation of accounting principles with a thorough experience of railway operation and finance: in this virtually unique position, he had a strong claim to be ranked with Lardner as an early railway theoretician. His preoccupation with the need to determine profits and to investigate in full the nature of railway assets set important precedents. The concept of a balance between replacement accounting and provision for depreciation was novel, and if not in accord with modern practice, it did indicate the unsuitability of the cash accounting methods which smaller railways had used in earlier decades. Although it was true that some firms had experimented with depreciation funds from the beginning of the century, Huish's efforts contrasted with the rather negative attitude towards capital accounting that had been prevalent during the classic period of the 'Industrial

---

1 See R. M. Robbins, 'Dr. Lardner's *Railway Economy*', *Railway Magazine*, xcvi (1950), 153–5; D. Solomons, 'The Historical Development of Costing', in Solomons (ed.), *Studies in Costing* (1952), 33–4; and Pollins, in Littleton and Yamey, *op. cit.*, 339, 349.

2 L.N.W. Mins, 14 July 1849, LNW1/21, BTHR.

3 Lardner, *op. cit.*, 38–44, 84–100, 106–12; Huish, *On Deterioration of Railway Plant and Road*, 11–12, 16, 23, 30–3, 40–2. G. R. Hawke, in *Railways and Economic Growth in England & Wales 1840–1870* (1970), relies heavily on Lardner, and defends the source from its critics (pp. 93–9). But he makes no mention of the connection with Huish. For example, Hawke rightly confirms the use made of Lardner by Karl Marx in formulating his views on depreciation (*Kapital*, vol. II (Berlin, 1961), 164, 173, 175–7), but Lardner's opinions owed much to Huish's work.

Revolution'.[1] The creation of modern accounting conventions has been linked with the growth of joint-stock companies,[2] and Huish's views can be seen as an early manifestation of this trend.[3]

The report on moving stock, which effectively settled the national debate, was certainly Huish's own work. It is more difficult, however, to establish the influence he exerted in the compilation of the permanent way report, where he was rather a collaborator and co-ordinator in a statistical exercise undertaken by several men.[4] There is also evidence of disagreement within the executive. An outstanding feature of the report of 1849 was the repeated reference to the adverse effects of increased traffic, locomotive weights, and train speeds. As early as 1847 Norris had stressed the problems associated with a low fares traffic policy, and in 1848 Carr Glyn warned a General Meeting of the possible financial outcome.[5] Finally, Robert Dockray, one of the company's resident engineers, reported in August 1848 that increased traffic would cause the track to deteriorate.[6] Huish nevertheless persisted in his stress upon the provision of express trains, and his sponsorship of heavy goods trains helped to cause an underestimate of the damage sustained by the track. By 1849, however, it was clear that he, in common with the other officers, recognized the inevitability of increased costs. It was stated to be

> no longer a matter of argument that the effect on the rails and other parts of the permanent way produced by the increased weight and speed of the engines and trains, has become very marked: and the concurrent testimony of those who are engaged in the practical part of the repairs, proves that the deterioration of the road has increased very rapidly since the period of the introduction of the heavy engines . . . there is no longer a doubt that the immoderate damage to both the road and the stock, from high speed, outweighs, in positive loss to the Company, the additional fare received . . .[7]

1 S. Pollard, *The Genesis of Modern Management* (1965), 241–5. There had been a general disregard of "careful and consistent profit calculation and asset valuation": B. S. Yamey, 'The Development of Company Accounting Conventions', *Three Banks Review*, XLVII (1960), 25.
2 *Ibid.*, 22.
3 I do not wish to imply that no firms or companies employed sophisticated costing methods before the London & North Western. The efforts of Josiah Wedgwood are a notable exception to the general rule, see N. McKendrick, 'Josiah Wedgwood and and Cost Accounting in the Industrial Revolution', *Economic History Review*, 2nd ser., XXIII (April 1970), 45–67.
4 See Huish's letter to the Works Ctee, 13 Apr. 1849, LNW1/281, BTHR.
5 L.N.W. General Meeting, 18 Feb. 1848, LNW1/1, BTHR.
6 Whitehead, *Railway Management. The Proof!*, 39–43.
7 Huish, *On Deterioration of Railway Plant and Road*, 37.

Dockray continued to criticize Huish's management, and in March 1850 he accused him of neglecting to provide for track repairs. But the truth of this accusation is not apparent, for the company was stated to have "regularly provided for deterioration out of revenue" before 1849, its maintenance costs per route-mile exceeding those of several other companies.[1] Dockray may well have been obsessive in his concern, and it should be remembered that Huish's rôle was to take an overall view of the company's position, such that the best possible revenue-cost situation could be reached.[2] Other sources indicate that the management was becoming increasingly concerned with economy, and it does not seem likely that the permanent way would have been exempted from such a prescribed policy. The reports, then, suggest a preoccupation with problems which, if handled carefully, would have secured a firm footing for future business activity. It is more difficult, of course, to judge the practical outcome of the policies suggested.

The directors seemed fully aware that dividends, previously maintained by a favourable traffic position and a 'cheap money' situation, would become seriously affected by further capital expenditure, pricing constraints, competition, and rising operating costs. Accordingly, a Committee of Investigation was created in 1848, under Admiral C. R. Moorsom, which, in consultation with Huish and the executive, made a number of positive proposals to reduce costs. In six reports, ideas were put forward for the concentration of departments, the rationalization of staff duties, and the use of company lands and other unused resources.[3] Carr Glyn also mentioned publicly four specific areas of attention, namely, permanent way maintenance, locomotive power, firemen's wages, and coke.[4]

Huish was active in effecting the changes which followed. He arranged a merger of parcels offices at Liverpool and secured the appointment of Norris as superintendent of the North Union Railway, measures which saved the company nearly £1,000 per annum. He reported on the reorganization of duties between Norris, Dockray, and Bruyeres, to free Woodhouse for the supervision of the newly-built Leeds & Dewsbury and

1 Dockray's diary, 8 Mar. 1850: R. M. Robbins, *Journal of Transport History*, VII (Nov. 1965), 113; Huish, *On Deterioration of Railway Plant and Road*, 43.
2 Dockray claimed that Huish had once opposed his suggestion for a reserved fund for permanent way renewal: Dockray, letter to Moorsom, 10 Nov. 1860, quoted in R. M. Robbins, 'From R. B. Dockray's Diary–III', *Journal of Transport History*, VII (May 1966), 156.
3 Moorsom Ctee Reports, 13 May–14 Oct. 1848, L.N.W. Special Ctee Mins & Reports, LNW1/50, BTHR.
4 L.N.W. General Meeting, 11 Aug. 1848, LNW/1, BTHR.

Huddersfield & Manchester lines, thus obviating the need for further staffing. In May 1850 he claimed to have saved £1,050 a year by merging the passenger and goods departments of the Southern Division.[1] The control of company stores became more concentrated, following the creation of a Stores Committee in September 1848, but there was still room for improvement: Huish's suggested measures to centralize the responsibility for checking stores accounts in 1849 was a further advance.[2] If the Moorsom Committee provided the stimulus, Huish provided specific proposals for specific cost problems.

Huish was similarly involved in the company's policy on ancillary activities. He arranged contracts with the firm of W. H. Smith, leasing the right to sell newspapers (at £1,500 per annum) and granting the firm the privilege of advertising at the railway stations.[3] He was also responsible for the administration of leases affecting Birmingham's railway hotel, and a number of refreshment room sites.[4]

The problem of track costs has been discussed above: that of locomotive and coke costs was also closely investigated by the company, and the statistics supplied to the Merchandise Committee, 1847–50, claimed a steady fall in average per mile coke and power costs, for both passenger and goods trains.[5] Coke consumption costs involved not only the highly technical questions of performance but also the more rudimentary economics of purchasing. The Great Western had undertaken its own coke manufacture in 1838, and a few companies followed suit.[6] The London & North Western itself possessed coke ovens at Camden and Peterborough, but found that it was often economically advisable to buy by special contract. This experience was shared by many companies in the north of England, close to the coal-fields, and at least one railway discovered that it was cheaper to purchase coke than to manufacture it.[7] Huish was involved in arranging contracts for the supply of coke, but he also suggested other ways in which costs might be reduced, and was not

---

1 L.N.W. Sthn. Road & Traffic Ctee Mins, 15 May 1850, LNW1/144, BTHR.
2 L.N.W. Mins, 9 Sept. 1848, LNW1/20; Stores Ctee Mins, 8 Feb. 1849, in Special Ctee Mins, LNW1/50, BTHR.
3 L.N.W. Mins, 15 July 1848, LNW1/20; Smith's letter to Huish, 28 Aug. 1848, in Moorsom Ctee Report, 9 Sept. 1848, LNW1/50; L.N.W. contract with Smith, LNW3/100; and Sthn. Road & Traffic Ctee Mins, 15 Jan. 1851, LNW1/144, BTHR.
4 L.N.W. Works Ctee Mins, 12 July, 12 Apr. 1850, LNW1/282, BTHR.
5 See table 16, above.
6 Whishaw, *op. cit.*, 160, 233, 297–8, 347.
7 The chairman of the Edinburgh & Glasgow Railway said in 1847 that coke cost the company 29s. per ton to produce, but that it could be obtained by contract for 22s. 6d.: Salt, *op. cit.* (1848), 28. Cf. Hawke, *Railways and Economic Growth . . ., op. cit.*, 395.

opposed in principle to company control of manufacture. However, although the company produced its own locomotives and rolling stock, its rails, and (on the northern division) its track maintenance were supplied by outside firms, while all general stores—from uniforms and tickets to iron and bricks—were obtained by the contract system.[1]

The Moorsom Committee was extremely interested in revising wage scales, gratuities, and other labour costs. As a direct result of Huish's efforts, a new wage classification was constructed, the apprenticeship system became more closely regulated, and a number of pay adjustments were made. Important revisions affecting workmen, ticket collectors, signalmen, and porters were agreed, but the limit of this policy was reached in August 1848 when an attempt to reduce gratuities for enginemen, and to alter their scale of promotion, resulted in a strike notice.[2] Further evidence shows that Huish figured in other specific areas of possible reduction. For example, he sponsored the introduction of the electric telegraph to facilitate an increase in traffic capacity without the need for additional tracks, and implemented a number of plans to economize on track use.[3] These measures, when taken with his efforts to promote traffic exchange via the Clearing House, and his support for the improved goods system, point clearly to a firm intention to increase operational efficiency.

Can the management's activities be subjected to statistical measurement? Such an exercise is always dangerous, but the London & North Western's accounts and reports do permit a rudimentary investigation of the company's business activity. Statistics of traffic receipts, for example, clearly indicate a rise in the output of transport services. Table 17 shows that the company's net income from traffic rose steadily as its activities increased. But total net income on all business operations fell by about 10 per cent between 1846 and 1851, and this may be taken as a more accurate indication of the company's experience. Nevertheless, this compares well with the performance of the Midland Railway, for example, although company comparisons are extremely dangerous, because of the lack of uniformity in expressing costs. The comparative success of the

1 See L.N.W. Stores Ctee Contracts, e.g. in 1851, LNW4/110, BTHR.
2 L.N.W. Mins, 9 Aug. 1848, LNW1/20; *Herapath's Railway Magazine*, 5–19 Aug. 1848.
3 L.N.W. Mins, 14 Nov. 1846, 14 Oct. 1848, LNW1/20, BTHR, and see Chapter VII. Huish claimed that the introduction of the telegraph would save £2,000 p.a. On the economy of track use, he proposed the diversion of a train via Birmingham to save £3,000 p.a.: Nthn. Road & Traffic Ctee Mins, 2 Nov. 1849, LNW1/158, BTHR.

Table 17
Three indices of net income, 1846–51 (1846–7 = 100)

1. London & North Western Railway

Year July–June	Net traffic income	Total net income	[*]
1846–7	100	100	—
1847–8	101.5	97.5	93.5
1848–9	102.8	95.3	93.8
1849–50	108.2	91.0	88.5
1850–1	115.4	92.2	88.6

2. Midland Railway (independent index)

1846–7	100	100
1847–8	95.0	89.3
1848–9	—	—
1849–50	99.2	33.4
1850–1	105.1	50.9

3. Great Western Railway (independent index)

1846–7	100	100
1847–8	101.3	100.7
1848–9	100.1	100.5
1849–50	81.8	82.7
1850–1	94.3	97.4

Source: Company Accounts, RAC1/164, 233, 290, BTHR. Net traffic income is traffic revenue *minus* traffic costs: total net income is total company revenue *minus* total costs (as interpreted by each company). L.N.W. data are in the Appendix, table 48.
* If rail renewal costs are included.

Great Western in retaining total net income may well be due to an understatement of total costs. Of course, rising traffic income may merely express expanded activities or increases in rates, but given the difficult situation after the 'Mania', involving *falling* passenger receipts from 1847 to 1849, the London & North Western's performance in holding on to its net income position appears to be satisfactory. Table 18 sets out the annual rate of return on receipts. As regards the company's traffic data, operating costs are shown to have remained static in the period, being about 35 per cent of gross receipts, a position shared by the Midland and Great Western railways, and probably reflecting the lowest operating ratio that could safely be achieved by the larger companies at this time. More attention should be paid to the rate of return on total revenue, however, since all the companies experienced difficulties in assigning certain costs to the traffic accounts. On the London & North Western, the rate of return fell from 55 to 43 per cent, suggesting that the increased output of transport services was accompanied by sudden and significant cost burdens. In fairness to the company, it should be noticed that costs appear to have been more than equitably spread over the period—indeed, profits may well have been understated in some years—and that the Midland and Great Western companies do not seem to have followed this course. The former clearly understated its costs when Hudson was chairman, making no provision for depreciation or renewal: the effects of the policy can be seen in the very low rate of return on total revenue, 1849–51.

Table 18
Annual percentage rate of return on receipts, 1846–51

1. London & North Western Railway

Year July–June	Gross traffic receipts	Net traffic receipts	Percentage rate of return on traffic receipts	Operating costs %
1846–7	£2,100,348	£1,368,764	65.2	34.8
1847–8	2,140,036	1,388,864	64.9	35.1
1848–9	2,156,219	1,407,531	65.3	34.7
1849–50	2,239,785	1,480,973	66.1	33.9
1850–1	2,384,869	1,579,087	66.2	33.8

	Total revenue	Net income	Percentage rate of return on total revenue *		Total costs %	*
1846–7	2,141,486	1,168,607	54.6	—	45.4	—
1847–8	2,194,092	1,139,127	51.9	49.8	48.1	50.2
1848–9	2,216,865	1,113,396	50.2	49.4	49.8	50.6
1849–50	2,312,784	1,063,235	46.0	44.7	53.0	55.3
1850–1	2,484,857	1,077,169	43.3	41.7	56.7	58.3

2. Midland Railway

	Gross traffic receipts	Net traffic receipts	Percentage rate of return on traffic receipts	Operating costs %
1846–7	£ 983,697	£ 688,086	69.9	30.1
1847–8	991,830	653,865	65.9	34.1
1849–50	1,142,718	682,312	59.0	41.0
1850–1	1,176,283	723,191	61.5	38.5

2. Midland Railway (continued)

	Total revenue	Net income	Percentage rate of return on total revenue	Total costs %
1846–7	1,003,166	490,393	48.9	51.1
1847–8	1,066,181	438,067	41.1	58.9
1849–50	1,210,327	163,552	13.5	86.5
1850–1	1,236,035	249,643	20.2	79.8

3. Great Western Railway

	Gross traffic receipts	Net traffic receipts	Percentage rate of return on traffic receipts	Operating costs %
1846–7	£ 986,559	£ 647,601	65.6	34.4
1847–8	1,028,774	655,870	63.8	36.2
1848–9	998,989	647,977	64.9	35.1
1849–50	813,863	529,471	65.1	34.9
1850–1	877,569	610,993	69.6	30.4

	Total revenue	Net income	Percentage rate of return on total revenue	Total costs %
1846–7	1,008,709	610,109	60.5	39.5
1847–8	1,053,996	614,436	58.3	41.7
1848–9	1,028,149	613,363	59.7	40.3
1849–50	838,957	504,338	60.1	39.9
1850–1	910,776	594,052	65.2	34.8

Source: Company Accounts, RAC1/164, 233, 290, BTHR. Operating costs do not include taxes, rates, legal expenses, guarantees, loans, rail renewal costs, where these items appear separately in the accounts.
* Includes rail renewal costs.

It is impossible to obtain satisfactory measures of productivity: the surviving data are not sufficiently informative to permit the complex calculations necessary for even a partial analysis. Nevertheless, the crude investigations which can be made are not entirely without relevance. In table 19, estimates of the rate of return on London & North Western capital are not necessarily an accurate reflection of the company's return on capital employed. It is far from easy to adjust the data for annual valuation changes, or to deflate the figures by relevant price indices. But all the percentages obtained (crude though they may be) exhibit a falling trend, as one would expect: certainly, the company had not attempted to

Table 19
London & North Western annual percentage rate of return on estimated capital 1846–51

Year July–June	A Net traffic receipts	1 Share capital 'called up'	$\frac{1}{A}$ %	2 Capital spent on 'lines open'	$\frac{2}{A}$ %	3 Capital spent including subsidiaries	$\frac{3}{A}$ %	4 Total capital spent	$\frac{4}{A}$ %
1846–7	£1,370,773	£12,167,539	11.26	£13,951,224	9.83	—	—	£20,010,466	6.85
1847–8	1,388,864	14,044,574	9.89	18,145,624	7.65	£21,244,057	6.54	22,885,120	6.08
1848–9	1,407,531	16,446,817	8.56	18,599,162	7.57	—	—	—	—
1849–50	1,480,972	18,561,069	7.98	22,504,818	6.58	25,457,808	5.82	28,699,566	5.16
1850–1	1,579,087	19,470,615	8.11	24,531,640	6.44	28,637,154	5.51	29,291,814	5.39

Year July–June	B Net income	1	$\frac{1}{B}$ %	2	$\frac{2}{B}$ %	3	$\frac{3}{B}$ %	4	$\frac{4}{B}$ %
1846–7	£1,168,607	as above	9.60	as above	8.38	as above	—	as above	5.84
1847–8	1,092,664*		7.78		6.02		5.14		4.79
1848–9	1,095,621*		6.66		5.89		—		—
1849–50	1,034,465*		5.57		4.60		4.06		3.60
1850–1	1,035,078*		5.31		4.22		3.61		3.53

Source: Company Accounts, RAC/1 233, BTHR. Column 1 does not include loan capital; column 2 omits expenditure on subsidiary companies, some of which were yielding revenue; column 3 estimates are also unsatisfactory, since they do not reflect total capital spent on *all* lines open and yielding revenue; column 4 includes a certain amount of unproductive expenditure. The capital sums are those at the *end* of each year (i.e. 30 June).
* Takes into account expenditure on rails.

deny that further expenditure would alter the relation of profits to capital. Of course, it would be more significant to calculate the rate of return in relation to the amount of capital used in the productive process in each year, but the material does not lend itself to such an examination. The company was working a number of lines which it controlled by lease, and others with which it had formed only a tenuous relationship. It is very difficult, in the absence of informative accounts, to make a distinction between revenue earned on these lines and revenue earned on the company's own network.[1]

The most common partial measure of productivity is, of course, the relation of output and net income to labour resources. Table 20 purports to show that, in the period, earnings per man-hour declined—a result of using men on less productive portions of newly-opened railways—but that the economies and wage-cuts introduced by the company *did* effect a fall in wage costs per man-hour. The inquiry is based, however, upon many indeterminates, and such a crude calculation should not be taken as an accurate indication of company performance.[2]

Table 20
London & North Western labour costs and earnings per man-hour, 1848–51

Year	Manpower*	Wage-bill†	Average wage	Wage per man-hour‡
1848–9	6,735	£350,878	£52.10	4.17d.
1850–1	9,538	392,843	41.19	3.30d.

Year	Gross earnings§	Net earnings ‖	Gross per worker	Net per worker	Gross per man-hour	Net per man-hour
1848–9	£2,156,219	£1,284,078	£320.2	£190.7	2.134s.	1.271s.
1850–1	2,436,215	1,468,349	255.4	153.9	1.703s.	1.026s.

Source: Company Accounts, RAC1/233, BTHR, and Accounts and Papers, P.P.1850, LIII, 1852, LXVIII.
* Manpower taken as at 30 June 1849 and 1851: does not include managerial and secretarial staff, whose wages are not included.
† Wage-bill includes sundry items, where these are not separated in the accounts.
‡ Man-hours calculated with an estimate of a 60-hour week, 3,000-hour year.
§ Traffic receipts and dividends from other railways.
‖ Gross earnings minus operating costs, losses on other lines, taxes, rates.

1 It is also difficult to make a similar distinction regarding the employment of capital resources.
2 The weakness of an inquiry based upon revenue instead of output (i.e. the volume of transport services) is explained by Hawke, *Railways and Economic Growth* . . ., *op. cit.*, 311–12.

Only from the mid-1850s do statistics exist which make possible a closer study of the company's achievements.[1] Our conclusions for the years 1846–51 must, therefore, be tentative. The available information reveals trends that are in themselves not startling, namely, falling rates of return on revenue and capital, and falling earnings per unit of labour. But it does seem that the attention to costs suggested in the company's records had positive effects, and, given the difficult circumstances of railway operation after the 'Mania', the overall performance of the London & North Western may be judged as most satisfactory. A great deal of this achievement may fairly be attributed to the energy and perspicacity shown by Huish and his executive.

Sometimes the company went too far in its attempt to economize— safe operation, in itself an item of saving, was endangered by the reduction in firemen's wages[2]—but its general attitude to costs was far sounder than that of the other major companies, and its system of audit, if far from perfect, was the best organized in the country.[3] It appears, therefore, that Huish's encouragement of operating efficiency and a more sophisticated cost accounting system was not only unusual for an executive officer, but was also accompanied by a degree of success.

1 Before 1851 there are only isolated examples of train-mile figures, while no passenger-mile statistics are available before 1852–3.
2 Carr Glyn estimated that the cost of compensation for accidents amounted to £10,000 in the last six months of 1848: L.N.W. General Meeting, 16 Feb. 1849, LNW1/1, BTHR.
3 Note Huish's efforts to improve the audit, L.N.W. Audit Ctee Mins, 12 Jan. 1849, LNW1/432, BTHR, and the evidence of Herapath, Spackman, and Swift, *S.C. on Audit of Railway Accounts*, P.P.1849, X, QQ. 674–6, 1208, and 2493.

6

The London & North Western Railway 1851-60

The effects of severe competition

part I

Chapters Six and Seven deal with the progress of the London & North Western from the managerial reorganization of 1851 to Huish's resignation in 1858 and the administrative changes which followed. This chronological treatment is again appropriate in that it corresponds with more general trends in British railway affairs, and, in particular, with the period of intense competition between the major companies.

Rail mileage in the United Kingdom, which had almost doubled between 1846 and 1851, grew more slowly in the 1850s, increasing by just

under 50 per cent from 1851 to 1860.[1] Construction and the consequent
search for traffic were closely linked to competitive-rivalries. Companies
tended to build for existing traffic channels, instead of seeking new ones,
and this resulted in an unnecessary duplication of routes and excess
traffic capacity. The result was "simply to divide without materially increasing the traffic, and thus to diminish the receipts, without . . . a
corresponding saving in expenses."[2] Executive management, especially
within the larger companies, became excessively complex, for not only
did increased traffic at reduced rates, with the constant pressure of rising
costs, create operating hazards, but the proliferation of co-operative
expedients between companies made 'diplomatists' of most general
managers. What characterizes the 1850s most of all is the willingness of
traffic managers to evade or ignore agreements and to indulge in sporadic
pricing battles. The struggle for the excursion traffic to the Great Exhibition of 1851 was a notable early example, and the theme of agreement
versus rate-war was repeated in 1853, 1856, and 1857–8, while Parliament
again hesitated and then failed to take necessary action. Under its
auspices inter-company friction reached a new scale of intensity. By
opposing large amalgamations Parliament prevented the major companies from achieving the best solution to competitive pressures. The
hostility towards this device shown during the sitting of the Cardwell
Committee in 1852–3 defeated a number of important projects, yet such
was the capriciousness of the ruling body that the North Eastern Railway
—the first company with a regional monopoly—was sanctioned a year
later.[3]

   The London & North Western was prominent in the events of the
1850s. At the height of its influence in 1855, it saw its position increasingly
under attack. Two events were very significant—the Great Western's
extension to Birmingham and Liverpool, and the Great Northern's grip
upon south Yorkshire and the East Coast route to Scotland. Competition
was thus created for traffic over which the company had enjoyed a predominance and, as table 21 shows, its share of United Kingdom railway
activity, although still large, gradually declined, and its business performance in general suffered a setback.[4] Although the company's traffic

1 U.K. mileage, 6,890 at the end of 1851, amounted to 10,433 at the end of 1860:
  Accounts & Papers, P.P.1852, XLVIII, 1861, LVII.
2 L.N.W. General Meeting, 15 Aug. 1855, LNW1/2, BTHR.
3 Admittedly, the N.E. was considered to be largely outside the main area of inter-
  company conflict, and the amalgamation was *de facto* before its sanction: Cleveland-
  Stevens, *op. cit.*, 222–5.
4 See Chapter VII.

increased, keeping pace with expansion generally, the figures below conceal the additional pressure caused by increased capitalization and reduced profit margins. The company's concern about these trends can be seen in the attempt to check costs, and to make use of detailed statistical analysis in order to isolate areas for special attention.

Table 21
London & North Western's share in United Kingdom railway activity

	L.N.W. 1851–2	Share of U.K. activity %	L.N.W. 1858–9	Share of U.K. activity %
Passenger revenue	£1,480,221	18.5	£1,473,420	13.8
Goods revenue	1,395,253	18.7	2,234,853	16.0
Total traffic revenue	2,875,476	18.6	3,708,273	15.0
Capital (shares called up and loans)	30,134,818	12.1	35,680,200	11.0
Labour force (lines open)	8,952	13.2	14,891	12.8
Stations	226	10.0	428	12.4

Source: Accounts & Papers, P.P.1852, XLVIII, 1852–3, XCVII, 1859, Sess. 1, XXV, 1860, LXI. Labour and station statistics taken at 30 June 1852 and 1859, capital data at 31 Dec. 1851 and 1858.

The 'Euston Confederacy', created in 1849–50, reached the zenith of its influence in railway affairs in the mid-'fifties, enhanced by the operation of the 'Octuple' and 'Ten Towns' pooling agreements, by which disputed traffic north and south of York was divided between the rival East and West Coast routes. Huish's precise part in this ingenious but precarious experiment in co-operation is difficult to detach from the labyrinth of conferences and agreements. His work was closely associated with that of other managers, for the inter-company conference was a favourite means of settling problems. He also operated in close consultation with his Board, and we must not follow other writers in underestimating the rôle of the company's successive chairmen—especially Carr Glyn and Lord Chandos—and of other prominent directors. Finally, in seeking to attribute responsibility, we must admit that it is extremely hard to assess the extent of bad faith—the degree to which managers deliberately evaded the terms of contracts which were not legally binding.

Huish was certainly influential in directing the 'Confederacy', even if his rôle was not the dictatorial one previously assigned to him. His efforts to combat competition, culminating in convulsions of intrigue and volte-face, were a key factor in the decline of the company's fortunes after 1856. His isolation in 1857 and 1858, and the collapse of the company's system, showed the railway world that co-operation was not merely valuable but essential, and that, to succeed, it should be based upon both equality and trust. To operate with any degree of profit, a railway company had to stabilize its relations with others and avoid rate-wars. In this situation, quality of service became an important factor. As Huish stated, "the time is past for simply providing accommodation, and relying on the public availing themselves of it. Successful rivalry, until combination is effected, daily depends more and more on the mode in which the service is performed . . .".[1] This was undoubtedly so, but in Huish's time rate-cutting, intimidation and other unwise expedients were also part of a manager's armoury.

Directors and shareholders alike were soon frustrated with a policy which became increasingly untenable. Huish and other executives were made scapegoats in a change of heart, the origins of which may be traced to a memorandum of 1853, where the directors considered the possibility of creating an association of companies to stem rivalries. It is easy to connect Huish with the statement's description of "officials [who] identified with a single undertaking rarely suffer from the cost which their personal triumphs inflict on many undertakings."[2] In the years 1851 to 1860 the London & North Western and the other major companies began to realize that they must make the best of the situation created by Parliament's attempts to encourage competition in the industry by co-operating among themselves. The Railway Clearing House prospered, and its activities expanded: conferences of passenger superintendents and of general managers began in November 1850 and January 1851 respectively. However, the House, although a significant potential force for inter-company peace, could not compel agreement. This remained the prerogative of each management.

In other spheres, the trends of the late 1840s were continued. Recruitment was becoming a matter for the industry itself, especially for skilled and semi-skilled grades. Ancillary activities grew, with particular atten-

1 M. Huish, 'Report to the Chairman and Directors of the London & North Western
  Railway on the Traffic for the Half-Year Ending 30th June 1855' (1855), confidential
  printed report, L.N.W. Company Reports, LNW1/756, BTHR, 19.
2 L.N.W. Memo., RCA4/1, BTHR.

tion to shipping links, engineering products, and hotels. Basic equipment, however, was still largely contracted for, and the system was even applied experimentally to the working of trains.[1]

1 Company organization

The London & North Western's organizational structure, created in February 1851, continued to evolve as the size and scope of management increased. When the regional committees, which had represented the constituent companies, were discarded, the central Board of Directors at Euston became the leading policy-making body. Composed of 30 members, it was large and therefore potentially unwieldy, but the management was loth to lose the experience of former regional directors, and the expansion of standing committees after 1851 required a large pool of men to draw on. There were over 30 such committees by 1852, headed by three with major responsibility for working arrangements—the Road & Traffic, Locomotive, and Works Construction & Estate, which each presided over three sub-committees representing the Southern, Northern, and North-Eastern divisions of the line. Nine additional committees supervised other business affecting the whole North Western network: these were the Audit, Finance, Stores, Rates, Parliamentary, Capital Expenditure, Church & Schools, and the newly-created Special Affairs Committee (December 1850, for inter-railway negotiations) and Permanent Way Committee (September 1852, for the supervision of maintenance over the whole line, on the expiry of the ex-Grand Junction contracts).[2]

Fixed committees for specific areas of managerial attention formed a notable feature of the new organization. Problems of subsidiary lines, joint undertakings (including stations), and traffic arrangements were dealt with in this way, since to have continually created and recreated *ad hoc* committees would have been tedious and might have strangled administrative decision. The nature of so-called special committees is more obscure, for they were omitted from the list published annually with the roll of directors and officers. There are references in the Board minutes however to a Special Salaries Committee, and an Hotels & Refreshment

---

1 Engine drivers worked their locomotives on a contract basis on the Eastern Counties Railway in 1852, and on the Southern Division of the L.N.W. in 1854: *Lawson's Merchant's Magazine*, I (1852), 186; *Herapath's Railway Magazine*, 3 June 1854.
2 Information on Committees from 'Roll of Directors and Officers', 1852–67, LNW4/50, and L.N.W. Mins, *passim*, LNW1/21–3, BTHR.

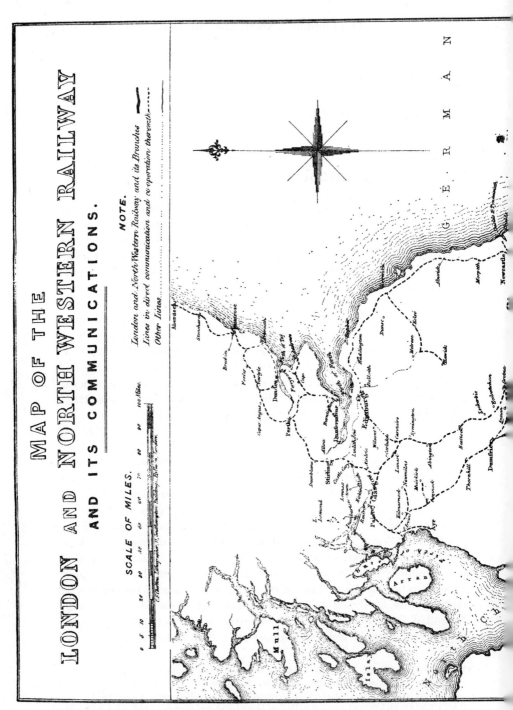

Map 5. London & North Western Railway, 1855–6,
from the London & North Western Committee of Consultation Report, February 1856

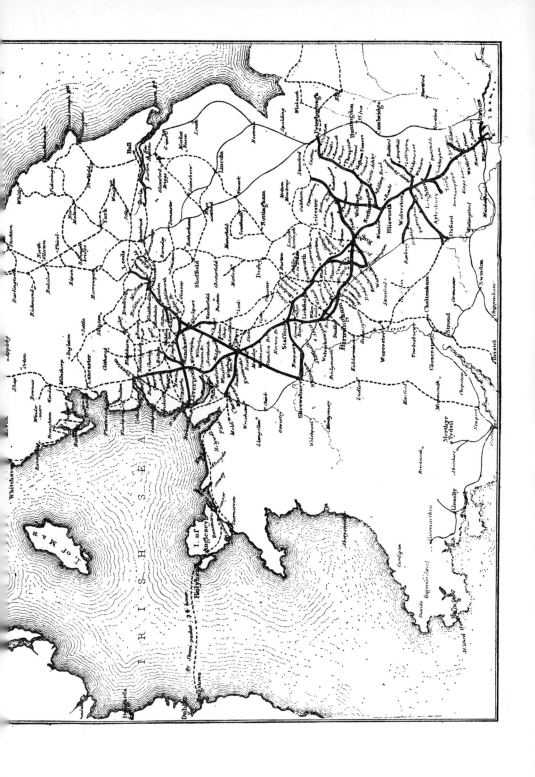

Rooms Special Committee, which were probably sub-committees whose meetings were occasional.[1]

It also seems that the system of *ad hoc* committees continued unaffected by these changes, and that, throughout the 'fifties, these were created for a variety of special purposes, some, as before, involving a partnership of director and executive officer.[2] Despite the existence of over 20 special area committees, business before the Board often fell outside their jurisdiction. *Ad hoc* bodies were therefore set up to consider such matters as special negotiations, experiments with services, and the utilization of assets.[3]

Some directors became acquainted with a wider range of administrative details, because of the increase in standing committees. Nevertheless, the Board and its major committees became more and more dependent on executive officers for information and policy decisions. Thus, an apparent move towards centralized control in February 1851 disguised a trend towards autonomous regional administration which was in progress at executive level. The existence of separate departments for each division of the railway reinforced this, as did the control of subsidiary companies by distinct managerial units, as, for example, those for the Shropshire Union and Chester & Holyhead Railways.[4] Potential friction between the directorate and its executive was thus accentuated as business expanded, and the membership of the various committees suggests the growing frustration of certain 'reformist' directors with the freedom enjoyed by the leading officers. In 1852, for example, C. R. Moorsom, Richard Moon, and Edward Tootal were among those with the most committee positions, and they figured strongly in the changes after 1855, being committed to a policy of reducing costs and achieving a tighter control of active management.

The sheer mass of minute books makes it difficult for the historian to make a precise judgment on the working of the organization, especially as regards responsibility, and the definition of duties. Well over a hundred relevant volumes survive for the period, and because the amount of

1 L.N.W. Salaries Ctee, LNW1/134–5; Hotels Ctee, see L.N.W. Mins, 13 Mar. 1852, 9 July 1853, 9 June 1855, LNW1/22, BTHR.
2 E.g. a committee of three directors and Huish dealt with Irish communication: L.N.W. Mins, 13 Dec. 1851, LNW1/21, BTHR.
3 E.g. L.N.W. Mins, 13 Mar. 1852 (re Manchester bonded warehouses), 14 Oct. 1854 (re passenger fares), and 13 Mar. 1858 (re Wolverhampton joint station), LNW1/22–3, BTHR.
4 R. S. Skey was head of the S.U. executive committee: L.N.W. Mins, 4 Aug. 1852, 10 Feb. 1855, LNW1/22. Poole became goods manager of the C. & H.: L.N.W. Road & Traffic Ctee Mins, 7 Apr. 1852, LNW1/140, BTHR. Both railways retained separate boards of directors.

business conducted precludes an exhaustive analysis, it is difficult to decide whether, for example, series end by accident or design, or whether procedure is prescribed or accidental. Nevertheless, there is little doubt that supervision continued to be effected principally by the committees, presided over by the central Board of Directors. It is also suggested, although this is hard to test empirically, that the company made less use of *ad hoc* committees for the settlement of matters involving other companies. The work of the Special Affairs Committee and other special area teams tended to encourage this, halting a feature of organization popular before 1851. The Board itself shunted off a growing number of items of business, placing them with subordinate committees, while it remained free to deal with the formulation of strategic inter-railway policy. The mechanics of internal management were therefore largely delegated. In 1852, for example, the Board redirected questions of pricing and fire insurance to committee level, a policy which became frequent, and which enhanced the status of executive officers called in to advise directors.[1]

A further important development was the increasing tendency for the Chairman or Deputy Chairman of the Board (or both) to reserve matters for their special attention. This was true of Carr Glyn, George Anson, and Lord Chandos, a fact which weakens the assertion, frequently made in the past, that Huish was solely responsible for the important inter-railway problems of the 1850s. Thus in April 1853 Anson and Benson, Chairman and Deputy Chairman at that time, decided to settle the problem of traffic from Liverpool to the Potteries, while from July 1854 Chandos, successor to Anson, became responsible for negotiations relating to Irish traffic.[2]

Executive management showed little drastic change up to 1855, with Huish remaining head of a pyramid structure containing two secretaries, three passenger and three locomotive superintendents, and four goods managers.[3] On the death of Eborall, Huish sponsored a successful plan to abolish the central goods district, which was replaced by a sub-region under Mills in December 1853, and from September 1852 Woodhouse was given control of permanent way maintenance over the entire company network.[4] With these exceptions the overall organization of the executive varied little from its pre-1851 appearance, although the duties of each officer altered, since the wider scope of company activities required

1 L.N.W. Mins, 12 Aug. and 7 Feb. 1852, LNW1/22, BTHR.
2 L.N.W. Mins, 9 Apr. 1853, 15 July 1854 *et seq.*, LNW1/22, BTHR.
3 See table 22, compiled from L.N.W. Roll of Directors and Officers, 1852–5, LNW4/50;
   Bradshaw's Railway Manual and Shareholders' Guide, 1851–5.
4 L.N.W. Road & Traffic Ctee Mins, 9 Dec. 1853, LNW1/140; L.N.W. Mins, 18 Sept.
   1852, LNW1/22; Permanent Way Ctee Mins, 18 Sept. 1852, LNW1/290, BTHR.

further delegation of responsibility. With Huish personally unable to supervise the entire management, there were moves to give goods agents and station masters increased power to handle traffic matters, and a concerted effort was made to create a greater exchange of information by senior officials. There is evidence of the existence of a committee of executive officers, and an executive goods conference, clearly separate from meetings arranged by the Clearing House. References to them are made in the Board and Road & Traffic Committee minutes, and their chief aim appears to have been to secure uniform practice in all departments.[1]

Table 22
Major executive structure of the London & North Western, 1851–5

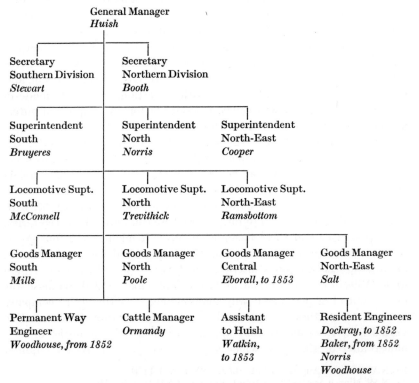

General Manager			
Huish			

Secretary Southern Division *Stewart*	Secretary Northern Division *Booth*		
Superintendent South *Bruyeres*	Superintendent North *Norris*	Superintendent North-East *Cooper*	
Locomotive Supt. South *McConnell*	Locomotive Supt. North *Trevithick*	Locomotive Supt. North-East *Ramsbottom*	
Goods Manager South *Mills*	Goods Manager North *Poole*	Goods Manager Central *Eborall, to 1853*	Goods Manager North-East *Salt*
Permanent Way Engineer *Woodhouse, from 1852*	Cattle Manager *Ormandy*	Assistant to Huish *Watkin, to 1853*	Resident Engineers *Dockray, to 1852* *Baker, from 1852* *Norris* *Woodhouse*

1 Re Executive Officers' Ctee, see L.N.W. Mins, 7 Feb. 1852, LNW1/22; Road & Traffic Ctee Mins, 13 Jan. and 13 Oct. 1854, LNW1/140; re Exec. Goods Conferences, see L.N.W. Mins, 7 Apr. 1852, 15 Jan. 1853, LNW1/22, and Road & Traffic Ctee Mins, 17 Oct. 1851, 14 Jan. and 14 Oct. 1853, LNW1/140, BTHR.

The company had evolved a comprehensive managerial structure, but by 1853 it was evident that serious problems were resulting from the growing complexity of operations and the constant pressure to function profitably. Criticisms of inefficiency, strengthened by reports of executive dishonesty, caused action to be taken in 1855. Moorsom, who had previously led the investigations of 1848, and Moon, who was rapidly acquiring a reputation for inquiry into executive management, were prominent in the formulation of change. They were aware first of all that trivial matters still came before the Board, despite efforts to retain its time for policy decisions. Thus, on 9 December 1854, the Board considered compensation for a cow killed on the line, and granted a special gratuity to a guard, administrative minutiae which also illustrate the unwillingness to delegate responsibility where even small expenditures were concerned. Moorsom and Moon also pressed the Board to avoid unnecessary expense by instituting a tighter control of the means by which new expenditure was recommended and considered. The executive changes affecting goods and permanent way management may well have been a response to this. Certainly, the minutes give clear indication of Moorsom and Moon's preoccupation with the estimates of capital expenditure provided by Huish and his executive. In 1852, for example, Moon complained about the cost of Bletchley station, while in 1853 Moorsom checked Huish's report on proposed expenditure at Birmingham (New Street). There was also a closer examination of costs by *ad hoc* committees, in which the two directors figured strongly.[1] By August 1854 a committee had been set up to investigate wages, salaries, and stores, and the Road & Traffic Committee had declared that all operational costs were to be passed by the sub-committees before officers could proceed.[2]

A difficult situation was exacerbated by executive disruption. Edward Watkin, chief assistant to Huish, resigned in November 1853, to join the Manchester Sheffield & Lincolnshire Railway. McConnell's reorganization of the southern locomotive department met strong opposition, particularly from Carr Glyn, and in April 1854 Goalen, the audit officer, and Caitcheon, an audit official at Liverpool, were found guilty of embezzlement. The changes which followed were, therefore, a product of retrenchment fortified by a reaction to administrative difficulty. Indeed, the actions taken paralleled those of 1848, for a period of expansion (1846–8, 1851–5) was followed by strict economy and a thorough inquiry into the

---

1 L.N.W. Mins, 15 May 1852, 11 June 1853, 9 Dec. 1854, LNW1/22; Road & Traffic Ctee Mins, 14 July 1854, LNW1/140, BTHR.
2 L.N.W. Mins, 10 Aug. 1854, LNW1/22; Road & Traffic Ctee Mins, 9 Aug. 1854, LNW1/140, BTHR.

company's management. In both periods there was an attempt to impose centralization both as a means of control and as an instrument of economy, the Moorsom Committee of 1848 having a direct counterpart in Moon's committee of investigation of 1855. The latter period, however, was characterized by a directorial revolt against dependence upon the executive for information and policy. This can be traced in occasional clashes before 1855, as for example in the conflict over bone traffic in 1853.[1] Thereafter battle was joined, and Moon was eventually able to secure the resolution that "It would conduce to the more efficient administration of the affairs of the company if they could be brought under the more continuous control and direction of the Board, or of a portion of its members."[2]

The principal change in 1855 was the creation of an Executive Committee of 13 directors, including the Chairman, which from 22 March combined the former responsibilities of the Road & Traffic, and Locomotive Committees. The new committee, which had been suggested by Carr Glyn and Chandos, was intended to avoid mistakes caused by lack of information, by assuming control of all traffic matters. The committee met twice monthly, alternately at London and Birmingham, as Carr Glyn had recommended. It presided over the six traffic and locomotive sub-committees and considered the suggestions of the various executive meetings, becoming the main instrument of directorial control over day-to-day operation. The change marked a further move away from control by the central Board, which thereafter gave increased attention to financial problems. The other main change was the amalgamation of the Works Committee with the Permanent Way Committee, a further demonstration of the desire to integrate similar processes within the management structure.

Carr Glyn had warned, however, that although the Executive Committee might prevent discord, it would be "unwieldy",[3] and his view was soon confirmed, in 1856, when a Goods Committee of seven directors was forced to assume special responsibility for merchandise, cattle, and mineral traffic. This was to meet successively at Euston, Manchester, Birmingham, and Liverpool, and to report through the Executive Committee, rather than directly to the Board. Nevertheless, the Goods

---

1 The Executive Goods Conference recommended the ending of bone traffic in Dec. 1852: this was supported by the Road & Traffic Ctee (Mins, 14 Jan. 1853, LNW1/140) but vetoed by the Board (Mins, 14 Jan. 1853, LNW1/22), BTHR.
2 L.N.W. Mins, 12 Feb. 1858, LNW1/23, BTHR. Moon's position was later defended by D. Stevenson, *Fifty Years on the London & North Western Railway* (1891), 31–3.
3 Carr Glyn, letter to Chandos, 13 Feb. 1855, Glyn Mills & Co. Archives.

Committee represented the failure of a centralization policy, a fact which was reinforced by the decision to decentralize the supervision of accounts, in June 1855.[1]

Parallel changes occurred within the executive. The first meeting of departmental heads was held at Birmingham in January 1855, with Huish as chairman. Its object, said Huish, was "to endeavour to improve the general working of the line",[2] and in its work it was closely linked to the Executive Committee, to which recommendations were passed. These Birmingham 'Officers' Meetings', as they became known, reflected the improved status of the second-rank officials, and especially the station-master and goods-agent, whose views were held to be important in determining local services. The meetings were intended to provide Huish and the other chief officers with information from the localities, and to secure thereby a more uniform implementation of decisions affecting traffic. The executive organization of goods traffic was also thoroughly revised in 1856, under Mills of Camden, who became chief goods manager and co-ordinator of the four districts. Following the dismissals of Poole and Salt in September and October respectively, posts fell to new district goods managers at Camden, Birmingham, Liverpool, and Manchester.[3] Additional changes, agreed by the Board in January 1856, showed a concern to accelerate decisions on goods matters, by making Huish more accessible to officials responsible for the outlying districts.[4]

These changes, again, did nothing to stabilize the company's management. Directors continued to be frustrated by their dependence upon the executive and preached economy at every opportunity. Attempts to solve these fundamental problems led to further alterations, culminating in the superseding of Huish and others of the 'old guard' in favour of officers more amenable to pressure from the Board and its committees. Collisions between the directors and executive became more frequent after 1855. Chandos, for example, was forced to censure Huish in January 1855 over his long-standing dispute with McConnell. He wrote:

> In your position as Chief Executive Officer of the Company, it must be hardly necessary for me to point out that your orders carefully considered should be distinctly worded . . . that they may not be open to misrepresentation . . .

1 L.N.W. Mins, 9 June 1855, LNW1/22. The Goods Committee was created in March 1856, L.N.W. Mins, 15 Mar. 1856, LNW1/23, and see LNW1/523, BTHR.
2 L.N.W. Officers' Meetings, 15 Jan. 1855, LNW1/583, BTHR.
3 *Bradshaw's Railway Manual and Shareholders' Guide*, 1856.
4 L.N.W. Mins, 12 Jan. 1856, LNW1/23, BTHR.

—a warning similar to that given him by the divisional Locomotive Sub-committee as early as November 1852.[1] Huish's insistence upon the need to strengthen rather than cripple the executive, made in his report on Traffic of August 1855, suggested a further serious clash over staff policy, and his view that a liberal expenditure on staff was cheapest in the long run brought him into direct conflict with Moon, Moorsom, and Tootal. Moreover, as traffic problems became more acute, and Huish became less influential in railway circles, the directors showed a growing eagerness to intervene in inter-company negotiations. During talks with the Lanca-shire & Yorkshire Railway in 1856, for example, two directors were deputed to represent the company "in traffic questions which the man-agers of the two companies cannot agree".[2]

A spate of investigations, suspensions, and alleged frauds reinforced the directors' disillusion with the executive. Within two months two influential goods managers were dismissed, Poole for alleged negligence concerning frauds committed by his staff, Salt for neglect of duty and the wrongful use of stores. Both Woodhouse, the permanent way engineer, and Bruyeres, passenger superintendent of the Southern Division, suffered close investigation following allegations against them, but were sub-sequently declared innocent.[3] These incidents coincided with Carr Glyn's unofficial suggestions to Chandos, made in a series of private letters beginning in January 1856, that Huish might eventually be replaced. By 1857 it was clear that a serious crisis was imminent. A struggle over the future management of the locomotive departments ended with the dis-missal of another ex-Grand Junction official, Richard Trevithick, who was the Northern Division's locomotive superintendent. The aftermath of McConnell's experimental contract system for engine crews had caused Carr Glyn and other directors to consider the feasibility of centralizing locomotive operation under one man. There was some opposition, how-ever, and reports presented in May 1855 and March 1856 had been shelved. In addition, Moon's resolution suggesting the amalgamation of the Northern and North-Eastern divisions under Ramsbottom had been defeated, if only narrowly.[4] The company was, however, to cease opera-tion of the 90 miles of Lancaster & Carlisle Railway in July 1857, and in April Chandos presented a memorandum supporting the amalgamation of the northern divisions. In May, opposition from three ex-Grand Junc-

1 Chandos, letter to Huish, 11 Jan. 1855, L.N.W. Chairman's Letter Book, LNW4/-, and Sthn. Loco. Sub-Ctee, 9 Nov. 1852, LNW1/225, BTHR.
2 L.N.W. Mins, 9 Feb. 1856, LNW1/23, BTHR.
3 L.N.W. Mins, 13 Sept. and 11 Oct. 1856, 12 Feb. and 14 Mar. 1857, LNW1/23, BTHR; Glyn to Chandos, 14–19 Jan. 1856, Glyn Mills & Co. Archives.
4 By 11 votes to 8: L.N.W. Mins, 29 Mar. 1856, LNW1/23, BTHR.

tion directors was quashed and in August Moon's protégé, Ramsbottom, took control of the new department.[1]

Moorsom stated, in retrospect, that the crux of the company's difficulties had been the fact that administration—which had more and more been delegated to executives—had been hampered by the fitful interference of individual directors: "It is this which has spoilt our chief officers, destroyed their responsibility, and made them a sort of hybrid", he wrote in 1858.[2] Trevithick had also recognized this. In his letter of resignation of August 1857 he blamed the company's troubles upon the unsettled relations between directors and the executive, and his own dismissal not upon criticisms of his control of his department—the ostensible reason used by the directors—but upon disagreements over expenditure.[3]

A further reorganization of the company's committee system took place in 1858, under Moon's guidance. In February and March the Board created a 'Special Committee', to undertake the duties of the Special Affairs and Parliamentary committees, and decided to amalgamate other committees, in order to integrate the conduct of business more closely. In this way the number of major managerial units was reduced from 13 to six.[4] The most important change, however, and the culmination of Moon's policies, was the resignation in September of Huish himself. The directors were then able to impose a stricter control on his successor, William Cawkwell.[5] Opposition to Huish had of course been building up for some time. Moon complained in 1855 that he could not agree with him on policy matters; Moorsom was critical of Huish's conduct of outdoor management; and Carr Glyn even suggested to Chandos that there should be a capable person under him to take over "in the event of his retirement".[6] By 1858 the pertinacity which had served him well in internal

---

1 When McConnell retired in 1862, the Northern and Southern divisions were merged, with Ramsbottom as executive head. Moon's opposition to McConnell is apparent in his letter to Chandos, 20 Feb. 1860, HL2/R286/28, BTHR.
2 Moorsom to Chandos, 6 Sept. 1858, HL2/R211, BTHR.
3 Letter, 5 Aug. 1857, HL2/R379/2, BTHR. However, there was an element of 'whitewashing' in Trevithick's statements. Cf. criticisms of him in Moon's letter to Chandos, 5 May 1857, R286, and see his own letter to Stewart, 8 Jan. 1857, HL2/R379/1, BTHR.
4 L.N.W. Mins, 20 Feb. and 12 Mar. 1858, LNW1/23, BTHR. The new system involved the following committees: 1. Special Affairs & Parliamentary; 2. Capital & Finance; 3. Traffic (formerly Executive) & Goods; 4. Permanent Way & Works & Branch Lines; 5. Audit, Rating, & Superannuation; 6. Stores.
5 Huish's letter of resignation, 11 Sept. 1858, HL2/R373/7, and L.N.W. Mins, 11 Sept. and 9 Oct. 1858, LNW1/23, BTHR. Cawkwell had been observed by Glyn at the Clearing House: Glyn to Chandos, 12 Jan. 1858, HL2/R307/3, BTHR.
6 Moon to Chandos, 17 Oct. 1855; Moorsom to Chandos, 2 Nov. 1854, HL2/R211, R286, BTHR; Glyn to Chandos, 14 Jan. 1856.

administration was clearly resented by other railway companies. He was being openly smeared by their officials, and friction within the London & North Western made his position increasingly untenable. Arguments over traffic policy alienated Moorsom, while Moon's preoccupation with economy brought the directors into conflict with one of Huish's fundamental rôles as general manager—to recommend the expenditure necessary to attract business.[1] Pressure on Chandos proved decisive in September. Individual comments on the company's executive head were most illuminating. Moon told Chandos, "in getting rid of him, do not say much about his good qualities, for as far as to management, he has known none", and Glyn complained that "no-one co-operates with him, and even those co:s connected with the L. &. N.W. Co. leave the individual unsupported".[2]

There was some recrimination after Huish's departure, but in general it was felt that the company was entering a new era. The general manager was far from guiltless, of course, and there is much evidence to support Moon's view that Huish's "hauteur and acrimony" had contributed to the company's severe traffic problems in the later 1850s.[3] But in the context of organizational change, his fall was part of a replacement of the older-established officials by men more responsive to control by the directors. Huish, Trevithick, Poole, and Salt were all officers of great experience, respected in railway circles. But their comparative autonomy worried the Board, and its viewpoint was clearly expressed by Moorsom: "My opinion has long been that the company's affairs are such as to require the regular administration of persons *above* the position of executive officers".[4] It is also significant that a director was deputed to take Huish's place as company delegate to the Clearing House.[5] Huish's removal thus heralded the 'Moon Era' in London & North Western affairs: Chairman from 1861, he personified strict economy and a firm control on the executive. It is, however, dangerous to view the succeeding decades as something either permanent or novel in railway manage-

1 Moorsom to Chandos, 24 Apr. 1858, Ashton to Chandos, 17 Feb. 1858; and Moon to Chandos, 18 June 1858: "Cpt. Huish will resist the application of the knife to our expenses as far as he can". Huish replied to Moon with an attack on Ramsbottom: Huish to Chandos, 5 Mar. 1858, HL2/R211, R373/7, R286, R373/13/10, BTHR.
2 Moon to Chandos, 6 Sept., and Glyn to Chandos, 5 Sept. 1858, HL2/R286, R307/4, BTHR.
3 Moon to Chandos, 17 Dec. 1860, HL2/R286/31. Note Huish's letter to Carter, urging strong action against the Eastern Counties Railway in 1857, HL2/R373/6, BTHR.
4 Moorsom to Chandos, 2 Aug. 1858, HL2/R211/6, BTHR.
5 L.N.W. Mins, 9 Oct. 1858, LNW1/23, BTHR.

ment. The 1870s saw a further expansion of the committee system, and
Cawkwell speedily acquired a reputation for responsibility.

What was the precise nature of Huish's duties and responsibility, in
his last eight years of office? Certainly, he can be seen performing all the
rôles which had previously been assigned to him, but it is scarcely practical to quantify thousands of decisions and policies in order to obtain a
definite separation of customary and exceptional duties. Certain trends
are clear, however. Firstly, Huish's fundamental rôle as link between the
directors and the executive remained an essential feature of his work. He
continued to report regularly, both to the Board and to the major committees, and the increasing importance attached to this procedure was
underlined by specific instructions made on the creation of the Executive
and Goods Committees in 1855–6. The former quickly resolved that "the
general manager present a monthly report . . . with such suggestions as
he may deem necessary [and] that the supts. of the traffic and locomotive
departments make a monthly report to Huish".[1] Similarly, when the
Goods Committee was established, Huish was asked to attend all its
meetings and co-ordinate the ideas of officers each responsible for one
division of the railway.[2]

Huish also continued to act as a bridge between the various committees. This rôle was greatly extended after 1851 to include responsibility
for ensuring managerial continuity between the Board and its major
committees, sub-committees and their parent bodies, and subsidary committees and those with full powers. The use of this system of delegated
management was essential to the handling of a great variety of railway
matters and was especially vital to a large concern. Examples of Huish's
participation in decision-making illustrate both the complexity of the
system and its value as an instrument by which matters could be sifted
and dealt with according to their relative importance. He was especially
active in the affairs of the various traffic committees, and questions of
general principle were taken by him from regional sub-committees to
chief committee, and, if necessary, to the Board itself. In November 1851,
for example, the proposed coal sidings at Rugby were considered in turn
by sub-committee, committee, and Board, Huish providing the necessary
continuity in the form of statistics, estimates, and advice.[3] Some matters
did not need to proceed so far along the organizational chain of command:
when Bruyeres suggested to Huish that improved signalling was required

1 L.N.W. Executive Ctee Mins, 22 Mar. 1855, LNW1/148, BTHR.
2 L.N.W. Goods Ctee Mins, 4 Apr. 1856, LNW1/523, BTHR.
3 L.N.W. Road & Traffic Ctee Mins, 14 Nov. 1851, LNW1/140, BTHR.

at Weedon in 1854, the matter was settled by the sub-committee concerned. On the other hand, an application for promotion in 1857 was taken by Huish to both the Executive Committee and the Board.[1] Clearly, some problems involved very complicated permutations of organizational routing before a decision could be made, and the evidence makes it certain that Huish's influence was enhanced by his position as common factor.

Huish also acquired what was basically a new rôle, namely the task of linking the numerous executive conferences and committees. It has already been stated that he acted as representative for the conferences of officers interested in traffic management, submitting their proposals to the relevant committee of directors. Further light is shed upon his internal duties by the minutes of the Birmingham Officers' Meetings, from 1855, which show him as Chairman, and head of the executive, directing policy and receiving reports. The main advantage of this more prescribed system of executive authority appears to have been a closer consultation on traffic matters by the main departments. A more definite reporting system and a clearer conception of subordinate authority facilitated improved relations between the locomotive and traffic departments, while allowing Huish to familiarize himself with the work of the regions.[2] It was also his task to secure a more coherent pattern of traffic management over the company's entire system, by attending the numerous meetings convened to discuss inter-company problems. He was prominent as a Railway Clearing House delegate and founder member of the General Managers' Meetings, and organized regular meetings of companies concerned in several important traffic agreements.[3]

Huish's position within the managerial structure continued to be an exceptional one. He maintained a direct link with the Chairman, was asked to join *ad hoc* committees—although with less frequency—and his reports, on *Railway Accidents* (1852), the permanent way, train communication (1853), the electric telegraph (1854), and traffic (1855), were both important and influential.[4] There was also continuity in Huish's

---

1 L.N.W. Sthn. Divn. Road & Traffic Ctee Mins, 15 Mar. 1854, LNW1/145; Executive Ctee Mins, 13 Mar. 1857, LNW1/149; L.N.W. Mins, 14 Mar. 1857, LNW1/23; L.N.W. letters, etc., LNW8/42, BTHR.

2 L.N.W. Officers' Meetings, e.g. 15 Jan. 1855, LNW1/583, BTHR.

3 See Chapter VII.

4 M. Huish, *Railway Accidents, Their Cause and Means of Prevention*, a published edition of a paper read to the Institute of Civil Engineers, 27 Apr. 1852; M. Huish and others, 'Report on the Renewal Fund . . .', 1853; R.C.H. General Managers' sub-committee, 'Report on Communication between Passenger, Guard, and Driver', confidential report, 9 Mar. 1853, GEN3/96, BTHR; M. Huish, 'Report to the Road

attention to traffic matters (the provision of facilities and service alterations), staff control, pricing, complaints, accidents, and compensation.
He was still able to act on his own authority in certain spheres, as, for
example, in the adjustment of rates, and in negotiations with the Post
Office, telegraph companies, company agents, and firms with whom the
company had signed agreements.[1] But his authority was gradually
reduced, mainly by the resurgence of control by the directors, but also to
some extent by the growing independence of subordinate executives.

Contrary to the implications of writers such as Hamilton Ellis and
George Dow,[2] Huish never enjoyed a supreme command of company
policy in the 1850s, despite his considerable knowledge of railway operation and its technicalities. Supervision was always close at hand, for
special authority had to be granted and proposals sanctioned by the
Board or its committees before his opinions could be implemented. It is
true that he exerted a considerable influence, especially in the second
stage of management procedure—in the execution of traffic policy, for
example—but to dub him the arch-villain of the period is to ignore the
rôle of Carr Glyn, Chandos, Moorsom, and Moon, who became increasingly
active in both policy-making and executive action. Indeed, from 1853,
there is evidence of their intervention in matters previously assigned to
the general manager. Thus, certain important company negotiations
were handled by the directors, among them those connected with the
Midland 'Common Purse' agreement, and with Irish traffic. As early as
1851 Huish informed the Road & Traffic Committee that Carr Glyn had
himself authorized a travel concession, and Chandos was later prominent
in urging competition with the Great Western and in suggesting fares and
services on the Buckinghamshire line.[3] At the time of Huish's resignation,
Moon was concerning himself with two of the general manager's pre-
serves—goods rates and excursion traffic.[4] In fact, although Huish

---

& Traffic Committee on an Extension of the Electric Telegraph', March 1854,
LNW1/716, BTHR; Huish, Report . . . on the Traffic . . . (1855).

1 On rates, see L.N.W. Mins, 12 Sept. 1857, LNW1/23; Huish's letters to Saunders,
1852–4, HL1/30–2, BTHR; on the Post Office, Road & Traffic Ctee Mins, 11 Aug.
1852, LNW1/140, L.N.W. Mins, 10 Nov. 1855, LNW1/23, BTHR; on the telegraph,
L.N.W. Mins, 14 Aug. 1851, LNW1/21, BTHR; on agents, Road & Traffic Ctee
Mins, 13 June, 8 Aug., and 14 Nov. 1851, 10 Mar. and 12 May 1854, LNW1/140;
Huish to Chandos, 6 Apr. 1858, HL2/R373/13/13, BTHR; on firms, Road & Traffic
Ctee Mins, 7 Apr. 1852, Executive Ctee Mins, 24 Apr. 1855, LNW1/148, BTHR.
2 Ellis, *op. cit.*, 182ff.; G. Dow, *Great Central*, vol. I (1959), 137, 156–9.
3 L.N.W. Road & Traffic Ctee Mins, 11 July 1851, 10 Mar. 1854, LNW1/140; Chandos
to Huish, Dec. 1854, LNW4/-; L.N.W. Mins, 22 Feb. 1856, 9 May 1857, LNW1/23;
L.N.W. Fares Ctee Mins, 3 Oct. 1854, LNW1/54, BTHR.
4 Moon to Chandos, 17 Sept. 1858, HL2/R286/16, BTHR.

remained an authority in traffic policy, Chandos was anxious to vet any changes, and by 1858 was keeping a close check upon his manager's conduct.[1] Huish still enjoyed his own areas of special freedom, being entrusted with the negotiations for the renewal of the 'Octuple' and 'Ten Towns' traffic agreements, 1855–6, and influencing the strategy of the company's relations with other railways, as his letters to Chandos illustrate. But from 1855 his actions were subjected to increasing scrutiny, and it appears that despite his power to direct policy, decision-making became essentially a matter of partnership between the directors and himself.

Huish suffered, in the eyes of the directors, from the opposition to him displayed by certain officers, and especially McConnell, Poole, and Dockray, who resisted his interference in matters which were considered to lie within their province. Poole, whose influence in the goods department was considerable, was often critical of the "gallant Captain", while McConnell, who tended to organize his department independently of the company as a whole, frequently clashed with Huish over locomotive matters, a fact which distressed Chandos.[2] Dockray, arguing with him over engineering costs, claimed that "The Capt. is so random that one really cannot believe a word he says".[3] These incidents, when taken with instances of fraud, and serious accidents—that at Bicester in September 1851 was a notorious example of disregard for regulations[4]—may be interpreted as a symptom of the growing difficulty of supervising subordinate officials. Alternatively, the high-handed attitude of Huish may have had its adverse effects. The evidence is, however, too diffuse to permit a clear judgment. Certainly, delays in the execution of instructions given by Huish, and his dependence on other officers for information, can be traced to a variety of sources, and the complexity of his executive authority may be reflected in the diverse duties assigned to the secretaries, Stewart and Booth. The creation of a statistical department within the general manager's office in 1854 was a firm indication that Huish could no longer legislate for the vast area covered by the company without help, and proof that railway management required a more scientific basis if problems were to be identified and solved.[5]

1 As early as 1854, Chandos asked Huish to send him details of prospective Liverpool fares: Chandos to Huish, Dec. 1854, LNW4/-, BTHR.
2 Poole to Saunders, 2 Feb. 1855, HL1/32, BTHR.
3 Diary, 27 Nov. 1850, in Robbins, *Journal of Transport History*, VII (Nov. 1965), 113.
4 Simmons's Report to the Railway Department, 26 June 1852, Accounts & Papers, P.P.1852, XLVIII.
5 L.N.W. Salary Lists, General Manager's Department, 1853–8, LNW4/1, BTHR.

2 Passenger traffic

The conduct of passenger traffic during the 1850s was strongly influenced by inter-railway factors. Unprecedented competition between the companies affected most decisions on services and pricing, and after 1850 a large company found it impossible to operate in isolation. This made the task of individual managers extremely complex, and the subsequent strain on managerial resources coincided with a further marked expansion of the United Kingdom's passenger traffic (see table 23). The London & North Western maintained a significant, if declining, share of this activity (see table 24) and was thus faced with particularly intensive management problems.

Table 23
United Kingdom passenger traffic, 1851–9

Year July–June	Numbers carried	Gross receipts	Mileage open
1851–2	86,758,997	£7,984,651	7,076
1854–5	112,655,052	9,221,024	8,115
1858–9	143,758,902	10,691 988	9,796

Source: Accounts & Papers, P.P.1852, XLVIII, 1852–3, XCVII, 1856, LIV, 1859, Sess. 2, XXVII.

The London & North Western faced severe competition in three of its industrial strongholds—south Staffordshire, Lancashire, and Yorkshire —while its long-distance services depended upon the co-operation of neighbours. More than ever before, traffic decisions came to be taken in concert with other managements. A powerful motive was the desire to achieve some uniformity in passenger travel over the major routes, but, as far as Huish and his company were concerned, many of the service changes of the 1850s were a response to more progressive competitors, part of a growing attention to quality of service. Thus, improvements in train speeds and frequencies and wider opportunities for cheap travel were obvious expedients for a company whose lead in railway technology —and especially in locomotive and carriage design—had been lost, and whose routes although well-established were not always the most direct.

Huish gave particular attention to long-distance traffic, where returns were potentially higher. Indeed, the company's system rested upon its express trains to Scotland, Birmingham, and Lancashire, all of which were affected by competition. In order to retain traffic for the Euston

Table 24
London & North Western's share of United Kingdom passenger and goods traffic and receipts, 1851–9

Year July–June	Share of U.K. passenger traffic (numbers) BY CLASS					Share of U.K. passenger receipts BY CLASS					Share of U.K. goods receipts	Share of U.K. total traffic receipts
	First %	Second %	Third %	Parlt. %	Total %	First %	Second %	Third %	Parlt. %	Total %	%	%
1851–2	11.1	9.4	7.0	10.3	9.5	25.5	17.6	7.6	17.6	18.5	18.7	18.6
1852–3	11.1	8.9	9.6*		9.5	22.4	15.5	12.4*		16.4	18.0	17.3
1853–4	10.0	9.5	9.0*		9.2	20.0	14.6	11.3*		15.1	17.0	16.1
1854–5	8.6	9.0	8.1*		8.5	18.9	14.0	12.0*		14.6	16.5	15.6
1855–6	7.6	7.4	7.9*		7.7	18.0	13.2	11.8*		14.0	15.9	15.1
1856–7	6.9	7.4	7.4*		7.4	17.9	13.1	11.0*		13.7	15.5	15.0
1857–8	6.9	7.7	7.3*		7.4	17.4	14.1	10.6*		13.7	15.1	14.4
1858–9	6.6	8.3	3.8	8.8	7.5	16.8	15.0	7.2	11.7	13.8	16.0	15.0

Source: Accounts and Papers, P.P.1852, XLVIII, 1852–3, XCVII, 1854, LXII, 1854–5, XLVII, 1856, LIV, 1857, XVI and XXXVII, 1857–8, LI, 1859, Sess. 2, XXVII, 1860, LXI. Passenger totals include season tickets and excess fares. From January 1858 statistics for L.N.W. and its subsidiaries have been used. The goods figures here include horses, dogs, carriages, mails, and luggage. Mitchell and Deane, *Abstract of British Historical Statistics* (1962), **227**, observe that from 1854 passenger receipts included those for luggage and mails. It is nevertheless possible to exclude these from the calculations, and this has been done.
* L.N.W. share of third and parliamentary classes (not divided).

route, speeds were increased and the exclusive character of express trains was abandoned. For example, in anticipation of the Great Western's entry into Birmingham (in 1852) and Liverpool (in 1854) Huish arranged the acceleration of expresses, and urged the introduction of second-class carriages on all these trains, to conform to Great Western practice.[1] Similar decisions were made by the general manager, after an agreement to charge equal rates had been implemented in January 1855. With rates agreed, competition depended upon quality of service, and improvements were essential. In 1857, therefore, the Birmingham–Liverpool service was modified.[2]

The provision of express trains to Scotland brought Huish into a wider management arena. Since the London & North Western was the dominant partner in the West Coast route via Lancaster and Carlisle, Huish was influential in the decisions of conferences held to discuss the effects of competition with the East Coast route from King's Cross via York. He put particular pressure upon the Lancaster & Carlisle and Caledonian companies to improve timings and was at the centre of discussions to improve facilities. Indeed, any alteration of long-distance accommodation involved not only Huish and his Board, but a multitude of committees and conferences also, while conflicts with rival companies entailed tortuous negotiations both inside and outside the Railway Clearing House.[3]

The operation of this complex managerial framework can be seen in the disputes concerning improvements to the Anglo-Scottish service. After the opening of the Great Northern's 'Towns Line' in August 1852 the East Coast route reduced the journey time to Edinburgh from $12\frac{1}{4}$ to 11 hours. The West Coast companies followed suit, and seized the initiative by extending express accommodation to second- and third-class passengers. Huish, it appears, was not a supporter of this policy: he had opposed the Chester & Holyhead Railway's request for second-class carriage in 1851, and had chaired the meeting of the Octuple Committee which had rejected the proposal to carry second-class passengers on morning expresses to the North.[4] However, the pressure of competition with a faster route led him to abandon his objections. The London & North Western began to carry second-class passengers to Scotland by

1 L.N.W. Road & Traffic Ctee Mins, 17 Oct. 1851, 9 Jan. and 8 Oct. 1852, 10 Mar. 1854, LNW1/140; *Bradshaw*, 1850–4, TT2/1E-H, BTHR.
2 L.N.W. Executive Ctee Mins, 26 Feb. 1857, LNW1/149, BTHR.
3 See Chapter VII.
4 L.N.W. Road & Traffic Ctee Mins, 8 Aug. 1851, LNW1/140; Octuple Companies Ctee Mins, 4 Feb. 1852, RCH1/505, BTHR.

express, agreed to book third-class passengers through, and in retaliation against the Great Northern's fast night trains at ordinary fares introduced (in July 1854) third-class day travel from London to Edinburgh in 11 hours.[1] The Octuple Committee attempted to stabilize the situation by defining the speed of express trains, and by restricting third-class passengers to trains taking at least 15 hours to reach Edinburgh, but there is ample evidence to suggest that companies evaded such restrictions.[2] By 1855 Huish had effected the acceleration of his company's night mail and refused to abandon second-class express travel, proof of the change of policy necessitated by loss of traffic.[3]

Long-distance traffic provided Huish with his most difficult service problems of the 1850s. Not only were Scottish and Birmingham traffics affected, but sporadic rate-wars were waged in Lancashire and Yorkshire. Proposed changes could involve opposition from any of the major companies, disrupting traffic agreements and hindering the provision of through traffic exchange which was being encouraged by the Clearing House. In 1858, for example, the company, in struggling to retain its influence in Manchester and Liverpool, incurred the opposition of the Lancashire & Yorkshire and Caledonian companies.[4] Furthermore, the intervention of the Post Office in traffic matters added to Huish's difficulties. Delays caused by the unloading of mails affected Scottish services in particular, and demands to introduce new postal services and to limit the use of mail trains by passengers hindered his efforts to keep pace with rival companies.[5] By 1858, however, the London & North Western had acceded to several Post Office requirements regarding mail trains.[6]

It is not surprising to find that excursion and through-booking facilities were greatly extended. The eight years following the Great Exhibition saw at least one important event each year for which excursions were provided by the company. The most important were the Duke of Wellington's Funeral in 1852, the Dublin Industrial Exhibition of 1853, the Lady Godiva Show and Crystal Palace Exhibition of 1854, Birmingham's Music Festivals of 1855 and 1858, the London Cattle Show, 1856, and the

1 L.N.W. Road & Traffic Ctee Mins, 9 Jan. 1852, LNW1/140; Octuple Ctee Mins, 27 Oct. and 14 Dec. 1853, RCH1/505; and L.N.W. Timebill, July 1854, and Huish's letter to Seymour Clarke, 20 June 1854, in GN1/276/9, BTHR.

2 Octuple Ctee Mins, 10 July and 13 Dec. 1854, 2 June 1855, RCH1/505, BTHR.

3 Octuple Ctee Mins, 13 Dec. 1854, RCH1/505; L.N.W. Executive Ctee Mins, 11 May 1855, LNW1/148, BTHR.

4 L.N.W. General Traffic Ctee Mins, 23 July 1858, LNW1/168, BTHR.

5 L.N.W. Road & Traffic Ctee Mins, 11 Aug. 1852, 9 Aug. 1854, and 8 Aug. 1851, LNW1/140, BTHR.

6 L.N.W. Executive Ctee Mins, 11–24 May 1855, 10 Feb. 1858, LNW1/148–9; Traffic Ctee Mins, 25 June and 23 July 1858, LNW1/168, BTHR.

Manchester Art Treasures Exhibition of 1857. Huish was responsible for the provision of trains for all these events, with the assistance of an agent at Birmingham.[1] A competitive spirit surrounded the majority of special excursion traffics, improving the price and comfort of passenger travel for the poorer sections of the community. During the Great Exhibition and the Manchester Art Exhibition, in particular, the existence of severe rate-cutting enabled such passengers to take advantage of exceptional temporary accommodation at low fares. Huish claimed, for example, that his company had carried 775,000 people to and from London during the Great Exhibition, May–October 1851, and the agent reported that 90,000 had travelled in 145 special excursion trains.[2] Special excursions were also used as competitive expedients even when there was no important event to celebrate. In February 1856, and from August 1857 into 1858, passengers travelling from the north to London enjoyed cheap first- and second-class travel at high speeds and with improved comfort.[3]

The London & North Western also gave considerable attention, under Huish's administration, to the more lucrative regular holiday tickets offered to the wealthier members of society. Availability and coverage were greatly extended, and efforts to secure inter-company agreement were more successful in this sphere. The Octuple Committee made several regulations for excursion tickets from London to Scotland, for example.[4] Huish's record suggests, however, that managers could easily upset arrangements if they wished, for although he appeared anxious to agree upon reciprocal facilities, his co-operation depended more upon the state of relations between the companies in question than upon a regard for public needs. This is clearly visible in Huish's correspondence with Saunders of the Great Western in 1852, where the former's willingness to arrange excursion traffic was part of an attempt to induce his rival to make a positive traffic agreement.[5] Later, Huish accused the Great Western of acting contrary to the spirit of the 1854 Traffic Agreement in

1 E.g. L.N.W. Road & Traffic Ctee Mins, 14 Mar. 1851, 10 Feb. 1852, LNW1/140; Executive Ctee Mins, 24 Apr. 1857, LNW1/149; and *Midland Counties Herald*, 29 June 1854, 14 Aug. 1856.

2 Huish, *Railway Accidents* . . ., 16; L.N.W. Road & Traffic Ctee Mins, 10 Feb. 1852, LNW1/140, BTHR.

3 Huish even secured the cushioning of second-class carriages and the provision of footwarmers in 1858, in response to Great Northern practice: L.N.W. Executive Ctee Mins, 7 Jan. 1858, LNW1/149; Traffic Ctee Mins, 28 Mar. 1858, LNW1/168, BTHR.

4 Octuple Ctee Mins, 10 Mar. 1852, 10 July 1854, etc., RCH1/505, BTHR.

5 E.g. Huish to Saunders, 18 Oct. and 20–8 Oct. 1852, HL1/31, BTHR.

running an additional weekly excursion in 1857, at a time when the two companies were competing for the London–Liverpool traffic.[1]

By 1858 Euston provided regular tourist tickets for resorts in Ireland, North Wales, Yorkshire, and the Lake District, and was instrumental in opening up new holiday playgrounds, among them the Isle of Man, the Lancashire 'watering places', and Central Wales.[2] Huish also organized regular Easter and Whitsun excursions, connecting London, the Midlands, and the North. Through-booking was encouraged by a system of traffic agreements, and facilitated by the increased scope and efficiency of the Clearing House. In this way, Huish was able to secure improved travel facilities to Ireland (especially Belfast) and to the West of England, and in 1855 there was an attempt to obtain through-booking for passengers travelling to the Paris Exhibition.[3]

Huish also continued to take part in the development of the company's ordinary facilities. He remained responsible for new lines, for the protection of local traffic from dislocation caused by main-line competition, and for the organization of special facilities, such as royal trains. There is also evidence to show that he intervened in minor matters which required immediate attention. On the whole, however, he was bypassed when minor traffic changes were decided. Since the company's service was probably the most extensive in the world at this time, it is hardly surprising that subordinate officers were given considerable scope in settling local issues.

Passenger traffic varied widely in price and quality, and it is difficult to draw general conclusions on the London & North Western's services. Statistics from parliamentary sources, which include from 1852 a series of passenger-mile figures, make possible a rough analysis of the main trends of the company's accommodation policy and experience, although the results may be misleading. It is important to understand, for example, that the company's network expanded in the 1850s to include a number of branch-lines where the traffic circumstances differed from those of the main routes. Table 25 indicates that although the company carried an increasing number of passengers overall, gains were made in the second and parliamentary classes only, and the profitable first-class sector remained static. The decline in third-class passengers was probably a change of definition rather than of facility, and taking the third and

1 L.N.W. Executive Ctee Mins, 11 June 1857, LNW1/149, BTHR.
2 L.N.W. Timetable, 1857, TT19/1A, BTHR. (See line illustrations.) See also
  Midland Counties Herald, 1851–8, and especially 14 Aug. 1856, 18 June 1857.
3 L.N.W. Traffic Ctee Mins, 10 June 1858, LNW1/168; Road & Traffic Ctee Mins,
  13 Jan. 1854, LNW1/140; Executive Ctee Mins, 8 June 1855, 24 Apr. 1857,
  LNW1/148–9, BTHR.

October—1857.

LONDON AND NORTH WESTERN RAILWAY.

ART TREASURES
EXHIBITION.

The Public are informed that Parties taking

TOURIST TICKETS TO THE LAKES,
NORTH WALES,
THE ISLE OF MAN,
The Lancashire Watering Places, and Ireland,
BY THIS ROUTE,

(full particulars of which may be had on application at the principal Stations of the Line), are permitted to break their Journey at MANCHESTER.

BY ORDER,

General Manager's Office,
Euston Station.

MARK HUISH.

SEA BATHING.

ABERYSTWITH, TOWYN, & ABERDOVEY,
FROM LONDON IN 13 HOURS.

Messrs. TAYLOR & COMPANY'S well-appointed Four-horse Mail and other COACHES, in connexion only with the London and North Western, and Shropshire Union Railways, leave the Lion Hotel Coach Office, the George and Raven Hotels, and Railway Station, Shrewsbury, as under:—

THE GREYHOUND
Every MONDAY, WEDNESDAY, and FRIDAY, at 10.45 a.m.,
Via WELSHPOOL, NEWTOWN, AND LLANIDLOES,

After the arrival of the Fast 1st and 2nd Class Train, leaving London (Euston Station) at 6.15 a.m., Rugby, 8.25 a.m., Birmingham (New Street Station) 9.9 a.m., Worcester 7.55 a.m., Kidderminster, 8.25 a.m., Dudley, 9.0 a.m., Wolverhampton (High Level) 9.23 a.m., Macclesfield 6.25 a.m., Stoke, 7.50 a.m., Stafford 10.0 a.m., and from Liverpool, Manchester, and the North (see Time Tables and Bradshaw's Guide), returning the alternate days from the Gogerddan Arms Hotel, Aberystwith, at 7.0 a.m., in time for the UP FAST TRAIN arriving in London at 9.30 p.m., Birmingham, 7.0 p.m., Wolverhampton at 6.20 p.m., and for Trains leaving Stafford for Liverpool, Manchester, and the North.

THE ROYAL MAIL,

Daily from the Lion Hotel Coach Office, at 4.0 a.m., via Welshpool, Newtown, and Machynlleth, after the arrival of the Mail Trains from London, Birmingham, Wolverhampton, and the South, and from Liverpool, Manchester, Stafford, and the North; returning from the Belle Vue Hotel, Aberystwith, daily, at 11.0 a.m., arriving at Shrewsbury in time for the Mail Train from Birmingham, Wolverhampton, London, Liverpool, and Manchester.

THE ALLIANCE,

Daily (Sundays excepted), at 3.30 p.m., to Welshpool and Newtown, after the arrival of Trains leaving London at 10 a.m., Rugby 12.40 p.m., Birmingham 12.55 p.m., Wolverhampton (High Level) 1.25 p.m., Liverpool 11.15 a.m., Manchester 11.15 a.m., and Stafford 2.30 p.m. Returning from Newtown at 8.0 a.m., Welshpool at 9.30 a.m., arriving in Shrewsbury in time for the 1st and 2nd Class Train, leaving Salop at 1.9 p.m. for London, Birmingham, Stafford, Wolverhampton, Kidderminster, Worcester, and the South, and for Trains for Liverpool, Manchester, and the North.—For further particulars, see Time Bills and Bradshaw's Guide.

Passengers and Parcels can now be Booked Through, by Coach and Railway, at the Company's appointed Offices at and between Aberystwith and Shrewsbury to London, Birmingham, Wolverhampton, Rugby, Chester, Stafford, Liverpool, Manchester, and most Stations on the London and North Western Line, as under:—

At Aberystwith	The Belle Vue, and Gogerddan Arms.
,, Machynlleth	Wynnstay Arms.
,, Llanidloes	Queen's Head.
,, Newtown	Elephant and Castle, and Bear's Head.
,, Welshpool	Royal Oak.

By this the most direct and expeditious route, passengers are saved the inconvenience of re-booking, and are not subject to change of Carriage between Shrewsbury and London.

For Fares and Times of Departure, apply at the above Offices, or at the Lion Coach Office, Shrewsbury.

N.B.—The Company will do all they can to ensure punctual arrival, but they cannot guarantee it, and therefore do not hold themselves responsible should they arrive too late for these trains.

parliamentary figures together, there was, under Huish's direction, an absolute increase of over 40 per cent between 1851 and 1859. By 1858–9, lower-class passengers made up about 60 per cent of the total.

In table 26 the statistics of passenger-miles travelled indicate an absolute increase in all classes, although the period of comparison differs from that in table 25. Nevertheless, looking at the percentage shares, a shift of emphasis from the higher to the lower classes is again suggested. This assumption is, of course, borne out by the minute-books, and fits in with the general hypothesis that the company's services became more broadly based in response to competition. However, the passenger-mile statistics are important in qualifying the impression, given by other statistical measures, that the first and second classes were less important than the parliamentary traffic. In fact, as far as passenger-miles are concerned, the second-class predominated, with the first and parliamentary sectors of roughly equal proportions. The key to this conclusion is obtained from a study of the average distance travelled by each class: Table 27 demonstrates the continuing importance to the company of first- and second-class travel, and it may be suggested that the increase in the numbers of lower-class passengers was due mainly to the opening of cheap, short-distance branch-line facilities, rather than to the growing interest in longer-distance excursions.[1] The temporary increase in third-class passenger-mileage in 1854–5 is more difficult to explain, however. It appears that the average distance travelled by this class was more than double that in 1852–3. The reasons for this are not documented, but the company was certainly experimenting with low fares in a number of localities at this time.[2]

London & North Western passengers enjoyed improved facilities in the 1850s, but the price of exceptional services, granted under competitive constraints, was the constant possibility of temporary inconvenience. Huish was at the heart of some of the more notorious examples of 'obstruction'. He was responsible for deliberate blocking tactics at Wolverhampton in 1851–2, and at Manchester (London Road) in 1857–8, which were aimed at rival companies. There were frequent complaints of passengers being directed over circuitous routes so that the company might retain their custom.[3] Huish was also adept at browbeating minor

1 Cf. the findings of G. R. Hawke, *Railways and Economic Growth in England & Wales 1840–1870*, (1970), 51.
2 See below, p. 198.
3 Note the complaint of a lady sent from Liverpool to Oxford via Bletchley, instead of over the far shorter Great Western route from Birmingham: Huish's letter to Revd R. Walker, 29 Dec. 1852, HL1/31, BTHR.

October—1857.

LONDON AND NORTH WESTERN RAILWAY.

EXCURSIONS
TO
THE SEA-SIDE.

EXCURSION TICKETS FOR TWENTY-EIGHT DAYS,

Commencing in JUNE, and ending 31st OCTOBER, will be issued from the undermentioned Stations to

SCARBOROUGH, WHITBY,- FILEY,
BRIDLINGTON, OR HARROGATE,
AND BACK,

At the following REDUCED FARES, with the option of returning so as to arrive at the Station at which the Tickets were taken, on any day not exceeding 28 days from the date of issue.

STATIONS.	SCARBORO', WHITBY, FILEY, OR BRIDLINGTON.		TO HARROGATE.	
	1st Class.	2nd Class.	1st Class.	2nd Class.
FROM	s. d.	s. d.	s. d.	s. d.
London	51 0	35 0	43 0	32 6
Oxford	51 0	35 0	43 0	32 6
Northampton	45 0	33 0	35 0	27 0
Liverpool	33 0	24 0	20 0	15 0
Manchester	26 0	20 0	14 0	10 6
Huddersfield	21 6	15 6	9 0	6 6
Oldham	26 0	20 0	14 0	10 0
Stockport	27 0	21 0	15 0	11 0
Staleybridge	26 0	20 0	14 0	10 6
Macclesfield	28 0	22 0	15 0	12 0
Crewe	30 0	24 0	17 6	13 6
St. Helens Junction	30 0	23 0	17 6	13 6
Warrington	30 0	23 0	17 6	13 6
Stafford	32 6	24 0	20 0	15 0
Wolverhampton	35 0	25 0	22 6	16 0

The whole of these Tickets are issued by the Ordinary Trains of the Company. The First Class Tickets are available by ANY Train, and the Second by such Trains as have Second Class Carriages attached. They will not be recognised for the Return Journey, unless they have been presented and Stamped on the day of return, at the Railway Booking Office, at either Scarborough, Whitby, Filey, Bridlington, or Harrogate.

Passengers going to or returning from Scarborough or Whitby, are at liberty to break their journey by remaining One Night at York; and Passengers going to or returning from Filey or Bridlington, by remaining One Night either at York or Hull.

Children under Three years of age, Free; above Three and under Twelve, Half-fares.

BY ORDER,

General Manager's Office,
EUSTON STATION.   **MARK HUISH.**

LONDON AND NORTH WESTERN RAILWAY.

MANCHESTER
Art Treasures Exhibition.

Until Further Notice, or the Closing of the Exhibition, the Public are requested to take Notice that

RETURN TICKETS ISSUED TO THE EXHIBITION,

From Stations on this Line,

EIGHTY MILES FROM MANCHESTER,
WILL BE EXTENDED FOR SEVEN DAYS,

Including the day of Departure and that of Return.

General Manager's Office,
EUSTON STATION.

BY ORDER,

                                    MARK HUISH.

Table 25
London & North Western passenger numbers, by class, 1851–9

Year July–June	First	%	Second	%	Third	%	Parlt.	%	Total
1851–2	1,120,841	13.65	2,902,182	35.83	1,086,738	13.23	3,101,739	37.76	8,212,438
1852–3	1,275,099	14.08	2,985,300	32.96	1,088,291	12.02	3,706,679	40.93	9,057,069
1858–9	1,236,190	11.43	3,548,026	32.81	947,845	8.77	5,081,492	46.99	10,818,554

Source: Accounts & Papers P.P.1852, XLVIII, 1852–3, XCVII, 1859, Sess. 2, XXVII. Percentages refer to the share of each class in total numbers carried. The years 1851–2 and 1852–3 are taken to reduce the effect (in comparisons) of the exceptional Great Exhibition period.

Table 26
London & North Western passenger-miles, by class, 1852–8

Year July–June	First	%	Second	%	Third	%	Parlt.	%	Total
1852–3	63,755,290	28.38	80,000,394	35.62	16,233,022	7.23	64,623,371	28.77	224,612,617
1854–5	61,161,433	25.20	79,014,596	32.56	34,762,734	14.32	67,768,817	27.92	242,707,580
1857–8	68,372,553	26.71	90,069,671	35.19	23,117,118	9.03	74,396,991	29.07	255,958,333

Source: Accounts & Papers, P.P.1852–3, XCVII, 1854, LXII, 1854–5, XLVIII, 1857–8, LI.

companies into sending traffic by specified routes, as his relations with the Shrewsbury & Hereford Railway indicate.[1] Examples are legion, and were certainly not limited to the London & North Western: the Midland Railway once resorted to the sending of Scottish passengers via Morecambe and steamboat, to prevent the receipts from being pooled according to the English and Scotch Traffic Agreement.[2]

Table 27
London & North Western average distance travelled, by class, 1852–8 (in miles)

Year July–June	First	Second	Third	Parlt.	Total
1852–3	50.00	26.80	14.92	17.43	24.80
1854–5	47.72	23.34	35.72	17.35	25.45
1857–8	53.71	28.24	22.04	15.60	25.13

Source: Extracted from statistics of passenger numbers and miles, in Accounts & Papers, *cit.* tables 25–6.

It is hardly necessary to say that pricing was an exceptional difficulty for all managers. There could be little general theory to guide their actions, for a small alteration in the country's network might upset years of patient negotiation and many hours of tabulation in the manager's and audit departments. Huish's Report on Traffic of 1855 reflected this course of events. The result of five years' experience following the report of 1850, it confirmed his previous convictions about passenger and goods pricing under competitive pressure and illustrated them with a thorough statistical analysis. As before, he could offer no panacea for falling passenger income. Referring to his previous statement on the universal character of losses as traffic became more diversified, he added:

> I do not see that either increase of trains, variation of fares, or any stimulants which can be applied, will increase the passenger traffic in anything like the proportion of the expense which would be incurred . . . Traffic arrangements whereby the receipts are thrown into a common fund are the only means of mitigating the existing evil.[3]

1 E.g. G. Findlay's letter to Huish, 26 Oct. 1857, re booking to Manchester via Stafford, LNW8/26, BTHR.
2 English & Scotch Traffic Ctee Mins, 12 Jan. and 19 Feb. 1858, RCH1/508, BTHR.
3 Huish, 'Report . . . on Traffic . . .', 14.

This attitude, then, lay consistently behind Huish's actions in the 1850s, but he was aware of its shortcomings. His investigation of Great Western competition led him to believe that:

> . . . Great Western receipts have not increased to so large an extent as ours have diminished; an additional proof, if any were wanting, that the opening of a parallel line merely divides, and does not increase, the general Traffic, although the accommodation may, as in the present case, be doubled.[1]

Certainly, loss-making duplicate trains were run by the two companies after the traffic agreement of December 1854,[2] and elsewhere difficulties arose over the interpretation of agreements and pooling devices. The only other notable change since 1850 mentioned by Huish was the decline in express traffic in favour of ordinary first-class traffic, a result of the company's overall improvement in comfort and speed. The express fare differential thus offered a negligible benefit, and it is hardly surprising that passengers transferred to the cheaper accommodation. With successful competition dependent upon quality of service (especially relevant when prices were stabilized by agreement) companies found it more and more difficult to preserve class differences.

The general manager continued to handle pricing matters, although individual directors such as Smith and Chandos exercised a supervisory jurisdiction, especially as affairs became increasingly complicated by company rivalries. Huish, for example, was entrusted with the raising of fares after the signing of the 'Ten Towns' agreement, dealt with long-distance fares in particular, and fixed the initial schedules for newly-opened lines. In these tasks he often worked with interested directors, and sometimes acted as a result of their direct intervention. But he was almost always involved in the execution of pricing plans, and at liberty to adjust these in response to operating conditions. His influence was thus very great indeed.

The various analyses of passenger receipts serve as a useful indication of the general trend of the company's experience. As table 28 shows, the level of annual receipts changed very little between 1851 and 1859. The apparent rise in receipts in 1855–6 may be explained by the inclusion of the Buckinghamshire and North Union railways' returns for the first

1 Huish, 'Report . . . on Traffic . . .', 11.
2 *Ibid.*, 15. Note the London–Birmingham service of June 1856, in *Midland Counties Herald*, 5 June 1856, showing the following duplicates:
L.N.W.   6.15 a.m.   7.30 a.m.   2.00 p.m.   8.00 p.m.
G.W.R.   6.00 a.m.   7.40 a.m.   2.00 p.m.   8.10 p.m.

Table 28
London & North Western passenger receipts, by class, 1851–9

Year July–June	First	%	Second	%	Third	%	Parlt.	%	Total*	Total†
1851–2	£608,734	41.12	£530,441	35.84	£50,619	3.42	£281,483	19.02	£1,480,221	£1,431,938
1852–3	549,438	41.29	458,157	34.43	50,023	3.76	263,875	19.38	1,330,768	1,277,281
1853–4	541,438	40.35	467,883	34.87	47,961	3.57	272,899	20.34	1,341,644	1,292,113
1854–5	514,786	38.17	452,462	33.55	92,981	6.89	276,119	20.47	1,348,745	1,279,902
1855–6	524,142	37.89	448,552	32.43	91,640	6.63	306,882	22.19	1,383,202	1,344,521
1856–7	554,606	39.17	456,516	32.24	73,790	5.21	319,096	22.54	1,415,827	1,415,827
1857–8	533,311	37.23	500,518	34.94	82,209	5.74	304,292	21.24	1,432,590	1,381,185
1858–9	518,409	35.18	545,204	37.00	68,938	4.68	324,343	22.01	1,473,420	1,389,353

Source: Accounts & Papers, *cit.*, Company Accounts, RAC1/233, BTHR. Season tickets (not shown here) account for between 0.60% and 1.13% of total receipts.

* Total receipts as shown in Parliamentary Returns.

† Total receipts as shown in the company's own Accounts, where the class receipts are *not* given.

time, while the Chester & Holyhead Railway accounts were included from 1 January 1859, affecting the year 1858–9. Taking these changes into consideration, it appears that absolute gains in gross receipts in the second, third, and parliamentary classes were balanced by a fall in first-class revenue, which had the effect of stabilizing overall receipts, despite an increase in mileage worked, in passenger-mileage, and in train-mileage, which added greatly to costs.

The company's statistics of receipts per-mile and per train-mile suggest falling earnings.[1] The limitations of such analyses must, of course, be recognized—they are independent of loads and track capacity, for example—but they are reinforced by use of the available passenger-mile returns which show a fall in average receipts per passenger-mile (i.e. in the average fares per mile):

Table 29
London & North Western receipts per passenger-mile, by class, 1852–8

Year July–June	First	Second	Third	Parlt.	Total*	Total†
1852–3	2.07*d.*	1.37*d.*	0.74*d.*	0.98*d.*	1.42*d.*	1.36*d.*
1853–4	2.02	1.37	0.77	0.98	1.41	1.36
1854–5	2.02	1.37	0.64	0.98	1.33	1.27
1855–6	2.02	1.36	0.68	0.99	1.34	1.30
1856–7	2.01	1.38	0.77	0.98	1.38	1.38
1857–8	1.87	1.32	0.85	0.98	1.34	1.30

Source: Accounts & Papers, *cit.*, and Company Accounts, *cit.*
* Using total receipts as shown in Parliamentary Returns.
† Using total receipts as shown in the company's own Accounts.

The table indicates that the fall occurred in the first and second classes. The third class fluctuated—the experiments of 1854–6 clearly affected average fares—and the parliamentary returns were steady. The above figures are also substantiated both by the average-fare estimates presented to Parliament, and by extracted fare schedules from other sources, such as timetables.

The policy which Huish favoured in 1850, namely to develop lower-class receipts, appears to have met with some success, but at the expense of first- and second-class patronage. This was chiefly a response to the

1 Huish, 'Report . . . on Traffic . . .', 12, giving earnings per mile, 1846–54; L.N.W. Company Report, February 1862, re annual accounts for receipts per train-mile, 1851–9, RAC1/233, BTHR.

reduction of differences in comfort between the classes, and also to a relaxation of the definition of parliamentary trains (which were exempted from passenger duty and therefore attractive to the companies). The extent of *net* passenger revenue is more a matter of conjecture, of course, but there seems little doubt that first-class traffic, despite reduced fares, remained a very valuable feature for the company. The effect of sporadic rate-wars is a further imponderable. A trend towards lower-class accommodation and a fall in first-class fares could well be explained in competitive terms alone, rather than as a result of an abstract pricing policy designed to maximize revenue.

Comparison with average fares for the United Kingdom suggests that the London & North Western's fares under Huish's management were consistently lower than those of the other major companies, a fact which had been also true of the previous period. A table (table 30) compiled from parliamentary sources gives the company lower per-mile fares on all except the parliamentary class.

Table 30
Average fares per mile of major United Kingdom railways, 1852, 1855, 1858

| Period Jan.–June | Sample | Fares by class in pence per mile | | | |
		First	Second	Third	Parlt.
1852	10 railways excluding the L.N.W.	2.28	1.56	0.81*	0.89
1852	Stated L.N.W. average	2.04	1.36	0.81	0.98
1855	11 railways excluding the L.N.W.	2.10†	1.53	0.77‡	0.86
1855	Stated L.N.W. average	2.02	1.37	0.66	0.98
1858	11 railways excluding the L.N.W.	2.06	1.50	0.83§	0.93
1858	Stated L.N.W. average	1.79	1.30	0.80	0.98

Source: Accounts & Papers, *cit*. The companies in 1852 were: Great Western, Midland, Eastern Counties, Lancashire & Yorkshire, South Eastern, Great Northern, Caledonian, London & South Western, York & North Midland, York Newcastle & Berwick; re 1855 and 1858, the last two companies amalgamated to form the North Eastern, and the London Brighton & South Coast, and Manchester Sheffield & Lincolnshire companies were added.
* 7 railways.
† Omitting the Caledonian, average = 2.21*d*.
‡ 8 railways.
§ 8 railways.

There is a strong possibility of error due to the unweighted character of the averages, but the same trend is reflected in an estimate of average fares for the United Kingdom prepared by Mihill Slaughter, using the Government's Report of 1858. Comparing his data with the company figures in table 29, it appears that the company's first-, second-, and third-class fares were lower than the country's average, but that a higher charge for parliamentary passengers had the effect of raising the average overall fare above that of the United Kingdom, due to the difference in relative importance of the various classes.[1]

Within this general framework, it is impossible to investigate satisfactorily the relation of long- to short-distance fares. Huish was in favour of keeping the latter as high as possible, but competitive pressure, and especially the extension of period returns at reduced tariffs, worked against this. But statistics drawn from timetables, which might throw light on the company's actions, are suspect for a great many reasons. The selection of a sample is far from random, and only ordinary fares are quoted, thereby tending to raise any estimates of average fares. Data extracted for 1857–8 suggest that in normal circumstances the short-distance fares were lower than their long-distance counterparts, a situation which is verified by evidence on experimentation with local fares to test demand.[2] There are several examples of such tests in the 1850s, following Huish's recommendations in his report of 1850. The results, however, were generally disappointing. Fare cuts in the Coventry–Birmingham, Liverpool–Warrington, Manchester–Macclesfield, and Bedford areas were made in 1854, but gross receipts fell despite increased patronage. The Coventry–Birmingham fares, for example, were reduced to under $1d.$ a mile first- and to $\frac{1}{2}d.$ third-class, but reported losses in the first three months of 1855 caused their abandonment.[3] The introduction of services to Kew was also a failure by 1854,[4] while other potentially successful experiments could not be implemented because of difficulties with rival companies. Huish estimated that, in all, the experiments cost the company over £1,000 in lost receipts. Nevertheless, he did attack an

---

1 M. Slaughter, *Railway Intelligence*, vol. XI (1861), 286–9. In 1858, for example, average U.K. fares were said to be: first, $2.09d.$; second, $1.46d.$; third and parliamentary, $0.88d.$; average (all classes), $1.28d.$
2 See Appendix, table 57.
3 L.N.W. Special Fares Ctee Mins, 11 Aug. and 3 Oct. 1854, LNW1/54; L.N.W. Mins, 13 Jan. 1855, LNW1/22; Executive Ctee Mins, 13 Apr. 1855, LNW1/148; Road & Traffic Ctee Mins, 10 Nov. and 8 Dec. 1854, 12 Jan. and 9 Mar. 1855, LNW1/140, BTHR.
4 L.N.W. Road & Traffic Ctee Mins, 13 Jan. 1854, LNW1/140, BTHR.

outstanding obstacle to uniformity of charge—the six-mile clause[1]—and in early 1855 fares calculated in accordance with this were revised to conform to the standard company scale.

Comprehensive tests of long-distance pricing were very rarely possible, for the uncontrollable variables were many. The complexities of traffic agreements and the strong possibility of retaliation by rival companies acted as a strong disincentive. But the period after 1851 did see a great extension of pricing concessions to the public, and Huish followed other companies in extending the availability of return tickets, excursions, and tourist facilities to test demand, while also making special provision for a variety of seasonal and exceptional traffics.[2] Extensions of availability usually followed the onset of competition. Thus, the struggle with the Great Western for London–Birmingham traffic led Huish to recommend and secure first-class day tickets on express trains in 1851, and two- and three-day returns in the following year. The growth of excursion facilities in the same area was a further response to competitive pressures. The validity of holiday tickets was extended to include travel on any day and for a period of up to 28 days, and periodic excursions, such as those from Birmingham to London, which had begun as day returns, were being advertised in 1856 for periods from three to 19 days.[3] This was perhaps the inevitable outcome of a pricing stalemate in which excursion fares were fixed at very low rates,[4] and the same can be seen in other competitive areas, and especially in Lancashire. Here, ordinary trains were run at excursion rates, and Huish was forced to extend the validity of day tickets in response to the actions of competitors. Such activity looked forward to the ultimate pricing concession of the 1850s—the abolition of express fares, which was effected by the Midland on its ordinary trains in 1859 after Huish's resignation.[5]

The efforts made by Huish to retain as much of the market as possible by means of pricing agreements and traffic pools have received the most attention in previous writings. Certainly, the traffic pool was one of the most significant developments of the 1850s. Some aspects of the policy

---

1 On the six-mile clause, see above, p. 74, n.1.
2 E.g. for Irish harvestmen, troops, emigrants, and pauper children. See L.N.W. Road & Traffic Ctee Mins, 12 Sept. 1851, 30 June 1853, LNW1/140; Executive Ctee Mins, 26 Feb. 1857, LNW1/149, BTHR.
3 E.g. *The Times*, 4 July 1851; *Midland Counties Herald*, 10 June 1852, 28 July 1853, 8 May 1856, 28 May 1857.
4 Fares of 12*s.* and 7*s.* return were equivalent to 0.64*d.* and 0.37*d.* per mile. Longer-period tickets cost 20*s.* and 9*s.* 6*d.*, = 1.06*d.*, and 0.50*d.*
5 *Midland Counties Herald*, 16 Dec. 1858, and see GN1/282/12, BTHR.

have been considered above, especially in discussing passenger accommodation, but the intricate workings of the various pricing agencies (which considered both passenger and goods traffic), the effect on the London & North Western's business, and the rôle played by Huish remain to be investigated.

7

The London & North Western Railway 1851-60
The effects of severe competition part II

1 Pricing agreements

Pricing agreements were central to Huish's traffic policy in the 1850s. They were the chief instrument in an effort to maintain the London & North Western revenue position in the face of intensifying competition from alternative routes. The surviving material, although scanty, throws some light on Huish's participation in the various pricing conferences, and facilitates a rough estimate (if no more) of the financial implications of his efforts.

The system operated by the London & North Western depended on two major devices: firstly, the secret 'Confederate' traffic agreements, involving so-called 'friendly' companies (including the Midland, Lancashire & Yorkshire, and Manchester Sheffield & Lincolnshire), by means of which traffic and rates were regulated principally for the benefit of the Euston route; and secondly, the 'pooling' agreements, to which the Great Northern was a major party, in which the traffic receipts were divided in agreed and fixed proportions between certain routes and between specified companies (see map 6 on pp. 216–17).

Passenger traffic was in general far easier to arrange than goods traffic. The determination of price, class, and speed could often be solved easily, whereas managers frequently disagreed about the use of goods waggons, demurrage, and a variety of special concessions offered to consignors. On the other hand, it was easier to evade regulations affecting passengers, especially by means of re-booking devices.[1] Most of the agreements, whether relating to passengers or goods, contained the stipulation that equal rates be charged by each company over each route. But this alone soon proved to be inadequate, and Huish's main contribution to railway policy lay in the conception of the 'pooling' agreement which by securing for his company a fixed proportion of the available market prevented traffic from falling entirely to a quicker and more convenient route. Thus, whatever the behaviour of demand for the services of the competing companies, financial adjustments made through the Railway Clearing House guaranteed a fixed share of income. It was in this attempt to reduce the loss of profitable long-distance traffic that Huish helped to create an intricate system of traffic divisions.

Passenger traffic was undoubtedly of major importance in the early years of the pooling agreements. The Great Northern's goods traffic was at first meagre (except for south Yorkshire coal), and the London & North Western enjoyed the advantage of a well-organized and established mode of operation. The initial conflict arose over passenger services from Yorkshire to London during the Great Exhibition of 1851. The opening of the Great Northern upset the division of traffic previously agreed by Huish and the Midland Railway, and on the failure of the three companies to agree, the dispute was referred to the arbitration of William Gladstone. His decision of August 1851, which related to six key towns—York, Leeds, Sheffield, Wakefield, Doncaster, and Lincoln—awarded the majority of the passenger traffic to the Great Northern.[2] Huish was able to raise

1 See below.
2 See the 'Six Towns' Award, 26 Aug. 1851, in the Appendix. The events leading up to the decision are recounted in Grinling, *op. cit.*, 92–106, and H. G. Lewin, *The Railway Mania and its Aftermath* (1936), 428–36.

fares by 15–18 per cent, but price stability was short-lived. A struggle developed for control of the Nottingham traffic via the Ambergate Nottingham & Boston line, and while the respective directors squabbled over policy, Huish evaded Gladstone's award by encouraging re-booking, first at Normanton, and then at Peterborough, where the 'agreed' fares were cut by over 30 per cent.

The eventual outcome of renewed competition was the 'Ten Towns' agreement, which from May 1853 extended the division of traffic to include Nottingham, Newark, Stamford, and Peterborough. Nottingham passenger traffic was shared equally, but the bulk of the remainder was awarded to the Great Northern, Huish's reward being the exclusion of his rival from the east Midlands in general.[1] A further breakdown occurred in 1856. Huish, realizing the danger to the London & North Western of the 'Little' North Western Company's Skipton to Lancaster route, tempted Seymour Clarke, the Great Northern general manager, with an offer to extend the existing pool to the area west of Sheffield, hitherto a monopoly of the Euston interest, but his careful negotiations were wrecked by the intervention of Denison, the Great Northern chairman.[2] The 'Ten Towns' Agreement expired on 1 January, and a fierce rate-war followed in February, forcing the companies to submit to Gladstone's arbitration once more. His decision of April 1857 increased the share of passenger traffic due to the Great Northern route, extending the scope of the division to include Bradford, Halifax, and the Lincolnshire coast.[3] It was becoming clear by this time that Huish's stalling tactics were no longer of much practical worth in view of the very low percentage of passenger traffic awarded to the 'Confederacy'.

The second major pool covered traffic between England and Scotland. Huish played a prominent part in the creation of the 'Octuple' and 'Sextuple' agreements, which prescribed a 50 per cent share of the disputed London–Edinburgh passenger traffic for the West Coast route via Preston, 37 per cent of the remainder for the Midland's route via Rugby and Normanton, and divided certain traffics between intermediate points and with Glasgow among the northern companies.[4] These initial divisions, operative for five years from 1 January 1851, secured a more than satisfactory settlement for the London & North Western, and Huish also

1 See 'Ten Towns' Agreement, 29 Apr. 1853, Appendix.
2 These were published as propaganda by the L.N.W.: *Minutes and Correspondence between the London and North Western, Midland, and Manchester Sheffield and Lincolnshire Companies, and the Great Northern Railway Company* (1856).
3 See Agreement, 22 Apr. 1857, Appendix.
4 Octuple and Sextuple Agreements, 17 Apr. 1851; see Appendix.

Table 31
The re-booking device as applied to Peterborough, 1852

From	Single fare to Peterborough by Midland			Peterborough to London (L.N.W.) cheap return			Total single fare to London by Midland and L.N.W.			Agreed single fare quoted by G.N.			Difference saved by re-booking at Peterborough		
	First	Second	Third	First	Second	Third	First	Second	Third	First	Second	Third	First	Second	Third
	s. d.	s. d.	s. d.	s. d.	s. d.	s. d.	s. d.	s. d.	s. d.	s. d.	s. d.	s. d.	s. d.	s. d.	s. d.
SHEFFIELD	18 9	14 1	—	2 6	2 0	—	21 3	16 1	—	32 0	24 0	—	10 9	7 11	—
LEEDS	23 2	17 7	11 0	2 6	2 0	1 3	25 8	19 7	12 3	36 6	27 6	17 2	10 10	7 11	4 11
YORK	26 0	18 11	11 2	2 6	2 0	1 3	38 6	20 11	12 5	39 6	29 0	17 6	11 0	9 11	5 1

Source: Seymour Clarke to Huish, 13 Mar. 1852, Great Northern Correspondence, GN1/274/9, BTHR.

dominated the meetings of the Octuple Committee of general managers convened to arrange matters connected with the pool. Enforcement depended on goodwill, and there were examples of members of the committee breaking the agreements, by using alternative routes not set down in the division—such as that from Lancashire to the North-East via the Leeds Northern Railway[1]—but in general the Committee helped to stabilize fares and to secure agreement on the pricing of special services.

Huish's most famous achievement in the arena of railway diplomacy was to secure the revision and renewal of the Scottish pooling arrangements, despite the opposition of Denison, in a series of complicated negotiations between March 1855 and January 1856. He acted as chairman of the Octuple Extension Committee, which sought to redefine the percentages due to each route, and to extend the scope of the pool to include most of the traffic to Glasgow and the north of Scotland via Greenhill Junction. Not only was Huish hampered by a dispute between the major Scottish railways (the Edinburgh & Glasgow and Caledonian companies were contesting Edinburgh–Glasgow traffic, while the Scottish Central and Edinburgh Perth & Dundee companies fought for the northern traffic), but he also faced the growing concern of the Midland Railway about its future as a north–south line. Its route via Normanton had declined rapidly in the face of competition from the Great Northern, and, shackled by a comprehensive traffic agreement with the London & North Western involving a common fund for all receipts—the 'Common Purse' Agreement of 1854[2]—it was unable to make use of the 'Little' North Western route for Anglo-Scottish traffic other than that between the Leeds area and Glasgow. The potentialities of this line as a further London–Scotland route (via the Great Northern and Midland) had certainly not escaped Huish, and was the major reason for his anxiety to accelerate the negotiations. His rival Clarke seems to have been unaware of this, despite the growing discomfort of the Midland general manager, Allport, at the poor position in which his company was being placed with respect to London to York traffic bound for the North.[3]

The Extension Committee, which was limited to a membership of eight managers, was an ideal instrument for Huish's diplomatic skills. The proposed divisions of passenger traffic instituted by him on behalf of the West Coast companies were on the whole accepted, and included in

1 Octuple Ctee Mins, 13 July 1852, 6 Apr., 8 June, 27 Oct., 4 Dec. 1853, RCH1/505, BTHR.
2 L.N.W. Mins, 9 Sept. and 11 Nov. 1854, LNW1/23, BTHR; see Appendix.
3 Octuple Extension Ctee Mins, 18, 19, 21 Apr., 21, 22 May, 2 June 1855, RCH 1/508, BTHR.

the English and Scotch Traffic Agreement, effective from 1 January 1856, a great success for his policy at the expense of Denison, in particular, who had attempted to wreck the talks by suggesting a territorial traffic division.[1] The new agreement pooled traffic from the major English towns to Glasgow, Edinburgh, and the north of Scotland. The London & North Western retained the larger part of the Glasgow passenger traffic, but conceded 60 per cent of the London–Edinburgh and 50 per cent of the London–north Scotland receipts. Leeds–Edinburgh passengers were also to be directed principally by the East Coast route, but the West Coast continued to monopolize traffic between Liverpool, Manchester, and Scotland. The 'Little' North Western found itself restricted to a 20 per cent share of traffic from the area south of Glasgow to Peterborough and the eastern counties, as its only gain over the provisions of the agreement of 1851.[2] This company quickly realized that the agreement of 1856 was merely a device to restrict its growth, but its traffic manager complained in vain to the committee of managers: Huish, who missed only five of its meetings between January 1856 and his retirement, was able to protect his advantage until all confidence in his methods was destroyed.[3] In time his rivals discovered that the great concessions which the London & North Western claimed to have made in 1856 were part of an attempt to hide the shaky foundations on which its supposed pre-eminence in Anglo-Scottish traffic rested.

Within two years Huish's system of alliances and pools suffered an almost total collapse. The Midland became increasingly disillusioned with only a 15 per cent share of London–York passenger traffic, and it took the opportunity to assert its independence when, following a last-ditch effort to prevent an alliance between the 'Little' North Western and the Great Northern, the 'Common Purse' agreement of 1854 was revealed and declared illegal in May 1857. Thereafter, the Midland began to divert traffic from the scope of the 1856 pool by using the route via Morecambe, and, having opened its Leicester–Hitchin line (also in May 1857), started to run through trains into King's Cross as a temporary solution to its difficulties in using the congested Euston line. This change of heart was symbolized by the resignation of Allport in the autumn of 1857.[4] Huish also lost the co-operation of Watkin, his former aide, who as general

---

1 Octuple Extension Ctee Mins, 17–18 Apr., 2 June 1855, RCH1/508, BTHR.
2 English and Scotch Traffic Agreement, 1 Jan. 1856, see Appendix.
3 English & Scotch Traffic Ctee Mins, 8 June 1858, quoting letter from Whelon to Newcombe, 20 Apr., RCH1/508, BTHR.
4 English & Scotch Traffic Ctee Mins, 7 May, 7 July, and 8 Dec. 1857, RCH1/508; R.C.H. General Managers' Ctee Mins, 12 Nov. 1857, RCH1/71, BTHR.

manager of the Manchester Sheffield & Lincolnshire proved an equally able diplomatist. Difficulties over traffic interchange, especially at Manchester, led Watkin to consider a repudiation of the traffic agreement of 1854, which had made his company a virtual satellite of the 'Confederacy'.[1] After complex inter-company machinations Watkin opened Retford Junction to the Great Northern, bringing Huish's rival into Euston's Lancashire strongholds in August 1857. Finally, the Lancashire & Yorkshire company acquired several points of difference with the London & North Western, particularly over breaches of agreement concerning passenger traffic from Huddersfield to London, from Liverpool to Manchester, and to Belfast. It also considered itself adversely affected by the operation of the English and Scotch pool, and was reluctantly forced to join its members.[2]

In February 1858 the London & North Western was engaged in a struggle to retain the valuable London–Manchester and London–Liverpool passenger traffics. Huish's policy at this time was a curious mixture of calm reasoning and irrational outburst. Although he understood that the Manchester Sheffield & Lincolnshire's strategy in reducing London–Liverpool fares was to claim a benefit to the public and thereby gain parliamentary approval for its Garston project—which promised a further Manchester–Liverpool line—he refused Clarke's offer to limit competition to London–Manchester trains.[3] Further, despite his realization that it was inconsistent to pool traffic in the east and withhold similar facilities in the west, his fall was closely linked with the failure of his final desperate attempt to bar the Great Northern from Lancashire.[4] Denison and Watkin proved to be equally unscrupulous, and were more than a match for him during the parliamentary proceedings to consider a Bill to cement the union between the Sheffield company and King's Cross. The London & North Western's disregard for its allies—which, in fairness to Huish, was fully supported by Chandos—was brought into the open, and, in particular, the offer of a territorial division at the expense of the Manchester Sheffield & Lincolnshire was exposed.[5] Huish's resignation soon followed. The Great Northern and Sheffield companies signed an alliance

1 See 'Statement Explanatory of Six Heads of Complaint preferred against the London and North Western Company . . .', 1857, LNW4/59, BTHR.
2 English & Scotch Traffic Ctee Mins, 17 Apr. 1856, 7 May and 7 July 1857, RCH1/508, BTHR.
3 Huish to Chandos, 29 Jan. 1858, HL2/R373/13/6; L.N.W. Executive Ctee Mins, 27 Nov. 1857, LNW1/149, BTHR.
4 Huish to Chandos, 15 Feb. 1858, HL2/R373/13/9, BTHR.
5 Clarke's evidence, *S.C. on the M.S. & L. and G.N. Bill*, P.P.1857–8, XV, QQ.3115–40.

for 50 years, an equal rates agreement replaced the pooling of English traffic, and only the Anglo-Scotch pool remained as a legacy of Huish's efforts. Even this was severely shaken, for intermediate rates had been forced lower than the agreed through charges, facilitating re-booking at Manchester, Preston, and Huddersfield in 1858.[1] Despite the obvious desire to secure a continuous traffic flow over separate lines, collaboration did not prove to be very successful. The ambition of certain companies to improve their traffic prospects naturally prevented a stable situation, and although the growing importance of the Clearing House as an impartial body prevented several disputes from degenerating into rate-wars, company conflict continued into the 1860s and beyond.

Huish also used traffic agreements in other areas, notably in the west Midlands. Competition with the Great Western, South Staffordshire, North Staffordshire, and Shrewsbury companies was eventually stabilized, although recurrent disputes tended to nullify the financial advantages so gained. Birmingham was staunchly defended from the Shrewsbury railways, and efforts were made to restrict the use by other companies of the London & North Western's Stour Valley branch to Wolverhampton. Not only were such actions financially damaging, but they proved less effective with the Great Western, which, unlike the Great Northern, was in 1851 a well-established company with ample resources. For passenger traffic, Huish was soon forced to accept the principle of equal fares, and in fact he treated Charles Saunders (of the Great Western) with great respect, in a lengthy period of negotiation leading to the equal rates agreement of December 1854. This made no attempt to direct traffic by specific routes. The proportions of traffic gained depended on the facilities offered by the two companies: regulations were made to prevent re-booking, and excursion fares were to be mutually agreed. The agreement appeared to be satisfactory to both sides, stabilizing the competition for traffic over a wide area, from London to Oxford, Leamington, Birmingham, Wolverhampton, Chester, and Liverpool.

The South Staffordshire was on the whole an ally of the 'Confederacy', its allegiance being secured principally by the 'Four Towns' pooling agreement, which divided traffic between Birmingham, Wolverhampton, Walsall, and Dudley. Competition with the North Staffordshire was, however, intermittent during the 1850s, although that railway was a party to the 'Common Purse' agreement with the Midland, and had contemplated amalgamation with the London & North Western. Huish's tactics did not

---

1 Re-booking was a violation of clause 20. See English & Scotch Traffic Ctee Mins, 8 Dec. 1857, 9 Mar. and 8 June 1858, RCH1/508, BTHR.

find favour with a company which never doubted that he wished to destroy its traffic prospects.

The financial effects of Huish's policies are very difficult to gauge. Judgments may easily be affected by the failure to take account of independent economic variables—the existence of a trade depression in the autumn of 1857 is a particular complication. Nevertheless, isolated evidence does suggest that the pooling agreements helped to forestall losses which otherwise would have taken place, either from an inability to charge remunerative rates, or merely because of the inevitable filtering of traffic through improved channels of communication. The material concerning the operation of the 'Ten Towns' pool from June 1854 shows the remarkable short-term success of Huish's efforts to divert traffic from its natural routes, a feature which was certainly beneficial in the short run, although the large losses incurred during the Lancashire rate-war tended to negate this. A table (table 32) showing the divisions of passenger traffic awarded, and the *actual* percentages carried by the respective routes, indicates that in all cases the Great Northern carried in excess of its awarded share, and was thereby compelled to make a repayment to the 'Confederate' interests of £16,000 for the year June 1854–5 on passenger traffic alone.

Table 32
Operation of the 'Ten Towns' pool: passenger traffic, 1854–5 (sample)

Traffic between LONDON and	Gladstone's award of 1853		Actual traffic carried		Traffic division as settled	
	L.N.W./ Mid.	G.N.	L.N.W./ Mid.	G.N.	L.N.W./ Mid.	G.N.
	%	%	%	%	%	%
YORK	20	80	4.51	95.49	17.11	82.89
LEEDS	35	65	16.15	83.65	31.23	68.77
SHEFFIELD	40	60	16.46	83.54	35.30	64.70

Source: 'Ten Towns' Extension Ctee Mins, 26 Nov. 1855, in *Minutes and Correspondence* . . . (1856), 7.

Certainly, the Great Northern made every effort to carry in excess of the award, in order to strengthen its position when renewal was due, but since the agreement specified that only 20 per cent of the gross receipts would be allowed as expenses on excess passenger traffic, Huish was in fact reaping the benefit in repayments on operations conducted by his rival. The same process can be seen in the results of the Octuple pool, where Huish reported that the first ten months from 1 January 1851 had seen excess carriage by all the East Coast companies.[1]

The effect of competition and rate-war upon revenue is again largely a speculative matter. There are a few surviving estimates of losses in specific cases—the opening of the Midland's Leicester–Hitchin line was computed to have caused a reduction of £500 in the 'coaching' receipts for May 1857, while the rate-war of 1857–8 was said to have lost the company about £57,000[2]—but these are isolated examples, and of little help in framing a general picture. The most valuable data are to be found in Huish's traffic report of 1855, which examined the major areas of falling revenue, especially those affected by the appearance of the Great Western as a major competitor. Huish's investigation, summarized in table 33, showed a fall in the company's passenger revenue of almost £35,000 over the first half of 1855. 'Exceptional' factors were isolated, from which it emerged that gains from pooling agreements were more than offset by a fall in inter-company bookings. But the major losses were in ordinary station takings, especially at London, Birmingham, and Manchester, much of which could be attributed to the competition of the Great Western.

The effects of Great Western competition were also examined for the first six months of 1852, 1854, and 1855. Revenue from London–Birmingham passenger traffic fell by 40 per cent over the three-year period. Losses also occurred on traffic between London and Wolverhampton, Chester, Oxford, and Shrewsbury, the only major exception being the London–Liverpool traffic, where despite a fall in express takings, the increases in other classes made for a rise of 17 per cent.[3] Huish estimated that the total loss to the London & North Western from Great Western competition was about £70,000 per annum.[4] These statistics are in accord with the impression given by the minutes, and especially with Huish's repeated warnings in 1852 that unless fares were lowered the Birmingham –Liverpool traffic would be lost "as the traffic between Liverpool and Wolverhampton and Chester had been".[5] The fares quoted at the time of the cut-throat competition with the Shrewsbury companies did not leave either party an adequate margin for profit; nor did the standard fares

1 L.N.W. Road & Traffic Ctee Mins, 10 Feb. 1852, LNW1/140, BTHR.
2 L.N.W. Executive Ctee Mins, 11 June 1857, LNW1/149; L.N.W. General Meeting, 13 Aug. 1858, LNW1/2, BTHR.
3 Huish, 'Report . . . on Traffic . . .', 7–8, and see Appendix, table 58.
4 *Ibid.*, 8–10.
5 L.N.W. Road & Traffic Ctee Mins, 11 June 1852, LNW1/140, BTHR.

Table 33
**London & North Western 'coaching' receipts:
a comparison of the first six months of 1854 and 1855**

1. Schedule of lost revenue, 1854/5

Great Western competition	£16,137
O.W.W. competition	3,000
'Exceptional factors'*	5,048
Inter-company bookings	4,232
Minor stations	4,548
Parcels, dogs, horses	1,850
	34,815

2. 'Exceptional' elements, 1854/5

'Exceptional' gains		*'Exceptional' losses		
Revenue from:		Excursions		
Miscellaneous new sources	£1,590	(not repeated in 1855)	c.	£2,040
'Octuple' and 'Ten Towns'		Alteration of date of		
agreements	1,276	Parliamentary session	c.	2,000
New stations	1,170	Experimental fares (1854)		1,008
	4,036			5,048

3. Station takings, 1854/5 (sample)

Station gains		Station losses		Station losses	
Liverpool (G.J.)	£2,582	Birmingham	£5,569	Liverpool (L.&M.)	£1,380
Dudley Port	664	London	5,193	Manchester (Vic.)	1,337
Warrington	584	Wolverhampton	3,345	Birmingham (S.V.)	1,264
Leamington (Avenue)	409	Manchester (L.Rd)	2,842	Chester	1,107

Source: Huish, 'Report . . . on Traffic . . .', 3–11.

fixed by the eventual agreement with the Great Western compensate by
raising gross revenue, although, in per-mile terms, they were theoretically
high enough to ensure profitable operation, particularly for the London &
North Western, which enjoyed the shortest route in most cases (table 34).

As suggested before, the continued provision of duplicating transport
services, especially in the areas of highest profit, had an adverse effect
upon the company's passenger revenue, while there was a corresponding
neglect of minority interests in the framing of train timetables. Here,
competition was not necessarily beneficial to the public, nor did the competing railway companies derive any advantage.

It appears, therefore, that Huish's manipulation of traffic and pooling

Table 34
Equal passenger fares in the area affected by Great Western competition, January–June 1858

Journey from London to	Distance	Agreed fares (single)			Fares per mile		
		First	Second	Third	First	Second	Third
Birmingham	L.N.W. 113 miles	20s.	15s.	9s. 5d.	2.12d.	1.59d.	1.00d.
Birmingham	G.W.R. 129¼	20s.	15s.	9s. 5d.	1.86	1.39	0.87
Wolverhampton	L.N.W. 126	22s. 4d.	16s. 9d.	10s. 5d.	2.13	1.60	0.99
Wolverhampton	G.W.R. 141½	22s. 4d.	16s. 9d.	10s. 5d.	1.89	1.42	0.88
Shrewsbury	L.N.W. 162¼	27s. 4d.	20s. 6d.	12s. 11d.	2.02	1.51	0.95
Shrewsbury	G.W.R. 171	27s. 4d.	20s. 6d.	12s. 11d.	1.89	1.44	0.91
Chester	L.N.W. 179¼	33s	24s.	14s. 10½d.	2.21	1.60	0.99
Chester	G.W.R. 213¼	33s.	24s.	14s. 10½d.	1.86	1.35	0.84
Birkenhead	L.N.W. 194¼	35s. 6d.	26s.	16s. 1¼d.	2.19	1.54	0.99
Birkenhead	G.W.R. 228	35s. 6d.	26s.	16s. 3d.	1.87	1.32	0.85
Weighted average fare	L.N.W.				2.14d.	1.57d.	0.99d.
	G.W.R.				1.88	1.88	0.87

Source: *Bradshaw*, 1858; L.N.W. Company Timetable, 1858, TT2/2B & C, TT19/1B, BTHR. Great Western distances are taken from *Bradshaw*.

agreements brought to his company only short-term benefits in passenger traffic, and these were nullified to a great extent by a 12 per cent fall in receipts for 1858 (compared with 1857), amounting to £170,000.[1] It is not possible to measure the extent of Huish's savings before 1858, but these had in any case to be set against the money which the London & North Western itself paid to other companies in accordance with traffic agreements. This amounted to over £160,000 for passenger and goods traffic between July 1855 and December 1858.[2] Further, even during the operation of the important traffic pools, the machinery for enforcement was very inadequate. The Normanton meetings of passenger superintendents achieved very little in this period, lacking the attendance of London & North Western representatives. Some efforts were made to fix general pricing standards for exceptional traffics, but more important and effective work (such as service changes) was restricted in scope to the northern companies.[3] Even the more influential body of general managers concentrated upon goods affairs, discussing passenger policy only occasionally.

There are many examples of Huish's violation of agreements to favour his company, and it might seem that short-term benefits were thereby gained. But other companies were doing the same thing, and the effects of very low-priced express accommodation during periods of intense competition must have been damaging. The London to Sheffield fares of February 1856 were well below a penny a mile, while the notorious five-shilling return fares from London to Yorkshire in 1851 and from London to Lancashire in 1858 involved a mileage rate of about one-fifth of a penny.[4] Huish would have preferred to keep fares as high as possible, and his efforts to persuade the Great Western to maintain high day-return and excursion charges in 1852 illustrate this intention. Nevertheless, he failed to maintain high fares, and his failure is to be explained partly by intransigence—a refusal to accept that the newly-established railways had any right to take traffic from the London & North Western—and partly by the hostility of his rivals to his devious attempts to upset traffic agreements and alter traffic flows.

The major pooling agreements awarded the London & North Western

1 L.N.W. Company Accounts, see Appendix, table 55.
2 *Ibid.*, see Appendix, table 56.
3 R.C.H. Passenger Superintendents Meetings, 1851–9, RCH1/114, BTHR.
4 London–Sheffield single (177 miles): 11*s*. 3*d*. first, 5*s*. 8*d*. second, = 0.76*d*. and 0.38*d*. per mile; L.N.W. 5*s*. return fares from London–Manchester (378 miles) = 0.16*d*. per mile.

a far greater share of goods traffic, a reflection of the company's leading position in this service. The 'Six Towns' award gave the 'Confederate' interests 65 per cent of London–Leeds and 70 per cent of London–Sheffield goods traffic, its share in the remaining traffics being from 5 to 15 per cent higher than the corresponding passenger division. As a result of the 'Ten Towns' agreement, Huish secured 70 per cent of the Nottingham and Stamford traffic and two-thirds of the Peterborough trade (shared with the Eastern Counties), the latter surprising in view of the circuitous nature of the route via Northampton.[1] The share of the London–Edinburgh goods as secured by the Octuple agreement was also highly satisfactory, being 50 per cent for the West Coast route proper, and 25 per cent for the Midland route via Rugby.[2]

The altered arrangements after 1855 continued to provide Huish's company with higher goods than passenger percentages, a proof of the slowness with which the Great Northern developed all but its coal trade. The results of the 'Ten Towns' pool, 1854–5, noted above with regard to passenger traffic, proved slightly more favourable for Huish in respect of goods. The 'Confederacy' carried in excess of its share of Nottingham, Doncaster, and Halifax traffic, and its losses on the important York, Leeds, and Sheffield divisions were not so great as they had been for passengers. In fact, the monetary adjustment made by the Great Northern in favour of Huish amounted to only £8,355, about half that paid out for excess passenger traffic.

The revision of 1857 made substantial reductions in the London & North Western's goods position, especially in the share of Leeds, Wakefield, Sheffield, and Stamford traffics, but there were also a few adjustments in its favour, and the overall result was that the percentages remained at least double those for corresponding passenger traffic.[3] During the negotiations for the renewal of the Anglo-Scottish traffic pool, the dominant hold on most traffics possessed by 'Confederate' interests was not seriously challenged. Indeed, the generous offer of an equal share for the East Coast companies in important goods traffic between Leeds, Manchester, Bradford, and Scotland was withdrawn in favour of a 60–40 division, in Huish's favour.[4] The resulting 1856 Agreement, therefore, was a more than adequate device to protect a valuable goods network.

The organization of through goods traffic was recognized to be an extremely difficult task, and the minutes of various managers' committees

1 'Six Towns' and 'Ten Towns' agreements, see Appendix.
2 Octuple Agreement, see Appendix. Mineral traffic was not divided.
3 Agreement of April 1857, see Appendix.
4 Octuple Extension Ctee Mins, 27 Nov. 1855, RCH1/508, BTHR.

Table 35
Operation of the 'Ten Towns' pool: goods traffic, 1854–5 (sample)

Traffic between LONDON and	Gladstone's award of 1853		Actual traffic carried		Traffic division as settled	
	L.N.W./ Mid. %	G.N. %	L.N.W./ Mid. %	G.N. %	L.N.W./ Mid. %	G.N. %
YORK	25	75	17.99	82.01	23.61	76.39
LEEDS	65	35	49.75	50.25	61.96	38.04
SHEFFIELD	70	30	50.86	49.14	66.17	33.83
NOTTINGHAM	70	30	82.86	17.14	72.57	27.43

Source: 'Ten Towns' Extension Ctee Mins, 26 Nov. 1855, in *Minutes and Correspondence* . . . (1856), 8.

indicate clearly that goods pooling was given far greater attention than the passenger business. The early meetings of the Octuple Committee, for example, were devoted principally to the complications of agreeing upon a classification of goods, and to a consideration of traffic affected by the competition of coastal shipping.[1] The same was true of the equal rates agreement with the Great Western of 1854, a 'Northern Alliance' committee being set up under Huish's supervision to consider the adjustment of rates and special agreements. The London & North Western, Great Western, Oxford Worcester & Wolverhampton, Shropshire Union, and Bridgewater Canal were parties to an attempt to stabilize rates in the Birmingham and south Staffordshire area for a classification of over 730 items.[2]

There is hardly any evidence on the financial effects of goods pooling. Short-run benefits are suggested, and it also seems likely that the merchandise department of the London & North Western fared better than the passenger under the strain of competition, at least while Huish was general manager. For both types of traffic, however, pooling was but a temporary solution to an extremely difficult problem. The immature state of railway cartelization in the 1850s was proof of the fluid nature of the network and the equally fluid relations of its chief administrators. Huish himself admitted that traffic agreements lacked permanence,[3] and

1 Octuple Ctee Mins, 10–24 Sept., 22 Oct., 19 Nov., 10 Dec. 1851, RCH1/505, BTHR.
2 Northern Conference Mins, 19–23 Dec. 1854 *et seq.*, GW1/749, BTHR.
3 Huish's evidence, *S.C. on Railway and Canal Bills*, P.P.1852–3, XXXVIII, QQ.1212–13.

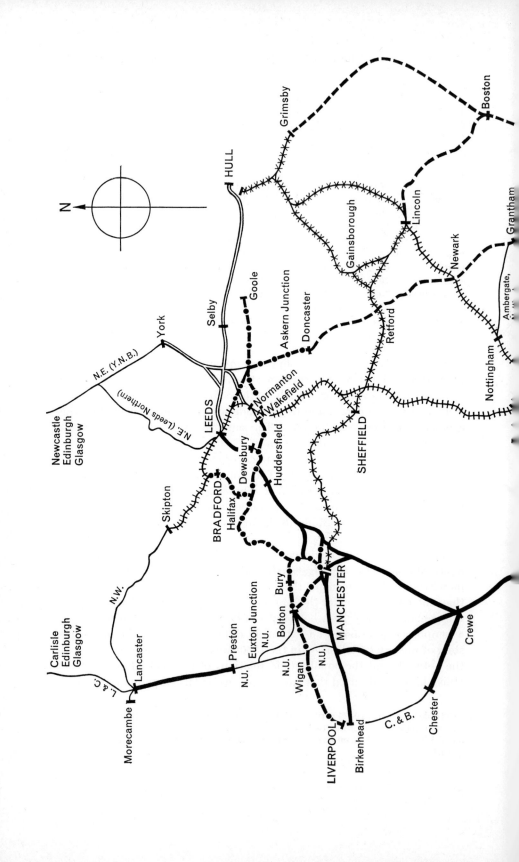

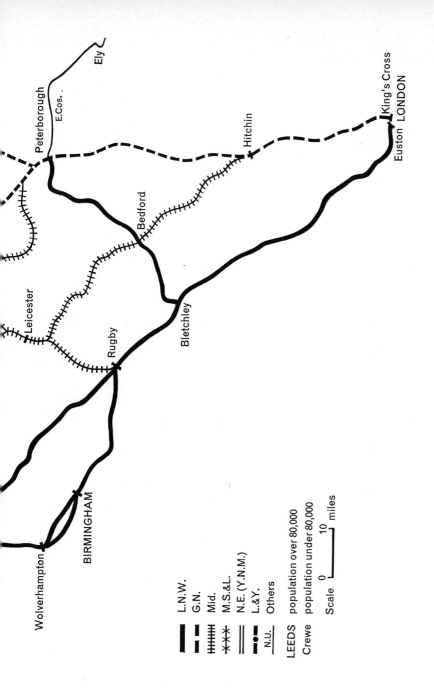

Map 6. Principal routes affected by 'Confederate'
and Great Northern pooling agreements in the 1850s. In 1854 the N.E. absorbed a
number of companies: names of these are given in parentheses, i.e. N.E.(Y.N.M.). The
N.U. (Preston-Wigan-Parkside and Euxton Junction–Bolton) was leased jointly by
the L.N.W. and L. & Y.

although his system collapsed, it should be remembered that amalgamation, potentially a more viable method of securing stability, was opposed
by Parliament. If, in these circumstances, we fault Huish's tactics, we
should also admire his 'Confederacy' as a bold example of strategic
planning in restrictive conditions.

2 Goods traffic

The study of pricing agreements has indicated that the London & North
Western continued to enjoy a predominance in goods traffic. What form
did this take, and how much can be attributed to Huish's management?
Here an attempt is made to answer both questions.

The company's goods traffic continued to expand after 1851, and gross
revenue increased steadily until the summer of 1857. There then followed
a temporary decline, attributed to a trade depression in Lancashire and
south Staffordshire and to the "reckless competition" for the profitable
London–Lancashire traffic, which affected receipts until 1859.[1] Nevertheless, the overall improvement in business was encouraging. A rise of 70
per cent in goods revenue between 1851–2 and 1858–9 kept pace with
additions to mileage operated, a feature which contrasted strongly with
the more static position of passenger traffic.[2] Not only did the company's
goods revenue come to exceed its passenger revenue,[3] but its share of the
United Kingdom's goods traffic became greater than its share of the
passenger traffic.[4]

The general picture, then, is one of growth. But not all goods items
enjoyed the same rates of growth. Receipts from coal traffic increased by
over 200 per cent between 1851 and 1859, while the merchandise (general
goods) and livestock traffics expanded by only about 50 and 60 per cent
respectively.[5] This caused a shift of emphasis in the goods account. Coal
receipts, which had contributed only about $4\frac{1}{2}$ per cent of total receipts in
1846 and 10 per cent in 1851, made up about 20 per cent by 1859. This

---

1 See Appendix, table 59, and L.N.W. General Meeting Reports, 19 Feb. and 13 Aug.
   1858, LNW1/2, BTHR.
2 Company Accounts, see Appendix, table 60.
3 See Appendix, table 55.
4 See Chapter V, table 24.
5 See Appendix, table 60.

was achieved at the expense of merchandise, for the share commanded by livestock traffic changed very little.[1]

The company did not distinguish between general goods and minerals (other than coal) in its merchandise accounts. Nor were receipts from other heavy items such as agricultural products separated. It is therefore difficult to test the hypothesis, raised in Chapter Five, that heavier freight was becoming increasingly important to the company. A number of isolated sources point to an increased concern with iron traffic, especially in south Staffordshire, while the discovery of extensive ironstone fields in Northamptonshire led Huish to negotiate a special contract in 1852 guaranteeing a shipment of 25,000 tons a year.[2] Huish also pressed the Road & Traffic Committee to provide for stone traffic at Hartshill, and the Goods Committee referred in 1856 to a "considerable" traffic in potatoes for the Birmingham and Liverpool areas. The negotiations with the Great Western Railway prior to the equal rates agreement of 1854 reveal that the London & North Western had made several special contracts to secure traffic in iron ore, pig iron, and other minerals, and the concern shown in the fixing of rates for grain and timber between Liverpool and Birmingham suggests a significant traffic in these articles. However, there is very little information on the quantities carried. From 1856 the parliamentary returns contain a more detailed analysis of goods tonnages and receipts, but here again coal is the only mineral to be isolated. Huish himself referred, in his report of 1855, to "large and increasing" profits from merchandise and mineral traffic, but made no attempt to distinguish between the two. Definite conclusions for the whole period are therefore likely to be dangerous, but it does appear from statistics for 1858 and 1859 that the company shared fully in the general increase of mineral traffic in the United Kingdom. The total mineral traffic carried by the railways (including coal) rose, for example, from 18 million tons in the last six months of 1855 to 27 million tons in the corresponding period of 1859. Of this latter tonnage the London & North Western carried nearly 8 per cent; at the same time, its share of the railways' total mineral receipts amounted to over 10 per cent.[3]

More information is available on the company's livestock and coal traffics. The former continued to be the responsibility of Fisher Ormandy,

1 See Appendix, table 59. Cf. the situation between 1846 and 1851, when the increasing share obtained by coal receipts was at the expense of livestock traffic: see above, p. 141.
2 L.N.W. General Meeting, 20 Feb. 1852, LNW1/2; Road & Traffic Ctee Mins, 9 Jan. 1852, LNW1/140, BTHR.
3 Accounts & Papers, P.P.1856, LIV, 1860, LXI.

the Cattle Manager, whose annual reports to Huish remained the chief means by which the General Manager supervised the business. Ormandy was responsible for the accommodation of the traffic, the organization of through services with other railways, and the implementation of seasonal service changes. He also had the authority to make pricing alterations for local traffic, although Huish continued to interfere in general rate changes, as he had done before 1851.[1]

The upward trend in both livestock traffic and revenue, begun in 1850, continued throughout the decade. Progress was halted in 1855 and 1857–8, however, by prolonged inter-railway competition.[2] Ormandy, in reporting a reduction in cattle traffic in 1855, pointed to the "fierce contest" of August 1855 for traffic from Liverpool to East Anglia, and a fall in the numbers sent to London from Leicester and Northampton.[3] The former was estimated to have cost the company £7,000 in lost revenue, while, in addition, the cattle traffic from the Aberdeen area was conceded to the East Coast route, at a cost of about £2,000 in 1855. Nevertheless, overall receipts did not fall in that year, and it appears that the increase in rates contemplated by Huish as early as 1853 and embodied in the tariff of 1 February 1855 was successful. Ormandy stated that the change had met with little opposition from the trade for most of the 82,000 rates in local use.[4] The average rate per waggon-mile was increased to 5.97d., and the deliberate surrender of the Aberdeen traffic was explained by its low yield of only about 3d. per waggon-mile.[5]

An estimate of the company's share of United Kingdom livestock traffic is available for the years 1856–9, obtained from Parliamentary Returns (table 36). It appears that about 16–18 per cent of the total animals and about 18–21 per cent of the receipts were obtained.

Ironically, it was the company's smallest livestock sector—the pig traffic—which commanded the largest share of United Kingdom traffic: in 1859, for example, over a third of the country's pig receipts was obtained. However, the data on receipts should be used with caution, due to the

1 See above, p. 146. On Ormandy's role see L.N.W. Road & Traffic Ctee Mins, 10 Feb. 1852, LNW1/140; Executive Ctee Mins, 13 Apr. 1855, LNW1/148, BTHR.
2 See Appendix, tables 55 and 61.
3 Ormandy, 'Report to the General Manager upon the Cattle Traffic of the London & North Western Railway for the Year 1855' (1856), confidential printed report, HL2/R102(3), BTHR, 177–8.
4 *Ibid.*, 184. On Huish's role see L.N.W. Road & Traffic Ctee Mins, 9 Sept. 1853; Executive Ctee Mins, 13 Apr. 1855, LNW1/140, LNW1/148, BTHR.
5 Ormandy, 'Report . . . upon the Cattle Traffic . . . for 1855', 178–80. See also G. Channon, 'The Aberdeenshire Beef Trade with London: a study in Steamship and Railway Competition 1850–69', *Transport History*, II (1969), 2–3.

Table 36
London & North Western's share of United Kingdom livestock traffic, 1856–9

	Number of animals				Gross receipts			
	1856 %	1857 %	1858 %	1859 %	1856 %	1857 %	1858 %	1859 %
Cattle	20.3	14.6	20.3	17.5	29.9	24.6	29.7	31.9
Sheep	23.0	15.9	16.3	15.2	33.6	31.2	28.3	31.1
Pigs	19.3	19.1	25.6	21.7	25.3	27.1	33.0	33.8
Total*	22.8	16.1	18.8	16.8	19.4	18.1	20.2	21.7

Source: Accounts & Papers, P.P.1857, Sess. 2, XXXVII, 1857–8, LI, 1859, Sess. 1, XXV, 1860, LXI.
*Total figures take into account 'unclassified' items: see Appendix, table 62.

large amounts which were not classified. About a third of the total livestock revenue distinguished by the railways fell into this category. Nevertheless, it is clear that the London & North Western's livestock traffic was of considerable importance, and it appears to have been protected fairly well from competition. The agreement which Huish inspired for the pooling of cattle receipts for traffic between southern Scotland and eastern England, operative from March 1853, secured much of the London traffic for the West Coast route, together with 50 per cent of the Eastern Counties and two-thirds of the London area division.[1] Ormandy reported in 1856 that the bulk of the traffic was being carried by the London & North Western via Lancaster, and that the receipts at competing points with the Great Western had also been maintained. Statistics provided by Ormandy on traffic handled at each station show the outstanding importance of the Irish cattle and pig trade handled at Liverpool. In 1855 the money taken there amounted to over £25,000, about half of the total local receipts; Irish business from the Chester & Holyhead Railway was similarly important, forming about 50 per cent of the traffic reaching the London & North Western from other lines.[2] This is not to deny that traffic *into London* was significant. The new cattle station built at Islington (opened in 1854) and the provision of a Metropolitan Cattle Market

1 Cattle Traffic Agreement, 28 Mar. 1853, between London & North Western, Great Northern, Newcastle & Carlisle, Lancaster & Carlisle, York Newcastle & Berwick, York & North Midland railways, LNW3/221, BTHR.
2 See Appendix, table 61.

(in 1855) were considered valuable developments in the retention of a remunerative trade.[1]

Coal traffic was also a leading sector of the goods traffic, as has been indicated above. Although sea and canal transport maintained an interest in its carriage, the railways increased their share of business, until by 1858 about 25 million tons were being conveyed annually. The London & North Western controlled about 10 per cent of the railways' tonnage and receipts.[2] Huish continued to play a decisive part in his company's arrangements, and he assumed particular responsibility for the negotiation of special bulk-consignment agreements. These were essential to the company, for the low coal rates imposed by Parliament precluded profit unless regular and large loads were guaranteed. The agreement with the Clay Cross company, referred to in Chapter Five, continued to operate: a similar agreement with the Ince Hall colliery was reached in 1853.[3] The terms offered included a $\frac{1}{4}d$. rebate (or "drawback") on a $\frac{3}{4}d$. rate per ton-mile for regular monthly consignments. Both collieries promised to send 45,000 tons a year. Huish was also interested in encouraging coal traffic in the Bolton area (estimated to be about 190,000 tons annually in 1856) and despite Lardner's much-publicized view that railway rates for journeys over 20 miles were prohibitive, it is clear that the London & North Western was eager to increase the average distance travelled by its coal trains. A General Meeting supported the policy in 1853, and the agreements with the Clay Cross and Ince Hall collieries specified traffics travelling over 80 and up to 200 miles.[4] The company also managed to tap the south Yorkshire coalfield, although the bulk of the traffic fell to the Great Northern Railway. The railways' coal traffic, if slow to develop on a long-distance basis, expanded rapidly in the 1850s, and the London & North Western was prominent in this development.[5]

1 L.N.W. Sthn. Road & Traffic Ctee Mins, 29 Mar. 1854, LNW1/145, BTHR, and Ormandy, 'Report . . . upon the Cattle Traffic . . . for 1855', 181–2.
2 In the years 1856–7 and 1857–8, L.N.W. coal tonnage was 2.3 and 2.5 million, or 8.8 per cent and 10.2 per cent of U.K. coal tonnage by rail. The company's share of coal receipts by rail amounted to 13.7 per cent and 10.5 per cent for the same years: P.P.1856, LIV, 1857, Sess.2, XXXVII, 1857–8, LI, 1859, Sess.1, XXV.
3 L.N.W. Agreements, LNW3/49–50; Road & Traffic Ctee Mins, 11 Mar. and 10 June 1853, LNW1/140, BTHR.
4 Lardner, *op.cit.*, 206–7, and see above, p. 141; L.N.W. Agreements, *cit.*
5 Cf. B.R. Mitchell, *Journal of Economic History*, XXIV (1964), 319, who refers to the slow growth of the railways' London coal traffic, and Hawke, *Railways and Economic Growth*, 166–73, who explains that railways first captured the inland coal traffic. The railways' London coal traffic grew rapidly after 1845: the L.N.W.'s traffic, only 1,600 tons in 1846, amounted to 152,000 tons in 1853; Huish, 'Report to the Road & Traffic Committee on an Extension of the Electric Telegraph' (1854), 6, printed confidential report, LNW1/716, BTHR.

Local goods rates were fixed chiefly by the goods managers concerned, and coal does not seem to have been an exception. Huish intervened directly, however, in matters concerning canal competition, and in problems involving accommodation, particularly in the London area. Competition by sea was, of course, an overriding problem, and one which faced all railways bringing coal to London. Huish was prominent in setting rates to meet this challenge, but resisted changes which might have threatened the stability envisaged by the inter-company pooling agreements. He also successfully negotiated a special coal traffic pool with the Grand Junction Canal in 1851, which divided the traffic between the canal and the London & North Western and Midland railways.[1] These examples make it clear that Huish intervened in important matters affecting coal traffic, and that delegation to regional goods managers was closely supervised.

A lack of comprehensive material prevents a similar analysis of the largest sector of the goods traffic—the merchandise, or general goods. Parliamentary statistics for 1858–9 reveal that the company carried over three million tons for the year beginning 1 July 1858, or about 11 per cent of the total United Kingdom traffic. Detailed information is at a premium, however. The great importance of the Liverpool traffic is certainly apparent. A set of station statistics indicates, for example, that in 1859 about 30 per cent of the company's merchandise trade originated in Liverpool, as did about 40 per cent of gross receipts (before deduction of terminal charges).[2] The outgoing London traffic must also have been considerable. The large depots at Camden and Haydon Square were reported to be fully utilized. No comparable data survive, however.

Huish's rôle does not appear to have altered significantly during the 1850s. He continued to arrange matters affecting the organization of the system in operation, and was especially entrusted with negotiations for new agency contracts in 1851 and 1857.[3] The agreement with Pickford & Co. and Chaplin & Horne of 1847 was replaced, after much bargaining, by that of 1 January 1852. The London & North Western was able to secure the performance of collection and delivery duties at a price much closer to actual cost, while the agents were guaranteed a larger annual salary, amounting to £10,000 (an increase of £2,500). On balance, however, the railway company appears to have derived the most benefit, for not only

1 L.N.W. Road & Traffic Ctee Mins, 8 Aug. 1851, LNW1/140, BTHR.
2 H. Bradshaw's Book of Liverpool Station Statistics (Tonnages and Receipts), 1856–9, LNW4/71, BTHR.
3 L.N.W. Road & Traffic Ctee Mins, 13 June and 8 Aug. 1851, LNW1/140; Huish to Chandos, 6 Apr. 1858, HL2/R373/13/13, BTHR.

were collection and delivery allowances cut, but the company reduced its commitment to pay bonuses if the agency duties were performed more cheaply. The credit for this success belongs to Huish.[1] The new arrangements were for the most part satisfactory, although terminal expenses in the London area were closely scrutinized by Huish in 1854, and the agents continued occasionally to forward goods by sea and canal.[2] The agreement of 1858 was the outcome of a further attempt to obtain agency services at actual cost. The system of allowances per ton was abandoned in favour of a direct payment by the railway company of the agents' expenses, and this was accompanied by a more thorough inspection of both the mode and efficiency of operation.[3] The company therefore continued to enjoy the advantages of entrusting its terminal duties to specialists over more than half of its network. In 1855 Huish reported that the system remained profitable, and he was quite prepared to combat objections of the kind met in 1848.

Huish remained a dominant figure in the planning of expanding freight services. He was, of course, dependent to some extent upon the reports and opinions of the principal goods managers, but all major policy matters passed through his hands, and some were the occasion for his special intervention. Surviving reports and minutes indicate that he was especially prominent in decisions to connect the railway with both the London and the Liverpool docks, to extend coal sidings and wharves in the London and Manchester areas, and to enlarge the major urban goods stations such as Birmingham and Manchester. Concern with the supply of waggons also brought him to the forefront of policy-making, and all the evidence points to the fact that his general strategy envisaged a large goods traffic with an extensive plant.

During the 1850s the organization of the company's goods business became increasingly blurred in its distinction between internal and external spheres of operation. Traffic problems could rarely be confined to the territory of a single company, and further service difficulties were raised by the growth of through traffic facilitated by the Railway Clearing House, which by 1855 handled about 175,000 different goods rates, its accounts for the last six months of the same year amounting to over £1,800,000 for goods and livestock alone. This figure, which represented about 70 per cent of the total traffic cleared, was over three times that for

1 Agreement of 1852, PIC3/3, BTHR; see Appendix.
2 L.N.W. Road & Traffic Ctee Mins, 10 Mar., 12 May, 14 July 1854, LNW1/140;
  Executive Ctee Mins, 24 May 1855, LNW1/148, BTHR.
3 Agreement of 1858, PIC3/4, BTHR; see Appendix.

the same period of 1848.[1] Membership also steadily increased, from about 50 companies at the beginning of 1851 to about 115 by the end of 1858, the latter including the Great Western, in spite of its broad gauge.[2] At the same time, the London & North Western's individual service was undoubtedly the most extensive in the world, with up to forty trains a day being worked over the busiest sections out of London and Liverpool by 1852.[3] In such a situation, therefore, the outcome of a large and diffuse business was a matching organization of executive conferences in both the internal and external spheres. An executive goods conference can be found as early as 1851, which with an officers' committee—first mentioned in 1852—considered accommodation and pricing problems affecting the London & North Western. From 1855, the Birmingham Officers' Meetings sought to rationalize the goods service in order to avoid waste and improve waggon-loads.[4]

A similar pattern may be traced in external management. The conference of goods managers, in existence since 1847, surrendered its dominant rôle in the Railway Clearing House to a committee of general managers, which from January 1851 was responsible (subject to the supervision of the Clearing House Committee) for through goods traffic control. When one also considers the existence of numerous special meetings of company officers, such as the 'Octuple', 'West Coast', and 'Northern Alliance' conferences, it is evident that the 1850s saw the beginnings of a concerted effort to achieve uniformity of practice within the railway industry.

The London & North Western, under Huish's leadership, made a positive contribution towards the integration of the country's goods traffic, although it should be recognized that this was done in order to protect its position of supremacy. Huish enjoyed a considerable influence among general managers, for although men like Seymour Clarke, Laws, and Allport shared his ability to control internal company affairs they lacked his overall acquaintance with the workings of the Clearing House system. Huish had been actively responsible for the creation of both the goods and general managers' conferences, and as a delegate to the Clearing House Committee was able to direct policies submitted from other

---

1 Morison's Report to the R.C.H. Ctee, 12 Mar. 1856, RCH1/4, and see above, pp. 144–5.
2 Computed from R.C.H. Ctee Mins, RCH1/2–4; the G.W. was admitted in March 1857, Mins, 11 Mar. 1857, RCH1/4, BTHR. Data extracted by Bagwell shows that by 1860 the route mileage operated by R.C.H. members was almost 70 per cent of the total U.K. mileage open, and that cleared receipts (passenger and goods) represented 24 per cent of total U.K. receipts: Bagwell, *op. cit.*, 295, 304.
3 Huish and others, 'Report . . . on Renewal Fund' (1853), 22–3.
4 L.N.W. Road & Traffic Ctee Mins, 17 Oct. 1851, LNW1/140; L.N.W. Mins, 15 May 1852, LNW1/22; Birmingham Meetings, 1855, *passim*, LNW1/583, BTHR.

meetings. London & North Western interests were thus more than adequately safeguarded, especially since Carr Glyn was the Committee's Chairman.[1]

During the 1850s, then, the London & North Western continued to play a decisive part in matters affecting through goods traffic. Questions involving mileage and demurrage charges for waggons, allowances for terminal duties, responsibility for loss or damage, and the equitable division of Clearing House costs, usually engaged Huish's personal attention. But the attempts to achieve uniformity of procedure always involved lengthy and tortuous discussions, and more often than not came to nothing. Indeed, the minutes of the Clearing House committees indicate that Huish himself was by no means blameless. Certainly, he showed a great anxiety to impress upon other companies the need for a more uniform waggon design, regular inspection of privately-owned waggons, and new procedures in connection with liability for damage—attitudes which he had adopted before 1851.[2] But there were also numerous examples of his disagreement with the efforts of others to legislate for the United Kingdom as a whole. He dissented from all resolutions which prejudiced the London & North Western's established advantage, both in regard to rate changes, and to alterations of through traffic arrangements in general. His opposition to experimental rates for newspapers, and for horses carried in cattle waggons, illustrates this, while the lengthy debate upon the advisability of terminating free passes for cattle dealers and drovers not only revealed Huish's opposition, but impressed upon the companies the continuing need to seek the agreement of companies outside the Clearing House.[3]

Huish's contribution was not a negative one, however, and he sponsored several important schemes to alter Clearing House regulations. In 1854 he raised the question of insurance and risk on valuable articles, and he acted as Chairman of the General Managers' meetings of June 1854 and November 1856, which dealt with a variety of problems, including terminal charges, damaged vehicles, and minor issues affecting mileage and demurrage regulations.[4] In fact, certain companies objected that some of the arrangements contemplated by Huish worked unfairly against them, as they had claimed in the past.[5] The smaller railways in

1 Glyn was Chairman from 1846 to 1873: Bagwell, *op. cit.*, 292.
2 Huish, at R.C.H. Ctee: Mins, 12 Mar. 1851, 13 June 1855, 10 Dec. 1856, RCH1/2–3, BTHR; and cf. above, p. 145.
3 R.C.H. General Managers' Ctee Mins, 1854–6, *passim*, RCH1/70–1, BTHR.
4 *Ibid.*, 2 June and 27 Sept. 1854, 12 Nov. 1856.
5 See above, p. 145.

the mining districts were violently opposed to the attempt to extend mileage and demurrage to coal and coke waggons, and the revised regulations of April 1852, which Huish had carefully nursed through the meetings of both General Managers and the Clearing House Committee, had to be rescinded in the following December.[1] Despite this and other cases of friction, the 1850s saw a consolidation of the progress made between 1847 and 1850, and although some basic points of difference remained, further strides towards an essential uniformity of traffic control were made, helped not only by Huish, but by Clarke, Allport, and Laws. Among the problems which were resolved during this period, a graduated mileage charge for waggon-use and a universally accepted definition of a 'ton' (for stone traffic) proved the most important. Indeed, such was the depth of inquiry into the possibilities of improvement that in 1855 a decimal monetary system was considered as a means to improve accounting.[2]

The external system of goods traffic control had its limitations, of course, and especially so in the realm of pricing, where responsibility for rate changes fell mainly to individual companies, and to special committees convened in connection with traffic agreements. The Clearing House classification of January 1852, which grouped over 700 items, was clearly an outstanding achievement in the effort to secure the acceptance of a general rating system, but there seems to have been far less agreement in the fixing of through rates. The immense complexity of goods rates, their vulnerability to competition, and the existence of many thousands of exceptional rates for special circumstances explains the reticence of the Goods Managers' Committee to interfere. This committee, which under Braithwaite Poole's leadership had fashioned the new classification, became involved principally in the revision of minor matters connected with it.[3]

Internal pricing was controlled by Huish under conditions similar to those in existence before 1851. Most local rate decisions were taken by the area goods manager, but Huish intervened whenever important traffics were involved. He was well aware of the peculiar difficulties attending the fixing of rates, and in particular of the impossibility of using a uniform mileage schedule, owing to the proximity of substitute modes of transport in all areas. It was also hard to adjust rates to suit

1 R.C.H. General Managers' Ctee Mins, 19 Nov. 1851, 4 Feb. 1852; General Managers Sub-Ctee Mins, 8 Dec. 1851, RCH1/70; R.C.H. Ctee Mins, 10 Dec. 1851, 9 June and 8 Dec. 1852, RCH1/2–3, BTHR.
2 R.C.H. Ctee Mins, 11 Mar. and 7 May 1857, 8 Feb. and 10 May 1855, RCH1/3, BTHR.
3 R.C.H. Goods Managers' Conferences, 1851–, RCH1/179–80, BTHR.

traffic circumstances, as he admitted in a letter to Stewart in January 1856:

> We have more than 450,000 rates in all . . . I will not say that none are too low, but . . . I cannot discover a point on our own line where any important change could be effected. A large proportion of our charges are at the parliamentary maximum, and where this is not the case, the rates are above those charged by Canal, and as high as the trade at present can bear.[1]

Huish's attitude did not change significantly during the 1850s, for he maintained a belief in a fluid pricing system, with freedom to charge differential rates according to circumstances. Complaints were, however, common, and it appears that the Board of Directors was anxious to remove certain inequalities of charge, as for example in the Birmingham–Banbury area, which was affected by Great Western competition.[2]

Some rates were increased, in spite of the accompanying obstacles, and Huish in fact assisted with both their conception and implementation. In 1851 he inspired a revision of the low rates granted to encourage Manchester businessmen to ship bale goods through the port of London, and organized the work of the executive goods conference which in 1853 suggested increases in the tariffs of several important commodities. Cattle rates were also raised in certain areas between 1853 and 1855, and iron rates were adjusted upwards in the areas affected by Great Western competition following the traffic agreement of 1854 (the rate between Birkenhead and Wolverhampton, for example, was increased by two shillings a ton).[3]

The direction of change was not generally upward, however, and there are parallel examples of Huish's action in reducing rates in response to demand. He was entrusted with the arrangement of special contracts granting preferential rates for guaranteed consignments and assured delivery dates—the 'time bargain'—and in addition to the coal contracts mentioned above he obtained special consignments of glass, from Chance Brothers of Birmingham, and ale, from Allsop and Bass of Burton.[4] His

1 Huish to Stewart, 29 Jan. 1856, HL2/R373/4, BTHR.
2 L.N.W. Executive Ctee Mins, 26 Apr. 1855, LNW1/148; L.N.W. Mins, 10 Oct. 1857, LNW1/23, BTHR.
3 L.N.W. Road & Traffic Ctee Mins, 11 July and 8 Aug. 1851, 14 Oct. 1853, LNW1/140; Executive Ctee Mins, 13 Apr. 1855, LNW1/148; Northern Conference Mins, 20–3 Dec. 1854, GW1/749, BTHR.
4 L.N.W. Road & Traffic Ctee Mins, 12 Mar., 7 Apr., 14 May, and 10 Dec. 1852, LNW1/140, referring to the Executive Goods Ctee Mins, 23 Mar. and 6 Apr. 1852, BTHR.

most important contribution lay in the arrangement of devices to meet the challenge of competition. In addition to his work in inter-company pricing (described above) he regulated the tolls and rates on the various canals controlled by the London & North Western with the intention of defeating canal competition on a broad front. By 1856 the company had acquired part-control (by means of joint leases with other railway companies) of the Leeds & Liverpool, Rochdale, and Huddersfield canals. When these are added to the Birmingham Canal Navigation and the Shropshire Union Canal, which the company owned directly, it is clear that Huish exercised an influence over many miles of important industrial waterway, and although all the canals, with the exception of the Huddersfield, made working losses, managerial control of their rates probably saved the company from more severe competitive difficulties.[1]

Huish also attempted to induce the outstanding independent canals to end competition by low rates, in order to stabilize tariffs at mutually acceptable levels. The division of coal traffic with the Grand Junction Canal in 1851, and the participation of the Duke of Bridgewater's Canal in the company's traffic agreement with the Great Western, were successful examples of this policy, although the railway had often to concede a lower differential rate. However, the effects of competition, which had caused the company considerable embarrassment before 1850, were greatly minimized. Minutes relating to Huish's control of rates show that not only were substantial efforts made to equalize railway and canal charges, but that the London & North Western, in common with other companies, was speedily gaining a hold upon heavy and mineral traffics (once a preserve of the canals) by means of its own extensive canal subsidiaries.

Inter-railway competition placed an equally severe strain upon goods pricing, and parallel steps were taken by Huish to secure as peaceful a traffic situation as was possible. A pool of merchandise traffic in the Lancashire area was arranged as early as September 1850, dividing business between the London & North Western, Lancashire & Yorkshire, and Manchester Sheffield & Lincolnshire railways on the basis of equal rates (later known as the 'Humber Agreement'). This, together with the previously mentioned passenger and goods agreements, was a clear indication of Huish's intention to protect his company's supremacy by means of inter-company controls. The more complex machinery involved in the

1 L.N.W. Company Accounts, RAC1/233, BTHR. Huddersfield Canal profits falling to the L.N.W. amounted to £29,000, 1851–60, but losses on the Leeds & Liverpool (and from 1856 the Rochdale Canal) were £31,000 over the same period.

organization of goods traffic discouraged recourse to rate-wars, and the members of Huish's 'Confederacy', while quite willing to cut passenger fares, were anxious to avoid disturbing goods rates.[1] Furthermore, the Great Western and London & North Western conducted their goods pricing on the basis of reciprocal action from 1855, and even after the latter had lost the good will of the Midland Railway, it was eager to stabilize coal rates to London, as the traffic agreement of February 1858 proved.[2]

Clashes of interest, re-booking devices, and physical hindrances to the traffic of competing companies were not problems to be solved easily, however, and the 1850s saw Huish as the most publicized if not the most notorious exponent of such devices to uphold the interests of a single company. It seems true, for example, that he was guilty of applying what Clarke termed "unfair cattle rates" in the Lincolnshire area and that, when forced to abandon low rates at Peterborough, he maintained them at nearby Wansford, thus encouraging drovers to divert cattle from the Great Northern line.[3] Evidence submitted to Parliament in 1858 also accused him of deliberate obstructionism during the 1850s, but his actions, though frequently suspect, were no more damaging than those of the Manchester Sheffield & Lincolnshire Railway in 1857, for example, when Watkin reduced what were already low rates between London and Lancashire.[4]

The existence of an effective competition by sea often upset the most meticulous arrangements for through traffic, and many inter-company squabbles originated in the desire of one company to cut rates in order to prevent losses, an action which threatened the structure of pooling agreements. Huish tended to deal harshly with smaller companies who wished to act in this way, and in 1855 he informed the Lancaster & Carlisle Railway that its proposed reduction of cotton rates between Leith and Liverpool would endanger the 'Octuple' and 'Humber' agreements.[5] Following the upward revision of Anglo-Scottish rates in 1855–6, Huish also led a resistance to the demand of the Aberdeen Railway for lower first-class

1 Huish, Allport, and Watkin, joint letter to Clarke, 26 Jan. 1856, in *Minutes and Correspondence* . . ., 22.

2 Agreement of 23 Feb. 1858, fixing equal rates from the Midlands to London (Euston or King's Cross), LNW3/59, BTHR.

3 Clarke to Stewart, 7 Aug. 1858, Clarke to Chandos, 10 Aug. and 10 Sept. 1858, LNW8/32–7, BTHR.

4 *S.C. on the Manchester Sheffield & Lincolnshire, and Great Northern Railway Companies Bill*, P.P.1857–8, XV, Edward Denison's cross-examination of Huish, QQ.6007–26, *et seq.*; Huish to Chandos, 29 Jan. 1858, HL2/R373/13/6, BTHR.

5 L.N.W. Executive Ctee Mins, 26 Apr. 1855, LNW1/148.

rates to London.[1] When, however, sea transport was found to have affected the London & North Western's own traffic in ale and iron from the Midlands to Scotland, Huish lost no time in suggesting and obtaining reductions at the meetings of the English & Scotch Traffic Committee in early 1858. Clearly, rate adjustments were still being considered principally in terms of individual gain.

It should not be thought that Huish's contribution to pricing was always either selfish or negative. The progress made by the Octuple and English & Scotch committees in fixing rates and classifying disputed items of traffic could not have been made without the support of the London & North Western. The most complex goods schedules were constructed, taking into account every conceivable class of traffic, and prescribing special rates for specially-defined items and for journeys affected by sea competition, in cases where agreement could be obtained. Although as suggested above the provisions of such schedules were never completely accepted, the general effect must have been beneficial to the railways concerned. The experience of the managers of the major companies in dealing with rates in committee was a valuable aid to the reconstruction of the 1852 classification in 1855, which proved a further step towards a general policy on goods traffic. Despite the hectic nature of the 1850s, and the seeming impossibility of securing agreement among companies whose interests were so often at variance, there appears much to support the contention that railway history was one not of legislation but of inter-company squabble, and that progress resulted from the companies' attempts to seek their own salvation.

In London & North Western terms, Huish's control of the goods system was successful, and despite the complexities of organization, and the ever-present threat of fresh competition, the service was praised for its punctuality and speed. As the minutes of the Birmingham Officers' Meetings from 1855 show, Huish urged that competitive goods trains be given priority to secure punctual and early despatch, and the results of his efforts can be gauged both from the slowness of the Great Northern and Great Western to break into the goods business and from favourable accounts in 1858 of the company's conduct of the prestige London–Manchester service.[2]

---

1 English & Scotch Traffic Ctee Mins, 11 Mar. 1856, etc., RCH1/508, BTHR.
2 L.N.W. Birmingham Officers' Meetings, 18 Oct. and 13 Nov. 1855, LNW1/583
  BTHR; evidence of William Warth, *S.C. on M.S. & L. and G.N. Bill*, P.P.1857–,8,
  XV, QQ.1065–9.

But despite the success of Huish's administration there was still some concern over the company's low rates, especially for coal and other mineral traffic. The debate initiated by Whitehead in the late 1840s was revived sporadically, and Huish, in his Report on Traffic of 1855, was prompted to defend the system and to reaffirm his opinion that the profits on both merchandise and coal were large and increasing. "Goods and coals", he said, had contributed "their fair quota of net revenue towards the dividend", and, reflecting that the percentage of profit was not the vital factor, he maintained his belief that the largest aggregate balance of profit was to be gained from a large traffic, even if margins were smaller.[1]

In spite of Huish's statements there appeared in 1856 a work of some notoriety which fiercely attacked the company's management. Entitled *A Review of the London & North Western Railway Accounts for the Last Ten Years, By A Manchester Shareholder*, the pamphlet suggested that "the Traffic is carried at an enormous loss": considerable attention was devoted to mineral, and especially coal, traffic, and the practice of preferential rate-fixing was strongly condemned.[2] The writer blamed the fall in dividends on the abandonment of uniform mileage rates, and he stated categorically that the coal and heavy mineral traffic did not pay. This argument was accompanied by an impressive array of statistical evidence drawn from the company's accounts, but there was a great deal of false reasoning, and Whitehead's error in making too much of a comparison of differing company conditions was repeated. It was certainly true that some rates were very low, and the company under Huish had attempted to increase coal rates in the Lancashire area, for example, in response to pressure for higher profit margins.[3] Huish had also admitted that although increased productivity had resulted from improved waggon-loads, earnings per waggon had in fact declined.[4] A survey of the gross earnings of the merchandise and mineral traffic between 1848 and 1853—extracted from Huish's Report on the Electric Telegraph of 1854—shows that the merchandise traffic produced 7–10 shillings per ton, while minerals yielded only about 1s. 6d. (table 37).

1 Huish, 'Report . . . on Traffic . . .', 16–17.
2 *A Review* . . ., 9, 12–21, 32–7.
3 L.N.W. Goods Ctee Mins, 17 Apr. 1856, LNW1/523, BTHR. Bradshaw's Book of Statistics shows a clear increase in the Bolton and Wigan rates in 1858: LNW4/71, BTHR.
4 L.N.W. Road & Traffic Ctee Mins, 14 Jan. 1853, LNW1/140, BTHR. Tonnage per waggon increased from 213 tons (1849) to 280 tons (1852), but earnings fell from £113 3s. to £111 0s. 5½d. (goods, coal, and cattle traffic).

Table 37
**London & North Western gross earnings per ton,
merchandise and mineral traffic, 1848–53**

Year	Merchandise earnings per ton	Mineral earnings per ton
1848	10.8s.	1.3s.
1849	10.7	1.4
1850	9.8	1.6
1851	8.1	1.6
1852	8.0	1.7
1853	7.4	1.8

Source: Huish, 'Report . . . on the Electric Telegraph' (1854), 10.

Mineral traffic was, however, conducted in owners' waggons, without terminal duties, and average yields were, unlike those for merchandise, rising steadily through the period investigated.

The "Manchester Shareholder" succeeded in proving very little beyond the obvious point that the company had not been able to increase its net profits to meet an extending capitalization. It was, however, wrong to suggest that low rates were profitable only for short distances and that a uniform and high tariff was necessary: both ran counter to the experience of managers for over a decade. On the other hand, it is extremely difficult, if not impossible, to *prove* that the company's low-priced traffic was in fact profitable. An account of net profits per train-mile made by Huish's department indicates that the goods traffic did make an overall contribution to profits, despite its higher working costs, but no effort was made to separate particular items of traffic, nor was this an easy thing to do.[1] Not only was a distinction between passenger and goods costs difficult to make, but the choice of statistical measurement could be misleading. It was stated after a further 50 years of experience that "Train-mile statistics alone are insufficient to support any allegations of inefficient management",[2] and it was recognized that even the superior ton-mile unit was of no value in determining the cost of transporting particular items.[3] It is with caution therefore that one should evaluate the work of writers who sought to prove that mineral rates of $\frac{1}{2}d$. per ton-mile *were*

1 L.N.W. Report, February 1862, RAC1/233, BTHR.
2 H. M. Ross, *British Railways, Their Organisation and Management* (1904), 99.
3 Albert Fink, cited in Ross, *op. cit.*, 112. See also G. L. Boag, *Manual of Railway Statistics* (1912), 20.

profitable, since their calculations depended on a high degree of approximation, for example regarding average net train loads.[1] The results of an examination of Huish's policy tend to be rather negative, but if it cannot be said that all the company's traffics were profitable, the overall position of the goods business appears to have been most satisfactory.

3 Management and business efficiency

The statistics for 1851–60 once again pose the basic problem of interpretation which runs through attempts to assess business performance in the nineteenth century. Although more consistent accounts were compiled, with an increased subtlety in the apportionment of working costs and in the choice of units to represent the overall output of transport services, it remains just as difficult to evaluate the effect of Huish's management upon the company's business record. There exists, as before, a wealth of descriptive evidence of Huish's attempts to improve performance, but this must be carefully balanced by use of the available units of measurement, however inexact they may appear.

The potential value of a competent general manager was of course considerable. Carr Glyn commented in 1855 that company efficiency was dependent upon the "practical knowledge and experience" of executive officers, and, indeed, the organization from that date was geared to allow Huish to suggest policies to improve efficiency and effect economy of operation—tasks which he had customarily performed.[2] The extraordinary pressures upon management in the 1850s did not affect this rôle, and in fact the company's records indicate that the general manager was constantly involved in the battle against rising costs, falling profit margins, and competition.

Before attempting an analysis of the data, a brief consideration of Huish's rôle as promoter of efficiency would be useful. The Board expected him both to increase revenue and to reduce costs, while providing adequate facilities for all types of traffic. This mammoth task demanded all the "research, tact, and skill" expected of the ideal manager.[3] In the 1850s, however, these aims were almost irreconcilable, and there

1 E.g. R. P. Williams, 'On the Economy of Railway Working', *Minutes of Proceedings, Institution of Mechanical Engineers* (1879), 110–11.
2 Carr Glyn to Chandos, 15 Feb. 1855, Glyn Mills & Co. Archives; L.N.W. Executive Ctee Mins, 22 Mar. 1855, LNW1/148, BTHR.
3 J.A. Fisher, *Railway Accounts and Finance* (1891), 4.

occurred a clash between the proponents of economy and those who wished to provide for new traffic. Huish attempted to balance the two policies, but he had no doubts as to the desirability of a large business, to be organized on the basis of a thoroughly reliable service to the customer. Management's dilemma centred upon the executive's encouragement of traffic in order to improve gross revenue, which at the same time necessitated further capital outlay and therefore increased pressure upon receipts to provide adequate returns.

The management of the train services was of paramount importance. Huish was the most influential single figure in improvements effected in the name of economy and consumer-satisfaction. He was responsible, for example, for the more extensive use of night goods and mail trains to ease congestion, and as Chairman of the Birmingham Officers' Meetings from 1855 he inspired several service changes: close attention was given to punctuality, the acceleration of essential servicing operations (such as cokeing and watering), the abandonment of unnecessary trains, the economical use of engine power, and the integration of branch-line and main-line working.[1] There are definite examples of a desire to meet petitions for improved services and to alter train times in response to seasonal needs, but the main preoccupation was with the rationalization of train diagrams to reduce expenses, and of train-loads to avoid the unproductive use of stock.[2]

Huish's published work on various aspects of management was as before a testimony to his exceptional control over working policy and to his wide knowledge of technical matters. His paper on *Railway Accidents* of 1852 proved a valuable apologia in defence of railway management, and a counterbalance to the undue publicity given to accident figures by the Railway Department of the Board of Trade. Huish laid particular stress upon the need for adequate safety systems. He favoured a firm and well-maintained permanent way, and outlined several technological developments designed to improve it, such as stone sleepers, fish-plates, and heavier rails.[3] Rail-makers were criticized for providing faulty material unequal to the task of supporting heavy traffic. Huish also discussed locomotive design (especially couplings and buffers), and fire, in his analysis of accident causes, but he found that by far the largest number of mishaps was caused by inattention to signals and neglect of

1 L.N.W. Birmingham Officers' Meetings, 15 Jan. and 12 Feb. 1855, etc. LNW1/583, BTHR.
2 *Ibid.* Train diagrams show the full details of routes taken by each locomotive and train for each section of line, over specified time-periods.
3 Huish, *Railway Accidents* . . . (1852), 4–6.

regulations. He therefore emphasized the need for proper observance of working regulations, a uniform signal design, and the use of the electric telegraph—all important opinions and part of a more scientific approach to problems of internal control.[1]

In 1853 Huish was asked to reconsider the position of the permanent way renewal fund in the light of increased company liabilities. The subsequent report to the Permanent Way Committee was a further example of the attempt to spread costs by means of an annual allocation from revenue. Huish, together with Woodhouse and Watkin, was directed to investigate the effects of extensive traffic development since 1849 and the consequent pressure upon the permanent way. Elaborate statistics were provided to show to what extent the 1849 estimate of the money required to replace the track had proved correct. Certainly, the company's situation had altered radically. As early as February 1850 a decision was taken to revise the estimated allocation to take account of increased mileage.[2] From November 1852 responsibility for the mainten- ance of the Northern Division passed from contractors to the company, and it was admitted also that previous calculations were upset by the fact that many rails had been lifted before fully worn out, because they had become unequal to the added stress of a larger traffic.[3] Technological developments came to affect the cost of relaying: the use of heavier rails and the adoption of fish-plating and firmer ballasting increased both material and labour costs, and the situation was exacerbated by a rise in the price of iron.[4]

Huish therefore suggested that the original estimate be revised up- wards, and the Board duly explained to the general meeting of 16 August 1853 that the annual sum required for renewal had been increased "after mature consideration".[5] The report contains further proof of Huish's enthusiasm for a depreciation fund as an accumulating fund rather than a means to meet current liabilities. It also demonstrated that under Huish's guidance the company's provision for renewal compared favour- ably with that of other leading railways.[6] But many of the companies

1 Huish, *Railway Accidents* . . . 14–17. Cf. Huish's evidence, *S.C. on Accidents on Railways*, P.P.1857–8, XIV,Q.1113: "I think the chief cause of accidents on railways is the necessity of adopting human agency in the conduct of a very vast machine . . .".
2 L.N.W. General Meeting, 22 Feb. 1850, LNW1/1, BTHR.
3 Huish and others, 'Report . . . on the Renewal Fund' (1853), 37–8.
4 *Ibid.*, 9–10, 38–40.
5 LNW1/1, BTHR.
6 Huish and others, 'Report . . . on the Renewal Fund', 4–5: the average sum per mile set aside by seven major companies in 1851 was £56 11s., while the L.N.W. set aside £60 7s., or with interest, £67 5s.

which had followed the London & North Western's lead in 1849 were induced, in the conditions of expansion of the 1850s, to revert to the easier method of "replacement accounting", and the London & North Western itself, having transferred part of its permanent way expenditure to capital in 1856, abandoned its depreciation fund entirely in 1865.[1] Great variations remained in the handling of accounts, and even in the early twentieth century there was much to criticize in the way railways manipulated capital and revenue accounts to suit business needs.[2] Nevertheless, if Huish's report was not part of a lasting contribution to accounting procedure, and if the rapid extension of the company's network invalidated his forecasts, the inquiry remains one of considerable analytical refinement, demonstrating the scientific basis on which many of Huish's management decisions were based. There was a marked attention to the compilation and use of statistics, and in calculating the annual sum required for rail renewal, great care was taken to balance the effects of a great many variables.[3]

Huish's reports on the electric telegraph of 1854 and on traffic of 1855 also contain valuable information on the state of railway operational technology in the 1850s. In his report of March 1854 the general manager made an extensive survey of the company's business, and offered suggestions to provide for an increased traffic with the safest and most economical mode of working. He began by summarizing the main problems facing all managements, and in doing so demonstrated his insight into the industry and its peculiar difficulties:

> The enlarged and rapidly increasing traffic of the line, notwithstanding the drains we have sustained by the opening of new routes, and competing railways; the necessity of continual improvements to keep pace . . . the increasing and somewhat indiscriminate rigour of Parliament and public opinion in regard to safety, celerity, and punctuality; and at the same time, the multiplied and multiplying causes of error and irregularity springing out of the expansion of a Railway System in detached parts, under distinct and often conflicting managements

1 H. Pollins, 'Railway Auditing—A Report of 1867', *Accounting Research*, VIII (1957), 22. Despite successive increases in the annual sums set aside from revenue, by 30 June 1856 only £399,747 had been provided to meet a total expenditure of £703,035, leaving a deficit of £303,288. The company's auditors accordingly transferred £214,227 of total expenditure to the capital account, as this sum was held to represent an "improvement" in the track beyond mere renewal: L.N.W. Reports and Accounts, RAC1/233, BTHR.
2 A. M. Sakolski, 'Control of Railroad Accounts in Leading European Countries', *Quarterly Journal of Economics*, XXVI (1910), 474–87.
3 Huish and others, 'Report . . . on the Renewal Fund', 8–42.

. . . combine to produce a problem of considerable perplexity".[1]

In the context of an increasing traffic, especially in the mineral business, Huish considered that the more "liberal use" of the electric telegraph would bring the "greatest relief from pressure",[2] and his support was undoubtedly instrumental in providing the London & North Western with a relatively advanced control of train movement. As early as 1846 he had urged the introduction of the telegraph on the congested London–Rugby line, to enable a 30 per cent increase in traffic capacity without the need for additional tracks.[3] A rudimentary system was introduced, and by 1851 it had been extended to certain intermediate stations, with the result that the large and irregular excursion traffic to the Great Exhibition was handled successfully.[4] The company had therefore helped to popularize the control of train movement by the automatic exchange of information, but the rapid increase in traffic over the London–Rugby section between 1846 and 1853 (48 per cent in trains and 139 per cent in freight tonnage) led Huish to consider and recommend the adoption of Edwin Clark's two-mile telegraph invention, the precursor of the modern block system of signalling. This, the result of discussions between Clark and Huish, envisaged the division of the line into short sections, each to be controlled by telegraphic signalling: trains were to be separated not by an interval of time (the former system) but by one of space, clearly a safer mode of operation.[5]

Clark's system was introduced on the London–Rugby line in 1855, providing the company with a further means to increase traffic capacity. However, the security intended by Clark did not materialize, chiefly because his invention was applied in a 'permissive' form, that is, two trains were allowed to enter the same section of track at the same time. A number of collisions occurred, though Huish claimed that it was the lack of trained staff and the tendency of the instruments to suffer short-circuiting that threatened the effectiveness of the system as a safety

1 Huish, 'Report . . . on the Electric Telegraph', 2.
2 *Ibid.*, 19.
3 L.N.W. Mins, 14 Nov. 1846, LNW1/20, BTHR; Huish, 'Report . . . on the Electric Telegraph', 3–4.
4 L.N.W. Mins, 14 Oct. 1848, 14 Feb. 1851, LNW1/20–1, BTHR; Huish, *Railway Accidents . . .* (1852), 16–17.
5 Huish, 'Report . . . on the Electric Telegraph', 5–11, 20–48, incorporating Clark's report of 18 Jan. 1854. See also M. Huish, 'Supplementary Report on the Extension of Telegraphic Communication' (1854), 3–12, including Clark's report of 14 June 1854, LNW1/716, BTHR. Clark's views were subsequently published as *Letter to Capt. Huish as to Proposed Improvements in the Electric Telegraph System* (1854). See also G. P. Neele, *Railway Reminiscences . . .* (1904), 82–90.

device.[1] Nevertheless, Huish had sponsored an important if imperfectly applied development in railway technology, and one which certainly enabled his company to operate a larger traffic without recourse to extensive capital works.[2] He stoutly defended Clark's system in his evidence to the Select Committee on Railway Accidents of 1858, claiming that it was the "nearest to perfection that can be arranged",[3] and although this was a fatuous remark, it indicates that the company successfully survived its early teething troubles. Huish also encouraged safety in other ways, notably in his constant campaign for uniformity in signals, and in waggon design. He was in favour of limiting train sizes, and devised a new and lasting system for controlling traffic on single-track lines.[4] Various regulations on the use of coloured lamps, and of safety points at sidings can be attributed to him.[5]

Huish clearly regarded safety and the use of technological aids as important factors in reducing costs per unit of operation. He also participated in a conscious drive to meet the difficulties of large-scale working over a wide area, by means of more intricate costing methods and a greater awareness of technical factors. The less favourable operating margins which faced the railways from the mid 1840s meant that there could no longer be a "cavalier attitude to exact costing and pricing".[6] It was thus essential for large concerns such as the London & North Western to improve their costing methods in general. The pressure upon management was unprecedented: as R. S. Edwards has stated, "Railways which made large scale industrial development possible combined practically all the problems—joint costs, integrated processes, depreciation, and obsolescence, heavy fixed investment and the control of a widespread organisation".[7]

1 Neele, *op. cit.*, 88.
2 Later experts claimed that the Huish-Clark 'partial block' system was in itself a costly innovation: Sir W. H. Preece, 'On the Block System of Working on Railways', paper read to the *Society of Telegraph Engineers*, 23 Apr. 1873, 6–7. Huish estimated the cost of the London–Rugby system at about £2,260 per annum: 'Report . . . on the Electric Telegraph', 40.
3 P.P.1857–8, XIV, Q.1116.
4 L.N.W. Road & Traffic Ctee Mins, 12 Dec. 1851, 9 Jan. 1852, LNW1/140, BTHR; Huish recommended the staff system for single-line working in 1853 after an accident at Oxford: *ibid.*, 14 Jan. 1853, and see Capt. Mallock, 'On the Block System . . .', *Society of Telegraph Engineers* (1873), 12. His support for greater security in train control can also be seen in his evidence to the *Royal Commission on Railways*, P.P.1867, XXXVIII, QQ.15853–6, 15934–52.
5 Neele, *op. cit.*, 91.
6 S. Pollard, *The Genesis of Modern Management* (1965), 245.
7 R. S. Edwards, 'Some Notes on the Early Literature and Development of Cost Accounting in Great Britain', *The Accountant*, xcvii (1937), 193.

The company continued to pay close attention to economy of operation and utilization of all possible resources. This was accompanied by the growing use of detailed statistical analysis, and in 1854 a special department was created in the general manager's office for this purpose.[1] It was at this time that such concepts as the passenger-mile, train-mile, and ton-mile first made their appearance as regular management aids. In particular, the costs of the locomotive departments—the largest single sector of operating costs—were dissected with some care, and from 1850 the cost of power per ton-mile and the cost of coke in terms of train- and engine-miles were calculated for each division of the railway.[2] Huish also provided estimates of oil and grease consumption, and average waggon-loads, to assist the various traffic committees of the period.

The problem of locomotive power and fuel costs, a complex feature of traffic management, caused the company some concern. The statistics after 1850 suggest that power costs per train-mile were rising, especially on the company's Northern Division. However, the train-mile unit can be misleading—an apparent rise in costs could be due merely to a change to longer, and therefore, fewer trains[3]—and, indeed, the *ton-mile* data (table 38) shows that the company was successful in reducing its power costs on all its divisions, at least after 1854.

Table 38
**London & North Western cost of locomotive power
per ton-mile, 1851–7**

Half-year ending	Southern Division	Northern Division		North-Eastern Division	
		(1)	(2)	(1)	(2)
31 May 1851	0.130*d*.	—	—	—	—
31 May 1854	0.128	0.116*d*.	0.116*d*.	0.124*d*.	0.136*d*.
31 May 1855	0.122	0.117	0.126	0.124	0.139
31 May 1856	0.115	0.110	0.123	0.119	—
31 May 1857	0.113	0.105	0.119	0.119	—

Source: L.N.W. Executive and Traffic Committees, LNW1/148–9, BTHR. The second calculations for the Northern and North-Eastern divisions have been adjusted to take account of variations in coke prices.

1 L.N.W. Salary Lists, General Manager's Department, 1854, LNW4/1, BTHR.
2 L.N.W. General Locomotive & Merchandise Ctee Mins, 1851–5, LNW1/222;
   Executive Ctee Mins, 1855–8, LNW1/148–9, BTHR.
3 For example, if two trains were merged, with no accompanying reduction in costs, the same service would appear to have cost twice as much per train-mile.

In the attempt to check costs in 1854, McConnell, the Locomotive Superintendent of the Southern Division, experimented with the contract system for enginemen, and with the use of coal as a locomotive fuel.[1] His ideas were not supported, however, and the contract system appears to have worked unfairly against the majority of enginemen, encouraging accidents by inducing men to work long hours in order to maintain their incomes.[2] The experiment with coal, although a valuable pioneer project, was opposed by the Locomotive Superintendents of the other divisions, on the grounds that it held no commercial advantage.[3] Nevertheless, the Southern Division continued to use a small amount of coal as fuel, and with the company's control of the entire maintenance of the track from 1852, further progress towards the control of necessary processes took place. Indeed, it was only a short time after Huish's departure that steel rails were being manufactured at the company's plant at Crewe.[4]

As the pressure of competition increased during the 1850s, and inflation contributed to the rise in the price of vital stores, it became necessary to reconvene the Moorsom Committee of Investigation. Huish again assisted the Committee in its work, and the report of November 1855, with its stress upon a rationalization of departmental duties and salaries, bore his stamp. However, the stimulus to economize was provided principally by the directors, and in particular by Moorsom and Moon, as part of the retrenchment policy which followed the administrative difficulties of 1854.[5] Huish continued to seek the more productive use of company resources. He promoted the lease of company land to a grain company at Peterborough, for example.[6] He also sought additional revenue from ancillary activities. In 1851 he arranged a more satisfactory contract which granted to W. H. Smith the right to sell newspapers and advertise at stations.[7]

---

1 J. McConnell's Report, 7 June 1854, cited in N. Caplan, 'An Essay in Railway Economy in 1854', *Railway Magazine*, cviii (1962), 494–6; McConnell, Report to the L.N.W. General Locomotive and Merchandise Ctee, 12 Mar. 1854, LNW1/222, BTHR.
2 *Herapath's Railway Magazine*, 12 Aug. 1854; Carr Glyn's letters to T. Smith, 20 Oct. 1854, and to Chandos, 10 Feb. 1855, Glyn Mills & Co. Archives.
3 *Ibid.*
4 L.N.W. Contract for use of the Bessemer Patent, 28 Mar. 1863, LNW3/89, BTHR.
5 See above, pp. 173–4.
6 L.N.W. Sthn. Road & Traffic Sub. Ctee Mins, 30 July 1851, LNW1/144, BTHR.
7 L.N.W. Road & Traffic Ctee Mins, 14 Nov. and 12 Dec. 1851, LNW1/140, BTHR: Huish negotiated a seven-year contract at £3,500 p.a. rising to £4,200 p.a., in place of the former contract at £1,500 p.a.

The directors were frequently interested in saving expense by revising wage scales and other items of labour cost. Huish, however, was sceptical of the benefit of indiscriminate economies, and the evidence reveals his support for an *increase* in the wage-bill in 1853, and his later defence of the need to maintain a high wage policy to attract and retain skilled labour, in the report of 1855. The harmful effects of economizing without care can be seen in the way long hours of work encouraged men to neglect train regulations, thereby contributing to serious and costly accidents at Bicester (1851), Oxford (1853), and Walsall (1854). The men responsible for the collision at Walsall had been on duty, it appears, for 19, 21, and 26 hours respectively.[1] Nevertheless, the management did make efforts to improve conditions of employment, creating a superannuation scheme for salaried staff in 1853, with contributions provided partly by the company.

It was particularly important to relate labour costs to fluctuations in business, if efficiency were to be maintained. Important evidence suggests that this was attempted, despite the difficulties of forecasting demand. In the Liverpool goods department, Huish supervised the regulation of labour costs to suit the amount of traffic handled. Evidence for 1857–9 indicates that the annual wage-bill per ton handled was kept fairly constant (at about 10d. per ton) and that the decline in traffic in 1858 was accompanied by a corresponding reduction in labour costs.[2]

It seems, therefore, that Huish continued to manage his company with a view to the increase of efficiency through the careful use of all the productive factors, and that his influence was far greater than that of other contemporary managers. The problem of assessing his performance with any accuracy is again most difficult, and although the descriptive evidence points to his untiring efforts to improve the company's business position, an evaluation of these efforts must rest upon a consideration of the available statistical evidence.

A survey of the company's traffic and total revenue and costs—as estimates of net income—between 1851 and 1860 probably masks as much as it reveals. It can be said, however, that under Huish's guidance, net traffic income (the "traffic balances"), although increasing, improved only slightly upon the position in 1851–2, and total net income fluctuated, as had been true of the period 1846–51, but was below the level of 1851–2 in four of the following eight years. In these terms, the company presents a rather static position in the 1850s, and it should be noted that the

1 Neele, *op. cit.*, 42–3.
2 See Appendix, table 63.

apparent improvement in the two years after Huish's resignation was due principally to the incorporation of the Chester & Holyhead and Lancaster & Carlisle railways in the accounts.

Table 39
Three indices of net income, 1851–60 (1846–7 = 100)

1. London & North Western Railway

Year July–June	Net traffic income	Total net income	*
1851–2	123.0	102.4	92.6
1852–3	116.6	92.9	87.9
1853–4	121.2	100.4	95.0
1854–5	123.6	96.2	90.6
1855–6	133.3	104.2	99.6
1856–7	142.5	106.6	
1857–8	126.1	87.8	
1858–9	132.0	87.8	
1859–60	173.1	106.3	

2. Midland Railway (independent index)

1851–2	105.5	68.3
1852–3	104.6	73.1
1853–4	112.1	82.0
1854–5	118.2	91.3
1855–6	126.7	101.6
1856–7	135.1	107.0
1857–8	140.0	114.1
1858–9	156.9	131.2
1859–60	173.9	148.5

3. Great Western Railway (independent index)

1851–2	109.8	114.7
1852–3	95.1	100.6
1853–4	114.9	120.8
1854–5	110.7	122.4
1855–6	134.6	141.4
1856–7	141.5	148.4
1857–8	145.3	152.7
1858–9	154.3	161.6

Source: Company Accounts, RAC1/164, 233, and 290, BTHR. Net traffic income is traffic revenue minus traffic costs: total net income is total revenue minus total costs (as interpreted by each company).
*Net income if rail renewal costs are subtracted: from 1856–7, rail renewal costs were not distinguished. L.N.W. data given in the Appendix, table 56.

Company comparisons again involve several pitfalls. Although the Midland and the Great Western appear to have experienced greater proportional income growth (particularly in *total* income), differences in the mode of compiling company accounts may well be responsible. Variation in the choice of costs attributable to traffic can be crucial, and the London & North Western, with its more rigorous costing policy, is likely to suffer in any crude comparison of performance.[1] The difficulties of using these income statistics to judge efficiency are intensified if comparisons are made of companies at different stages of development. The Great Northern Railway, for example, saw a doubling of its net income between 1851 and 1860, a far more satisfactory 'performance' than that of its three main rivals, but hardly surprising in view of its comparatively minor position in 1851.[2]

Table 40 provides estimates of the annual rate of return on traffic receipts and total revenue. The London & North Western's return on traffic receipts, which had remained roughly stationary from 1846–51, fell from about 65 to 57 per cent during the latter part of Huish's career. Similarly, the return on total revenue, which had been falling before 1851, declined further until by 1859–60 it stood at 28.9 per cent, almost half the figure for 1846–7.[3] Narrowing margins reflected both the serious burden of an increased traffic handled under more difficult business conditions and the effects of extending the concern to embrace less profitable subsidiaries (both railways and canals). The steady fall in the return on total revenue was accompanied by an ever-widening gap between operating and total costs. As the company increased the range of its activities, it incurred a greater proportion of costs which could not easily be allocated to particular traffics: rates and taxes, guarantees to other companies, and interest payments on loans were the chief items of expenditure. In 1846–7 these unallocable costs represented only 25 per cent of total costs: by 1859–60 this had risen to 44 per cent.[4] Lower rates of return, together with a larger business, were policies to which Huish was firmly committed, but the need in these circumstances for additional capital expenditure (exacerbated by competitive considerations) placed an additional strain upon the management.

1 Cf. the comments made in Chapter V, pp. 155–7. It should also be noted that the Midland's position in 1851 was in any case weak, and that the Great Western enjoyed considerably more freedom from competition than did the London & North Western.
2 With 1851–2 = 100, net traffic income was 206.8 and total net income 214.1 in 1859–60.
3 See table 18, pp. 157–8.
4 Extracted from the Appendix, tables 48 and 56.

Table 40
Annual percentage rate of return on receipts, 1851–60

1. London & North Western Railway

Year July–June	Gross traffic receipts	Net traffic receipts	Percentage rate of return on traffic receipts	Operating costs %
1851–2	£2,556,820	£1,683,514	65.8	34.2
1852–3	2,541,937	1,596,902	62.8	37.2
1853–4	2,726,366	1,658,344	60.8	39.2
1854–5	2,821,387	1,691,826	60.0	40.0
1855–6	2,974,922	1,824,089	61.3	38.7
1856–7	3,197,335	1,949,821	61.0	39.0
1857–8	3,014,302	1,725,896	57.3	42.7
1858–9	3,195,523	1,806,624	56.5	43.5
1859–60	4,067,997	2,369,774	58.3	41.7

	Total revenue	Net income	Percentage rate of return on total revenue *		Total costs %	*
1851–2	2,675,475	1,197,234	44.7	40.4	55.9	59.6
1852–3	2,665,743	1,087,744	40.8	38.5	59.2	61.5
1853–4	2,877,432	1,174,885	40.8	38.6	59.2	61.4
1854–5	2,920,228	1,126,484	38.6	36.3	61.4	63.7
1855–6	3,128,302	1,220,182	39.0	37.2	61.0	62.8
1856–7	3,361,577	1,245,863	37.1		62.9	
1857–8	3,199,042	1,026,439	32.1		67.9	
1858–9	3,386,425	1,025,685	30.3		69.7	
1859–60	4,292,508	1,242,001	28.9		71.1	

2. Midland Railway (extract)

	Gross traffic receipts	Net traffic receipts	Percentage rate of return on traffic receipts	Operating costs %
1851–2	£1,213,635	£ 726,077	59.8	40.2
1853–4	1,376,593	771,253	56.0	44.0
1857–8	1,670,320	961,120	57.5	42.5
1859–60	1,996,632	1,196,849	59.9	40.1

	Total revenue	Net income	Percentage rate of return on total revenue	Total costs %
1851–2	1,281,647	334,948	26.1	73.9
1853–4	1,462,575	401,966	27.5	72.5
1857–8	1,742,247	559,438	32.1	67.9
1859–60	2,044,602	728,456	35.6	64.4

Table 40 (continued)

3. Great Western Railway (extract)

	Gross traffic receipts	Net traffic receipts	Percentage rate of return on traffic receipts	Operating costs %
1851–2	£1,010,848	£ 710,785	70.3	29.7
1853–4	1,192,402	744,083	62.4	37.6
1856–7	1,509,777	916,129	60.7	39.3
1858–9	1,594,780	999,192	62.7	37.3
	Total revenue	Net income	Percentage rate of return on total revenue	Total costs %
1851–2	1,047,582	699,871	66.8	33.2
1853–4	1,241,859	736,880	59.3	40.7
1856–7	1,564,307	905,700	57.9	42.1
1858–9	1,648,392	986,041	59.8	40.2

4. Great Northern Railway (extract)

	Gross traffic receipts	Net traffic receipts	Percentage rate of return on traffic receipts	Operating costs %
1851–2	£ 598,450†	£ 333,054	55.7	44.3
1853–4	943,753	521,068	55.2	44.8
1857–8	1,207,621	629,790	52.2	47.8
1859–60	1,345,999	688,748	51.2	48.8
	Total revenue	Net income	Percentage rate of return on total revenue	Total costs %
1851–2	606,324	305,039	50.3	49.7
1853–4	957,264	499,843	52.2	47.8
1857–8	1,244,871	576,464	46.3	53.7
1859–60	1,366,538	653,024	47.8	52.2

Source: Company Accounts, RAC1/155, 164, 233, 290, BTHR. Operating costs do not include taxes, rates, legal expenses, guarantees, loans, and rail renewal costs, where these items have been separated in the accounts. Note: from 1855–6, L.N.W. gross traffic receipts do *not* include amounts paid to other companies for traffic carried in excess of traffic agreements.
* Includes rail renewal costs, separated until 1856–7.
† Estimated.

Differences in the methods of accounting alter significantly the estimation of annual costs and affect thereby the computed rates of return for other companies. The returns on total revenue of the Great Western and

Great Northern railways appear to be high, and one must suspect that these companies did not share the exact costing procedures developed by the London & North Western under Huish. However, the overall impression is of falling rates of return, whatever the accounting conventions used.[1]

Table 41
London & North Western's annual percentage rate of return on estimated capital, 1851–60

Year July–June	A Net traffic receipts	1 Share capital 'called up'	$\frac{1}{A}$ %	2 Capital spent on 'lines open'	$\frac{2}{A}$ %	3 Total capital spent	$\frac{3}{A}$ %
1851–2	£1,683,514	£20,413,189	8.25	£24,734,753	6.81	£29,574,697	5.69
1852–3	1,596,902	21,324,900	7.49	25,130,004	6.35	29,849,161	5.35
1853–4	1,658,344	21,747,600	7.63	26,070,704	6.36	31,422,063	5.28
1854–5	1,691,726	22,043,112	7.67	26,689,359	6.34	32,194,604	5.25
1855–6	1,824,089	22,111,433	8 25	26,960,776	6.77	32,477,089	5.62
1856–7	1,949,821	22,339,396	8.73	27,354,574	7.13	32,941,407	5.92
1857–8	1,725,896	22,875,501	7.54	28,087,829	6.14	34,160,658	5.05
1858–9	1,806,624	23,399,821	7.72	28,489,740	6.34	34,813,053	5.19

Year	B Net income	1	$\frac{1}{B}$ %	2	$\frac{2}{B}$ %	3	$\frac{3}{B}$ %
1851–2	£1,081,646*	as above	5.30	as above	4.37	as above	3.66
1852–3	1,027,310*		4.82		4.09		3.44
1853–4	1,110,361*		5.11		4.26		3.53
1854–5	1,059,149*		4.80		3.97		3.29
1855–6	1,163,516*		5.26		4.32		3.58
1856–7	1,245,863		5.58		4.55		3.78
1857–8	1,026,439		4.49		3.65		3.00
1858–9	1,025,685		4.38		3.60		2.95

Source: Company Accounts, RAC1/233, BTHR: column 1 does not include loan capital: column 2 omits expenditure on subsidiary companies (some of which were yielding revenue); and column 3 includes a certain amount of unproductive expenditure. The capital sums are those at the *end* of each year (i.e. 30 June).
*Takes into account expenditure on rails.

1 The Midland Railway showed an improvement in its returns on total revenue, but its position in the immediate post-Hudson period was exceptionally poor: the burden of guaranteed dividends to subsidiary companies was particularly severe, and provision for depreciation and renewal had been neglected.

Table 41 provides an indication of the London & North Western's return on capital, although the risk of inaccuracy found earlier also applies here.[1] The steady fall in returns from 1846 appears to have been arrested after 1851, and it is suggested that the management's efforts to check expenditure resulted in a stabilizing of returns until 1857–8. The last two years of the series, in which all the several calculations show a pronounced fall in returns, were characterized by the competitive outbursts which curtailed income growth and induced Huish's fall from grace. Thus, the general manager, having contributed to a largely successful attempt to stabilize returns, was also in part responsible for the violent competition which caused a collapse of revenue in 1857–8. In fairness, however, it must be admitted that a trade depression in the autumn of 1857 affected business, especially in the manufacturing North, and it may also be suggested that without Huish's mastery of diplomatic and administrative methods in railway management, the company would have experienced lower returns far sooner than it did.

The achievements of Huish's management may be assessed further by an examination of the results from the company's large number of subsidiary undertakings. The accounts indicate that considerable losses were made by many of them during the 1850s, but dividends received from profitable concerns in which the company retained an interest helped greatly to offset their effects. Losses on the leases of the Preston & Wyre, Shropshire Union, and Manchester & Buxton railways, and on the Leeds & Liverpool and Rochdale canals amounted to £340,000 over the nine years from July 1851: the net loss on guarantees to the Stour Valley Railway was £172,000 for the same period, while guarantees to the Buckinghamshire Railway amounted to £117,000 over the $4\frac{1}{2}$ years to June 1855.[2] However, dividends collected from seven railways, 1851–60, totalled an estimated £760,000, which surely must have covered the operating losses of the other subsidiaries. Thus, although the entire capital investment in other lines remained on balance unproductive, at least the company escaped the large net losses on subsidiaries suffered by several major companies.

Table 42 provides a further crude measure of productivity, in terms of labour costs and earnings per man-hour. Wages per man-hour rose from 1851, until in 1857–8 they exceeded the level of 1848–9.[3] At the same time both gross and net earnings per man-hour fell, although there was

1 See above, pp. 158–60.
2 Computed from Company Accounts, RAC1/233, BTHR.
3 In 1848–9 the average wage per man-hour was estimated at 4.17d.; see table 20, above, p. 160.

Table 42
**London & North Western labour costs and earnings
per man-hour, 1851–8**

Year	Manpower*	Wage-bill†	Average wage	Wages per man-hour‡
1851–2	8,936	£432,603	£48.41	3.87d.
1852–3	11,362	510,611	44.94	3.60
1854–5	12,774	620,877	48.60	3.89
1856–7	13,290	663,234	49.90	3.99
1857–8	12,532	666,116	53.15	4.25

Year	Gross earnings§	Net earnings‖	Gross per worker	Net per worker	Gross per man-hour	Net per man-hour
1851–2	£2,436,215	£1,468,349	£272.6	£164.3	1.817s.	1.095s.
1852–3	2,616,759	1,548,623	230.3	136.3	1.535	0.909
1854–5	2,899,866	1,361,562	227.0	106.6	1.513	0.711
1856–7	3,273,256	1,837,169	246.3	138.2	1.642	0.921
1857–8	3,125,610	1,651,858	249.4	131.8	1.663	0.879

Source: Company Accounts, RAC1/233, BTHR, and Accounts and Papers,
P.P.1852–3, XCVII, 1854, LXII, 1854–5, XLVIII, 1857, Sess.2, XXXVII, 1857–8, LI.
* Manpower taken as at 30 June 1852, 1853, 1855, 1857, 1858, does not include
  managerial and secretarial staff, whose wages are excluded.
† Wage-bill includes sundry items, where these cannot be separated.
‡ Man-hours calculated with an estimate of a 60-hour week, 3,000–hour year.
§ Traffic receipts plus dividends received from other concerns.
‖ Gross earnings minus operating costs, losses on other lines, taxes and rates.

some recovery in the last two years (1856– 8), which suggests that the management had some success in relating the size of its labour force to changing company requirements during a period of rising prices.[1] To venture more would in the circumstances be dangerous. The data are influenced by several variables, many of them unidentified.[2] Moreover, comparisons with other companies would prove rather inconclusive, unless parity of operating conditions could be established.

Ton-mile statistics—the most useful measurement of operating performance—exist only in terms of six-monthly periods used by the company's locomotive departments, that is, from December to May, and

[1] Both the Sauerbeck and Rousseaux price series show a marked rise in prices in 1853 and 1854: the price level of 1854 was maintained until Huish's resignation in 1858; see Mitchell and Deane, op. cit., 472, 474.

[2] A change in the relationship between the London & North Western and its subsidiary companies may be relevant here, since the size of the labour force would be affected.

from June to November. Since revenue and costs were calculated over the periods January–June and July–December, a correlation, with the object of estimating net earnings per ton-mile, is not possible. Huish's department did, however, calculate revenue *per mile* and *per train-mile*. Although the defects of these statistical units have been indicated above,[1] the data are a further indication of the company's operating experience. In table 43, the revenue from passenger and goods traffic is differentiated.

Table 43
London & North Western net revenue per mile, and gross and net revenue per train-mile, passenger and goods traffic, 1851–60

Year July– June	Passenger and mails revenue			Goods revenue		
	Net per mile	Gross per train-mile	Net per train-mile	Net per mile	Gross per train-mile	Net per train-mile
1851–2	£1,882	7s. 6¼d.	4s. 9d.	£ 826	6s. 2½d.	2s. 10d.
1853–4	1,580	6 6¼	3 10¼	1,009	6 5½	2 11
1855–6	1,542	6 8¼	3 11¼	1,177	6 9¼	3 2¼
1857–8	1,340	6 1¾	3 4¼	945	6 2	2 6¾
1859–60	1,131	5 11	3 3	1,014	6 1¼	2 8

Source: Company Accounts, RAC1/233, BTHR.

Passenger earnings show a steady downward trend, in response to the competition of the 1850s. But goods earnings, though subject to greater annual fluctuation, held up well, a creditable performance that reflects the company's lead in this department. The period 1857–8 saw a sharp fall in the earnings from both types of traffic, clearly a result of the collapse of Huish's system of inter-company agreements.

The several partial analyses of company performance support the contention suggested by the more circumstantial evidence, that Huish enjoyed some success in his efforts to stabilize the London & North Western's position in the face of severe competition. Although there was little improvement in net income, and rates of return continued to fall, the return on capital was stabilized until 1857–8, and earnings per unit of labour appear to have improved in the two years after 1856. Earnings on goods traffic were also maintained. Further, the demonstrably poorer results of 1857–8 (or, indeed, of 1857–60) suggest that the company's position would have deteriorated earlier without the much-criticized strategy of the 'Confederacy' and Huish's general efforts to stimulate

1 E.g. pp. 233–4, 240, and cf. Boag, *op. cit.*, 4, 22, 24–5, and Ross, *op. cit.*, 98–103.

efficiency in internal management. Indeed, Huish's preoccupation with inter-railway affairs did not appear to reduce his interest in supervising internal costs.[1] His activities in the 1850s revealed an increasing awareness of the intricacies of railway costing methods, and a firm resolve to relate decision-making to the findings of comprehensive statistical analysis. His efforts to achieve operating economies, while stressing the importance of maintaining the effectiveness of the company's plant, were both of theoretical value and practical worth.

1 The expenditure in Huish's own department was closely supervised. Costs (related to mileage operated) fell in the 1850s: office expenditure for the six months to 30 June 1851 was £21.73 per mile, and over the same period in 1858, £19.72: Company Accounts, RAC1/233, BTHR.

8

Conclusion

Huish's resignation in 1858 has often been held to represent the start of a new and more peaceful era in railway affairs, and it is an appropriate point at which to take stock of railway management in a broader context. In this final chapter, a brief consideration of Huish's activities after 1858 is followed by a general account of his work as manager, and some concluding observations on the significance of both his management and that of the London & North Western in the development of British management practice.

1 Huish in exile, 1858-67

Huish gave up his post as general manager in November 1858 and thereafter ceased to influence company policy. He was called upon to give
occasional advice on minor matters,[1] but the wholehearted opposition of
Richard Moon, chairman from 1861, and the curtailment of executive
freedom, prevented his return to favour. He did, however, retain an active
interest in railway management, and his experience proved of great value
elsewhere. On moving to the Isle of Wight he soon became involved in
railway politics. In 1860 the Isle of Wight Railway was authorized to
construct a line from Ryde to Ventnor, and as early as December of the
same year Huish attended a Board meeting, advising the directors on
problems of finance and construction.[2] On 1 January 1861 he was offered
£500 as a share qualification and a further £500 for his services in supervising land-purchase and construction, should he join the Board: this he
did in October.[3]

Huish's work as a director of the Isle of Wight Railway paralleled in
many ways his duties as secretary of the Glasgow Paisley & Greenock,
25 years earlier. He negotiated with the London & South Western and
London Brighton & South Coast railways for running powers over their
joint line from Ryde (St John's) to the steamer pierhead, and was prominent in the purchase of land and the supervision of contractors' costs—
these were tasks he had performed in Scotland.[4] Although failing health
prevented an active participation in management after 1863, his success
in curbing costs during construction helped to put the company on a
sound footing, and his negotiations with companies on the mainland
resulted in the creation of a profitable direct route from London and the
South to the resorts of Sandown, Shanklin, and Ventnor. Thus, Huish
made the transition from executive manager to director—a rare phenomenon at this time—but his work was limited to assisting a minor company
and lay outside important railway affairs. Had it not been for the intense
opposition of certain directors in 1858 he would certainly have followed
Richard Creed onto the London & North Western Board.

Huish's considerable experience was also harnessed by the Board of

1 See Huish to Chandos, 17 Jan. 1859, and Huish to Stewart, 21 Sept. 1860, 15 Dec.
  1863, HL2/R373/13/11, 15–16.
2 I.O.W. Mins, 7 Dec. 1860, IOW1/1, BTHR.
3 I.O.W. Mins, 1 Jan. and 3 Oct. 1861; I.O.W. General Meeting, 15 Aug. 1861,
  IOW1/2, BTHR.
4 I.O.W. Mins, 1861–3, *passim*, IOW1/2–3, BTHR.

Trade, which appointed him arbiter in several inter-company disputes. He was invited to settle a number of disputes over running powers, particularly in Ireland,[1] and in 1866 he gave evidence on the same subject to the Select Committee on the Cornwall Railway.[2] He was also called in to decide on minor problems arising from the joint use of railway facilities.[3] These activities placed Huish in the position of 'railway sage'. His evidence to the Royal Commission on Railways in 1866 ranged widely over several problems of railway management. Questioned on running powers, he suggested that these had often been conceded to forestall the creation of duplicate lines, and were in this sense acceptable.[4] However, he gave firmer support for company amalgamation, as a means to secure ease of operation and higher profits.[5] He also advocated uniformity in operating regulations and a uniform system of signalling, in the interests of safety.[6]

Huish also professed a concern for the conditions in which railwaymen worked. His sympathy for the cause of a half-day holiday was publicized in 1856, when it was revealed that he had closed certain London & North Western offices in Manchester, Liverpool, and London on Saturday afternoons.[7] Huish was described as "a gentleman . . . whose character stands high for Christian principle",[8] and although this may not have been evident to his opponents in the railway world, in retirement he was able to indulge his Nonconformist ideals. He favoured, for example, the provision of religious instruction for the 'labouring classes' and in 1863 obtained the appointment of a Scripture Reader for men constructing the Isle of Wight Railway.[9]

Huish's business interests in the 1860s were not confined to railways. He was prominent, for example, as Chairman of the Electric & International Telegraph, and Clifton Suspension Bridge companies. Unfortunately, there is very little evidence about his precise rôle within

1 Huish claimed to have settled four or five such disputes, among them that between the Dublin & Meath and Dublin & Drogheda railways in 1866: Huish's evidence, *R.C. on Railways*, P.P.1867, XXXVIII, QQ.15853, 15857, 16012.
2 *S.C. on Central Cornwall Railway Bill*, 1866, QQ.101–71, PYB1/344, BTHR.
3 In January 1865, for example, he decided the rent to be paid by the M.S. & L. for the use of the G.N. station at Doncaster.
4 *R.C. on Railways*, P.P.1867, XXXVIII, QQ.15852, 15866, 15885–91. Running powers granted the right to operate trains over the lines of other companies on payment of agreed tolls.
5 *Ibid.*, QQ.15904–6, 16082.
6 *Ibid.*, QQ.15855–6, 15929–52.
7 Huish, letter to John Lilwall, 10 July 1856, published in J. Fitzgerald, *The Duty of Procuring More Rest for the Labouring Classes* . . . (1856), 56.
8 *Ibid.*
9 I.O.W. Mins, 5 June 1863, IOW1/3, BTHR.

these organizations, but it does appear that he controlled the policy of the telegraph company for some time, particularly in its dealings with rivals, such as Reuter, and with railway companies.[1] The Clifton Bridge company, a revival of an unsuccessful project of the 1830s, owed much to the active promotion of interested railwaymen and engineers. Huish, together with William Barlow and John Hawkshaw, took advantage of the availability of equipment originally intended for Hungerford Bridge and organized subscriptions for a new Act of 1861, authorizing an expenditure of £35,000; under his chairmanship the bridge was completed, and opened in December 1864.[2] These examples suggest the hypothesis that experience gained in the railway industry was transferred to associated enterprises.[3]

2   Huish as manager

Huish, always a controversial figure, continues to excite the censure of those historians who have concentrated their attention on the more discreditable episodes of railway history. Although "The blackening of Mark Huish as the archfiend of railway diplomacy" has been declared a "boring sport, indulged in by lesser and ill-informed writers",[4] many still brand him as persistently or uniquely 'unscrupulous', 'dictatorial', or 'Machiavellian', using a variety of epithets which do little to provide us with an objective assessment of his managerial career.[5] Extreme criti-

---

1 Board Agenda Book No.3, Private Letter Book, 1866, Electric & International Telegraph Company, G.P.O.R.O.
2 *Illustrated London News*, 15 Mar. 1861, 7 Dec. 1864; W. Barlow, Memorandum, 12 Feb. 1867, HL1/24, BTHR.
3 Cf. G. R. Hawke, *Railways and Economic Growth in England and Wales 1840–1870* (1970), 385.
4 Review of Ellis, *British Railway History*, in *Stephenson Locomotive Society Journal*, xxxi (1955), 47.
5 A line of succession is evident, from E.T. MacDermot, *History of the Great Western Railway*, vol.I (1927), 318–20, 393, and the more objective Grinling, *op. cit.*, 92–4, 151–65, and H. G. Lewin, *The Railway Mania and its Aftermath* (1936), 440–4, to the more modern assessments of R. Lloyd, *Railwaymen's Gallery* (1953), 52–78; Ellis, *op. cit.*, 104, 182–211, 234–7; R. Hough, *Six Great Railwaymen* (1955), 111, 127, 134, 140; Dow, *op. cit.*, 182, 191; P. E. Baughan, 'Buxton Centenary—The Approaches from Derby and Burton-on-Trent', *Railway Magazine*, cix (1963), 678; and E. G. Barnes, *The Rise of the Midland Railway 1844–1874* (1966), 133. The faults of the 'railway historian' are revealed by Kellett, *op. cit.*, 135, and his 'Writing on Victorian Railways: An Essay in Nostalgia', *Victorian Studies*, xiii (1969), 90–6, and by Hawke's study of Lardner and his critics, *op. cit.*, 93–9.

cism, whether it be due to excessive hindsight or to bias in favour of individual companies, should certainly be avoided. Analysis of company management demands a wider perspective, and although in this book Huish's obvious intrigues, irrationalities, and miscalculations have certainly not been underestimated, they have been viewed in the context of the overall strategy of the London & North Western and the managerial options available to it. Huish was not the company's sole policy-maker, and he did not possess the 'dictatorial' influence so often ascribed to him. Nor did he necessarily endorse the policies which circumstances forced him to pursue. He recognized, for example, that inter-company relations could not be stabilized by pooling and other traffic agreements, but was compelled to face a situation created by a government which actively encouraged competition and blocked the path to company amalgamation.[1]

Huish's shortcomings should not of course be minimized. In his business dealings the "wily Captain", as Lewin called him,[2] frequently resorted to a mixture of brute force and guile.[3] His personality did not lend itself easily to the careful compromise, and his relations with both the directors and his own 'middle management' were often strained.[4] An intuitive manager, who was prepared to interfere with any employee and bend any rule should it suit him, he made strenuous efforts to retain personal control over as many of the company's affairs as possible. In this sense his actions may be considered regressive, since the company was pulled back towards the 'bossed' rather than the 'managed' firm by a man who had done much to set it on a progressive path.[5]

Nevertheless, the more positive aspects of Huish's career deserve our close attention. As General Manager of the London & North Western he became the foremost of an élite among Victorian business managers, enjoying a high social status and an exceptional salary. When he joined the Glasgow Paisley & Greenock Railway in 1837 he was paid £200 a year, a relatively modest sum: ten years later his salary was ten times that amount, far higher than the earnings of executive managers in the majority of British companies.[6] Huish's investments in railways were also

1 See above, pp. 164, 215, 218.
2 Lewin, *op. cit.*, 440.
3 In fictional terms Huish probably resembles Galsworthy's Elderson rather than Mrs Gaskell's Captain Brown: John Galsworthy, *The White Monkey*, 1924 (Heinemann, 1925, 43–52 &c), Elizabeth Gaskell, *Cranford*, 1851–3 (*Cranford and Other Tales*, Smith, Elder, 1906, 10–23).
4 See above, pp. 54, 78, 116, 175–8, 182.
5 Recently, one manager considered a staff of 400 to be the limit of personal control: A. Jay, *Management and Machiavelli* (1967), 16.
6 In the 1850s salaries of £1,000 were not uncommon among leading railway managers: such earnings normally exceeded the expectations of 'managers' (i.e. non-owners)

substantial. His will reveals a personal fortune of almost £40,000, an immense sum for a salaried official at this time.[1] Indeed, the *Middlesex Directory* of 1855 describes him as a member of the "gentry".[2] Huish's career thus represents the growing stature of the professional executive in British industrial and commercial management. He epitomized the evolution of the railway manager from the comparatively low-paid official, of diverse origins, limited status, and vague responsibilities, to the highly-skilled, well-paid specialist. Succeeding general managers of major railway companies could expect the final rewards of a seat on the Board, and in many cases, a knighthood.[3] In Huish's day the haphazard practices of the 1820s and 1830s were replaced by a clearer understanding of the executive's rôle and a recognition that the efficiency of the railways was closely associated with the practical knowledge of such men.

From the 1830s the railways provided the first real opportunity for training an administrative class in the techniques of large-scale business management, and Huish spanned the main stages of this development. He began his career as secretary of the Glasgow Paisley & Greenock, a small company in the course of construction. This railway typified the infant industry in its attempts to adjust to unfamiliar problems of size and control. Huish was able to take advantage of the management's lack of experience to control a wide variety of business matters and participate fully in policy-making, before an established procedure had been created.[4] As secretary and manager of the Grand Junction, Huish became the executive head of an early trunk railway wrestling with more complex problems of administrative responsibility. A more sophisticated managerial structure resulted, with a measure of delegation to paid officers and some clearly-defined areas of responsibility, but the failure of the Board of Directors to avoid trivial matters reduced the management's effectiveness as an instrument of control.[5] Finally, as Manager of the London & North Western Huish led one of the most advanced executive structures of the early Victorian period. Business was carefully divided among a large number of committees and delegated to executives

---

in other industries. Pollard suggests that top managers earned between £500 and £2,000 p.a. in the period 1790–1830, but concedes that "Many, if not most, of these men were partners in their firms", *op. cit.*, 144.

1 Huish's will, February 1862, Somerset House, London.
2 *Middlesex Directory*, 1855, Guildhall Library, London.
3 E.g. the careers of William Cawkwell, George Findlay, James Allport, Edward Watkin, Henry Oakley, William Birt, and James Thompson.
4 See Chapter III.
5 *Ibid.*

who were themselves organized on a committee basis. It was Huish's principal task to link the various administrative bodies and keep the presiding Board of Directors informed of the company's activities. In the 1850s the company made several positive contributions to managerial theory and practice within the industry, and Huish himself inspired developments in accounting, statistical analysis, and technology.[1]

Huish was indeed an exceptional manager, with a far wider command of railway problems than was customary. His influence over the general councils of the industry was rarely matched by other executives. He believed, for example, in the railway control of goods traffic, and emphasized the need for a large volume of traffic and a high quality of service: both proved to be policies fundamental to competitive railway operation for the rest of the century. He was one of the few executives to act as a company delegate to the Railway Clearing House—a position normally open only to directors—and as such promoted the Goods Managers' and General Managers' Conferences, which became a vital channel for the confidential exchange of railway management policy.[2] The 'Euston Confederacy' was very much his own solution to the traffic problems of the 1850s, a shortlived but bold and imaginative piece of strategic planning. The pricing and pooling agreements embraced by this alliance system represented a major development in railway history, and formed the basis for the more successful rates conferences of the 1860s and beyond.[3]

The pressures of the 1850s—increasing competition, rising costs, and governmental pricing constraints—made the manager's task more difficult, but they also stimulated improvements in management techniques. Here Huish's contribution was also considerable. He was one of the first managers to devise methods of accounting and control appropriate to a large railway company. His published reports, dealing with a variety of technical and general business matters, were a testimony to his importance not only as a practical manager but also as a railway theoretician. As chief executive of the largest joint-stock company of the day his advice was often sought by representatives of other railways, and his views naturally attracted attention in both the daily press and specialist journals. The Board became increasingly dependent upon him for information and policy, and his resignation in 1858 may be attributed in part

1 See Chapters V and VII.
2 See above, pp. 144–7, 224–7.
3 E.g. the English & Scotch Rates Conference, and the Normanton Rates Conference. Huish's role in inter-company affairs was such that Denison, chairman of the Great Northern, complained of executives able "to determine the principles or conditions on which negotiations are to be conducted, and treaties made . . .", *The Times*, 12 Feb. 1856.

to the directors' resentment of the exalted position of a man whose command of day-to-day problems was frequently too comprehensive to be seriously challenged.[1] Huish, then, was the outstanding product of the scope allowed to managers of the early railways. He exploited the vast opportunities offered to excel in an industry where experience was slight, and change rapid and considerable. While we must await detailed studies of other managers, none of Huish's contemporaries appears to have equalled either his predominance in railway affairs or his range of managerial interests.

3 Huish, the London & North Western, and the development of management practice

Any evaluation of business management practice is a tricky exercise, and in an historical investigation the problems are intensified. How do we decide who did what? Who influenced whom? To what extent were decisions and actions systematically formulated, and how novel were the techniques applied? These questions become more difficult to answer the larger and more complex the organization, the patchier the evidence, and the further back in history we go. There is also a strong temptation to see the history of management primarily as a linear process, a continuous development from the intuitive entrepreneur, acting instinctively, to the modern executive, master of the complexities of management science. Our studies suggest, however, that there have been several discontinuities, several 'ebb and flow' movements, with techniques discovered and developed, only to be abandoned, and later re-discovered.[2] Taking full account of such difficulties, an attempt will be made in these concluding passages to assess the management of Huish and his company in the context of modern management theory and practice. Two main questions will be raised: how 'modern' was Huish's personal management? and, Did the London & North Western contribute to the overall development of management practice?

1 See above, pp. 173–82.
2 The 'ebb and flow' process has been argued, for example, by McKendrick, who considers that "many advanced techniques had existed in the late eighteenth century, but had atrophied . . .": N. McKendrick, 'Josiah Wedgwood and Cost Accounting in the Industrial Revolution', *Economic History Review*, 2nd ser., XXIII (1970), 46. The railways' (and especially the London & North Western's) experience with depreciation funds and ton-mile statistics is a relevant example of such a process, see above, pp. 148–55, 236–41.

How does Huish compare with the chief executive of the current text-books? The short answer is, very well. His activities were similar to those expected of today's top managers in large-scale companies, and he certainly comes close to George Steiner's ideal, the charismatic "leader of men . . . a business statesman in dealing with government and community leaders; a thoughtful person who can look ahead and know how to get there; a man of action who can make decisions for prompt compliance; an innovator; and a vigilant seeker of opportunities who is willing to come to grips with and solve problems."[1] As General Manager of both the Grand Junction and London & North Western railways Huish appears as the self-assured taker of calculated risks, the creative, persuasive negotiator, at the centre of company planning, and responsible for the company's total efforts.[2] In this latter rôle he certainly conforms to one of the most important functions of the modern chief executive—"to identify and specify aims for the entire enterprise".[3] He was both theoretician and practical manager—both "yogi" and "commissar"[4]—a dedicated company man responsible for the general welfare and overall business policy of the companies he served.[5]

On closer examination, however, certain doubts as to Huish's 'modernity' emerge. Today's chief executive is expected not only to lead his company, but also to co-ordinate the efforts of other managers, who enjoy a range of delegated responsibilities.[6] Huish certainly helped to encourage the delegation of authority from directors to executives in the railway industry, but was himself anxious to dominate policy-making and reluctant to delegate matters to his subordinate officers. In this he remained the intuitive entrepreneur, resembling the owner-manager of the small firm. The results of Huish's zealous internal management may be compared with the warning given to modern managers by Frank Pace: "If you did try to know everything that was happening and controlled your men that tightly, your men would leave you or would lose their initiative

1 G. A. Steiner, *Top Management Planning* (1969), 89.
2 Cf. *ibid.*, 128–30.
3 *Ibid.*, 141. Cf. 64: "The job of a top manager essentially concerns the way in which his total organization reacts to its environment to achieve the objectives set for the organization. His concern is with the totality of the enterprise and how it operates in its environment." See also C. I. Barnard, *The Functions of the Executive* (Cambridge, Mass., 1938), 231–3, and R. A. Gordon, *Business Leadership in the Large Corporation* (Berkeley and Los Angeles, 2nd ed. 1966), 5, 106–14.
4 Cf. Jay, *op.cit.*, 111–17.
5 Cf. P. A. Baran and P. M. Sweezy, *Monopoly Capital. An Essay on the American Economic and Social Order* (New York, 1966), 15–16, 25–6, 37–8.
6 Cf. Gordon, *op. cit.*, 3–5, 52–3, 106–7.

which made them effective."[1] To be fair to Huish, the balance between individual initiative and group consensus is a very delicate one. It poses a dilemma which continues to worry modern managers and their theorists. From about 1850 Huish withdrew to his Euston office, adopting a more remote stance. He was however criticized for it, Moorsom suggesting to Chandos that management might be improved "If we had a manager who, instead of sitting all day on a tripod, like a Delphian oracle of old-fulminating prophecies, were to occupy himself out of door on the line . . . and learn by his knowledge the real facts . . . ".[2] But this criticism of Huish as the office-bound manager unacquainted with the railway's operation was misplaced. He was surely moving, if reluctantly, towards a necessary function for the chief executive of a large company—to co-ordinate activities at the centre, and to spend more time on general planning. His increasing involvement with railway politics, government committees, and management publicity suggests this process of 'corporate planning', designed to promote the company's interests within its business environment.[3]

Huish, then, approximates to the modern chief executive to an extent remarkable for a founder member of a new profession, a man merely on the threshold of a nascent science. But although his management represents a useful model of executive behaviour, his example may not have impressed contemporary managers critical of the activities which accompanied his fall from office. This being so, we should extend our inquiry to the total management experience of the London & North Western, and the railways in general, in Huish's day. How important was the railways' contribution to business management? How new were the management techniques adopted before 1860? Was experience passed on to other companies and other industries?

It has been suggested that the London & North Western displayed several relatively advanced features of management, and it has been argued that a new attitude to large-scale business management came with the growth of the railway industry. But it is hard to establish precisely that the techniques developed were of decisive importance elsewhere in the economy, and even more difficult to establish that experience was actually transferred to other industries. Dr Hawke, in his recent examination of the railways and economic growth, considers the claims for the railways as pioneers in business management, and shows a sceptic-

1 Quoted in Steiner, *op. cit.*, 94.
2 Moorsom to Chandos, 2 Nov. 1854, HL2/R211, BTHR.
3 Cf. Steiner, *op.cit.*, 90; Kenn Rogers, *Managers—Performance and Personality* (1963), 105–6.

ism similar to that extended by Pollard to management's rôle in the Industrial Revolution.[1] Other writers, however, have little doubt that the railways sponsored important developments in business management practice.[2] The debate raises all the complex problems of the management process discussed above, and many of the issues require a great deal of further research before any firm judgments can be made. Here it is possible to mention only some of the arguments and suggest only a few of the available hypotheses.

How new were the techniques developed by the London & North Western? Clearly, there are immense problems in determining management innovation. For example, the company under Huish's guidance led the railways' drive towards a greater degree of cost-consciousness, accompanied by improvements in statistical analysis and accounting procedures. But other historical investigations have uncovered parallel achievements, which must make us wary of attributing too much to the railways. In the late eighteenth century Josiah Wedgwood used cost accounting to aid decision-making, and in the 1840s Alexander Blair's statistical analyses and strategic planning models for the Bank of Scotland were no less advanced.[3] Hawke, indeed, doubts whether railway management offered possibilities for acquiring *any* particular management skills, either in organization, accounting, marketing, or costing.[4] But while isolated companies established advanced management procedures both before and after the coming of the railways, before 1860 no single industry appears to have offered that coherent response to problems of large-scale management which the railways developed, and which was exemplified by the London & North Western. The large railway company faced at an early stage all the major difficulties of big business, and the general character of its management was influenced by both the size and the variety of these difficulties.

It remains true that there were few examples of a professional managerial class in British businesses in the nineteenth century. As Professor Payne has remarked of the period before 1914, "the structure of many British companies inhibited the ascent of the brilliant salaried official.

1 Hawke, *op. cit.*, 384–8; Pollard, *op. cit.*, 271; and see McKendrick, *loc. cit.*, 46.
2 E.g. Edwards, 'Some Notes on the . . . Development of Cost Accounting in Great Britain', *loc. cit.*, 193; M. Zinkin, 'Galbraith and Consumer Sovereignty', *Journal of Industrial Economics*, XVI (1967), 3–4, quoted by Hawke, *op. cit.*, 386.
3 McKendrick, *loc. cit.*, 45–67; T. R. Gourvish, 'The Bank of Scotland 1830–45', *Scottish Journal of Political Economy*, XVI (1969), 288–305.
4 Hawke, *op. cit.*, 385–7.

Leadership by inheritance applied in a great range of industrial activities".[1] This was even more the case before 1870. Such a charge could not, however, be levelled against the railways. The upward mobility offered by the London & North Western and other railways, though not a phenomenon completely new to industry,[2] was effectively denied to the majority of managers in Huish's day. The divisional system of organization may not have been a new development, but it is misleading to equate the highly-developed structure of the London & North Western, encompassing 15,000 men spread over most of England, with the more modest collieries and ironworks, where capital and labour inputs were on a much smaller scale.[3] Positive innovations, such as the executive committee, the partnership of directors and executives for specific tasks, and the planned routing of decisions, were developed by the company, and it is difficult to imagine smaller industrial concerns requiring a similar range of sophisticated procedures before 1860.[4]

Hawke contends that forward planning was not found on the railways.[5] But although definitions are always troublesome, the activities of Huish and his company certainly merit the name 'planning', and a great deal of it appears to have been 'forward'. General business strategies were created, cost and traffic trends were projected, and the General Manager was at the centre of a vast network of planning procedures, devised by both his line and staff managers.[6] Further research will probably confirm the impression that Huish was by no means a unique example of the manager as planner on the early railways.

Doubts have also been expressed about the railways' rôle in the development of accounting techniques. But here too it is difficult to accept Hawke's suggestion, based upon the rather flimsy evidence offered by Pollard, that the railways were no more successful than other industries in developing satisfactory accountancy, and that "the need to develop exact costing techniques was less pressing".[7] The London & North Western appears to have been one of the pioneers of several advances, not least of which was the formulation, by Huish and others,

1 P. L. Payne, 'The Emergence of the Large-scale Company in Great Britain, 1870–1914', *Economic History Review*, New ser., xx (1967), 538.
2 Cf. Pollard, *op. cit.*, 145.
3 *Ibid.*, 24 *et seq.*; Hawke, *op. cit.*, 386.
4 See above, pp. 109–16, 167–82.
5 Hawke, *op. cit.*, 386.
6 See above, pp. 258–61 and cf. Steiner, *op. cit.*, 34, 37–9. Plans were developed not only by Huish and his staff but also by the company's goods managers (such as Poole and Salt) and locomotive superintendents (such as McConnell).
7 Hawke, *op. cit.*, 387; Pollard, *op. cit.*, 239–41, 245–6, 248–9.

of procedures to determine depreciation and plant valuation.[1] Moreover, in responding to more difficult business conditions after 1847, the company placed greater emphasis on analysis for costing control, and made a deliberate attempt to spread costs over time and stabilize dividends.[2] It is true that some techniques were imperfectly developed, and some were soon abandoned. But the company's record remains impressive, both for its internal management, and for the encouragement it gave to other railways through publication of its problems and solutions. Further studies may establish a firmer link between the major railways and management accounting than the one suggested here.

It is also difficult to be certain, as Hawke appears to be, that the railways did not demand the marketing skills required in other industries.[3] Certainly, some companies enjoyed local monopolies, and many services could be provided without a careful consideration of consumer demand. But in the 1840s and 1850s competition intensified, the railway map was constantly changing, and as a result the product offered by individual companies was also subject to continual change. Problems of pricing, quality of service, 'sales' agreements, and public relations were all clearly important in Huish's management, and strenuous advertising was often necessary to promote competitive services. Efforts to 'control the market', encouraged by Huish and other managers, suggest that railway marketing demanded skills at least as complex as those needed elsewhere.[4]

The early railways, and especially the London & North Western, made the first concerted attempt to solve the overriding problems of large-scale business, and developed important and possibly novel practices of business management. But there are strong doubts that these were taken up by companies in other industries. Hawke indicates that there existed opportunities to exchange information by means of managerial mobility, but he also suggests that movement between industries was not exceptionally characteristic of railway managers, and certainly not true of leading executives.[5] This is, of course, hardly surprising. The railways were a specialist, prestige industry, where salaries were high, and the inducements to move very small. Huish was one of the last of the 'old school' of managers, recruited from outside: thereafter, both top and middle managers were internally recruited, trained within the industry,

1 See above, pp. 148–53, 236–7 and cf. G.A. Lee, *Transport Finance and Accounting* (1965), 20–4, 34–5.
2 See above, pp. 148–55, 234–42.
3 Hawke, *op. cit.*, 384.
4 See above, pp. 201–18 and cf. Kellett, *op. cit.*, 65–7, 134–6, and W. S. Barry, *Managing A Transport Business* (1963), 162–76.
5 Hawke, *op. cit.*, 384–5.

and ended their careers as top managers or directors of the companies they had served. In later life they appear to have offered little to other industries. Indeed, the record of other businesses—as regards executive status, for example—suggests that the likelihood of an extensive and successful interchange of ideas and techniques is remote.

But if the idea of a widespread and direct transference of management techniques is rejected, we cannot dismiss so easily the railways' indirect influence on business. Railway management attracted considerable public attention, and Huish and his company were prominent in publicizing important general features of business management.[1] The possibility also remains that particular companies benefited from contact with the railways and their managers. A detailed investigation of several managerial careers is surely needed before we can be certain that railway executives did not participate in other businesses—Huish certainly did so[2]—and that directors did not apply their experience of railways to other ventures.

The experience of Huish and his company thus marks an important chapter in the development not only of railways but also of business management practice as a whole. Indeed, the leading contribution of railways was not confined to Britain. The work of Professor Chandler, for example, has done much to indicate the importance of American railroads in promoting large-scale business techniques,[3] and it is interesting to find that the management of Huish and the London & North Western has very close parallels with that of Daniel McCallum, General Superintendent of the Erie Railroad, and the Baltimore & Ohio, Erie, and Pennsylvania railroads. These companies resembled the London & North Western in their size, geographic extent, and complex organization, and in both countries a rise in executive status accompanied the development of line and staff procedures, detailed planning systems, and the growing use of accounting methods and statistical analysis to aid effective administration.[4] There was, also, a parallel response to competition and general

---

1 Huish, Salt, and Poole as executive writers established a pattern of leadership for the company which was maintained by G. Findlay, *The Working and Management of an English Railway* (1889), D. Stevenson, *Fifty Years on the London & North Western* . . . (1891), and G.P. Neele, *Railway Reminiscences* (1904).
2 See above, pp. 255–6.
3 E.g. A. D. Chandler, 'The Railroads: Pioneers in Modern Corporate Management', *Business History Review*, xxxix (1965), 17–40, Chandler and S. Salsbury, 'The Railroads: Innovators in Modern Business Administration', in B. Mazlish (ed.), *The Railroad and the Space Program. An Essay in Historical Analogy* (Cambridge, Mass., 1965), 127–62, and Chandler, *The Railroads: The Nation's First Big Business* (New York, 1965), 97–128.
4 Chandler, 'The Railroads: Pioneers . . .', *loc. cit.*

economic pressure.[1] All this indicates that Huish's career was not an isolated example of the way in which planned management made a valid contribution to the more effective operation of the railways as businesses, and in doing so brought the industry closer to principles of modern management behaviour. In Britain some techniques did not develop very far, some were even abandoned, and the railways remained exceptional firms.[2] But it is perhaps not too much to apply to Britain Chandler's claim that "railroads created modern administration—that is, they moved business activity away from organizations run by entrepreneurs with the aid of personal trustees, relatives, and the like to corporations, with a systematized, bureaucratic management."[3]

1 The L.N.W.'s reorganizations of 1848 and 1855 were similar to that of the Erie in 1853—responses to more difficult business situations, *ibid.*, 27–8.
2 In Britain it was not until the twentieth century that amalgamations took place to bring other industrial companies remotely close to the capitalization of railway companies. In 1905, for example, the largest industrial company, Imperial Tobacco, had a capital of only £17.5 million: Payne, *loc. cit.*, 539–40.
3 Chandler and Salsbury, *loc. cit.*, 128. Cf. Gordon, *op. cit.*, 73–5.

Appendix

Appendix

1 Statistical tables

Table 44
Grand Junction revenue statistics, 1841–5

Period half-year	'Coaching'*	Livestock	Coal etc.	Merchandise	Rents	Total revenue
July–Dec. 1841	£192,437	£4,419	£1,462	£39,883	£3,608	£241,816
Jan.–June 1842	161,358	6,785	1,209	36,003	2,277	207,635
July–Dec. 1842	161,445	6,813	1,337	35,882	2,358	207,637
Jan.–June 1843	132,976	9,333	1,120	39,198	2,464	185,093
July–Dec. 1843	155,861	8,867	1,170	44,218	2,826	212,944
Jan.–June 1844	139,031	7,810	1,161	45,273	2,152	195,429
July–Dec. 1844	161,480	8,203	1,708	55,687	2,090	229,169
Jan.–June 1845	151,199	11,350	2,185	59,390	2,199	226,326
July–Dec. 1845†	285,028	16,092	8,300	121,738	4,106	435,268

Source: Company Accounts, GJR1/7, BTHR. Figures rounded to nearest pound.
* Includes passenger, carriages, mails, parcels, and horses traffic.
† Revenue includes returns from the Liverpool & Manchester, Bolton & Leigh, and
  Kenyon & Leigh railways.

Table 45
Grand Junction revenue and costs statistics, 1841–6

Period half-year	Gross traffic receipts	Operating costs*	Total gross revenue†	Total costs	Final balance (net income)
July–Dec. 1841	£238,208	£ 90,514	£241,816	£104,998	£136,817
Jan.–June 1842	205,358	77,235	207,635	93,974	113,661
July–Dec. 1842	205,479	61,489	207,837	88,367	119,470
Jan.–June 1843	182,629	63,739	185,093	80,320	104,772
July–Dec. 1843	210,118	68,196	212,944	85,767	127,176
Jan.–June 1844	193,277	66,930	195,429	84,309	111,120
July–Dec. 1844	227,079	77,692	229,169	96,593	132,576
Jan.–June 1845	224,127	81,114	226,326	96,636	129,869
July–Dec. 1845‡	431,162	138,650	435,268	180,499	254,768

Source: Company Accounts, GJR1/7, BTHR.
* Excludes rates, taxes, permanent way maintenance, legal and compensation costs, and, from July–Dec. 1843, costs of Crewe gas works, etc.
† Includes rents and interest.
‡ Data includes returns from the amalgamated railway companies (cf. table 44).

Table 46
Grand Junction goods traffic statistics, 1841–6

Period half-year	Total goods receipts	Merchandise receipts %	Livestock receipts %	Coal receipts %
July–Dec. 1841	£ 45,764	87.1	9.7	3.2
Jan.–June 1842	43,997	81.8	15.4	2.8
July–Dec. 1842	44,032	81.4	15.5	3.1
Jan.–June 1843	49,642	78.9	18.8	2.3
July-Dec. 1843	54,255	81.5	16.3	2.2
Jan.–June 1844	54,244	83.5	14.4	2.1
July–Dec. 1844	65,598	84.9	12.5	2.6
Jan.–June 1845	72,925	81.4	15.6	3.0
July–Dec. 1845	146,130*	83.3	11.0	5.7
Jan.–June 1846	162,769*	82.3	11.9	5.8
Weighted average 1841–6:		82.7	13.4	3.9

Source: Company Accounts, GJR1/7, BTHR.
* Includes receipts from amalgamated railway companies.

Table 47
London & North Western revenue statistics, 1846–51

Period half-year	Passengers	Horses/dogs*	Parcels	Merchandise†	Livestock	Coal	Mails
Jan.–June 1846	£611,616	£18,751	£44,827	£261,877	£30,245	£14,397	n.s. §
July–Dec. 1846	672,659	19,110	55,679	290,547	37,793	15,758	
Jan.–June 1847	600,240	17,791	52,358	294,363	21,940	22,105	
July–Dec. 1847	652,392	17,666	56,050	317,459	38,916	26,201	£21,442
Jan.–June 1848	583,279	16,859	49,087	291,762	22,084	25,952	20,930
July–Dec. 1848	635,005	17,248	55,059	329,310	36,883	27,580	22,192
Jan.–June 1849	559,569	16,805	50,051	335,899	20,312	28,810	21,491
July–Dec. 1849	629,136	17,263	52,296	345,394	37,068	28,089	20,355
Jan.–June 1850	589,890	17,538	46,765	372,757	25,988	37,213	20,026
July–Dec. 1850	640,699	16,258	52,303	399,163	36,570	42,009	20,285
Jan.–June 1851	637,378	17,238	45,352	385,325	23,290	45,102	28,893
July–Dec. 1851	851,259‡	15,146	50,808	398,529	34,369	46,098	24,338

Source: Company Accounts, RAC1/233, BTHR.
* And private carriages.
† From July–Dec. 1847 the figures are net of collection and delivery charges, as per the agency agreements.
‡ Includes revenue from excursions to the Great Exhibition.
§ n.s. 'Mails' were not separated in the accounts until July–Dec. 1847.

Table 48
London & North Western revenue and costs statistics, 1846–51

Period half-year	Gross traffic receipts	Operating costs*	Total gross Revenue†	Total costs (includes rail renewal)	Balance	Final balance (including rail renewal costs)
Jan.–June 1846	£981,417	£384,624	£1,002,270	£467,341	£534,929	n.s. §
July–Dec. 1846	1,091,549	347,115	1,110,795	456,884	653,910	n.s.
Jan.–June 1847	1,008,799	384,469	1,030,691	515,998	514,697	n.s.
July–Dec. 1847	1,130,129	378,771	1,160,085	552,693	647,855	£607,392
Jan.–June 1848	1,009,907	372,401	1,034,007	548,735	491,272	485,272
July–Dec. 1848	1,123,280	382,141	1,154,019	568,067	596,202	585,952
Jan.–June 1849	1,082,939	366,547	1,062,846	553,177	517,194	509,669
July–Dec. 1849	1,129,605	381,390	1,164,396	647,149	536,018	517,247
Jan.–June 1850	1,110,180	377,422	1,148,388	681,170	527,217	517,218
July–Dec. 1850	1,207,289	390,362	1,248,499	714,522	557,076	583,977
Jan.–June 1851	1,177,580	415,420	1,236,358	735,257	520,093	501,101
July–Dec. 1851‡	1,420,543	450,002	1,479,404	880,489	729,514	648,915

Source: Company Accounts, RAC1/233, BTHR.
* Excludes rates, taxes, legal expenses, interest on loans, guarantees.
† Includes rents, dividends from other lines, etc.
‡ Great Exhibition year, 1851.
§ n.s. Until July–Dec. 1847, rail renewal costs were not shown separately.

Table 49
Passenger traffic statistics, 1846–51

1. Great Western, Midland, Eastern Counties railways:
share of U.K. traffic

| Company | Year July–June | Share of U.K. passenger traffic receipts BY CLASS | | | | | Share of U.K. goods receipts | Share of U.K. total traffic receipts |
		First %	Second %	Third %	Parlt. %	Total %	%	%
G.W.R.	1846–7	13.90	17.79	—	14.28	13.10	8.30	11.20
G.W.R.	1850–1	8.77	10.96	—	5.94	8.21	4.26	6.30
Mid.	1846–7	7.96	8.06	9.68	11.09	8.35	9.77	8.91
Mid.	1850–1	5.67	6.99	14.80	6.06	7.18	9.41	8.26
E. Cos	1846–7	5.56	6.29	7.08	4.08	5.76	5.92	5.82
E. Cos	1850–1	5.42	5.35	5.00	4.84	4.25	4.95	5.10

Source: P.P.1847–8, XXVI, 1852, XLVIII.

2. Great Western, Midland, Eastern Counties railways:
passenger and goods traffic, share of total receipts (gross)

Company	Year July–June	Passenger receipts/ total receipts %	Goods receipts/ total receipts %
G.W.R.	1846–7	70.72	29.28
G.W.R.	1850–1	67.33	32.67
Mid.	1846–7	56.95	43.05
Mid.	1850–1	44.90	53.05
E. Cos	1846–7	59.81	40.19
E. Cos	1850–1	53.05	46.96

Source: P.P. as above.

Table 50
London & North Western passenger and goods traffic: share of total gross receipts, 1846–51

Year July–June	FROM PARLIAMENTARY RETURNS		FROM COMPANY ACCOUNTS	
	Passenger receipts/ total receipts %	Goods receipts/ total receipts %	Passenger receipts/ total receipts %	Goods receipts/ total receipts %
1846–7	58.43	41.57	60.60	39.40
1847–8	53.72	46.28	57.74	42.26
1848–9	50.01	49.99	55.40	44.60
1849–50	48.72	51.28	54.42	45.57
1850–1	49.09	50.91	53.59	46.41

Source: P.P. *cit.*, Company Accounts, RAC1/233, BTHR. Note: Passenger receipts do *not* include receipts from parcels, mails, horses, and dogs traffic, in either set of figures. The goods percentages in the P.P. returns are probably inflated by the inclusion of receipts for collection and delivery (these charges were subtracted in the company accounts after July 1847).

Table 51
Statistics relating to the controversy over the London & North Western's goods traffic, 1848–9

1. L.N.W. merchandise traffic accounts, 1846–7

RECEIPTS	Half-year to 31 December 1846	Half-year to 31 December 1847
Goods (not coal, cattle)	£288,612	£389,063
Carrier rents (London and Birmingham line)	2,722	—
Total	£291,334	£389,063

EXPENSES		
Waggons	£ 9,732	£12,654
Wages	32,374	45,277
Stores	4,646	5,833
Miscellaneous	13,280	14,831
Carrying expenses	—	71,603
Total	£60,032	£150,198
Net profit	£231,301	£238,865

Source: Huish, 'Confidential Report . . . upon . . . the Merchandise Traffic' (1848), HL2/R99B, BTHR.

Table 51 (continued)

2. L.N.W. revenue account statistics, 1847–8

Passenger receipts (including parcels, mails, horses, dogs)	£1,417,659
Goods receipts (minus terminal costs)	722,376
Working expenses (not rates, taxes)	751,172

Source: Huish, *Letter to George Carr Glyn* . . . (1848), 8, checked in Company Accounts, RAC1/233, BTHR.

3. J. Whitehead's table of London & North Western rates, 1849

Journey London–Birmingham class of goods	Previous rate (L. & B.)	Present rate* (L.N.W.)
1	11s. 8d.	11s. 8d.
2	14s. 0d.	17s. 6d.
3	18s. 8d.	22s. 6d.
4	23s. 4d.	27s. 6d.

Source: Whitehead, *Railway Management—The Proof!* . . . (1849), 6.
* Minus 10s. a ton collection/delivery charges.

4. Proposed rates for the London & North Western, and the Grand Junction Canal, September 1848

Journey London–Birmingham Class of goods	G.J.C.	L.N.W.
1	20s.	21s. 8d.
2	25s.	27s. 6d.
3	30s.	32s. 6d.
4	35s.	37s. 6d.
5	40s.	45s. 0d.
Iron, undamageable	15s. 10d.	16s. 8d.
Iron, damageable	18s. 4d.	21s. 8d.

Source: L.N.W. Loco & Merchandise Committee Mins, 8 Sept. 1848, LNW1/221. BTHR.

Table 52
Grand Junction Canal tonnage receipts, 1845–57

Year	Receipts taken at Paddington Wharf, London		Total receipts, entire canal, 12 months
	January	June	
1845	£1,798	£1,327	£106,101
1846	1,180	776	82,044
1847	1,133*	1,050	86,356
1848	1,160*	933	79,374
1849	1,542	1,105	83,748
1850	943†	1,315	81,565
1851	1,565	1,075	79,585
1852	—	—	77,813
1853	—	—	79,617
1854	—	—	82,356
1855	—	—	71,679
1856	—	—	73,886
1857	—	—	70,521

Source: Grand Junction Rate Book, GJC4/5, BTHR.
* Frost.
† Severe frost.

Table 53
London & North Western goods traffic statistics, 1846–51

Period Half-year	Total goods receipts	Merchandise receipts %	Livestock receipts %	Coal receipts %
Jan.–June 1846	£306,519	85.4	9.9	4.7
July–Dec. 1846	344,098	84.4	11.0	4.6
Jan.–June 1847	338,408	87.0	6.5	6.5
July–Dec. 1847	382,576	83.0	10.2	6.8
Jan.–June 1848	339,789	85.9	6.5	7.6
July–Dec. 1848	393,773	83.6	9.4	7.0
Jan.–June 1849	385,021	87.2	5.3	7.5
July–Dec. 1849	410,551	84.1	9.0	6.9
Jan.–June 1850	435,958	85.5	6.0	8.5
July–Dec. 1850	477,742	83.6	7.7	8.7
Jan.–June 1851	453,817	84.9	5.1	10.0
July–Dec. 1851	478,996	83.2	7.2	9.6
Weighted average 1846–51	—	84.7	7.7	7.6

Source: Company Accounts, RAC1/233, BTHR.

Table 54
London & North Western livestock traffic, 1846–51

1. London & North Western, and United Kingdom livestock traffic in 1847

	L.N.W.	U.K. (estimated)	L.N.W. receipts
Cattle	161,171	500,000	£25,435
Sheep	399,998	2,000,000	16,622
Pigs	150,674	390,000	17,223

Source: Hyde Clarke, *Contribution to Railway Statistics* . . . (1849), 11–15.

2. Livestock traffic carried by the L.N.W., 1848–50

Year	Cattle	Sheep	Calves	Pigs	Total	Total receipts
1848	170,898	490,946	24,098	133,246	819,288	£59,006
1849	170,956	567,665	21,381	143,487	903,489	57,748
1850	230,454	623,382	26,659	194,198	1,075,293	64,439

Source: Ormandy, 'Report upon the Cattle Traffic . . . for 1849', 40, and 'Report upon the Cattle Traffic . . . for 1850', 41.

3. Livestock traffic carried to Smithfield Market, London, 1849

Carrier	Cattle	Sheep	Calves	Pigs	Total
L.N.W.	55,545	285,016	4,607	9,721	354,889
E. Cos	57,391	275,334	4,113	10,661	347,499
By road	39,336	523,992	10,000*	50,000*	623,328
Continental imports	33,555	125,269	1,949	11,315	172,091
Total†	223,443	1,534,620	79,526	53,393	1,890,982

Source: Ormandy, 'Report upon the Cattle Traffic . . . for 1849', 2.
* Estimate.
† Includes figures from other railways, and transport by sea.

Table 55
London & North Western revenue statistics, 1851–60

Period Half-year	Passengers	Horses/dogs	Parcels	Merchandise	Livestock	Coal	Mails
Jan.–June 1851	£637,378	£17,238	£45,352	£385,325§	£23,290	£45,102	£23,893
July–Dec. 1851	851,259	15,146	50,808	398,529	34,369	46,098	24,338
Jan.–June 1852	580,679	18,364	44,758	390,992	25,568	50,916	24,986
July–Dec. 1852	676,755	16,310	49,669	447,957	40,555	54,726	24,325
Jan.–June 1853	600,526	18,215	46,680	458,508	23,999	59,883	24,325
July–Dec. 1853	681,370	18,348	54,032	501,219	46,557	70,345	24,325
Jan.–June 1854	610,743	20,024	49,050	519,172	28,020	78,392	24,325
July–Dec. 1854	691,554	17,140	55,233	546,890	54,404	84,906	24,325
Jan.–June 1855	588,348	18,697	48,927	551,315	30,013	88,926	24,705
July–Dec. 1855	707,846	17,811	56,477	580,702	51,885	100,254	26,821
Jan.–June 1856*	636,676	20,011	54,938	596,549	36,433	115,363	30,650
July–Dec. 1856	749,610	18,834	61,588	615,774	63,754	142,602	30,427
Jan.–June 1857	666,217	19,979	52,837	608,772	37,653	140,556	30,510
July–Dec. 1857	799,465	20,323	59,987	577,008	56,192	136,601	30,482
Jan.–June 1858	581,720	17,838	52,417	524,380	35,252	138,009	30,429
July–Dec. 1858	703,915	18,240	62,084	558,884	49,379	158,932	30,475
Jan.–June 1859†	685,438	20,652	61,074	633,213	47,688	169,627	45,592
July–Dec. 1859‡	924,540	24,997	76,485	931,954‖	91,879	=	54,349
Jan.–June 1860	795,152	24,301	69,259	1,011,398‖	54,416	=	57,812

Source: Company Accounts, RAC1/233, BTHR.
* North Union and Buckinghamshire receipts included.
† Chester & Holyhead receipts included.
‡ Lancaster & Carlisle receipts included.
§ Merchandise figures are net of collection and delivery charges.
‖ Merchandise figures include "minerals".

Table 56
London & North Western revenue and costs statistics, 1851–60

Period half-year	Gross traffic receipts	Operating costs*	Total gross revenue†	Total costs (includes rail renewal)	Balance	Final balance (including rail renewal costs)
Jan.–June 1851	£1,177,580	£415,420	£1,236,358	£735,257	£520,093	£501,101
July–Dec. 1851	1,420,543	450,002	1,479,404	830,489	729,514	648,915
Jan.–June 1852	1,136,277	423,304	1,196,071	763,340	467,720	423,731
July–Dec. 1852	1,309,799	454,299	1,366,903	809,265	596,754	557,638
Jan.–June 1853	1,232,138	490,736	1,298,840	596,754	490,990	469,672
July–Dec. 1853	1,396,198	503,089	1,468,304	865,571	645,369	602,733
Jan.–June 1854	1,330,128	564,893	1,409,128	901,500	529,516	507,628
July–Dec. 1854	1,470,454	566,089	1,523,945	936,341	631,380	587,604
Jan.–June 1855	1,350,933	563,472	1,396,283	924,738	495,104	471,545
July–Dec. 1855	1,541,500[a]	553,434	1,588,459	954,893	690,232	633,566
Jan.–June 1856	1,490,622[b]	597,399	1,539,843	1,009,893	‡	529,950
July–Dec. 1856	1,682,591[c]	615,668	1,740,745	1,067,215		673,530
Jan.–June 1857	1,556,518[d]	631,846	1,620,832	1,048,499		572,333
July–Dec. 1857	1,682,060[e]	669,363	1,750,551	1,131,469		619,082
Jan.–June 1858	1,379,999[f]	619,043	1,448,491	1,041,134		407,357
July–Dec. 1858	1,581,861[g]	657,092	1,649,826	1,121,368		528,458
Jan.–June 1859	1,663,287[h]	731,807	1,736,599	1,239,372		497,227
July–Dec. 1859	2,104,206[i]	828,604	2,183,609	1,548,887		634,722
Jan.–June 1860	2,012,341[j]	869,619	2,108,899	1,501,620		607,279

Source: Company Accounts, RAC1/233, BTHR.
* Excludes rates, taxes, legal expenses, interests on loans, and guarantees.
† Includes rents, dividends from other lines, etc.
‡ From Jan.–June 1856 no separation of rail renewal costs is made.

a Deducting money paid to other companies = 1,511,355
b Deducting money paid to other companies = 1,463,567
c Deducting money paid to other companies = 1,658,818
d Deducting money paid to other companies = 1,539,017
e Deducting money paid to other companies = 1,658,803
f Deducting money paid to other companies = 1,355,499
g Deducting money paid to other companies = 1,561,471
h Deducting money paid to other companies = 1,634,052
i Deducting money paid to other companies = 2,072,194
j Deducting money paid to other companies = 1,995,803

Table 57
London & North Western long- and short-distance passenger fares, 1857–8

1. Short-distance fares

Journey	Miles travelled	Fares per mile (as charged Oct. 1857–Dec. 1858)			
		Express	First	Second	Third
Euston–Kilburn	3	—	2.00*d.*	1.33*d.*	—
Euston–Willesden	6¼	—	1.92	1.44	0.96*d.*
Euston–Harrow	11½	—	2.09	1.57	1.00
Bolton–Daubhill	1¼	—	4.80	3.20	0.80
Bolton–Chequerbent	3½	—	2.57	1.71	0.85
Shrewsbury–Upton	3¾	—	2.13	1.60	0.93
Shrewsbury-Walcott	6¼	—	1.92	1.44	0.96
Banbury–Farthinghoe	4	—	2.25	1.50	1.00
Leamington–Kenilworth	4½	—	2.22	1.33	0.78
Stamford–Seaton	10½	—	1.71	1.14	0.86
Weighted average		—	2.19	1.50	0.92

2. Long-distance fares

		Express	First	Second	Third
Euston–Rugby	82¾	4.13	2.25	1.67	0.99
Euston–Oxford	78¼	—	1.69	1.28	0.81
Euston–Birmingham	113	—	2.12	1.59	1.00
Euston–Crewe	158¼	2.73	2.24	1.59	0.99
Euston–Stafford	133½	2.74	2.25	1.62	0.99
Euston–Shrewsbury	162½	2.44	2.02	1.51	0.95
Euston–Chester	179½	—	2.21	1.60	0.99
Euston–Manchester	189	—	2.22	1.59	0.99
Euston–Birkenhead	194½	—	2.19	1.54	0.99
Euston–Liverpool	202	2.67	2.20	1.60	0.99
Euston–Wolverhampton	126	—	2.12	1.59	1.00
Euston–Preston	210¼	2.55	2.10	1.57	0.99
Euston–Fleetwood	231	2.68	2.18	1.57	1.00
Euston–Edinburgh	401¼	2.60	2.20	1.59	0.99
Euston–Glasgow	405¼	2.58	2.19	1.58	0.99
Euston–Aberdeen	541¾	1.99	1.77	1.33	0.89
Weighted average		—	2.19	1.59	0.99

Source: London & North Western timetables, TT19/1A, B, BTHR.

Table 58
The effects of Great Western competition on London & North Western passenger revenue, 1852–5

1. London and Birmingham, London and Liverpool traffic, 1852–5

Period Half-year	Journey examined	Express	Gross receipts by class			Day returns		Total
			First	Second	Third	First	Second	
Jan.–June 1852	London–Birmingham	£7,305	£7,894	£11,984	£5,769	£1,333	£1,436	£35,724
Jan.–June 1854	London–Birmingham	3,934	7,828	6,033	5,870	1,302	1,062	26,031
Jan.–June 1855	London–Birmingham	2,812	5,712	6,916	3,660	920	1,264	21,826
Jan.–June 1852	London–Liverpool	17,242	7,635	9,659	10,433	134	85	45,250
Jan.–June 1854	London–Liverpool	15,383	13,555	10,266	12,159	202	135	51,702
Jan.–June 1855	London–Liverpool	14,172	13,466	10,703	14,353	185	122	53,003

2. Total effects of Great Western competition, 1852–5

Period Half-year	Traffic at competing points with G.W.	Stour Valley traffic	Shrewsbury–Birmingham traffic	Total loss from 1852 (A+B+C)	'Real' loss over six months at competing points proper (taking into account an increase in London–Liverpool traffic of £7,753 (E) (D+E)	Estimated losses over 12 months
Jan.–June 1852	£127,274					
Jan.–June 1854	116,227					
Jan.–June 1855	105,312					
Loss 1854/5	10,914					
Loss 1852/5	21,961 A	5,223 B	2,192 C	£29,376 D	£37,129	£70,000

Huish, 'Report . . . on Traffic . . .' (1855), 7–10.

Table 59
London & North Western goods traffic statistics, 1851–60

Period Half-year	Total goods receipts	Merchandise receipts %	Livestock receipts %	Coal receipts %
Jan.–June 1851	£453,817	84.9	5.1	10.0
July–Dec. 1851	478,996	83.2	7.2	9.6
Jan.–June 1852	467,477	83.6	5.5	10.9
July–Dec. 1852	543,328	82.4	7.5	10.1
Jan.–June 1853	542,391	84.5	4.5	11.0
July–Dec. 1853	618,122	81.1	7.5	11.4
Jan.–June 1854	625,584	83.0	4.5	12.5
July–Dec. 1854	682,201	80.2	7.4	12.4
Jan.–June 1855	670,255	82.3	4.4	13.3
July–Dec. 1855	732,543	79.3	7.0	13.7
Jan.–June 1856*	748,346	79.7	4.9	15.4
July–Dec. 1856*	822,131	74.9	7.8	17.3
Jan.–June 1857*	786,974	77.4	4.7	17.9
July–Dec. 1857*	771,801	74.8	7.5	17.7
Jan.–June 1858*	697,593	75.2	5.0	19.8
July–Dec. 1858*	767,196	72.8	6.5	20.7
Jan.–June 1859†	850,529	74.4	5.7	19.9
July–Dec. 1859‡	1,023,834	91.0§	9.0	§
Jan.–June 1860‡	1,065,815	94.8§	5.2	§
Weighted average	1851– 1858	78.8	6.1	15.1
Weighted average	July 1851– June 1859	79.4	6.1	15.5

Source: Company Accounts, RAC1/233, BTHR.
* Includes receipts from North Union, Buckinghamshire lines.
† Includes receipts from Chester & Holyhead Railway.
‡ Includes receipts from Lancaster & Carlisle Railway.
§ Merchandise and Coals not separated.

Table 60
London & North Western traffic receipts—percentage variations, 1851–60

Period	Passenger traffic %	Passenger, parcels, and mails traffic %	Merchandise traffic %	Coal traffic %	Livestock traffic %	Total goods traffic %
1851–2/1857–8	−3.5	−1.1	+39.5	+183.1	+52.6	+55.2
1851–2/1858–9	−2.9	+1.2	+51.0	+238.7	+61.9	+70.9

Source: tables 55 and 56.

Table 61
London & North Western livestock traffic, 1850–5

1. Livestock traffic carried by the L.N.W., 1850–5

Year	Cattle	Sheep	Calves	Pigs	Total	Total receipts
1850	230,454	623,382	26,659	194,198	1,075,293	£64,439
1854	300,976*	878,492	40,923	299,762	1,522,737†	86,369
1855	261,043*	899,941	34,568	300,364	1,499,934†	88,351

Source: Ormandy, 'Report upon the Cattle Traffic . . . for 1850', 41, and 'Report upon the Cattle Traffic . . . for 1855', 178.
* 'Oxen'.
† Total includes horses: 2,584 (1854), 4,018 (1855).

2. Analysis of livestock traffic in 1855:
traffic handled at local stations, and received from other lines

Place	'Local traffic' receipts		Company	'Foreign traffic' receipts	
	1854 £	1855 £		1854 £	1855 £
London (Islington)	665	760	C. & H.	11,397	13,990
Liverpool	24,600	25,116	Aberdeen	3,685	1,331
Birmingham	1,699	1,757	G.S.W.	2,771	2,929
Manchester	1,586	1,888	Mid.	2,062	1,627
Northampton	4,553	3,869	L. & C.	1,224	1,318
Shrewsbury	3,600	2,655	Cale.	1,040	1,315
Aylesbury	1,251	1,098	S. & H.	660	1,227
Mkt. Harborough	1,114	840	O.W.W.	805	1,035
Peterborough	876	1,155	Etc.		
Rugby	854	1,186			
Etc.					
Total (all local stations)	58,931		Total (all railways)	25,266	26,631

Source: Ormandy, 'Report . . . upon the Cattle Traffic . . . for 1855', 186–91.
Only the chief revenue-earning stations and foreign railways are included in the table.

Table 62
Livestock traffic statistics, 1856–9

Year	Cattle	Sheep	Pigs	Total	(Unclassified)
1. Numbers, London & North Western Railway					
1856	404,649	1,576,894	296,072	2,377,614	—
1857	345,239	1,126,818	303,642	1,775,699	—
1858	471,717	1,127,964	524,617	2,124,298	—
1859	459,067	1,213,143	475,472	2,147,682	—
2. Numbers, United Kingdom railways					
1856	1,997,748	6,843,603	1,537,459	10,450,625	—
1857	2,364,729	7,084,773	1,593,226	11,047,100	—
1858	2,323,305	6,938,160	2,048,622	11,326,006*	15,922*
1859	2,618,423	7,994,245	2,192,945	12,805,613	
3. Gross receipts, London & North Western Railway					
1856	£50,212	£38,986	£10,989	£100,287	—
1857	48,961	33,402	11,484	93,847	—
1858	56,031	28,918	16,459	101,410	—
1859	71,455	41,449	19,695	132,599	—
4. Gross receipts, United Kingdom railways					
1856	£167,848	£115,939	£43,424	£517,515*	£188,304*
1857	199,046	107,090	42,447	517,356*	168,767*
1858	188,472	102,267	49,881	501,396*	160,775*
1859	223,884	133,288	58,245	609,783*	194,303*

Source: P.P.1857, Sess.2, XXXVII, 1857–8, LI, 1859, Sess.1, XXV, 1860, LXI.
* Total figures include unclassified traffic.

Table 63
Liverpool: weekly wages and tonnages handled, showing average cost per ton, 1857–9

1857 Tons	Wages		1858 Tons	Wages		1859 Tons	Wages	
14208	£654		9469	£546		14612	£627	
15200	664		10138	539		14080	645	
15877	669		11616	549		14128	656	
14511	656		12089	553		15461	629	
16396	647		12877	562		15023	630	
16460	652		13873	571		15792	643	
16047	667		13470	585		15333	646	
15955	651		12993	577		15594	650	
15047	646		15044	579		16554	651	
15517	656		13855	573		17677	647	
15514	666		12035	556		16290	643	
16254	658		12434	560		17120	654	
16663	648		13960	570		17268	662	
15506	644		13760	574		17745	704	
14466	654		11033	561		16168	690	
14690	631		13559	571		16706	659	
14501	641		14563	583		15885	653	
16405	633	1857	16008	593	1858	12757	650	1859
15615	629	Average	15551	580	Average	15886	642	Average
16023	626	10.656d.	14472	574	10.012d.	18862	670	10.097d.
15047	625	per ton	13822	570	per ton	16972	651	per ton
16165	626		16133	559		16500	660	
14253	616		13623	557		16218	678	
14284	628		14124	566		16679	696	
14011	632		13928	567		15008	644	
14592	639		13712	564		14752	660	
15693	627		13450	567		14878	641	
14793	635		14744	569		16231	653	
13943	620		14341	576		16616	713	
14951	634		13572	579		16509	701	
15406	623		14464	579		16137	658	
15136	614		14474	575		19560	665	
16652	621		14315	582		16987	681	
14430	625		13391	582		16771	674	
15180	629		14406	576		15630	659	
14819	624		14604	581		15551	662	
15217	628		14733	591		15264	674	
16216	622		15408	599		16049	699	
14109	625		15560	598		16586	689	
14716	634		13821	587		16679	711	
14512	622		13592	590		16437	703	
13394	619		13646	589		17752	703	

Table 63 (continued)

1857 Tons	Wages	1858 Tons	Wages	1859 Tons	Wages
13096	£625	14281	£587	17160	£696
15126	617	14492	591	17478	726
13090	611	14475	587	18538	767
13029	605	13462	597	17050	756
11664	596	15431	597	16602	734
11486	578	14892	641	16775	758
11400	552	15205	632	17395	729
10552	554	14626	621	17882	746
11796	552	15637	626	16596	738
11745	557	14409	648	17232	824
Total					
761352	£33807	723572	£30186	841415	£35400

Source: Bradshaw's Book of Liverpool Station Statistics, LNW4/71, BTHR.

2 Agreements and contracts

London & North Western's goods traffic agency agreement with Pickford & Co. and Chaplin & Horne, 1 January 1847 (extract)

1. Pickford, Chaplin & Horne to be merchandise agents, on terms below . . .
2. Duties: collection and delivery to and from goods stations to and from any town or place within 7 miles of the L.N.W.; collection of invoices, accounting, guarantees, and risk of bad debts, loading, unloading, etc.
3. Remuneration: Allowances for collection/delivery duties, per ton:

AT London (Camden)	8s.
Birmingham, etc.	2s. 6d.
Manchester	2s. 6d.
Wolverhampton, etc.	2s. 6d.
Whitmore	6s.

   Subject to a correct six-monthly statement of actual costs . . . there being a clear intention that all services OFF the railway are to be performed at the cost price . . .
4. Inducements to the Agents to cheapen the allowances offered to them: in respect of any saving: 15% on first 6d. saved per ton
   10% on all sums saved after 6d.
5. Salary for other services:

On the first 100,000 tons handled per year out of Camden:	1s. per ton
On each ton handled beyond 100,000:	6d. per ton
On goods handled at stations on the L.N.W. where the agents were once carriers (e.g. Manchester, Birmingham):	4d. per ton
On goods handled at stations where the G.J. was or the L.N.W. are now carriers (e.g. Liverpool):	3d. per ton
On goods passing between stations where the L.N.W. or G.J. were carriers at one end, the agents at the other (e.g. goods from Wolverhampton–Coventry, Whitmore–Manchester):	4d. per ton

   The L.N.W. guarantee the agents £7,500 per annum.
6. All rates to be fixed by the L.N.W., and the agents not to deviate from these without the express authority of the company.
7. Except at Liverpool, Manchester, Preston, Wigan, Chorley, Parkside, Warrington, Hartford, Crewe, Chester, Stafford, etc., collection and delivery to be performed by the agents.
8. Contract for five years.

Source: L.N.W. Agreements, LNW3/3, BTHR.

London & North Western's goods traffic agency agreement with Pickford & Co. and Chaplin & Horne, 1 January 1852 (extract)

1. Pickford, Chaplin & Horne to be merchandise agents, on terms below . . .
2. Duties: collection and delivery within 7 miles of the L.N.W.; invoicing, accounting, risk, etc.
3. Remuneration: Allowances for collection/delivery duties, per ton:

AT London, Camden (including loading/unloading)	7s.
London, Camden (collection/delivery only)	5s. 6d.
London, Haydon Square (including loading/unloading)	4s. 6d.
London, Haydon Square (collection/delivery only)	3s.
Birmingham, etc.	2s. 6d.
Manchester	2s. 6d.
Wolverhampton (at present)	2s. 6d.
Wolverhampton (when central station opened)	2s.
Other stations	2s. 6d.

   Subject to a correct six-monthly statement of actual costs . . .
4. Inducement to the Agents to cheapen allowances: in respect of any saving, $7\frac{1}{2}\%$ of same.
5. Salary for other services:

On the first 100,000 tons handled per year out of Camden and other London stations, including Haydon Square:	6d. per ton
On each ton handled beyond 100,000:	3d. per ton
On goods handled at other stations:	2d. per ton

   The L.N.W. guarantee the agents £10,000 per annum. If earnings are less than £10,000, the L.N.W. will make up the deficiency; if over £10,000, the agents to pay to the L.N.W. $\frac{2}{3}$rds of the excess until the same amounts to £11,000; and all above £11,000 is to be paid to the L.N.W.

Source: Pickford & Co. Agreements, PIC3/3, BTHR.

London & North Western's goods traffic agency agreement with Pickford & Co. and Chaplin & Horne, 1 January 1858 (extract)

1. Pickford, Chaplin & Horne to be merchandise agents, on terms below . . .
2. Duties: collection and delivery within 7 miles of the L.N.W.; invoicing, accounting, risk, etc.
3. L.N.W. can undertake on three months' notice collection and delivery itself at or for any station except London, Birmingham, Coventry, Leeds, Manchester, Northampton, Oxford, Wolverhampton . . . except, where both Pickford and Chaplin & Horne act as agents, the L.N.W. cannot assume control of the duties of only one agent.
4. Remuneration: The actual sums disbursed, plus 5% on the agents' stock employed—the agents charging for the present the average cost for renewal and interest . . . The agents to pay monthly to the L.N.W. the balance due . . .
5. Inducement to the Agents to reduce costs: the L.N.W. to allow the agents $7\frac{1}{2}\%$ off rate saved off the lowest expenses of the average of the two agents' costs during the last two years under the former agreement of 1 January 1852.

6. Salary for all other services:
   On the first 100,000 tons handled per year at Camden
   and other London stations: 6*d*. per ton
   On tonnage handled beyond 100,000 and up to 200,000: 3*d*. per ton
   On goods handled at other stations: 2*d*. per ton
   The L.N.W. guarantee the agents £10,000 per annum. If computed salary exceeds
   £10,000, the agents to pay to the L.N.W. ⅔rds of the excess up to £11,000; and all
   above £11,000 to be repaid to the L.N.W.

Source: Pickford & Co. Agreements, PIC3/4, BTHR.

The 'Octuple' traffic agreement, 17 April 1851

An agreement between companies carrying between London and Edinburgh:
London & North Western, Lancaster & Carlisle, Caledonian, North British, York
Newcastle & Berwick, York & North Midland, Midland, Great Northern.
The following routes to Scotland defined:
1. Euston via L.N.W. to Preston, via. L. & C., Cale. to Edinburgh (WEST COAST).
2. Euston via L.N.W. to Rugby, via Mid. to Normanton, via Y.N.M. to York, via
   Y.N.B. to Berwick, via N.B. to Edinburgh (EAST COAST).
3. G.N. to Lincoln and Knottingley (via direct 'towns line' when built), via Y.N.M.
   to York, via Y.N.B., N.B. to Edinburgh (EAST COAST).

Schedule of divided traffic (mails and mineral traffic EXCLUDED)

LONDON-EDINBURGH traffic divided equally between the WEST and EAST coast routes.
Subdivision of EAST COAST share:

Passenger Traffic		Goods Traffic	
G.N./	L.N.W./Mid./	G.N.	L.N.W./Mid./
Y.N.M.	Y.N.M.	Y.N.M.	Y.N.M.
%	%	%	%
33⅓	66⅔	50	50

On the opening of the 'towns line':

Passenger Traffic		Goods Traffic
G.N./	L.N.W./Mid./	as above
Y.N.M.	Y.N.M.	
%	%	
63	37	

All traffic for places north of York and south of Edinburgh from London to go by
EAST COAST. If a route carries more than its share, a deduction will be made, allowing
20% of passenger receipts, and ¼*d*. per ton-mile on goods traffic. Equal rates and
fares to be charged, by agreement. For 5 years, from 1 January 1851.

Source: L.N.W. Agreements, LNW3/4, BTHR.

The 'Sextuple' traffic agreement, 17 April 1851

For the arrangement of traffic other than provided for by the 'Octuple' Agreement, agreed by the London & North Western, Caledonian, Lancaster & Carlisle, Midland, York Newcastle & Berwick, North British.

Schedule of divided traffic (ALL traffic, except mails from Birmingham)

1. Through traffic, Birmingham and L.N.W. road stations to Edinburgh:
   50% WEST, 50% EAST coast, via York.
2. G.N. road stations, and stations common to the G.N. and Mid. to Edinburgh and Glasgow, or stations on N.B., or E. & G., or north of Edinburgh:
   100% EAST coast, via York.
3. L.N.W. traffic to Glasgow:
   100% WEST coast.
4. Normanton and Mid. stations south of Normanton to Edinburgh, and stations on E. & G. (except Glasgow):
   100% EAST coast.
5. Mid. stations north of Normanton to Edinburgh, stations on E. & G.:
   100% WEST coast (except re 12, below).
6. Mid. to N.B. stations, except Edinburgh:
   100% EAST coast, via Y.N.B.
7. Leeds, Bradford, etc. to Glasgow:
   100% WEST coast, via 'Little N.W.'.
8. Y.N.M., Y.N.B. to N.B. stations (including Edinburgh), E. & G. (including Glasgow):
   100% EAST coast.
9. Liverpool, Manchester to Y.N.B., N.B. stations (except Edinburgh):
   100% EAST coast, via York.
10. Mid. to Y.N.B. stations—traffic to go via York.
11. L.N.W. stations north of Wolverhampton but south of Newton Jnc. to Newcastle, and Y.N.B., to go via York; L.N.W. stations south of Wolverhampton to Newcastle, etc. to go via Mid. and Derby.
12. Nothing to restrain N.B., Y.N.B. from arranging with other companies re Leeds–Edinburgh traffic, stations between, also on E. & G., except Glasgow.

No company to make or quote through fares, or rates and fares with steamboats in connection with traffic to which this agreement refers (17). Equal rates and fares, to be fixed by the common consent of not less than four companies (18). For 5 years, from 1 January 1851.

Source: L.N.W. Agreements, LNW3/5, BTHR.

Gladstone's 'Six Towns' traffic award, 26 August 1851

Division of Passenger and Goods Traffic (but not mails, and minerals) affecting the London & North Western, Midland, Manchester Sheffield & Lincolnshire, and Great Northern railways.

Schedule of divided traffic

Traffic between LONDON and	Proposal of L.N.W. 19 March 1851 L.N.W./Mid.		Proposal of G.N. 19 Feb. 1851 G.N.		Gladstone's Award L.N.W./Mid.		G.N.	
	Pass. %	Goods %	Pass. %	Goods %	Pass. %	Goods %	Pass. %	Goods %
YORK	30	40	80	66⅔	20	25	80	75
LEEDS	40	60	66⅔	50	35	65	65	35
WAKEFIELD	40	60	66⅔	50	25	40	75	60
DONCASTER	25	40	85	85	5	10	95	90
SHEFFIELD	In abeyance				40	70	60	30
LINCOLN	25	40	85	75	15	25	85	75

Source: L.N.W. Agreements, LNW3/12, BTHR; *Herapath's Railway Magazine*, 6 Sept. 1851.

The 'Ten Towns' traffic agreement, 29 April 1853

An extension of the 'Six Towns' award, dividing traffic to Nottingham, Newark, Stamford, and Peterborough between the London & North Western, Midland, and Great Northern railways.

Schedule of divided traffic

Traffic between LONDON and	L.N.W./Mid. Pass. %	Goods %	G.N. Pass. %	Goods. %	
NOTTINGHAM	50	70	50	30	
NEWARK	20	45	80	55	
STAMFORD	30	70	70	30	
PETER-BOROUGH	10*	66⅔*	90	33½	* This traffic shared by the L.N.W. and E. Cos.

G.N. not to carry over the Mid. lines—Nottingham–Rugby, Nottingham–Derby, Nottingham–Mansfield, Nottingham–Erewash Valley, Nottingham–Lincoln— EXCEPT to Newark, Lincoln, and Southwell. L.N.W. and Mid. companies not to carry to Grantham, or to places between Grantham and Nottingham, or on the G.N. line between Peterborough and Retford, and Gainsborough, EXCEPT to Newark, Lincoln, Retford, and Gainsborough.
"The late impediments at the Midland station at Nottingham as to through traffic, etc. shall be done away with, and free access given to the omnibuses to meet the Great Northern trains."
Agreement operative from 16 May 1853 to 1 January 1856.

Source: L.N.W. Agreements, LNW3/15, BTHR.

The 'Common Purse' agreement, 1854

Agreement between the London & North Western, and Midland railways, also included the Manchester Sheffield & Lincolnshire, North Staffordshire, and North Western ('Little N.W.') railways.

1. Organization through a Joint Ctee with fullest powers.
2. Entire receipts to be pooled as a common fund, from 1 July 1854, excluding working expenses and credits under agreements with other co.s.
3. A Central Audit to examine and settle receipts.
4. A periodic division of earnings, each company being credited with its own local traffic, and its share of through traffic.
5. Before division, each company to be allowed as working expenses 35% of passenger, and 45% of goods and minerals receipts.
6. L.N.W. traffic is: the whole of the main line, branches, the Huddersfield Canal, part-leases of the North Union, and Preston & Wyre railways, the Buckinghamshire, and Shropshire Union railways, and shares in the Manchester & Buxton, M.S.J.A., and North Staffordshire, etc.
7. M.S. & L. traffic to be taken at actual receipts of the year June 1853–4 plus £20,800, the estimated value of the Barnsley extension traffic.
8. The Common Fund to include a division received from the Chester & Holyhead Railway, and any excess traffic from the North London Railway above 5%.
9. Mid. traffic is: the whole of the main line, branches, the 'Little N.W.', Ashby Canal, and a portion of the Manchester & Buxton.
10. Receipts of the above railways and canals to be ascertained for the year 1853–4 plus £25,000 to Midland receipts, £20,800 to M.S. & L. receipts.
11. The percentages of receipts enjoyed by the L.N.W. and Mid., after the deduction of allowances, to govern future division from 1 July 1854; if the M.S. & L., 'Little N.W.', and North Staffs. cease to be in alliance, the proportion will be changed.
12. For 10 years, from 1 July 1854.

Source: L.N.W. Mins, 11 Nov. 1854, LNW1/22, BTHR.

The English and Scotch traffic agreement, 1 January 1856

A renewal and extension of the 'Octuple' Agreement of 1851–5, dividing
traffic between the London & North Western, Lancaster & Carlisle, Caledonian,
Midland, Great Northern, North Eastern, and North British railways.
The following routes to Scotland defined:

1. Euston via L.N.W. to Preston, via L. & C., Cale. to Edinburgh and Glasgow
   (WEST COAST)
2. Euston via L.N.W. to Rugby, via Mid. to Normanton, via N.E., N.B. to Edinburgh
   (EAST COAST)
3. King's Cross via G.N. to York, via N.E., N.B. to Edinburgh (EAST COAST)

Schedule of divided traffic (Passenger traffic includes parcels; goods includes livestock,
minerals; Mails, coal, and coke EXCLUDED)

Traffic From	To Edinburgh —&c.				To the North of Scotland				To Glasgow			
	WEST		EAST		WEST		EAST		WEST		EAST	
	P.	G.	P.	G.	P.	G.	P.	G.	P.	G.	P.	G.
	%	%	%	%	%	%	%	%	%	%	%	%
LONDON	40	50	60	50	50	50	50	50	80	60	20	40
LIVERPOOL	100	100	—	—	100	100	—	—	100	100	—	—
MANCHESTER	100	60	—	40	100	60	—	40	100	100	—	—
LEEDS	$33\frac{1}{3}$	50	$66\frac{2}{3}$	50	50	50	50	50	$66\frac{2}{3}$	60	$33\frac{1}{3}$	40
BIRMINGHAM	75	$66\frac{2}{3}$	25	$33\frac{1}{3}$	90	$66\frac{2}{3}$	10	$33\frac{1}{3}$	100	100	—	—
Places between MANCHESTER and LEEDS*	$33\frac{1}{3}$	60	$66\frac{2}{3}$	40	50	60	50	40	80	60	20	40
BRADFORD	$66\frac{2}{3}$	60	$33\frac{1}{3}$	40	$66\frac{2}{3}$	60	$33\frac{1}{3}$	40	75	70	25	30
HULL, GRIMSBY	†	$33\frac{1}{3}$	100	$66\frac{2}{3}$	†	$33\frac{1}{3}$	100	$66\frac{2}{3}$	†	$33\frac{1}{3}$	100	$66\frac{2}{3}$
SHEFFIELD, NOTTINGHAM, HITCHIN, PETERBOROUGH, STAMFORD, NEWARK, DONCASTER, and RETFORD	5	20	95	80	5	20	95	80	20	$33\frac{1}{3}$	80	$66\frac{2}{3}$
Midland stations un-named above	$33\frac{1}{3}$	50	$66\frac{2}{3}$	50	100	100	—	—	100	100	—	—

Notes: * Not Bradford.
   † No through booking allowed by the west coast route.

Supplementary Divisions:

YORK TRAFFIC (divided between L.N.W., G.N., N.E.)

	WEST		EAST	
	Pass. %	Goods %	Pass. %	Goods %
LONDON–YORK portion of LONDON–EDINBURGH traffic	15	25	85	75
LONDON–YORK portion of traffic LONDON– stations north of YORK but south of EDINBURGH*	15	35	85	65
From stations north of YORK but south of EDINBURGH to DONCASTER, RETFORD, LINCOLN, HITCHIN, etc., for portion south of YORK†	5	20	95	80
Ibid. to NOTTINGHAM, SHEFFIELD	60	60	40	40

* NOT stations on Leeds Northern west of N.E. main line.

† Mid.'s share of York–Hitchin traffic not to start until the Leicester–Hitchin line is open.

TRAFFIC VIA PETERBOROUGH: Re distance due Lancashire–Peterborough, or any E. Cos station:

L.N.W. %	'Little N.W.'/Mid. %
80	20

The Scottish Central, and Edinburgh Dundee & Perth companies to be free to join within seven years—the traffic then to be divided as follows:

	S.C./E. & G.		E.D.P.	
	Pass. %	Goods %	Pass. %	Goods %
Of traffic allotted to the WEST COAST route:	90	75	10	25
Of traffic allotted to the EAST COAST route:	66⅔	50	33⅓	50

E. & G. to be included when hostility between itself and the Cale. ceases.

The Agreement does not include traffic between York and Leeds, or any station on the Leeds Northern west of the N.E. main line, or any station south of the N.E.'s southern termini, or passenger traffic between Glasgow and Hull, Grimsby, and the north of Scotland and Hull, Grimsby.
For 14 years, from 1 January 1856.

Source: English & Scotch Traffic Ctee Mins, RCH1/508, BTHR.

Gladstone's revised award, 22 April 1857

London & North Western, Great Northern, Midland, and Manchester Sheffield & Lincolnshire railways.

Schedule of divided traffic (not mails, minerals)

Traffic Between	G.N.		L.N.W./Mid.	
LONDON	Pass.	Goods	Pass.	Goods
and	%	%	%	%
YORK	90	75	10	25
LEEDS	75	48	25	52
WAKEFIELD	85	85	15	15
DONCASTER	95	88	5	12
SHEFFIELD	80	42	20	58
LINCOLN	85	75	15	25
NOTTINGHAM	50	25	50	75
STAMFORD	95	70	5	30
PETERBOROUGH	90	55	10*	45*
NEWARK	90	55	10	45
HALIFAX	85	57	15	43
BRADFORD	80	42	20	58
HULL	92	87	8	13
GRIMSBY	95	90	5	10
GAINSBOROUGH	95	90	5	10

* Divided between the L.N.W. and E. Cos.

Allowances for carrying in excess of the award: 20% of gross passenger, and 20 or 30% of gross goods receipts. Re-booking prohibited, e.g. at Masborough (for Sheffield), and Normanton (for Wakefield).
For period 1 March 1856 to 28 February 1870.

Source: GN1/280/7/11, BTHR.

Select bibliography and sources

A Unpublished sources

British Transport Historical Records Office, London

(This office is now administered by the Public Record Office.)

Minutes, Reports and Accounts, Correspondence, and Papers of:

Eastern Counties Railway	1839–45
Grand Junction Railway	1833–46
Great Northern Railway	1846–60
Great Western Railway	1833–60
Isle of Wight Railway	1859–66
London & Birmingham Railway	1830–46
London & North Western Railway	1846–65
Liverpool & Manchester Railway	1826–45
Manchester & Leeds Railway	1836–45
Midland Railway	1844–60
North Eastern Railway	1854–60
Pickford & Company	1837–60
Railway Clearing House	1842–60

Complete references are provided in the footnotes.

Scottish Record Office, Edinburgh

(This office now houses the collection of the British Transport Historical Records Office, Edinburgh.)

Minutes, Reports and Accounts, Correspondence, and Papers of:

Glasgow & Paisley Joint Railway	1837–42
Glasgow Paisley & Greenock Railway	1837–42
Glasgow Paisley Kilmarnock & Ayr Railway	1836–41

Complete references are provided in the footnotes.

Public Record Office, London

Board of Trade General Department Papers, Miscellanea, and Commercial Department Correspondence and Papers, Ref: BT1, BT6, BT11.
Ministry of Transport: Railway Department Correspondence, Papers, and Minutes, Ref: MT2, MT6, MT11, MT13.

House of Lords Records Office, London

Minutes of Evidence, House of Commons Select Committees on Railway Bills:
1837 vol. 13   Glasgow Paisley & Greenock Railway
1845 vol. 82   Trent Valley Railway
1846 vol. 84   London & Birmingham, Grand Junction, etc. Amalgamation

Glyn Mills & Co. Archives, London

Letters and Documents of George Carr Glyn, Lord Wolverton (1797–1873).

Post Office Record Office, London

Electric and International Telegraph Company: Board Agenda
Books, Letter Books, 1861–6.

India Record Office, London

East India Company Cadet Papers, 1823, Ref: L/MIL/9/153.

B Published sources

Local & Personal Acts of Parliament

Glasgow Paisley & Greenock Railway	1837–42
Grand Junction Railway	1833–46
London & Birmingham Railway	1843
London & North Western Railway	1846–60

Parliamentary Papers

(i) Select Committees, Royal Commissions:

S.C. on Communication by Railway, P.P.1839, X, 1840, XIII.
S.C. on Accidents on Railways, P.P.1841, VIII.
S.C. on Railways, P.P.1844, XI.
S.C. on the South Eastern Railway Petition, P.P.1845, X.
S.C. on the Oxford Worcester & Wolverhampton, and Oxford & Rugby Railway
    Bills, P.P.1845, XI.
House of Lords, S.C. on the Management of Railway Promotion, P.P.1846, XIII.
S.C. on Railway Acts Enactments, P.P.1846, XIV.
Royal Commission on the Gauge of Railways, P.P.1846, XVI.
House of Lords S.C. on the Audit of Railway Accounts, P.P.1849, X.
S.C. on Railway and Canal Bills, P.P.1852–3, XXXVIII.
S.C. on Accidents on Railways, P.P.1857–8, XIV.
S.C. on the Manchester Sheffield & Lincolnshire, and Great Northern Railway
Companies Bill, P.P.1857–8, XV.
Royal Commission on Railways, P.P.1867, XXXVIII.

(ii) Accounts and Papers:

P.P.1843, XLVII	P.P.1852, XLVIII
1845, XXXIX	1852–3, XCVII
1847, XXXI	1854, LXII
1847, LXIII	1854–5, XLVIII
1847–8, XXVI	1856, LIV
1847–8, LXIII	1857, XVI
1849, XXVII	1857, Sess. 2, XXXVII
1849, LI	1857–8, LI
1850, XXXI	1859, Sess. 1, XXV
1850, LIII	1859, Sess. 2, XXVII
1851, XXX	1860, LXI
1851, LI	1861, LVII

Contemporary newspapers and periodicals

Birmingham Journal	1839–41
Glasgow Saturday Post	1840–1
Greenock Advertiser	1837–41
Illustrated London News	1858–67
Liverpool Courier	1839–46
Liverpool Mail	1839–41
Liverpool Times	1841–6
Manchester Guardian	1841–6
Midland Counties Herald	1841–59
Morning Chronicle	1848–9
Morning Herald	1848–9
Times	1840–60
Bradshaw's Railway Companion	1839–45
Bradshaw's Railway and Steam Navigation Guide	1843–59
Bradshaw's Railway Manual and Shareholders' Guide	1848–60
Herapath's Railway Magazine	1839–60
Lawson's Merchants' Magazine	1852
Railway Chronicle	1844–9
Railway Gazette	1845–51
Railway Magazine and Annals of Science	1835–8
Railway Record	1845–59
Railway Times	1837–60

C Secondary sources

Anon., *Railways: their Uses and Management* (1842).

Sir W. M. Acworth, *The Elements of Railway Economics* (1932).

P. S. Bagwell, *The Railway Clearing House in the British Economy 1842–1922* (1968).

W. S. Barry, *Managing a Transport Business* (1963).

G. L. Boag, *Manual of Railway Statistics* (1912).

R. P. Brief, 'The Origin and Evolution of Nineteenth-Century Asset Accounting',
Business History Review, XL (1966).

A. K. Butterworth, *A Treatise on the Law Relating to Rates and Traffic on Railways and Canals* (1889).

W. H. Chaloner, *Social and Economic Development of Crewe, 1780–1923* (1950).

A. D. Chandler, 'The Railroads: Pioneers in Modern Corporate Management', *Business History Review*, XXXIX (1965).

E. D. Chattaway, *Railways, Their Capital and Dividends* (1855–6).

E. Clark, *Letter to Capt. Huish as to Proposed Improvements in the Electric Telegraph System* (1854).

Hyde Clarke, *Contributions to Railway Statistics, in 1846, 1847, and 1848* (1849).

E. Cleveland-Stevens, *English Railways: Their Development and Their Relation to the State* (1915).

P. Deane and W. A. Cole, *British Economic Growth, 1688–1959* (1962).

G. Dow, *Great Central*, vol. I (1959).

P. Eckersley, *Railway Management. Observations on Two Letters to George Carr Glyn, Esq.* (1848).

R. S. Edwards, 'Some Notes on the Early Literature and Development of Cost Accounting in Great Britain', *The Accountant*, CVII (1937).

Sir G. Findlay, *The Working and Management of an English Railway* (6th ed., 1899).

W. Galt, *Railway Reform, its expediency and practicality considered* (1844).

T. R. Gourvish, 'Captain Mark Huish: A Pioneer in the Development of Railway Management', *Business History*, XII (1970).

T. R. Gourvish, 'The Railways and Steamboat Competition in Early Victorian Britain', *Transport History*, IV (1971).

C. H. Grinling, *The History of the Great Northern Railway 1845–1902* (1903).

G. R. Hawke, 'Pricing Policy of Railways in England and Wales Before 1881', in Reed, q.v.

G. R. Hawke, *Railways and Economic Growth in England and Wales 1840–1870* (1970).

M. Huish, *A Letter to George Carr Glyn, Esq., M.P. . . . On Some Points of Railway Management* (1848).

M. Huish, *On Deterioration of Railway Plant and Road* (1849).

M. Huish, *Railway Accidents, Their Causes and Means of Prevention* (1852).

W. T. Jackman, *The Development of Transportation in Modern England* (1916).

J. R. Kellett, *The Impact of Railways on Victorian Cities* (1969).

P. W. Kingsford, 'Railway Labour 1830–1870', unpublished London Ph.D. thesis, 1951.

D. Lardner, *Railway Economy: A Treatise on the New Art of Transport, its Management, Prospects, and Relations, Commercial, Financial, and Social* (1850).

P. Lecount, *A Practical Treatise on Railways* (1839).

C. E. Lee, *Passenger Class Distinctions* (1946).

H. G. Lewin, *Early British Railways. A Short History of their Origin & Development 1801–1844* (1925).

H. G. Lewin, *The Railway Mania and its Aftermath 1845–1852* (1936).

London & North Western Railway, *Minutes and Correspondence between the London and North Western Railway, Midland, and Manchester, Sheffield and Lincolnshire Companies* (1856).

London & North Western Railway, *A Review of the London & North Western Railway Accounts, for the Last Ten Years. By a Manchester Shareholder* (1856).

G. McDonnell, *Railway Management, with and without Railway Statistics* (1854).

R. C. O. Matthews, *A Study in Trade Cycle History. Economic Fluctuations in Great Britain 1833–1842* (1954).

B. R. Mitchell, 'The Coming of the Railways and United Kingdom Economic Growth', *Journal of Economic History*, XXIV (1964), also in Reed, q.v.

G. P. Neele, *Railway Reminiscences* (1904).

G. Ottley, *A Bibliography of British Railway History* (1965).

H. Parris, *Government and the Railways in Nineteenth Century Britain* (1965).

P. L. Payne, 'The Emergence of the Large-scale Company in Great Britain, 1870–1914', *Economic History Review*, 2nd ser., XX (1967).

S. Pollard, *The Genesis of Modern Management* (1965).

H. Pollins, 'A Note on Railway Constructional Costs 1825–1850', *Economica*, new ser., XIX (1952).

H. Pollins, 'Aspects of Railway Accounting before 1868', in A. C. Littleton and B. S. Yamey (eds.), *Studies in the History of Accounting* (1956), also in Reed, q.v.

H. Pollins, 'Railway Auditing—A Report of 1867', *Accounting Research*, VIII (1957).

B. Poole, *Twenty Short Reasons for Railway Companies being themselves the Carriers of Goods* (1844).

M. C. Reed (ed.), *Railways in the Victorian Economy* (1969).

R. M. Robbins, 'From R. B. Dockray's Diary', *Journal of Transport History*, VII (1965–6).

H. M. Ross, *British Railways, Their Organisation and Management* (1904).

S. Salt, *Facts and Figures, principally relating to Railways and Commerce* (1848).

W. E. Simnett, *Railway Amalgamation in Great Britain* (1923).

M. Slaughter, *Railway Intelligence* (1849–61).

A. Smith, *The Bubble of the Age: or the Fallacies of Railway Investments, Railway Accounts, and Railway Dividends* (1848).

G. A. Steiner, *Top Management Planning* (1969).

D. Stevenson, *Fifty Years on the London & North Western Railway* (1891).

'A Sufferer' (pseud.), *Railway Policy, A Letter to G. C. Glyn, Esq.* (1848).

W. W. Tomlinson, *The North Eastern Railway, its rise and development* (1914).

G. L. Turnbull, 'The Railway Revolution and Carriers' Response: Messrs. Pickford & Company 1830–50', *Transport History*, II (1969).

Veritas Vincit (pseud.), *Railway Locomotive Management* (1847).

F. Whishaw, *The Railways of Great Britain and Ireland* (1840).

J. Whitehead, *Railway Management. A Letter to George Carr Glyn, Esq., Chairman of the London and North Western Railway* (1848).

J. Whitehead, *Railway Management. A Second Letter to George Carr Glyn, Esq., in reply to Capt. Huish's letter* (1848).

J. Whitehead, *Railway Management. The Proof! A Third Letter to George Carr Glyn, Esq.* (1849).

J. B. Williams, *On the Principles of Railway Management* (1846).

R. P. Williams, 'On the Economy of Railway Working', Minutes of Proceedings, *Institution of Mechanical Engineers* (1879).

Index